£10-00

VÉZELAY
The Great Romanesque Church

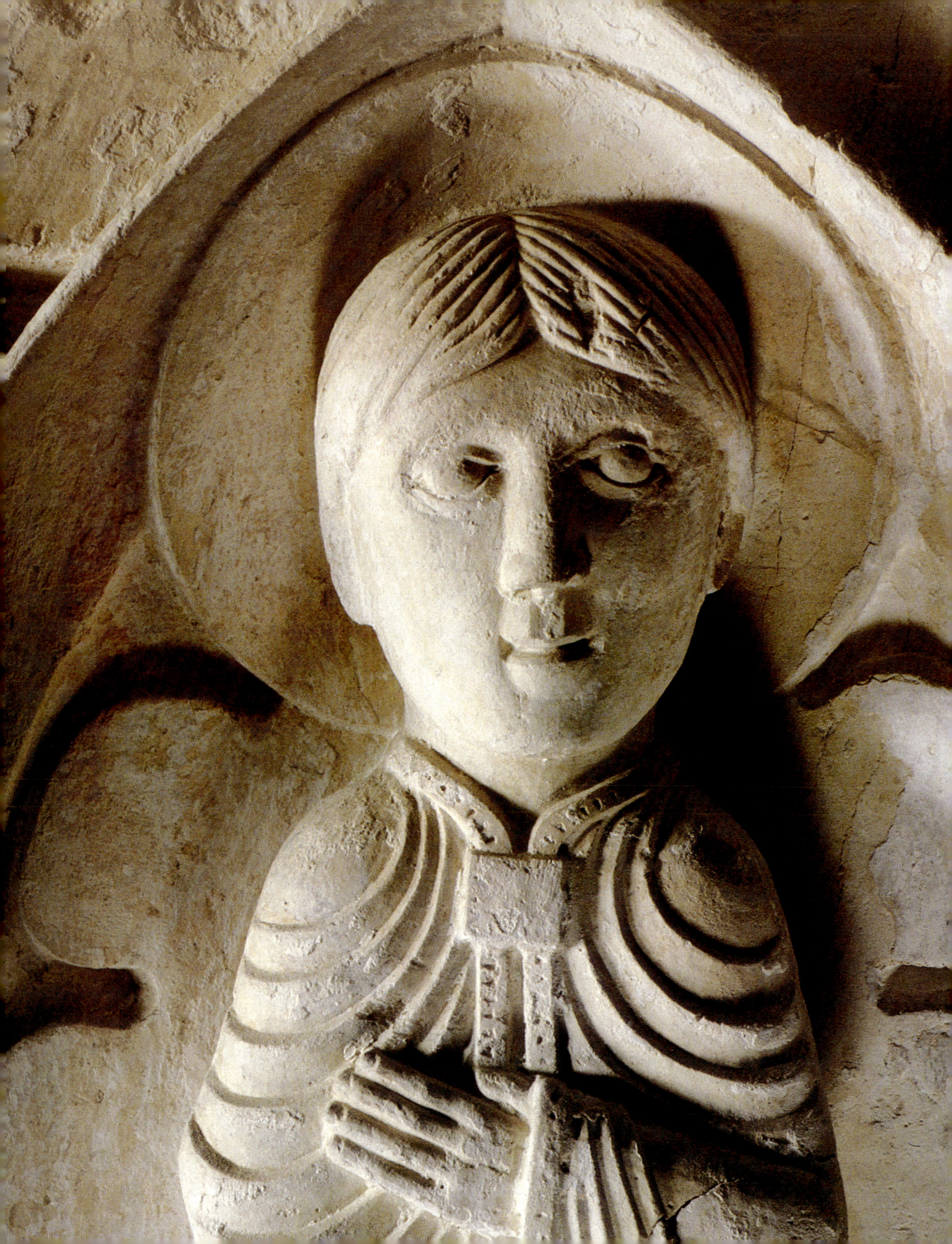

VÉZELAY

The Great Romanesque Church

BY VÉRONIQUE ROUCHON MOUILLERON

PHOTOGRAPHS BY DANIEL FAURE

TRANSLATED FROM THE FRENCH
BY LAUREL HIRSCH

HARRY N. ABRAMS, INC., PUBLISHERS

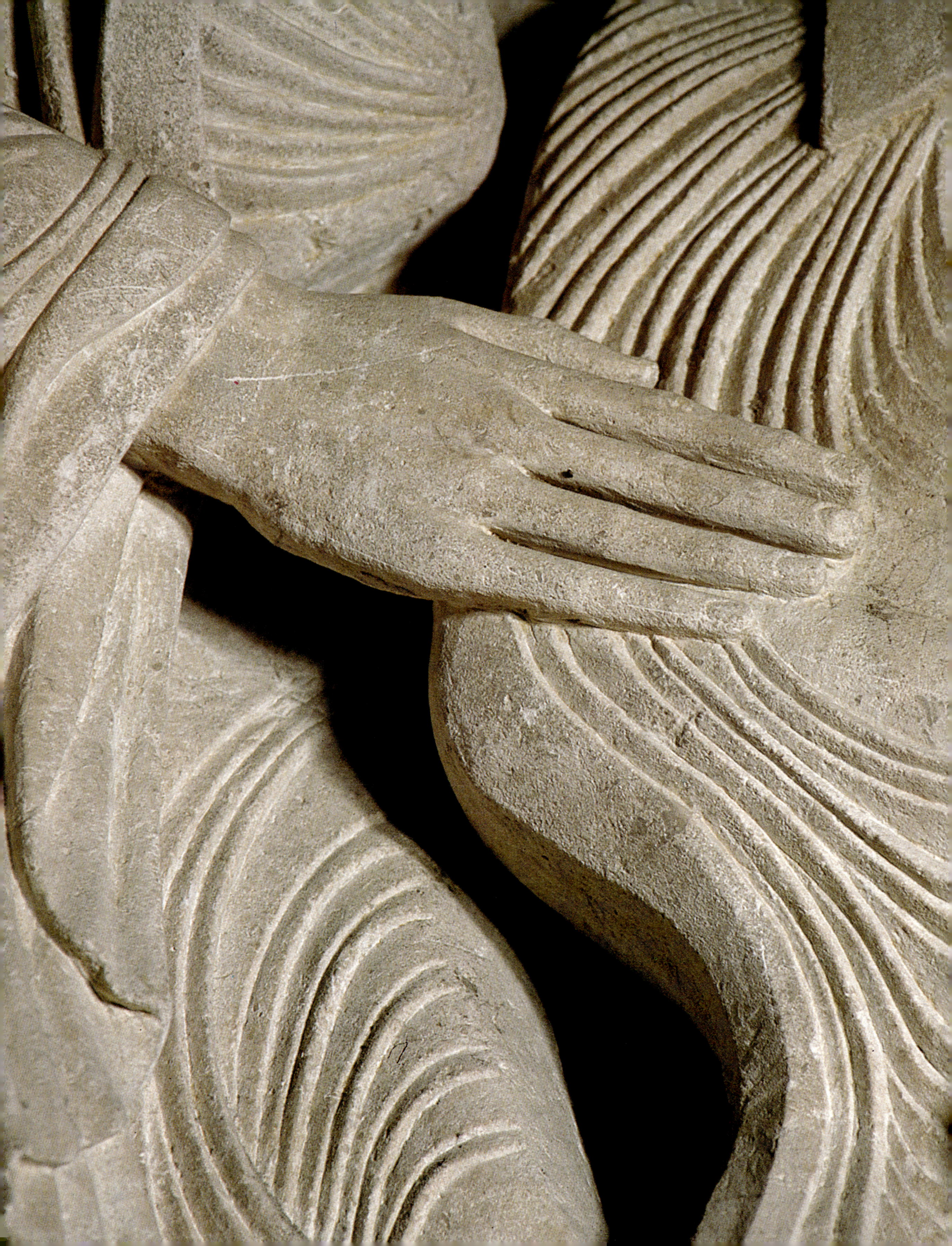

CONTENTS

"VÉZELAY,

On Easter Sunday, 1146, Bernard, abbot of the monastery of Clairvaux, came to the Burgundian town of Vézelay to preach the Second Crusade, a task entrusted to him by Pope Eugenius III. Bernard, who would later be canonized as St. Bernard of Clairvaux, was renowned even in his youth for his dazzling eloquence. Destined for a brilliant career as a scholar and cleric, at age twenty-two he had applied to enter the monastery at Cîteaux, the mother house of the austere Cistercian order. By joining the Cistercians, the young man was choosing to follow the strict observance of the ancient Rule of St. Benedict rather than the more worldly life of the powerful and wealthy Cluniac order, whose mother house was the Burgundian Abbey of Cluny. The Cistercians, a reformed branch of the Benedictines, had been founded in 1098, and the order was thus in its infancy when Bernard applied for admission in 1112. The new order demanded retreat from the world, manual labor, silence, and the elimination of all ornament, both from the monastery buildings and from the dress of the monks themselves. Impressed by the spirit of this brilliant young man, the monks of Cîteaux accepted him as a member, and not long after, sent him to found a new Cistercian house at Clairvaux, in the Champagne region.

During the course of the twelfth century, the Cistercian movement, which was part of a general tendency felt throughout Europe in this period toward a reformed monasticism and a return to earlier traditions, weakened the powerful influence of the monastery of Cluny, which had dominated ecclesiastical life in Western Europe from the end of the tenth century. St. Bernard in particular, who was abbot at Clairvaux until his death in 1153, remained an influential figure in ecclesiastical matters throughout his life, even emerging from retirement on occasion to intercede in the affairs of the church, as well as in those of the Capetian kings. Thus, the monk who stood before the church at Vézelay in the white habit of his order to preach the crusade on March 31, 1146 was one of the most powerful religious figures of the mid-twelfth century.

A man of asceticism and spirituality, and at the same time of eloquence and action, Bernard committed the full force of his energies to the crusade. The term "crusade" itself was not yet in use at the time (the earliest known use of the word is from the mid-thirteenth century); medieval Latin texts generally speak of "the journey to Jerusalem" or "the route to the Holy Sepulcher." Indeed, crusades were conceived as a form of pilgrimage to the sacred places of the Holy Land. Clearly, however, they were also military ventures, intended to free the pilgrimage sites and to bring relief to Christians living in the Islamic East. Thus they served both as acts of piety for penitent sinners and as wars to free Jerusalem. The Christian faithful of the time saw no contradiction in these two objectives, and the first call to the crusades, launched by Pope Urban II at Clermont in 1095, was met with enormous enthusiasm by Christians in the West. The first crusaders set out immediately, gathering crowds of people as they went. Whether armed or civilian, commoner or knight, vassal or baron, all were driven either by conviction or intrigue.

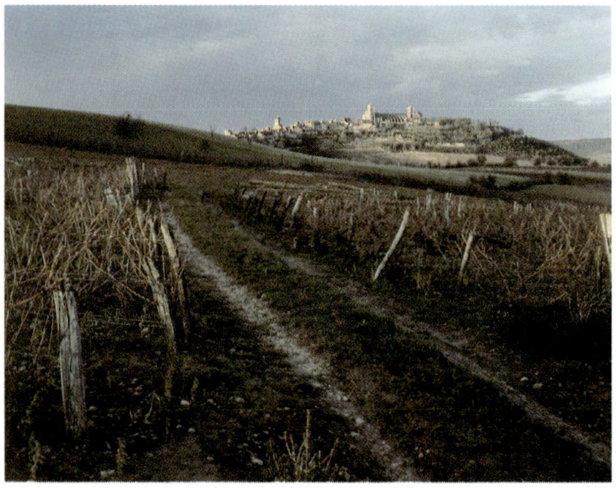

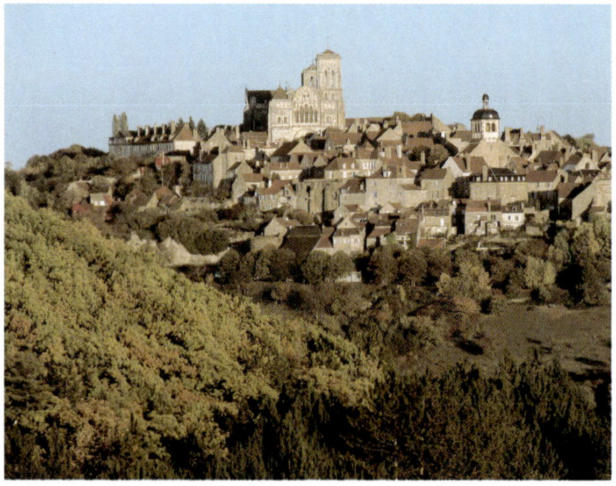

the illustrious monastery"
—Bernard of Clairvaux

In 1099 Jerusalem was taken by the army of Godfrey of Bouillon, and from then on Western Christians believed that they must retain the conquered territory at all costs, including the cities taken along the way to Jerusalem. This conviction would give rise to the primary justification for the Second Crusade when the city of Edessa (Urfa) in southeastern Asia Minor was recaptured by the Arabs in 1145. The Christians of Western Europe were convinced that it must be freed, and that they were obliged to leave everything behind them to follow in the steps of Christ to the Holy Land. Thus this Second Crusade was simultaneously spiritual, political, and military. Driven by the oratory of St. Bernard, its cause was undertaken by Louis VII of France, as well as by a number of other princes. Upon setting out for Jerusalem, Louis VII entrusted the regency of his kingdom to Suger, the abbot of Saint-Denis.

A CHANGING SPIRITUAL AND POLITICAL CLIMATE

The second quarter of the twelfth century saw the rise of the influence of two great monastics: Bernard of Clairvaux, and Suger, abbot of the royal abbey at Saint-Denis, immediately north of Paris. Bernard's domain was primarily spiritual, while that of the Suger was chiefly political. The discordant personalities of these two men express the divergent aspirations of their age. Even more significantly, so do their almost antithetical notions of monastic life. Their views of the role of art, and its place in a house of worship, were deeply conflicting. Suger wrote, in defense of religious art, that "the multicolored beauty of precious stones carries me far from worldly concerns, and by transposing the material with the spiritual, I achieve a high level of meditation." In response, Bernard wrote: "Only contemplation, in all its varied and diverse forms, is everywhere, whether we derive greater pleasure from reading these marbles or reading from manuscripts, whether we prefer to spend the day admiring their details or contemplating the law of God."

Suger was religious in the style of the monastery at Cluny, whose church and cloister overflowed with precious objects, textiles, altarpieces, and sculpted capitals, all created for the greater glory of God. St. Bernard, by contrast, was utterly opposed to capitals carved with monsters and demons, which, he believed, disturbed the monks' prayers; he also rejected the carving of images of the saints into pavements, and all other sources of expense and "ineptitude" in the monastery buildings. Indeed, the complete absence of such decorations is the very definition of the Cistercian style.

It should be noted that St. Bernard's condemnation was directed at the monasteries; secular churches, whose congregations were chiefly lay people, escaped his interdiction, since they presumably needed the crude tool of imagery to reach untutored minds. The Cistercian monasteries, by contrast, were reclusive, voluntarily distancing themselves from all contact with the laity and the secular clergy. However, as Suger would no doubt have objected, the royal abbey at Saint-Denis was an exception. It was, after all, the site

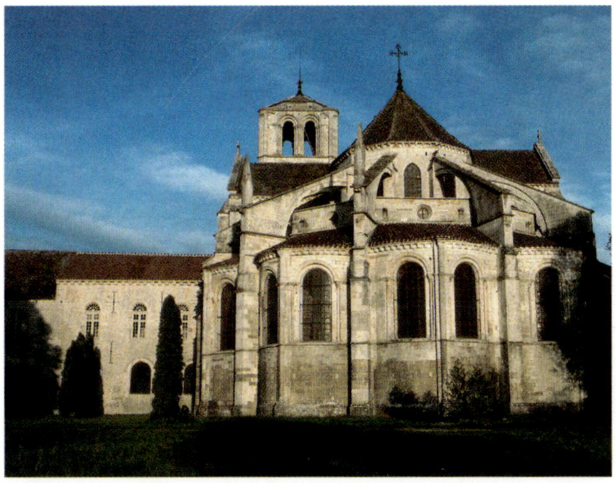

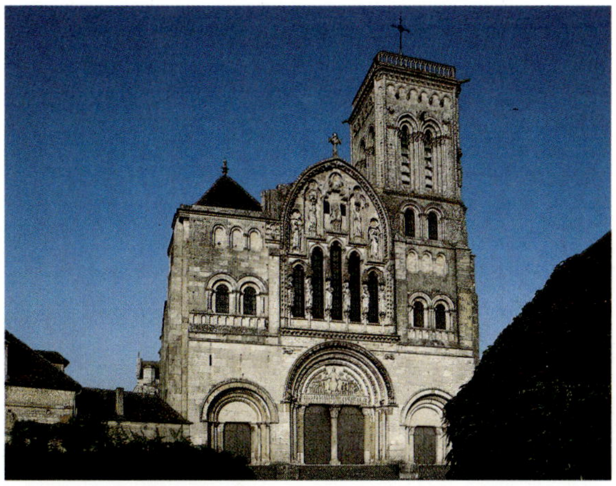

of the tombs of the Capetian kings, and an important pilgrim church as well. A monastery with such important ties to the world was more powerful than Cluny and all its affiliates.

VÉZELAY AS A PILGRIM CHURCH

Although it was St. Bernard who was called to preach at Vézelay, the abbey there, with its richly carved portals and capitals, was certainly no child of Cîteaux, and indeed there was no spiritual link between it and the Cistercians. On the contrary, Vézelay was a dependency of the Abbey of Cluny. It stood, however, at the beginning of one of the four major "French roads" to the Pyrenees, the route to the shrine of St. James at Compostela, in northern Spain. Thus Vézelay offered a distinct advantage for anyone wanting to reach a large number of people.

European Christianity considered three holy places worthy of special veneration: the Holy Land, a destination that remained so distant that it was rarely visited before the crusades; Rome, the seat of the Western Church, where there were innumerable sanctuaries and relics; and the town of Compostela in northern Spain, the site of the tomb of St. James the Greater, one of the first disciples of Jesus and the apostle to Iberia. The pilgrimage to Santiago de Compostela drew great masses of the faithful from all of Europe. Those coming from the north generally traveled along the road from Paris, through Tours and Bordeaux; those from the south, along the road from Arles, through Toulouse. Other pilgrims came from Clermont or Cluny, converging at Le Puy, where the road from the Auvergne began. A fourth, Burgundian, route began at Autun or Vézelay. All of these routes were designed to pass near churches that housed important relics, which the pilgrims would invariably honor with a visit. Of particular note were those of St. Martin at Tours, visited by pilgrims coming from the north; those of St. Foy at Conques, for the pilgrims coming from the Auvergne; and those of St. Martial at Limoges, for those coming from Burgundy. At Vézelay, the relics of St. Mary Magdalene were venerated.

Mary Magdalene is mentioned in the Gospels as a friend and disciple of Christ, and the first person to see Jesus on Easter morning after the Resurrection. Medieval hagiographers conflated her with two other women described in the Gospels: Mary, the sister of Martha of Bethany and Lazarus, whom Jesus raised from the dead; and the penitent sinner who anointed Christ's feet at the feast of Simon the Pharisee (Luke 7:36ff; identified as Mary of Bethany in John 11:2). According to her medieval legend, Mary Magdalene left the Holy Land after Christ's Ascension and traveled to Provence, where she converted masses of people to Christianity, and then became a hermit, living out her days in a cave at Saint-Baume, not far from Aix.

Despite this persuasive story, during the first half of the ninth century pilgrims began to venerate the saint at Vézelay. Former prisoners, attributing their liberation to her intervention, came to the abbey and brought their chains with them as votive offerings. Later, miraculous cures were said to have occurred at the church, and the rumor spread that the Magdalene's body was entombed beneath the high altar. To put an end to the conflicting statements coming from Provence, in the eleventh century the monks at Vézelay presented a document, undoubtedly a forgery, which supposedly confirmed an ancient transfer of the saint's relics to Burgundy. The abbey church, formerly dedicated to the Virgin Mary and to Saints Peter and Paul, was reconsecrated to Mary Magdalene. In 1220, however, the Provençal monks of the abbey at Saint Maximin near Aix upstaged the Vézelay tradition by orchestrating the rediscovery of Mary Magdalene's relics in their own abbey-church. From that time, Vézelay attracted fewer of the faithful.

THE BASILICA FLOURISHES

For the two and a half centuries from the years 1040 to 1280, the church of the Magdalene was responsible for the wealth and celebrity of its Burgundian abbey. Founded in the Carolingian period (ca. 858), the monastery had remained of modest importance before the pilgrimages to venerate the Magdalene had caused it to blossom. With its growing wealth, came an expansion of the old Carolingian church; a new choir and transept were built, and were consecrated in 1104. The work, which was interrupted by a violent revolt of the local population over abusive taxation, did not resume until after 1120, when, on the eve of July 22—Mary Magdalene's day—the townspeople burned down the church's ancient nave. Abbot Renaud de Semur, later abbot of Aubri, oversaw the construction of the new triple-aisled nave, which was begun in 1120 and completed in 1138. During this period, work first began on the tympana—the semicircular stone overdoors to the portals to the nave—which were richly decorated with sculpture, and continued with the capitals of the nave columns, which were also richly carved. A vast rectangular

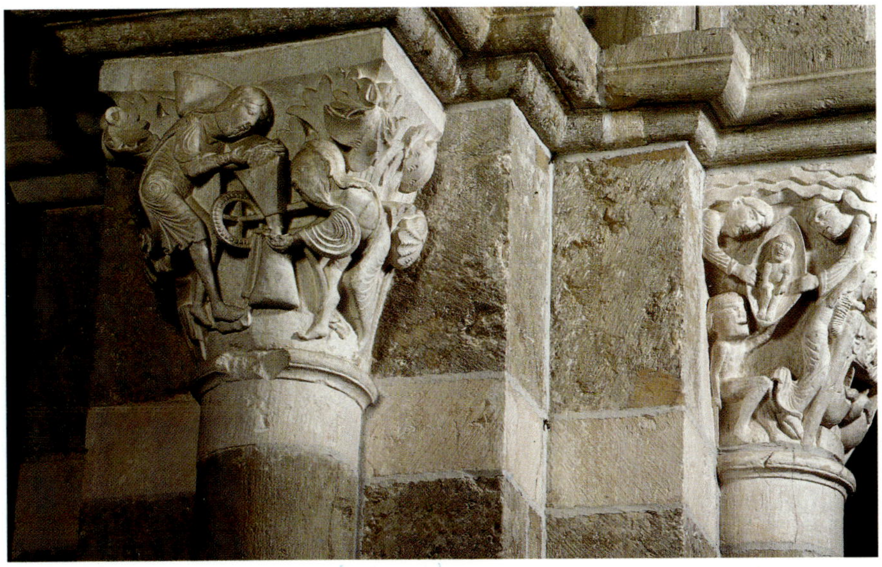

narthex or vestibule, as wide as the nave itself, was soon added to the church. The structure remained in the same state through the 1190s, at which point the abbey was overflowing with riches. Tastes, however, had begun to change. The Romanesque transept and choir were pulled down and reconstructed in the Gothic style. It is this blending of the Romanesque and Gothic that today remains the marvel of the interior of the basilica.

Famous as a site sacred to the Magdalene, Vézelay can attribute its great wealth to a single legal statute. In 863, soon after its founding, the abbey was made a dependency of the Holy See, under the direct control of the pope himself. The abbey was thus independent of any local ecclesiastical or civil authority. When it began to flourish, the pope placed Vézelay under the control of its powerful neighbor, the great abbey at Cluny. In a world becoming ever more feudal, it was a great privilege to be independent of all local authority, whether that of the bishops of Autun or the counts of Nevers.

Cluny itself owed obeisance only to the pope and to the king, and it was this autonomous status that accounted for its power and wealth during the eleventh century. Its religious power was owed to the reformation of the Church achieved by Pope Gregory VII (1073–1085), of which the monks of Cluny were the most faithful supporters and successful implementors. Its political and material strength lay in the fact that Cluny was a mother abbey, with no less than eight hundred affiliates throughout France, its congregations composed of powerful lords endowed with vast estates, capable of challenging a kingdom. Finally, Cluny's spiritual and artistic strength lay in its expansion of the pilgrimages to Compostela by prescribing the routes and developing the monasteries that served them. The monastery at Vézelay, as it was situated within the sphere of Cluny's power, owed its own expanding wealth and artistic influence to the mother Abbey. With Vézelay's strength and prosperity firmly established, in 1162 the pope rescinded the right of the abbots of Cluny to supervise the finances of Vézelay, and from that point on, Vézelay enjoyed total independence as an equal of Cluny.

EASTER 1146

On Easter, 1146, the holiest day of the Christian calendar, a crowd had gathered around Bernard of Clairvaux. The vast crowd filled even the smallest paths that climbed the hill, hoping to hear the mass given at the tomb of Mary Magdalene. It was in this grand setting, with the basilica in the background, its choir and transepts in the Romanesque style, its new nave and narthex in the new Gothic manner, with sculpture everywhere, that the abbot presented his sermon.

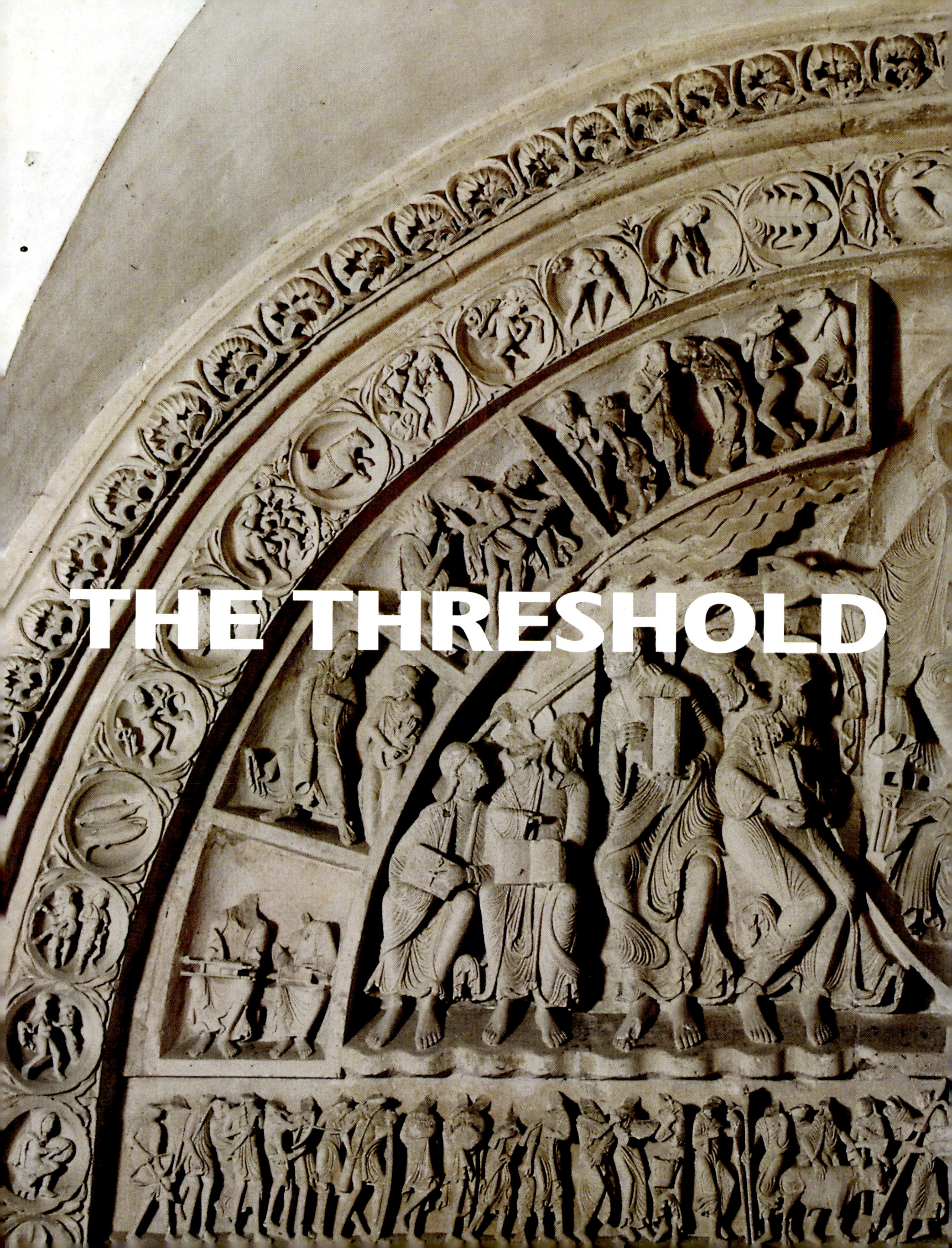

THE THRESHOLD

The Church Reaches Out to the World

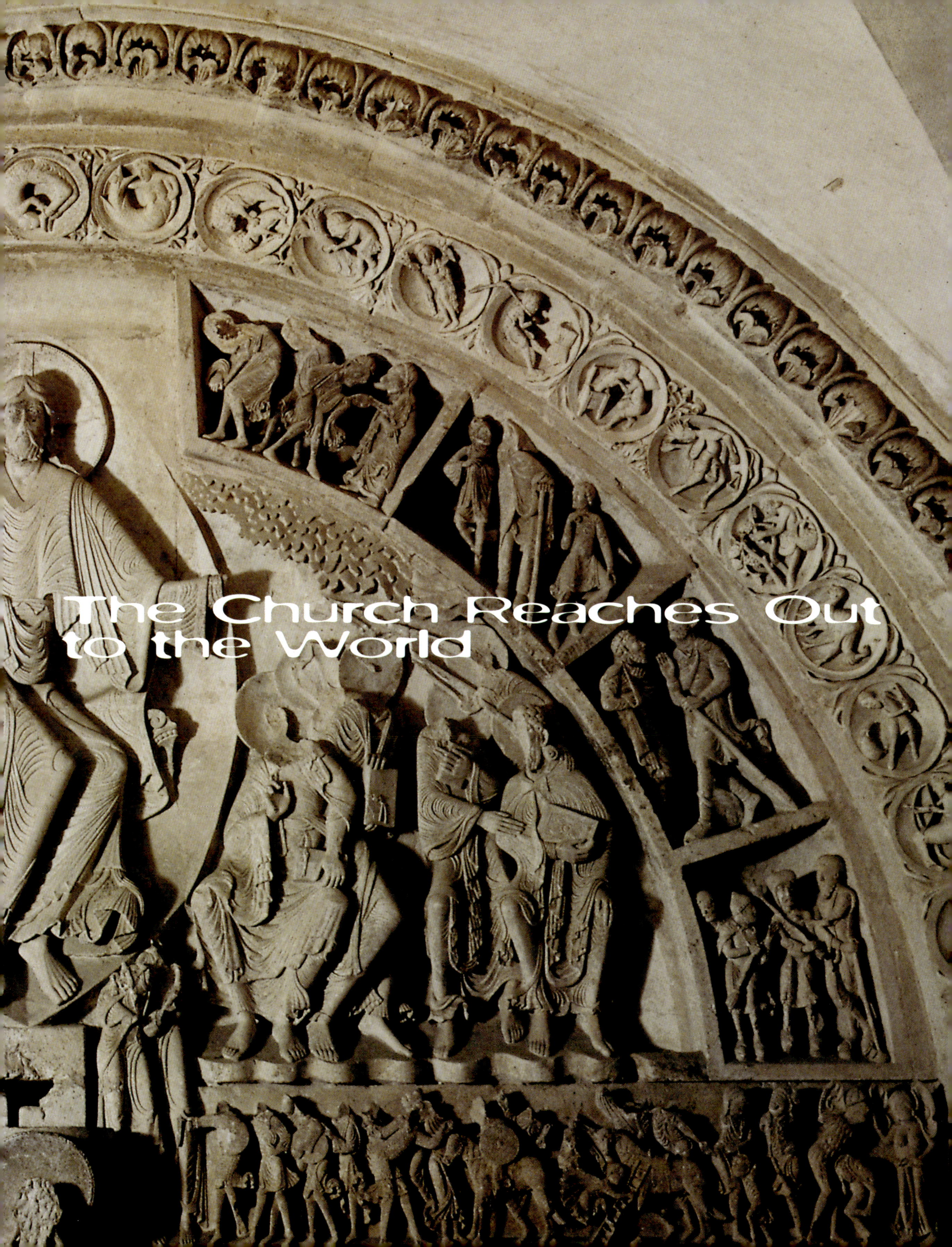

The symbolic and artistic threshold of the basilica has always been in the narthex, in the Romanesque sculpture of the three doors that lead into the nave. The enormous tympanum of the central portal, and the smaller tympana of the aisle doors, were built and carved sometime around 1220 or 1225. Compared with these, the tympana of the façade are scarcely worth mentioning. There, the aisle doors are utterly devoid of sculpture, and the central portal, which was destroyed by the hammers of revolutionaries in 1793, presents only a poor nineteenth-century copy of a Romanesque Last Judgment. The tympana at the entrance to the nave, however, belong to a group of great sculpted portals carved in the first quarter of the twelfth century. Most of these magnificent doorways are in Aquitaine and Burgundy, but other fine examples are also to be found all along the pilgrim routes to Compostela, and in the abbeys and priories of the Cluniac order. Along with those of Moissac, Conques, Autun, and the now-vanished façade of the monastery of Cluny, the tympana at Vézelay are the most renowned members of this family of splendid Romanesque overdoors.

The great size and importance of the central portal at Vézelay make it the most prominent feature of the narthex. The door is both wider and taller than the aisle doors, and it is divided in two at the center by a sculpted pier. This pillar once carried a figure of St. John the Baptist, which was almost completely destroyed during the Revolution. The columns that support the springing of the arch at left and right are extended upward by a register of figures carved in relief. The tympanum, of a size unprecedented when it was carved, is slightly more than nineteen feet, eight inches in diameter. Supported by a massive horizontal lintel profusely carved with figures, the tympanum has at its center an immense figure of Christ flanked by the apostles and enclosed by an arc of eight historiated compartments. These scenes are framed by a series of moldings, including one row of carved foliage and another of figured medallions, emphasizing the semicircular form of the whole.

CHRIST AND HIS APOSTLES

The focus of the portal's composition is a colossal figure of Christ, which sits enthroned in the center of the tympanum. Recognizable by a halo inscribed with a cross, which alludes to the crucifixion, Christ is surrounded by a mandorla, a wide almond-shaped ellipsis that sets off his figure like a luminous aureole. His lightly flexed arms reach out to the left and right as if in a broad embrace, and rays of light emanate from his extended fingers to descend on the heads of the twelve apostles, who are gathered on either side in two groups. Each apostle holds a book; some of the books are open and some are closed. To the right

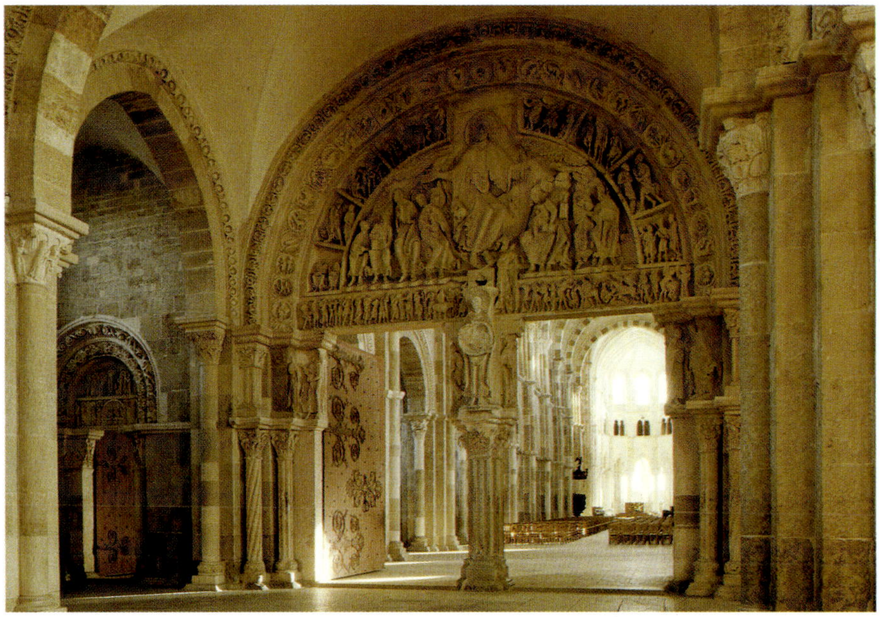

of Christ, distinct and immediately identifiable, is the figure of St. Peter, who holds the heavy key to the kingdom of Heaven. Seated in the foreground near Peter is a beardless disciple, similarly distinguished by his large size. He is clearly recognizable as John, whom tradition often elevates, along with Peter, to privileged rank. The animated postures of the other apostles seem almost to suggest the rhythms of a dance.

Since the apostles are shown receiving the divine light of Christ, the scene appears at first to be a traditional representation of Pentecost. According to the Book of Acts (chapter 2), the apostles gathered fifty days after Easter (the Greek word *pentekonta* means "fifty"), "And there appeared unto them cloven tongues like as of fire, and it sat upon each of them. And they were all filled with the Holy Ghost" (King James Version). This account does not mention the presence of Christ, however; moreover, the traditional iconography of the day of Pentecost includes certain specific features that are not present here: small flames above each head, the Holy Spirit in the form of a dove descending on the gathered disciples, and the figure of the Virgin Mary, who sits at the center of the assembled apostles. None of these features appears on the Vézelay tympanum, whose emphasis is almost entirely on Christ as the dispenser of spiritual fire. Thus it cannot be an image of Pentecost.

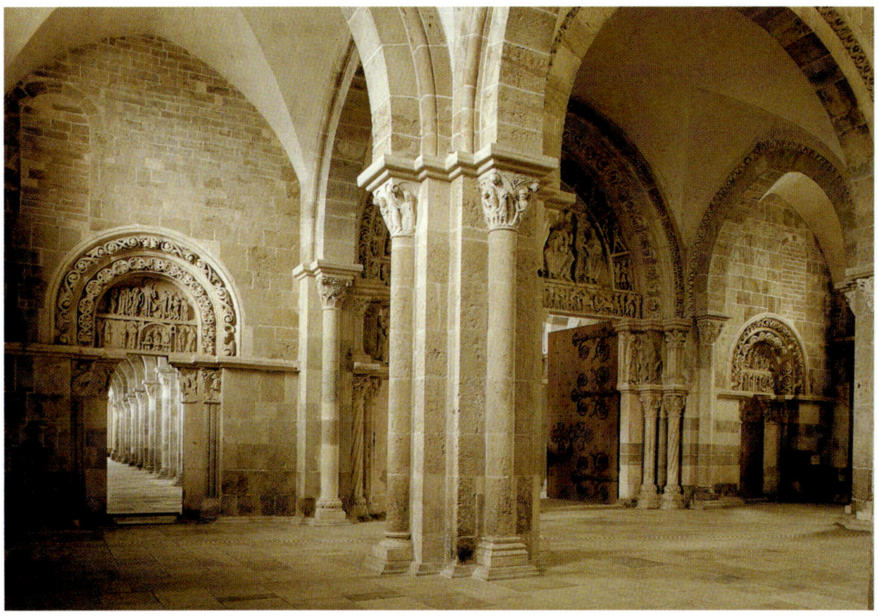

Rather than a narrative scene illustrating a precise moment of the descent of the Holy Spirit, the Vézelay tympanum represents a theophany, an atemporal vision of God, represented, according to the preferences of medieval theology and iconography, as Jesus, the Son of God and the Second Person of the Trinity. This theophany is, however, of a different type entirely than the roughly contemporary examples that appear on the tympana at Moissac and Autun. The Christ at Vézelay occupies an altogether different sphere than the Christ figures above those portals. Here he is not a Christ of the Last Days, neither the apocalyptic vision found at Moissac, nor the Final Judge of Autun. Instead, the Christ of Vézelay is shown in celestial and eternal glory, yet at the same time seemingly reabsorbed by the temporality of the apostles, restored to a worldly existence and brought to earth once again in this momentary vision. Infused with a tremendous sense of joy, the work comprehends both the transcendence and the immanence of the divine.

THE FIGURES ON THE LINTEL

Two long processions of small figures emerge from the ends of the lintel to meet at its center. Many and varied, they represent in miniature the peoples of the earth. On the section of the lintel to the viewer's right, next to and just below the Christ's mandorla, stand two elongated figures, hard to identify since their heads were knocked off by vandals during the French Revolution. These figures, so much larger than the others on the lintel, must surely represent the apostles Peter and Paul, whose presence evokes the debates in the early Church over the scope of the Christian mission. Paul believed from his conversion that Christ had intended that the Church should reach out to embrace all nations, including the pagan world. Other early Christians, including Peter, believed that the Christian message had been intended only for Jews, whose belief in the Messiah Christ had fulfilled. However, according to the Book of Acts, Peter had a dream that convinced him that the Christian message should be offered to the world, and that Christianity should be, not a "Church of circumcision" but a "Church of the gentiles" (from the Latin *gentes,* "nations"). Thus the presence of Peter and Paul on the lintel at Vézelay is surely meant to symbolize Christianity's expansion across the earth.

The lintel in effect presents a census of the peoples of antiquity, arranged according to a clear hierarchy, starting at the center of the composition and progressing outward. On the right half, near the center, Roman soldiers dressed in suits of armor and equipped with shields have come to pay their respects to the apostles. On the left side, a Roman priest is about to sacrifice a bull. A large procession, apparently of Greeks, follows. On both the extreme left and the extreme right are peoples of lower order. To the left, eight fierce archers, perhaps Scythians or Parthians, prepare to let loose their arrows, while to the right, African Pygmies are shown climbing ladders to mount their horses. To the right of them is a strange tribe of people with enormous ears, resembling animals, who, according to ancient tales, lived in far-off India. Here, then, "civilized" antiquity is portrayed by Greek and Roman soldiers and priests, who are set close to the figure of Christ, while the more "barbaric" peoples of the ancient world—Persian hunters, African tribes, and the mythical inhabitants of India—are placed at a greater distance from him. Thus, gathered upon the lintel are representations of every continent, every degree of civilization, and every level of ancient society.

The people on the lintel are certainly meant to represent folk of antiquity, however the "antiquity" presented is one of the medieval European imagination: a pagan world, in need of conversion. Moreover, the reliefs on the lintel express a message that complements that of the theophany depicted above them. Inscribed upon the tympanum are the words that the Bible records that Christ spoke to his apostles: "And ye shall be witnesses unto me . . . unto the uttermost part of the earth" (Acts 1, 8); and "Go ye therefore, and teach all nations, baptizing them in the name of the Father, and of the Son and of the Holy Ghost" (Matthew 28, 19). Thus, another moment from the Gospels, the Mission of the Apostles, has been fused with the traditional iconography of the day of Pentecost. Just prior to his Ascension, Christ blessed his apostles and sent them off to evangelize the earth, promising that after he left them he would send the Holy Spirit to help them. Following this, he ascended into heaven. In the Scriptures, several days pass between the Mission of the Apostles—Christ's call for them to carry the gospel to all of creation, made just before his Ascension—and the actual beginning of their mission, which took place on the day of Pentecost. On the central portal at Vézelay, the sculpture fuses the two incidents, the tympanum and lintel bringing together the dramatic intensity of both Christ's promise and its realization.

EIGHT STATES OF THE WORLD

Eight small scenes, separated into four symmetrical compartments, surround the arc of the tympanum. They, too, address the theme of universal mission, which is represented symbolically by an elementary numerology: the number four refers to the four points of the compass, while the number eight symbolizes regeneration and baptism. As on the lintel, the nations depicted stand for more than themselves. Each people shown is afflicted with a physical or mental defect that represents some moral or spiritual imperfection. Thus, the act of evangelism, portrayed on the lintel in its vast geographic and social reach, is shown on the tympanum as the agent of the power of salvation, capable of bestowing, upon conversion, a healing of body and soul.

The figures in these eight compartments, like those on the lintel, are arranged according to a certain hierarchy. The four lower compartments symbolize moral and spiritual behavior, and can be considered as a group. On the left, the two scribes whose heads have been knocked off, each of whom rests a portable desk on his knees, represent the apostles, or at least men faithful to Christ. The two figures immediately above them person-

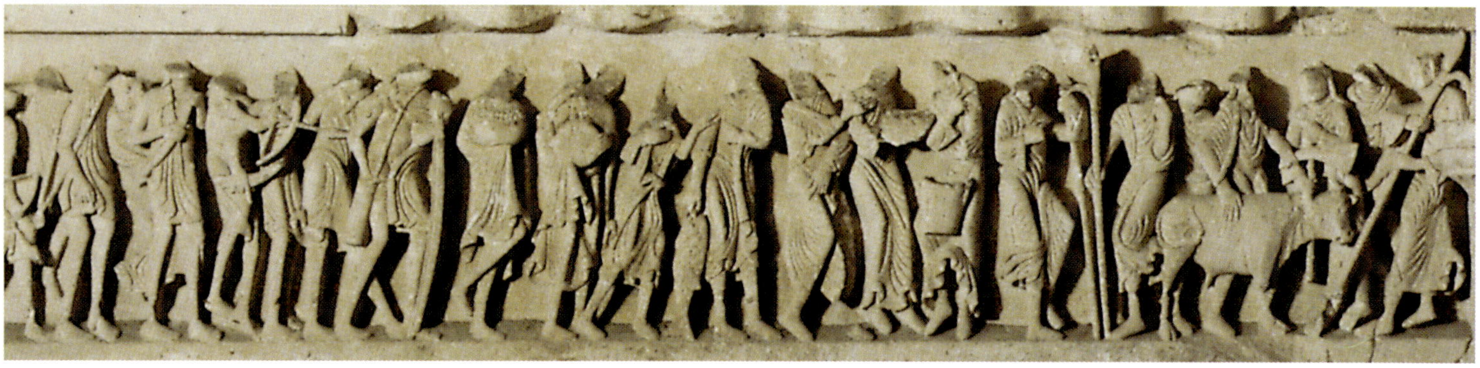

ify the Jews. In the corresponding compartments on the right, two attempted acts of persuasion are contrasted, both of which are rejected. In the upper one, an honest soldier is offered a bribe, which he refuses; in the lower compartment, a Christian tries to convert two Assyrian magi. The Byzantine soldier in the upper compartment refuses to be lead into wrongdoing, while the magi below refuse to be brought into the true faith.

The four upper compartments, which each correspond to physical and mental ills, are arranged according to their severity. The mute, the person lacking a sense of smell, the blind, the deaf, and the hunchbacked are personified by various nationalities: dog-headed men for the mute, pig-snouted Ethiopians for people without a sense of smell, and the mythical people of India with their enormous ears for the deaf. Less grievously deformed, Phrygians are shown with a club foot, a deformed knee, and a withered hand. Facing them are representations of mental ills: a man possessed, and a set of Cappadocian Siamese twins, presented naked and in an indecent pose. These were the classic maladies of the biblical repertoire, which would, according to prophesy, be healed with the coming of the Kingdom of God. They are listed in the Book of Isaiah, and it is remarkable to note the close correspondence between that text and the scenes on the tympanum: "Strengthen ye the weak hands, and confirm the feeble knees. Say to them that are fearful of heart, 'Be strong, fear not: behold your God will come with vengeance . . . The eyes of the blind shall be opened, and the ears of the deaf shall be unstopped.' Then shall the lame man leap as a hart, and the tongue of the dumb sing" (Isaiah 35, 3–6). Cures such as these have been associated with the Messiah from the time of the Old Testament prophets, and as a matter of course, to the miracles performed by Christ during his earthly life.

THE APOSTOLIC MISSION AND THE CRUSADES

Designed and executed some twenty years after the beginning of the First Crusade, the iconographic program of the Vézelay tympanum must be considered in terms of that great movement to mobilize the minds and spirits of Christians throughout Western Europe. Indeed, during the course of the twelfth century, Vézelay was the site of the launching of a crusade on more than one occasion. Not only was the abbey the place where Bernard of Clairvaux would first preach the Second Crusade, it was also the point of departure for the Third Crusade in 1190. The choice of iconographic themes at Vézelay can hardly have been accidental; the similarity between the evangelical mission of the apostles and the hoped-for triumph of the Christian faith in the Holy Land by the crusaders would scarcely have been overlooked. When Pope Urban II, a member of the Cluniac order, began the First Crusade in 1095, the venture was proclaimed at Clermont. The objective on this occasion was to deliver the tomb of Christ from the Muslims. For the Second Crusade, which was launched at Vézelay, Bernard of Clairvaux focused on a different objective. During his sermon he exclaimed: "Let the Christian people go and convert these pagan nations, and let them take advantage of those very treasures the crusades have brought to light."

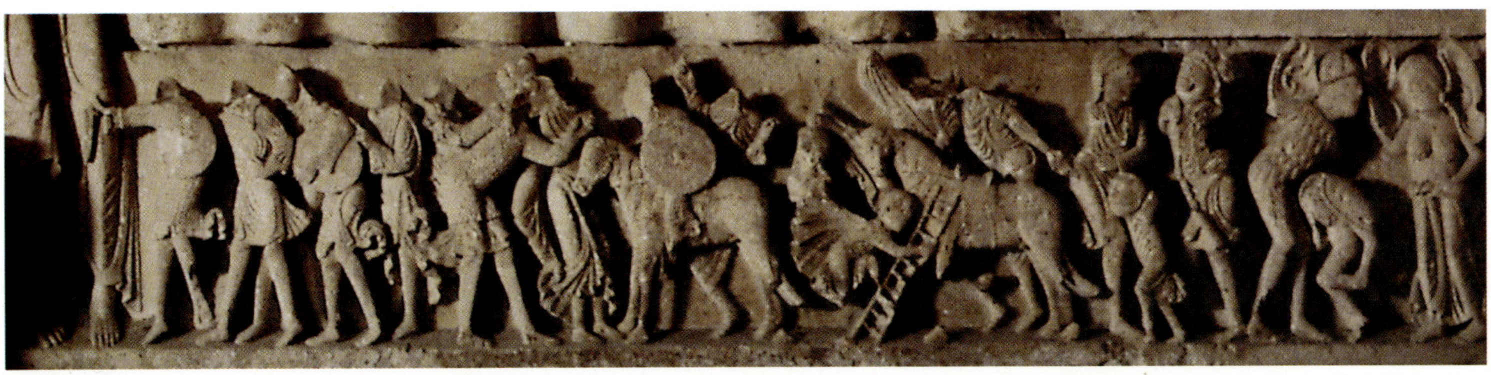

The Gift of the Holy Spirit

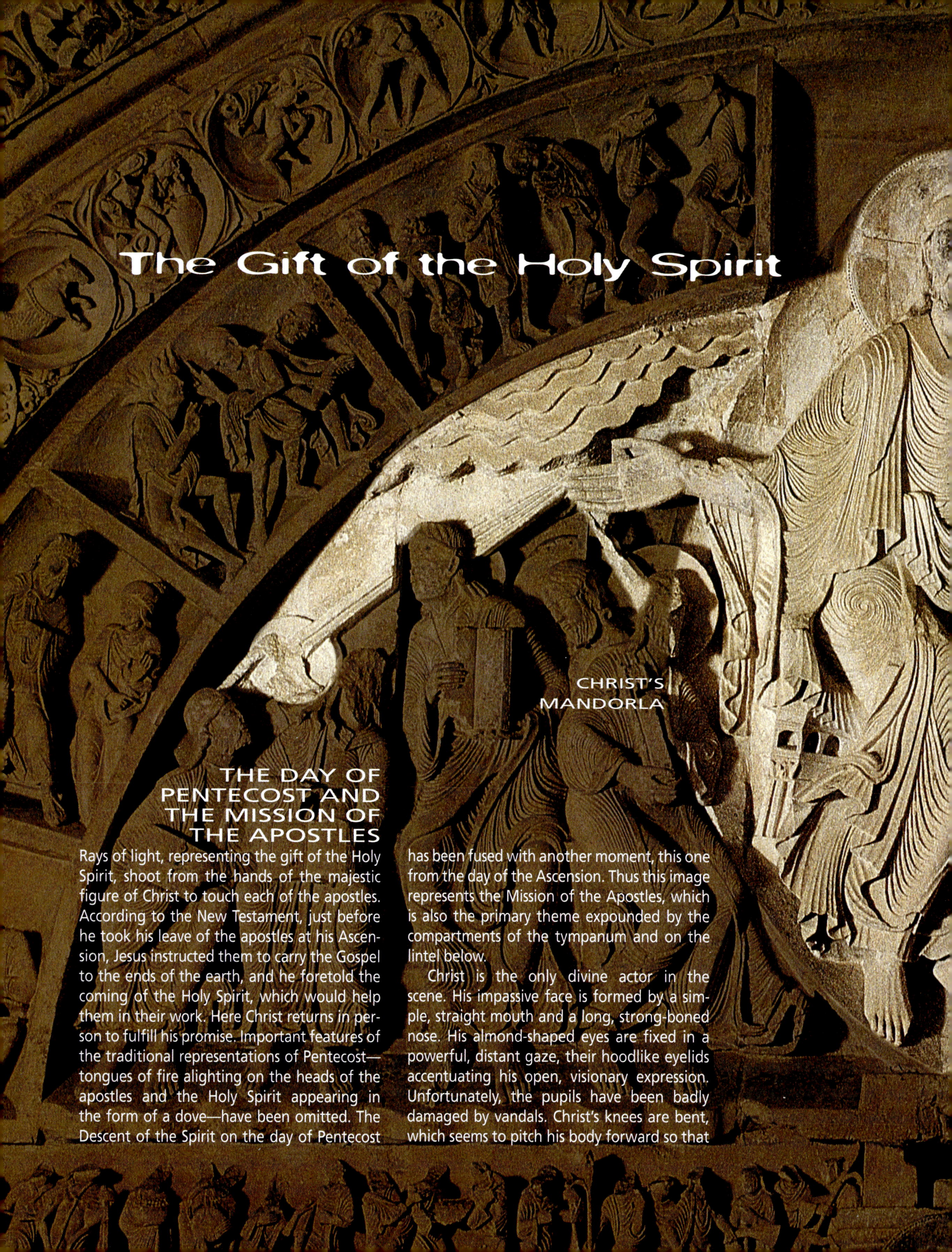

THE DAY OF PENTECOST AND THE MISSION OF THE APOSTLES

Rays of light, representing the gift of the Holy Spirit, shoot from the hands of the majestic figure of Christ to touch each of the apostles. According to the New Testament, just before he took his leave of the apostles at his Ascension, Jesus instructed them to carry the Gospel to the ends of the earth, and he foretold the coming of the Holy Spirit, which would help them in their work. Here Christ returns in person to fulfill his promise. Important features of the traditional representations of Pentecost—tongues of fire alighting on the heads of the apostles and the Holy Spirit appearing in the form of a dove—have been omitted. The Descent of the Spirit on the day of Pentecost has been fused with another moment, this one from the day of the Ascension. Thus this image represents the Mission of the Apostles, which is also the primary theme expounded by the compartments of the tympanum and on the lintel below.

Christ is the only divine actor in the scene. His impassive face is formed by a simple, straight mouth and a long, strong-boned nose. His almond-shaped eyes are fixed in a powerful, distant gaze, their hoodlike eyelids accentuating his open, visionary expression. Unfortunately, the pupils have been badly damaged by vandals. Christ's knees are bent, which seems to pitch his body forward so that

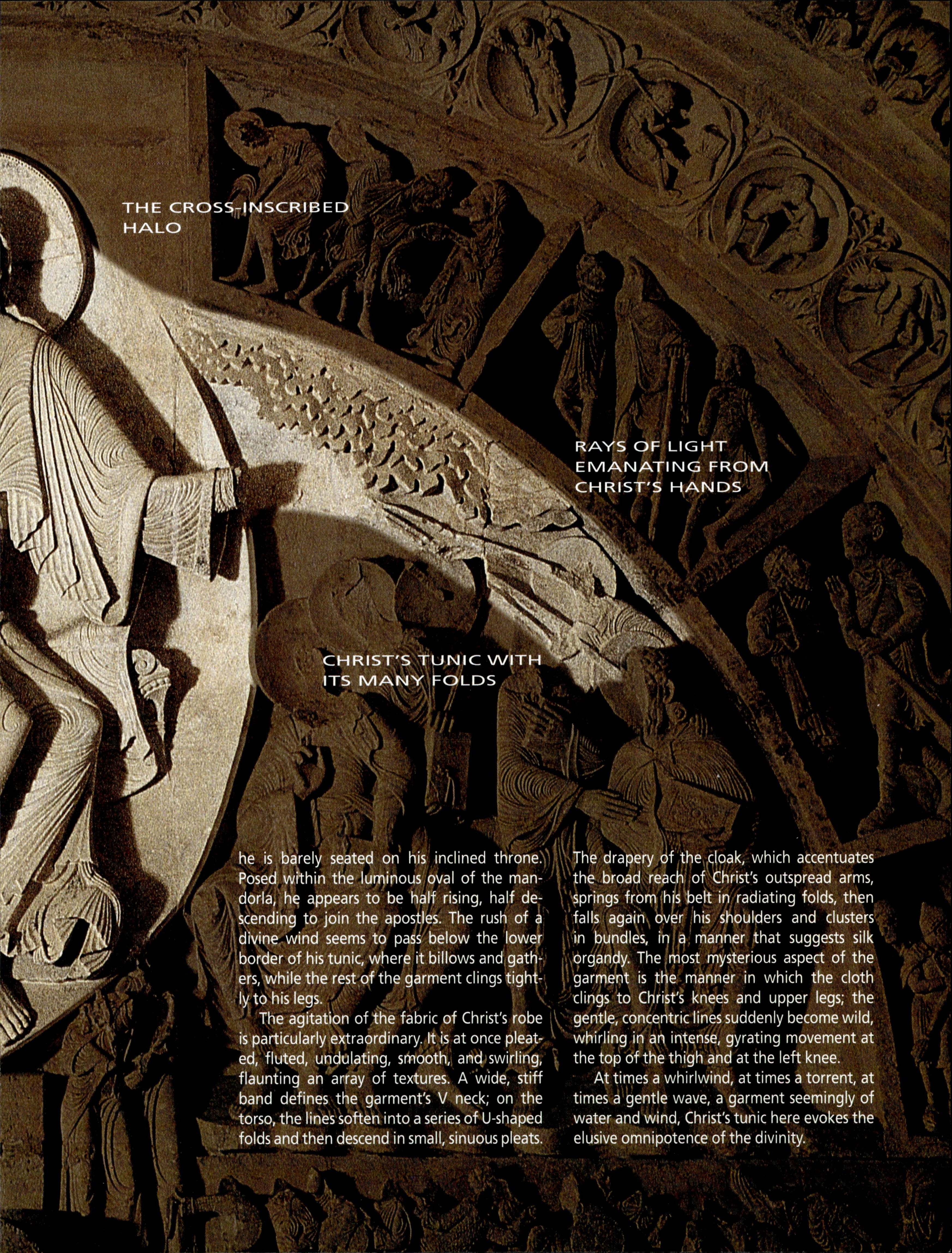

he is barely seated on his inclined throne. Posed within the luminous oval of the mandorla, he appears to be half rising, half descending to join the apostles. The rush of a divine wind seems to pass below the lower border of his tunic, where it billows and gathers, while the rest of the garment clings tightly to his legs.

The agitation of the fabric of Christ's robe is particularly extraordinary. It is at once pleated, fluted, undulating, smooth, and swirling, flaunting an array of textures. A wide, stiff band defines the garment's V neck; on the torso, the lines soften into a series of U-shaped folds and then descend in small, sinuous pleats. The drapery of the cloak, which accentuates the broad reach of Christ's outspread arms, springs from his belt in radiating folds, then falls again over his shoulders and clusters in bundles, in a manner that suggests silk organdy. The most mysterious aspect of the garment is the manner in which the cloth clings to Christ's knees and upper legs; the gentle, concentric lines suddenly become wild, whirling in an intense, gyrating movement at the top of the thigh and at the left knee.

At times a whirlwind, at times a torrent, at times a gentle wave, a garment seemingly of water and wind, Christ's tunic here evokes the elusive omnipotence of the divinity.

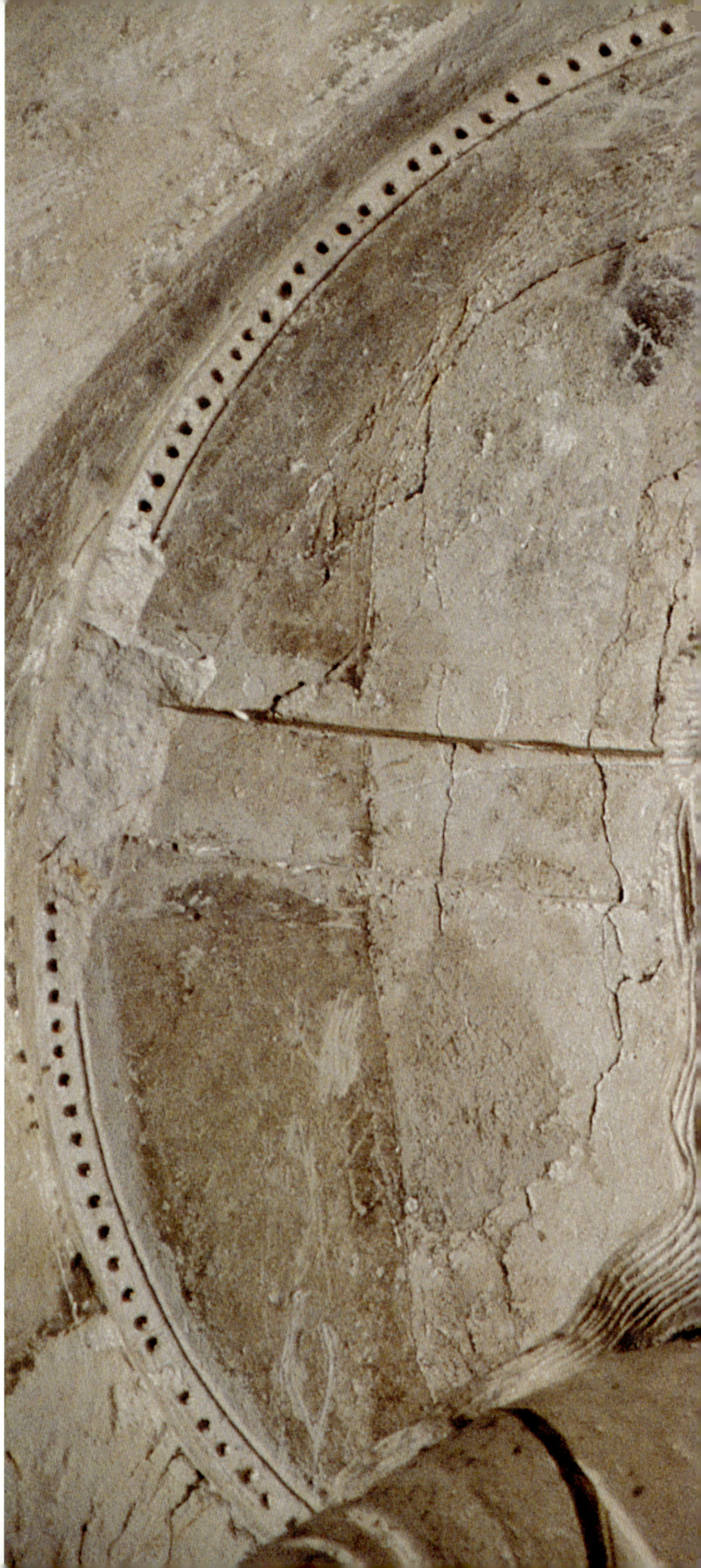

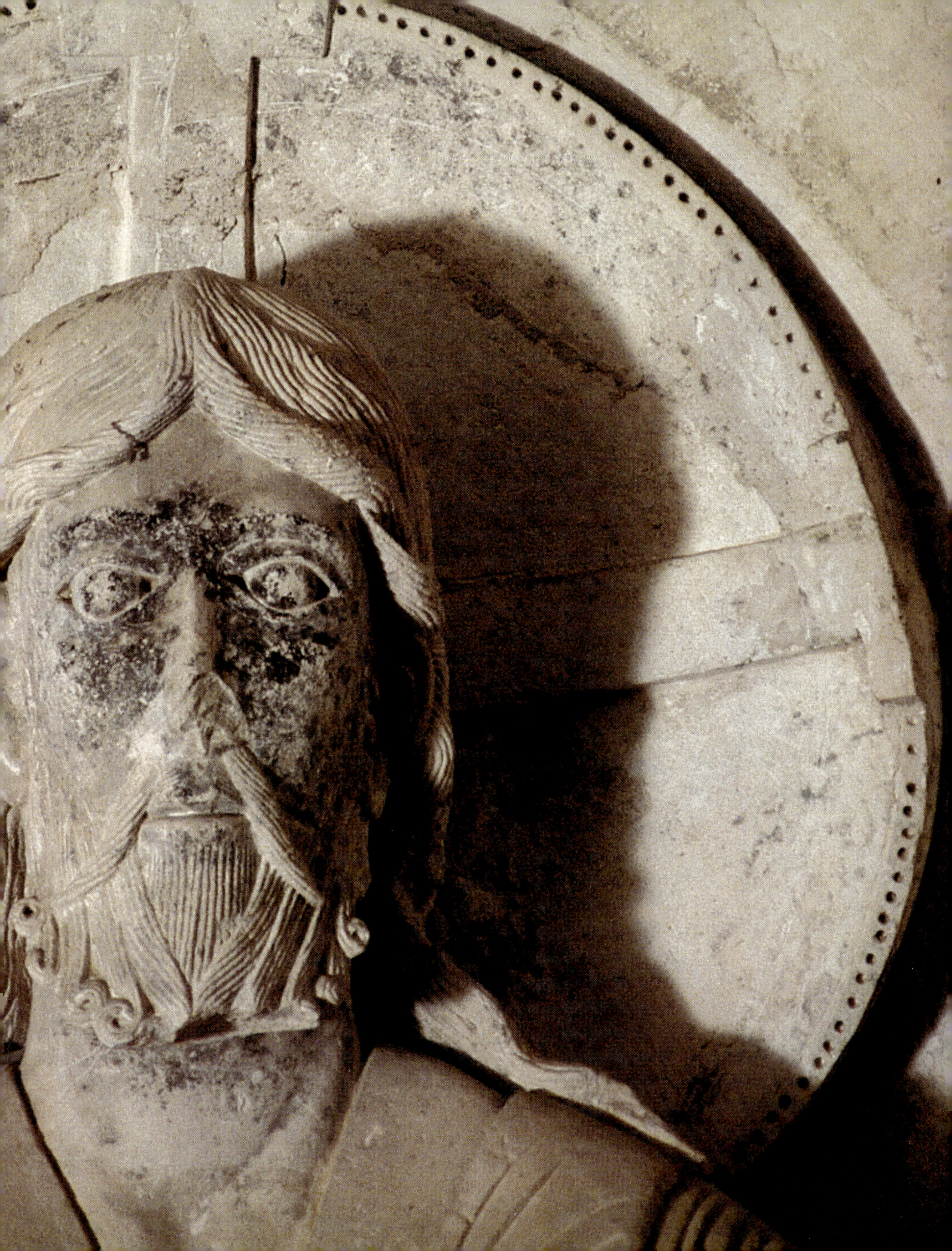

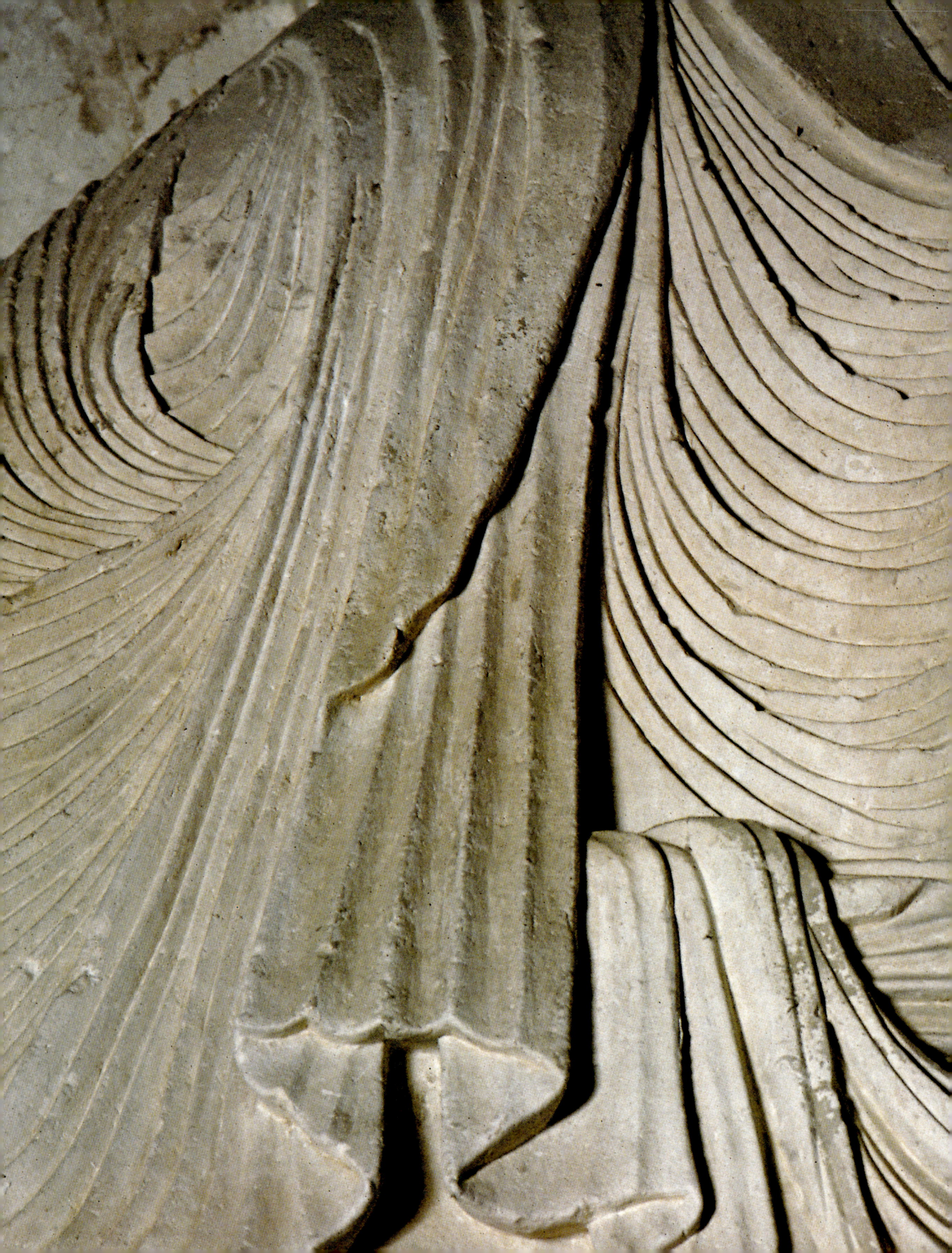

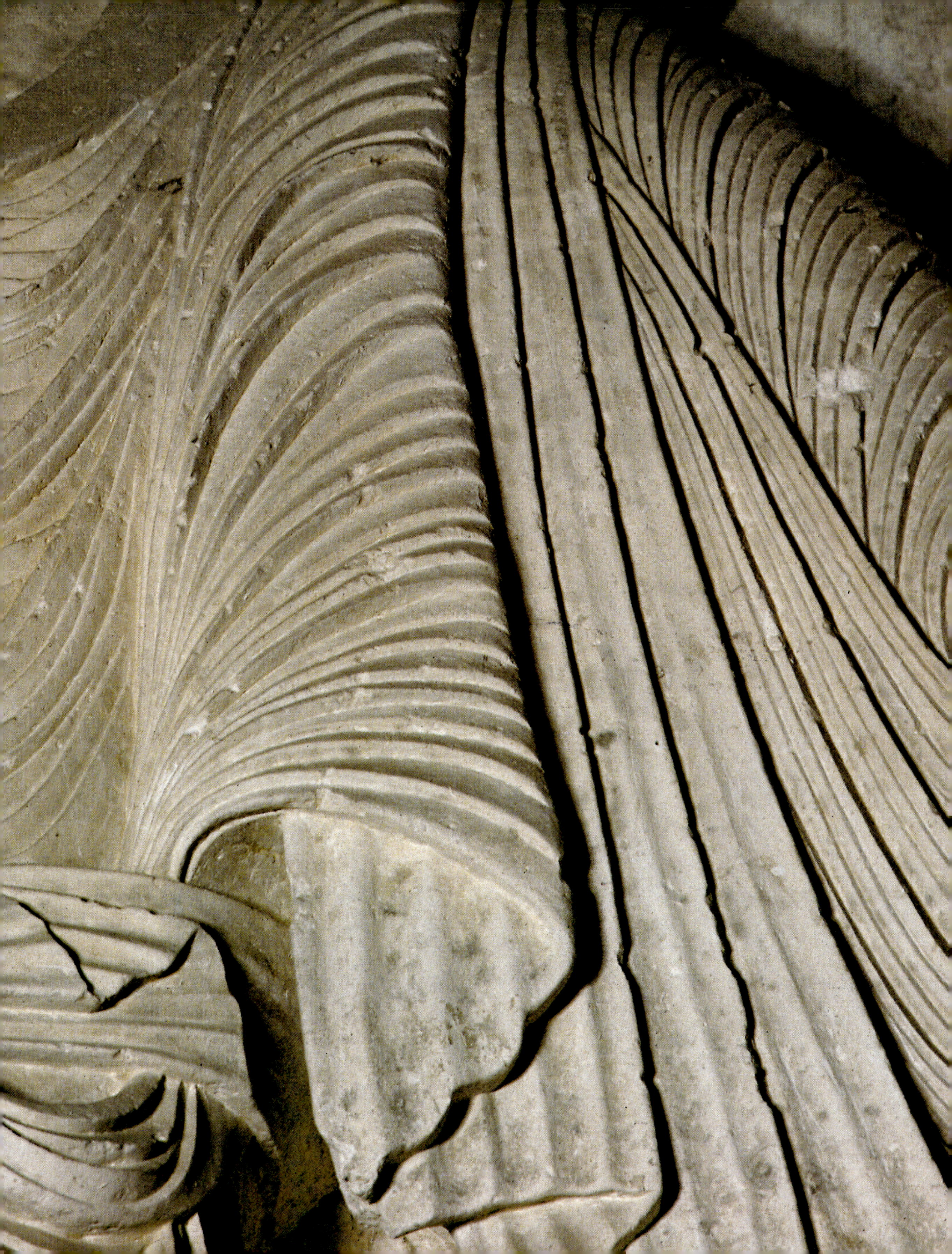

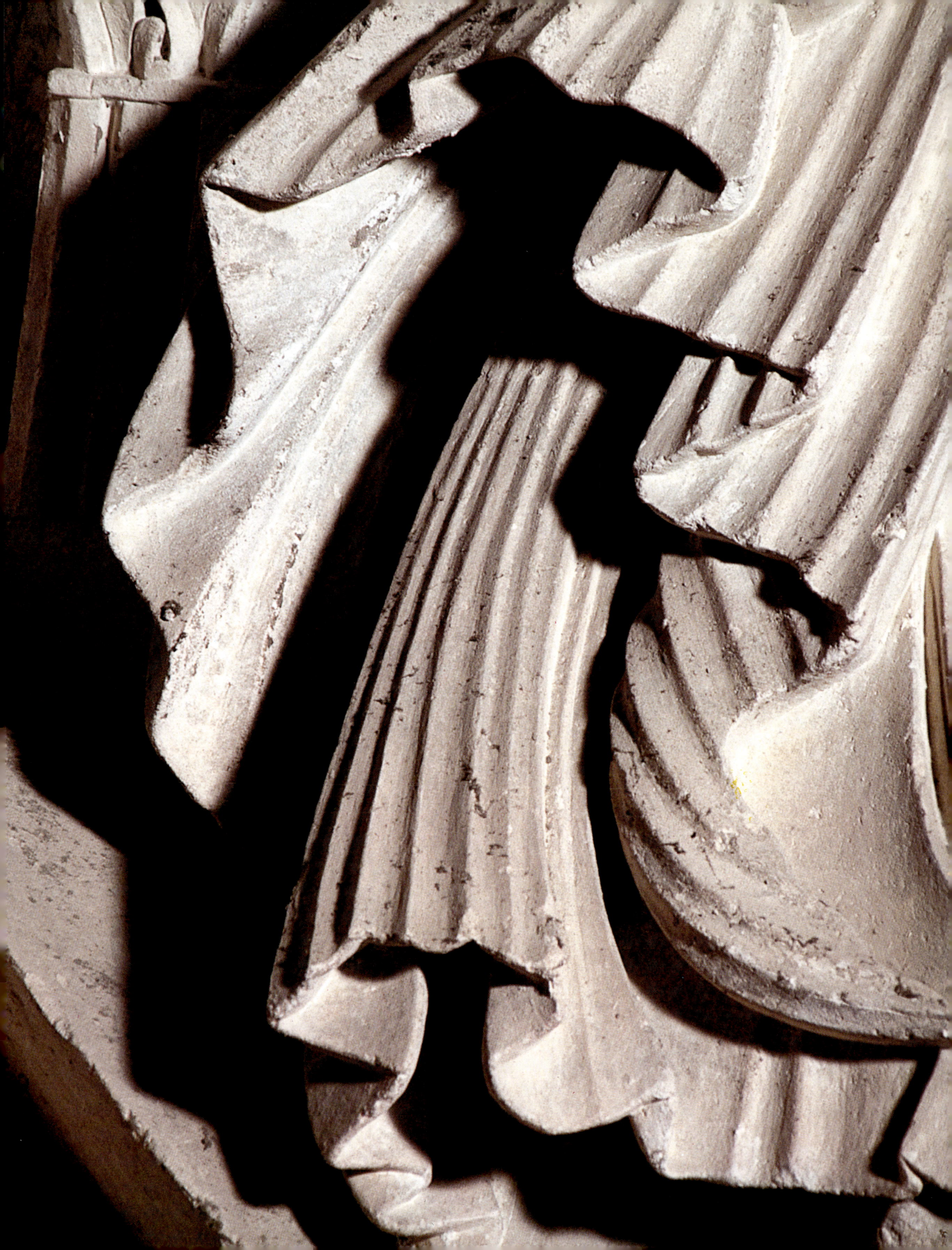

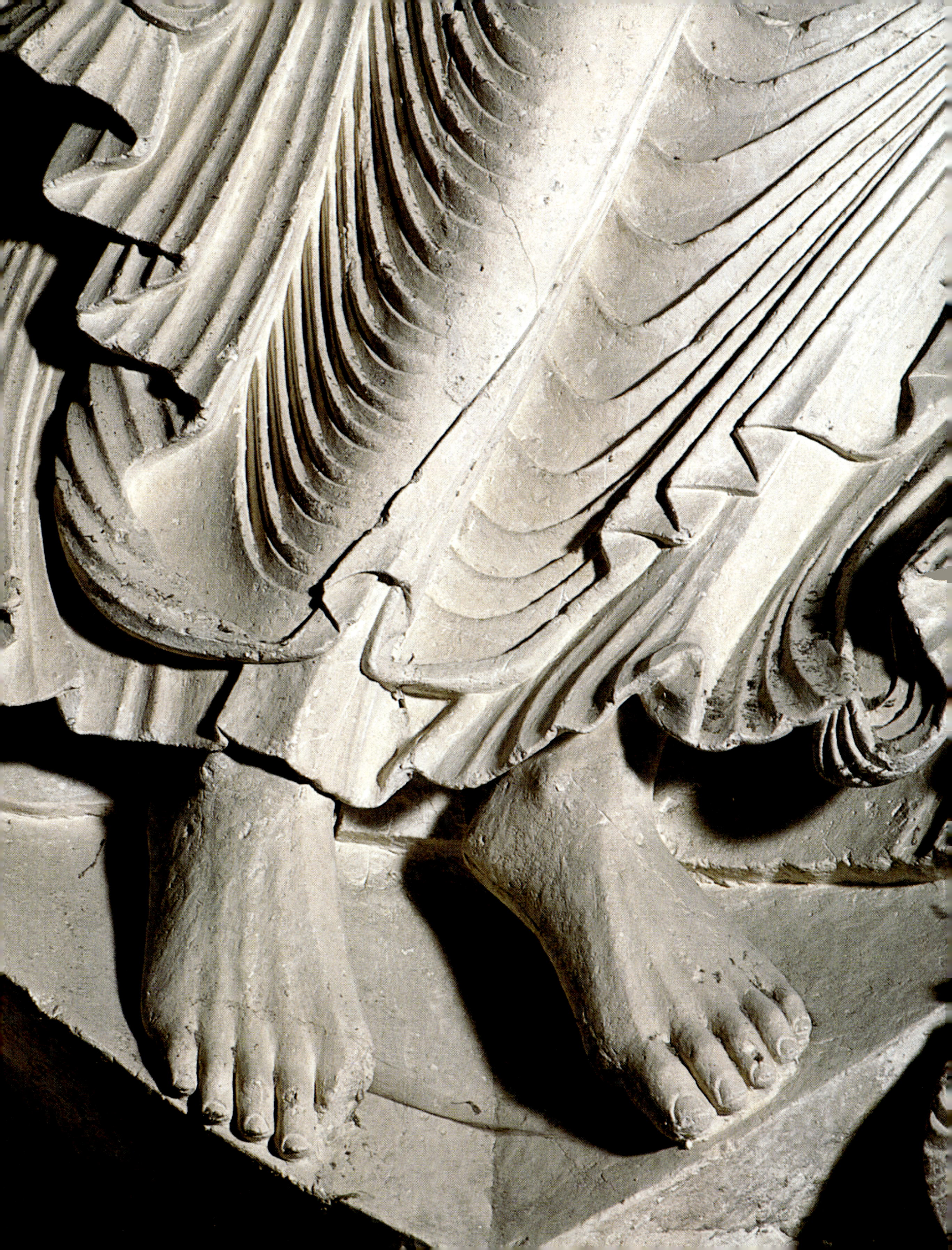

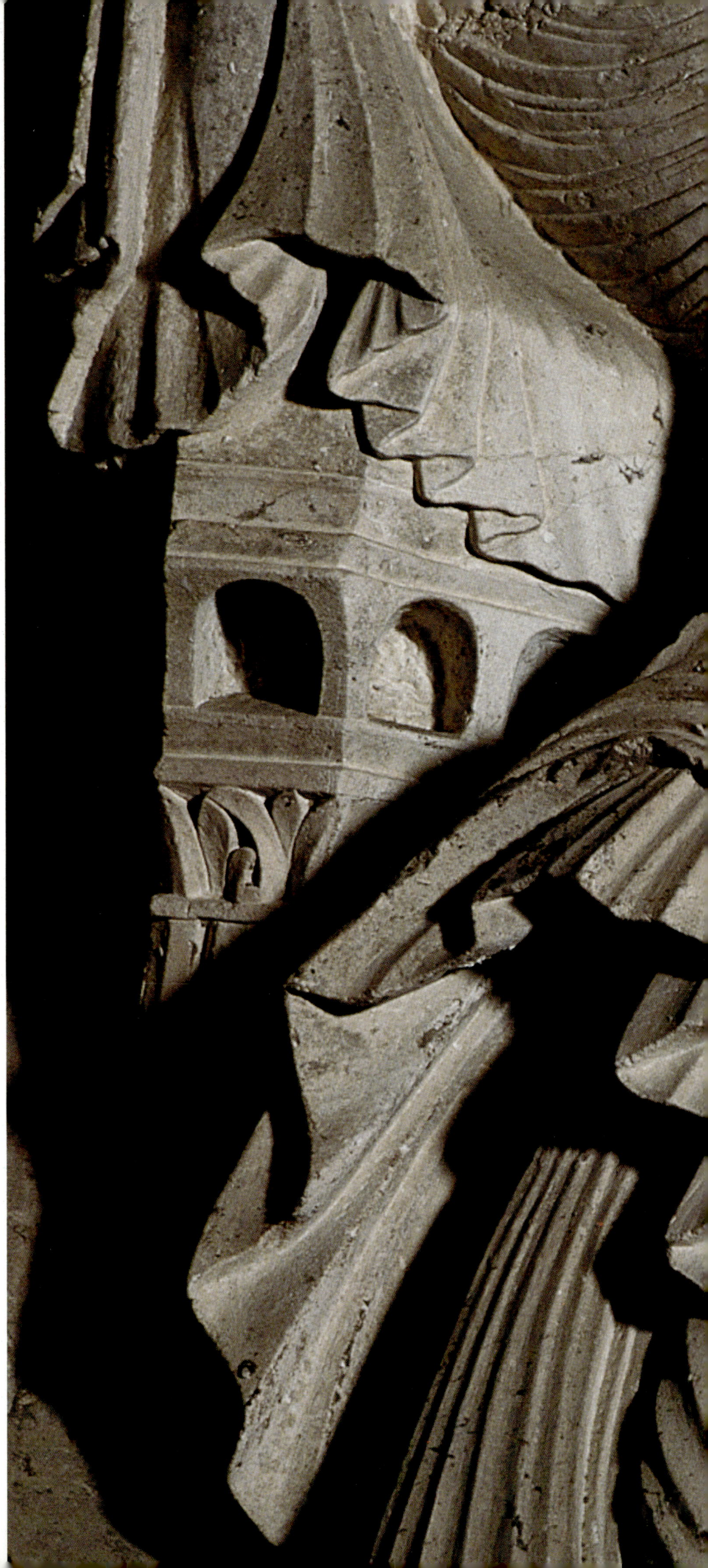

CAPITALS, ARCHES, AND
FLUTED PILASTERS ADORN
THE THRONE OF CHRIST

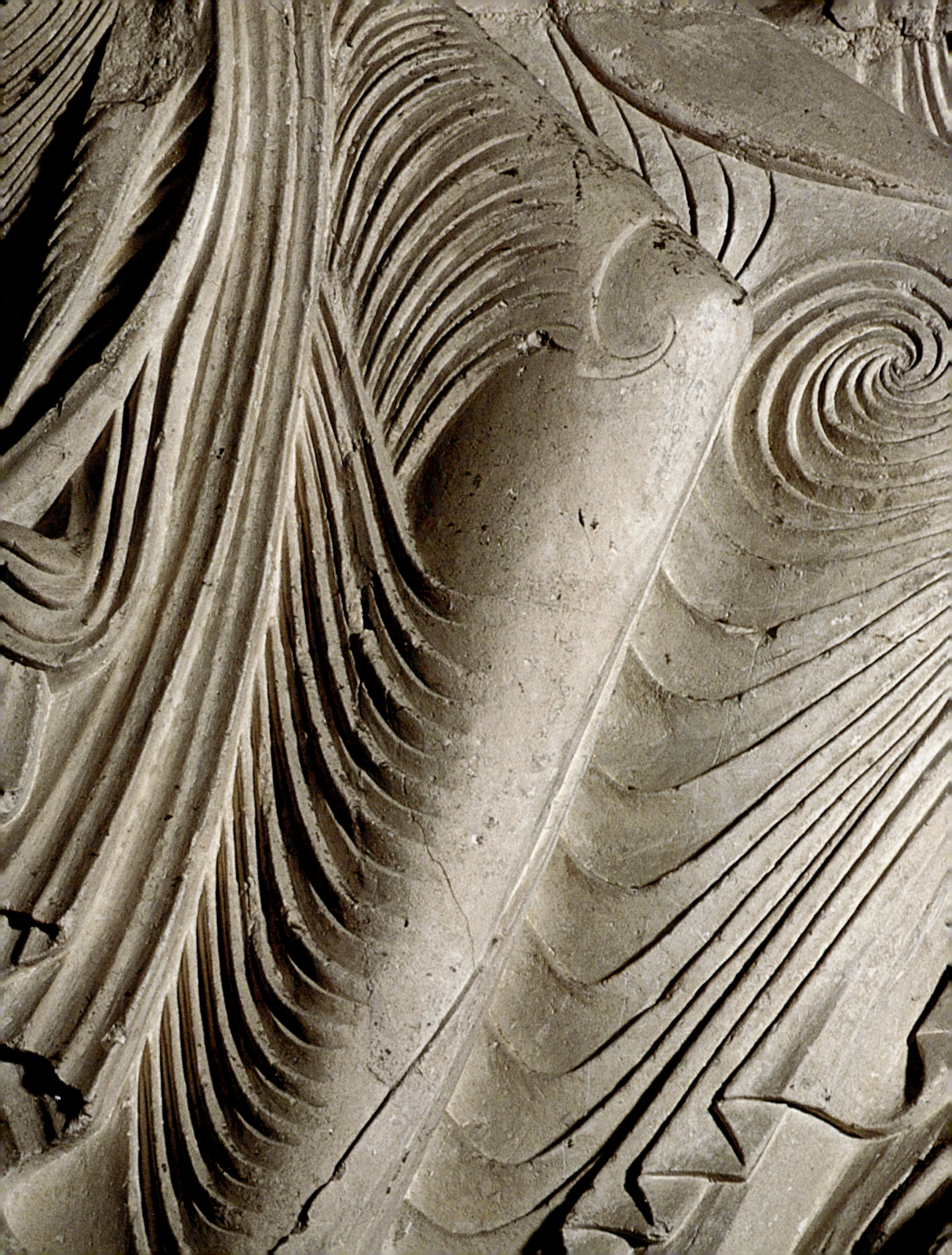

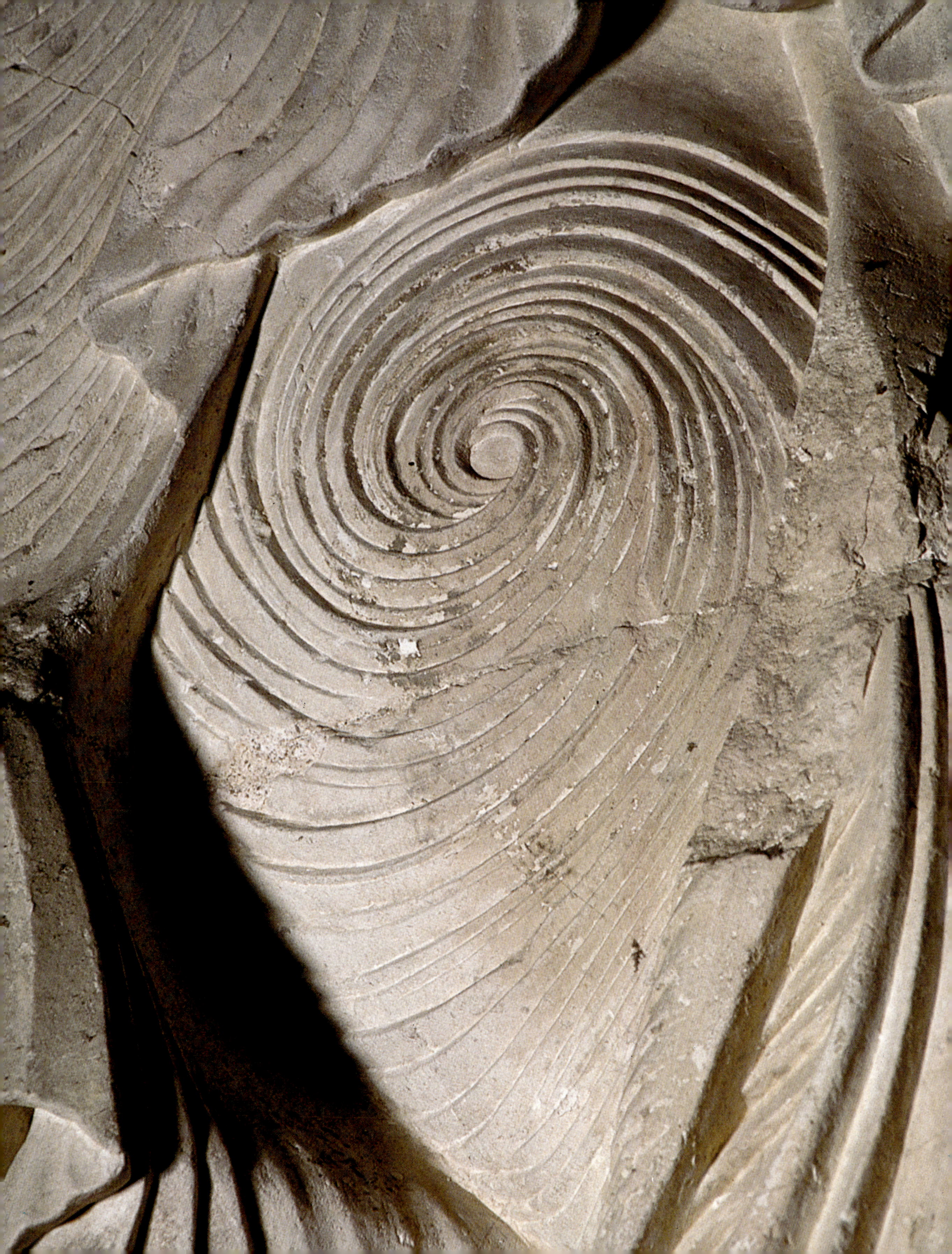

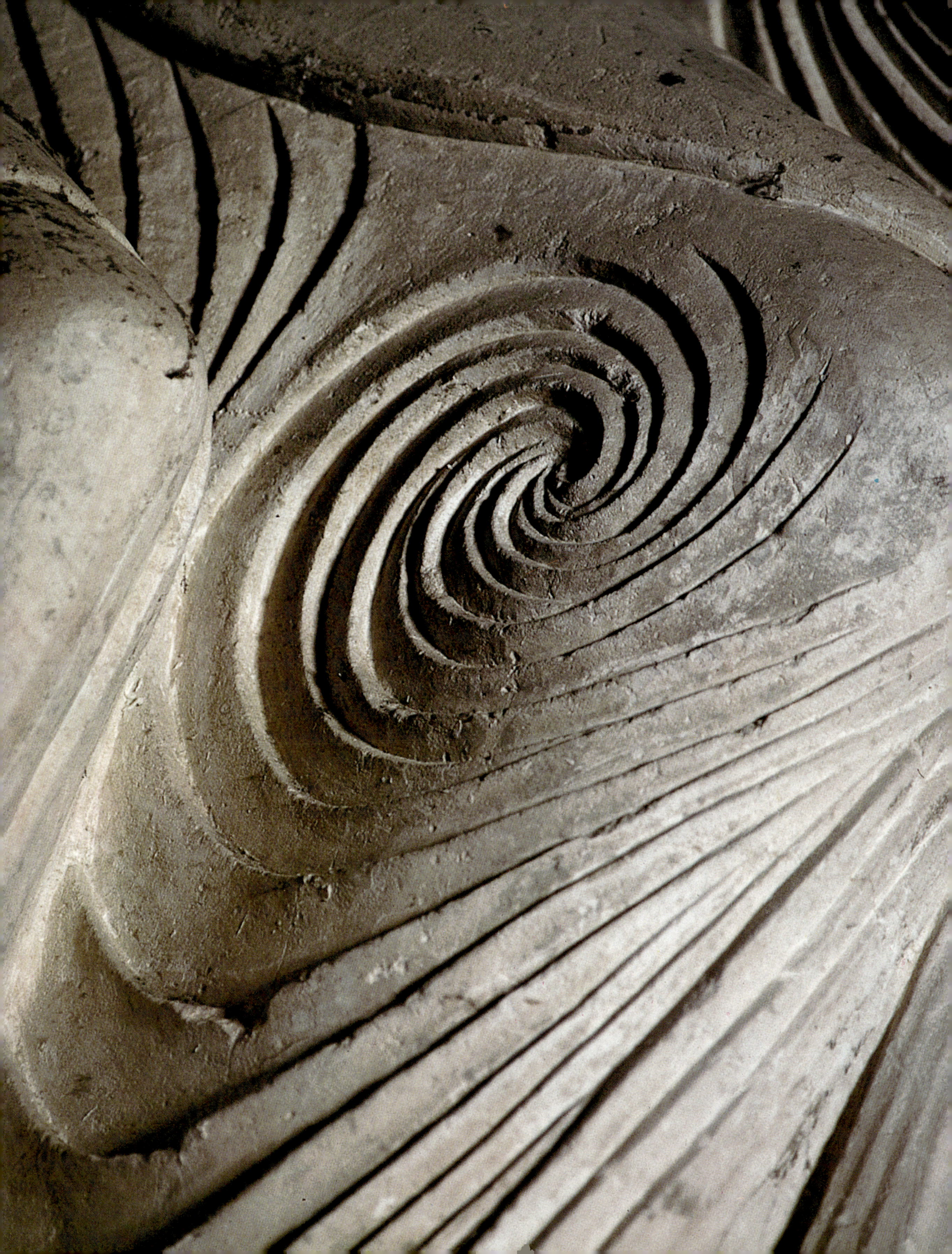

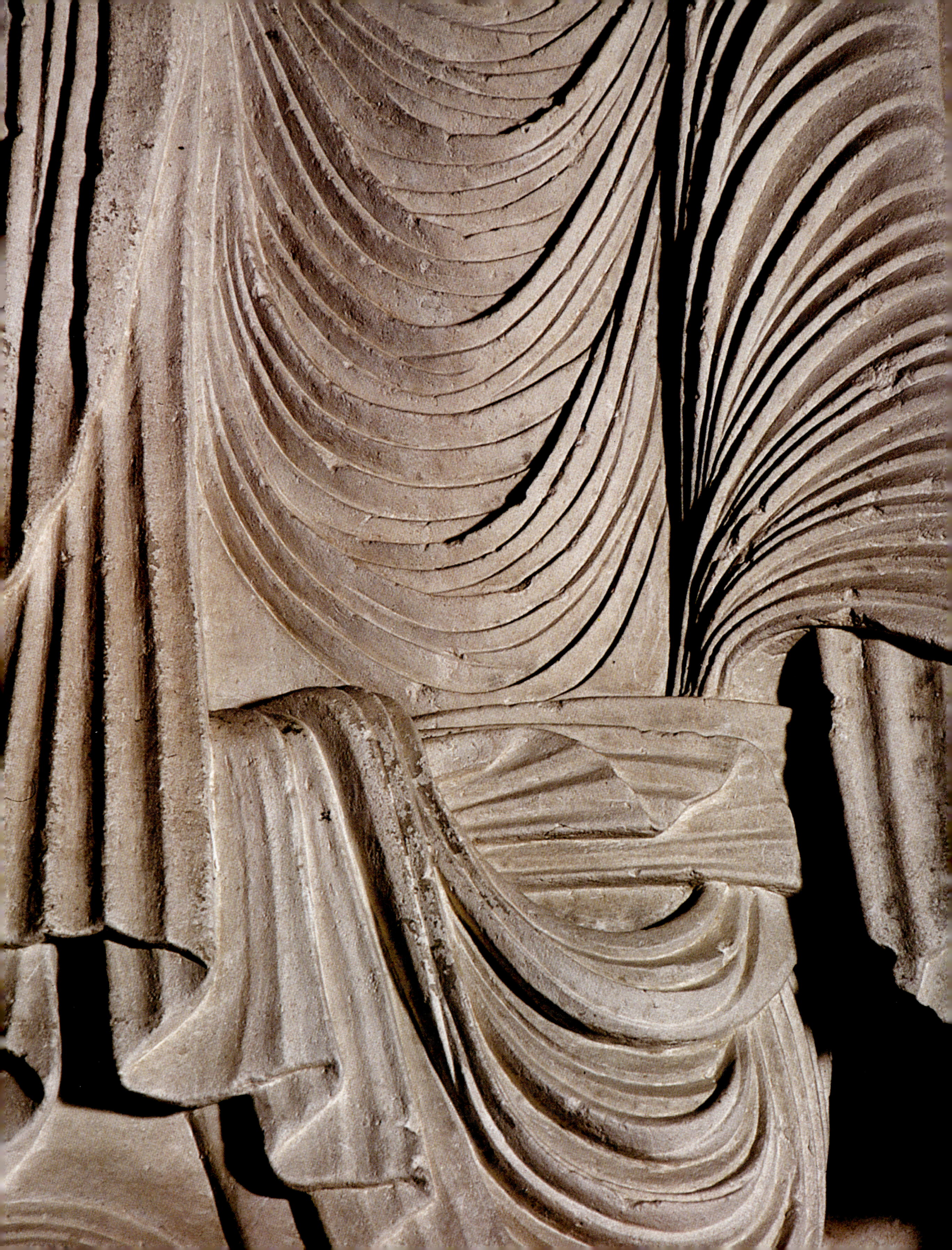

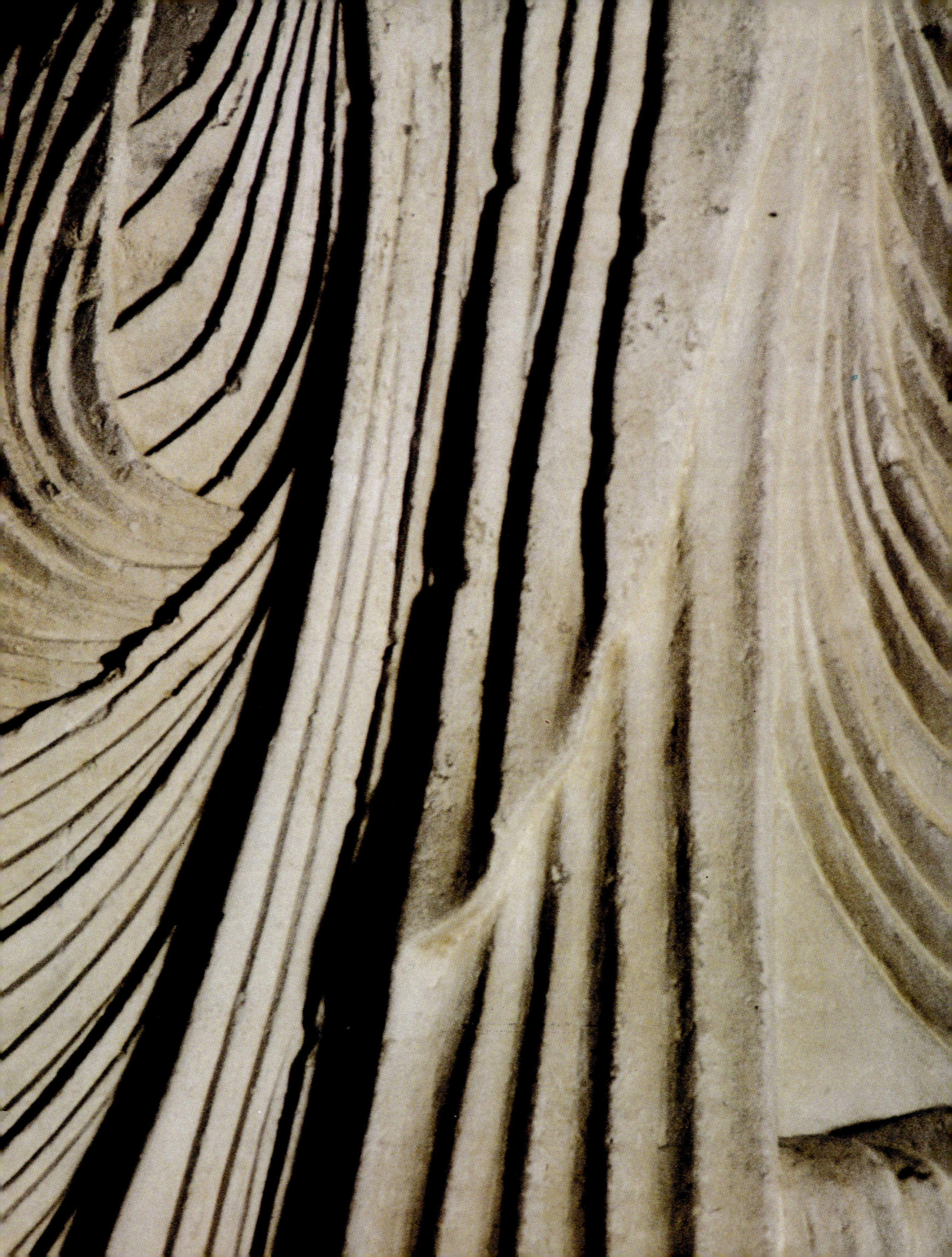

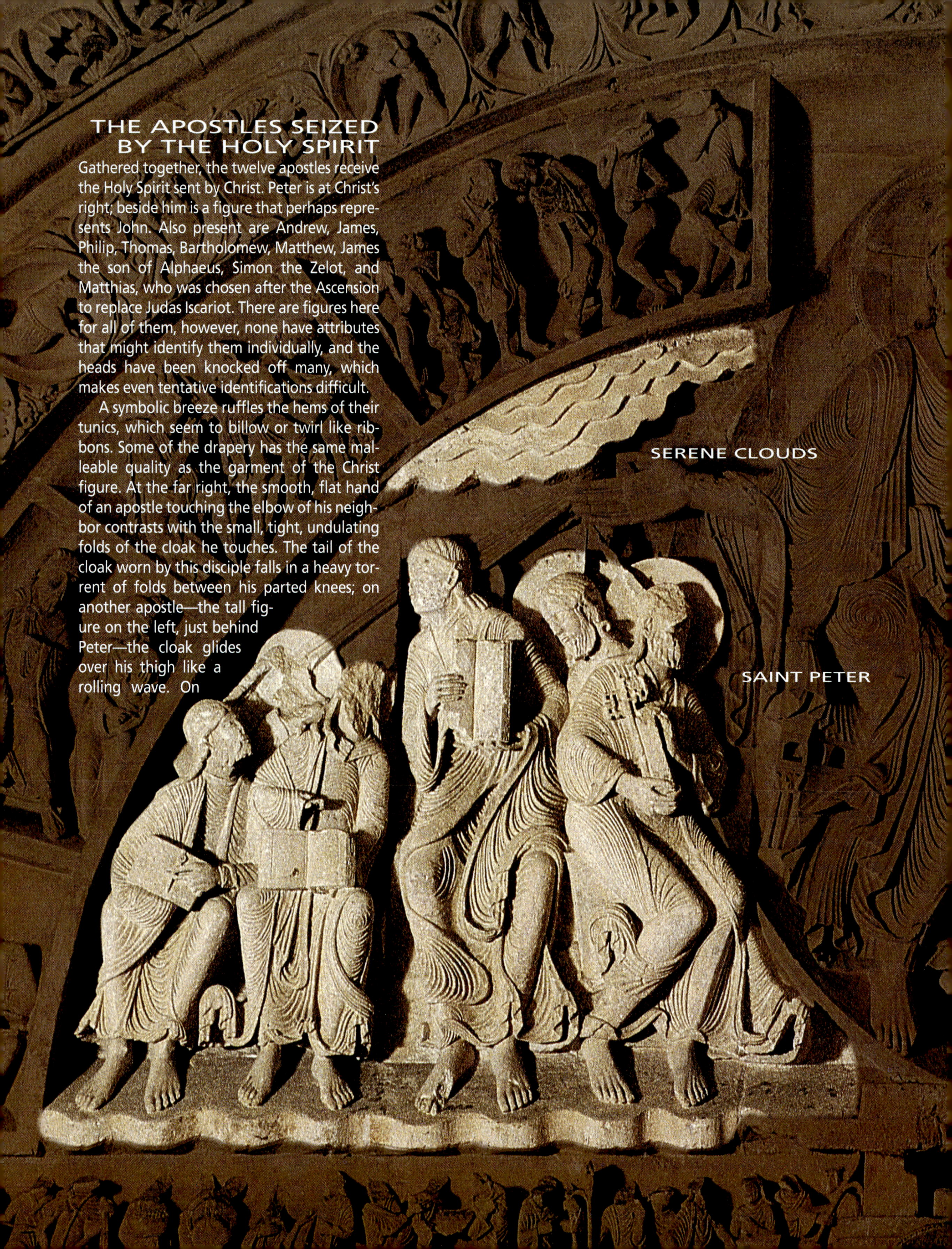

THE APOSTLES SEIZED BY THE HOLY SPIRIT

Gathered together, the twelve apostles receive the Holy Spirit sent by Christ. Peter is at Christ's right; beside him is a figure that perhaps represents John. Also present are Andrew, James, Philip, Thomas, Bartholomew, Matthew, James the son of Alphaeus, Simon the Zelot, and Matthias, who was chosen after the Ascension to replace Judas Iscariot. There are figures here for all of them, however, none have attributes that might identify them individually, and the heads have been knocked off many, which makes even tentative identifications difficult.

A symbolic breeze ruffles the hems of their tunics, which seem to billow or twirl like ribbons. Some of the drapery has the same malleable quality as the garment of the Christ figure. At the far right, the smooth, flat hand of an apostle touching the elbow of his neighbor contrasts with the small, tight, undulating folds of the cloak he touches. The tail of the cloak worn by this disciple falls in a heavy torrent of folds between his parted knees; on another apostle—the tall figure on the left, just behind Peter—the cloak glides over his thigh like a rolling wave. On

"And ye shall be witnesses unto me . . . unto the uttermost part of the earth."

another, the apostle seated just to the right of Christ's mandorla, the cloth falling between the legs falls into softly gathered pleats.

Each of the apostles carries a book of a different size, clearly representing the scriptures that they must carry to the ends of the earth. The books carried by the disciples seated to the left of Christ are closed. Some give the impression of having a precious silver or gold binding, while others, more simple, seem to be affixed with a metal or leather lock. To the far right of Christ, one apostle appears to be unlocking his book, while the others hold theirs open. The opposition of open and closed book is complemented by the asymmetrical representation of clouds that circle the tympanum. These clouds are at times serene and at times stormy. Within this duality must be read an allusion to the spiritual powers that Christ gives his apostles as he charges them with the evangelical mission: to condemn or absolve, to forgive a sin, or not. The side of the tympanum to Christ's right represents his power of salvation, while the side on his left speaks of his power to condemn.

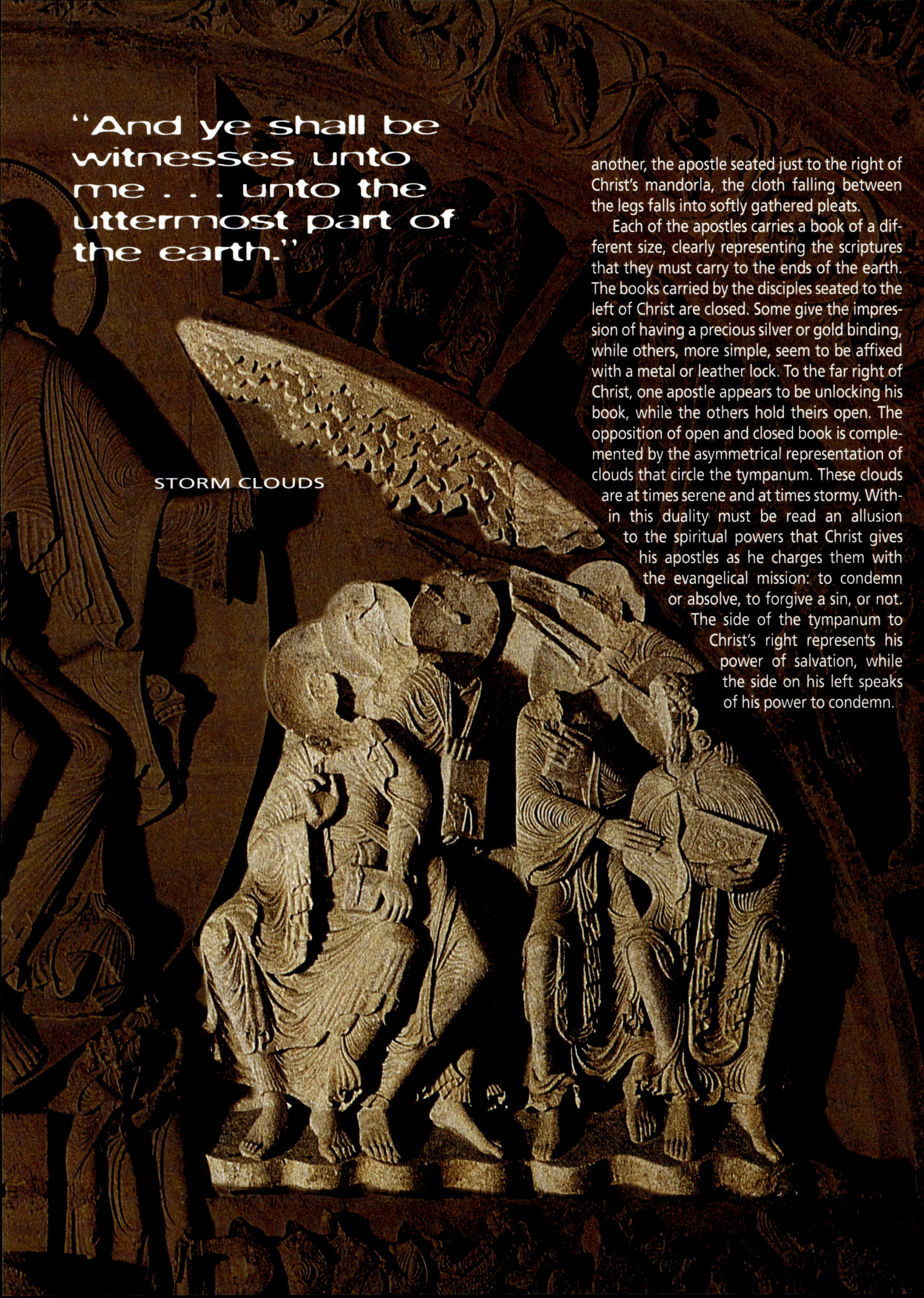

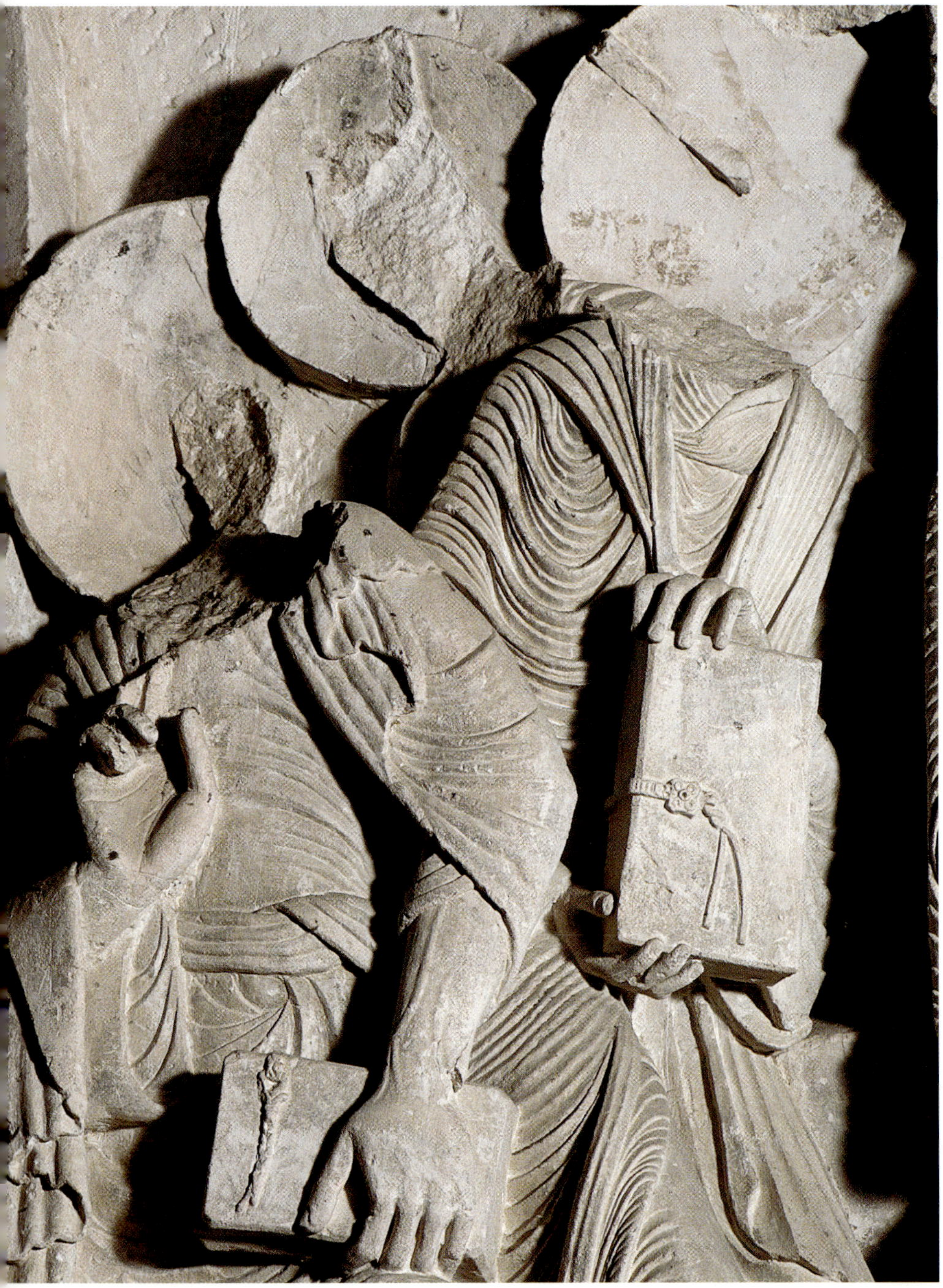

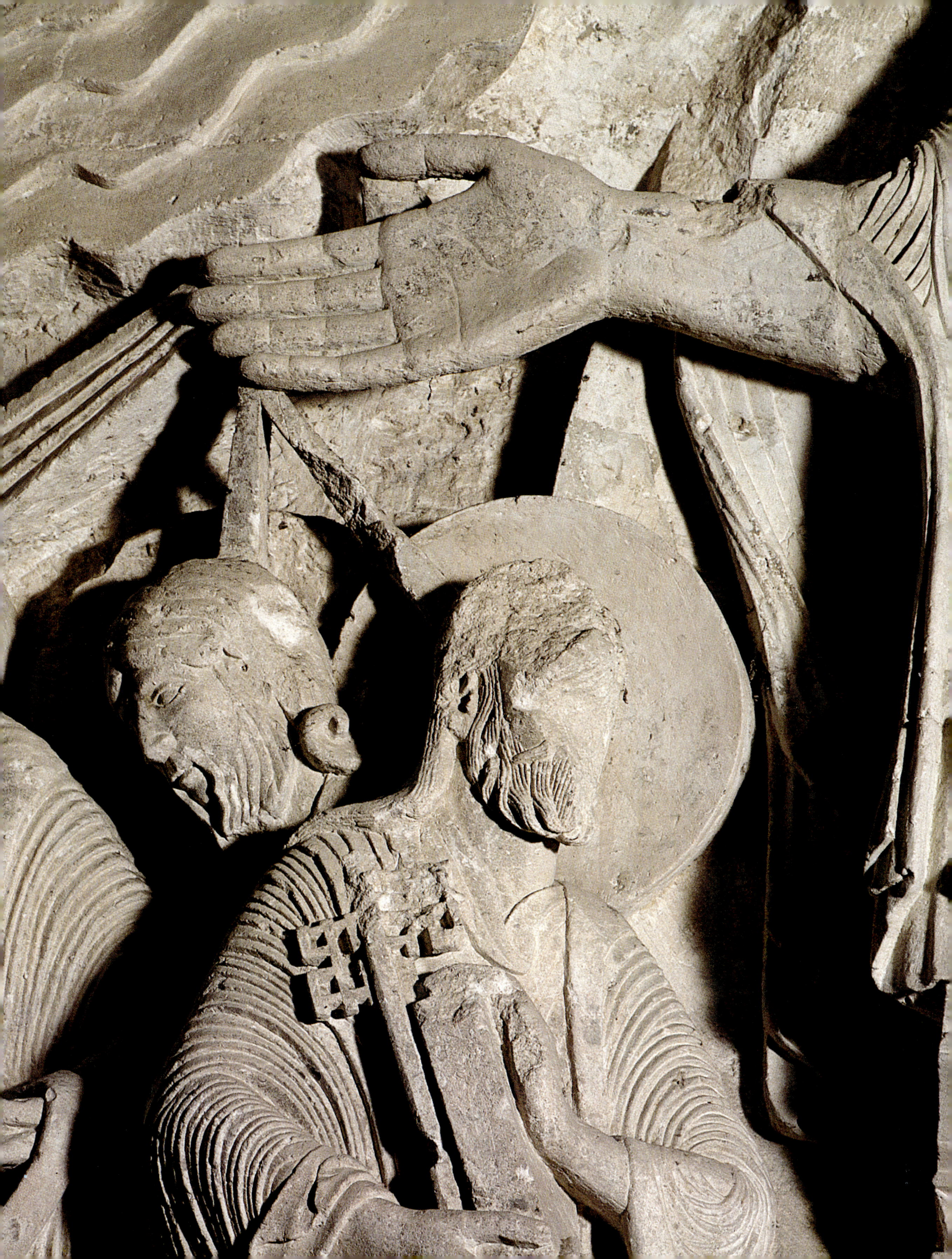

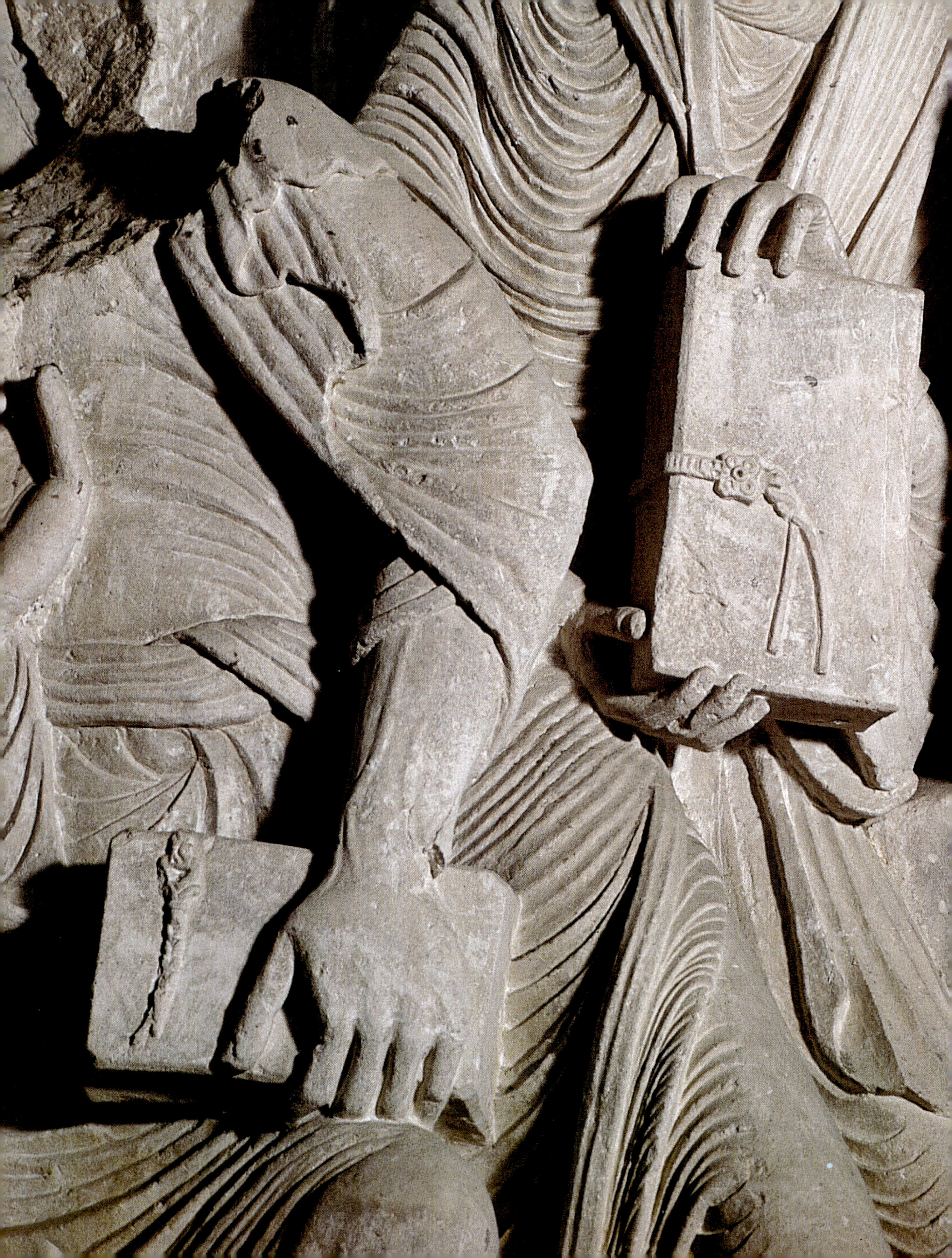

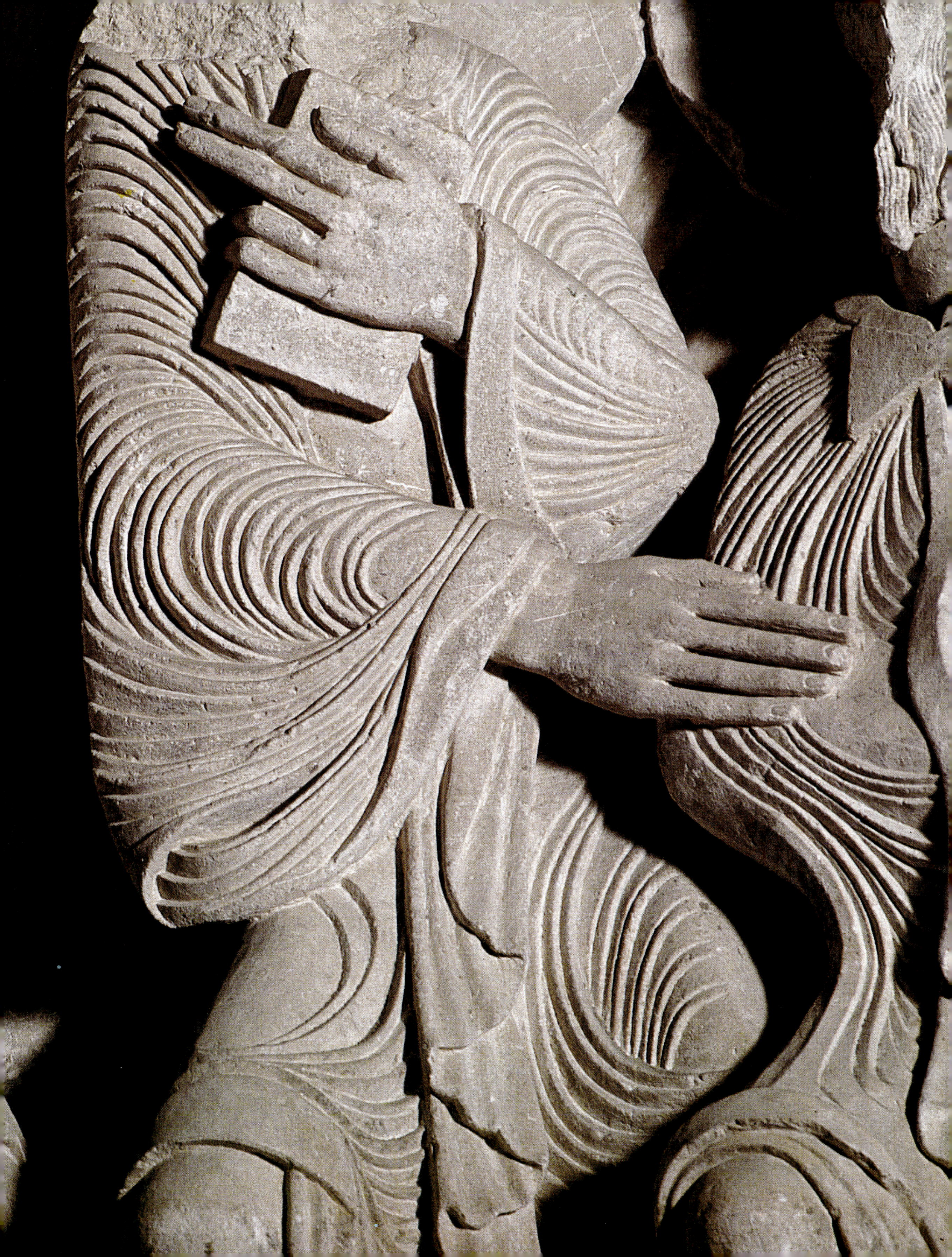

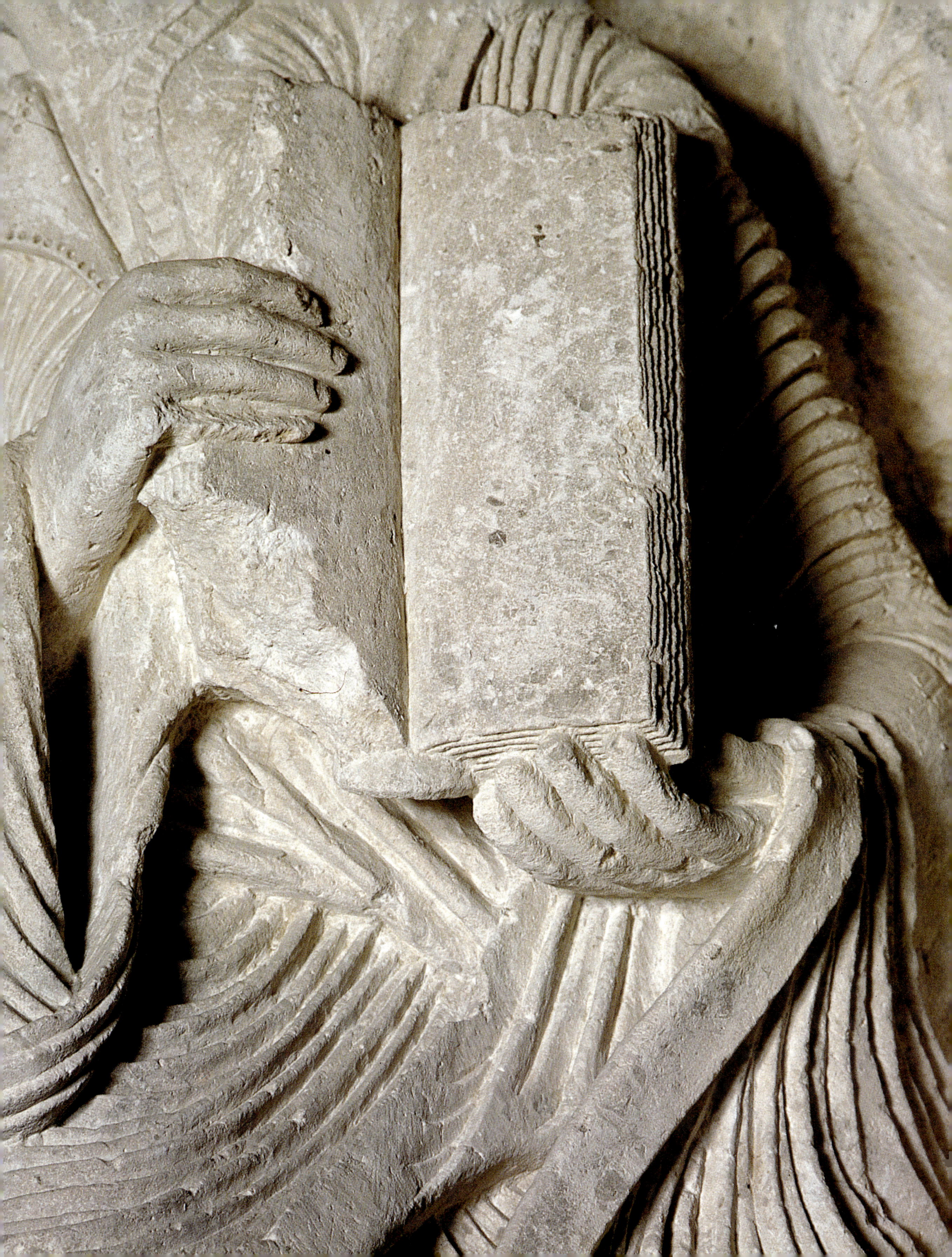

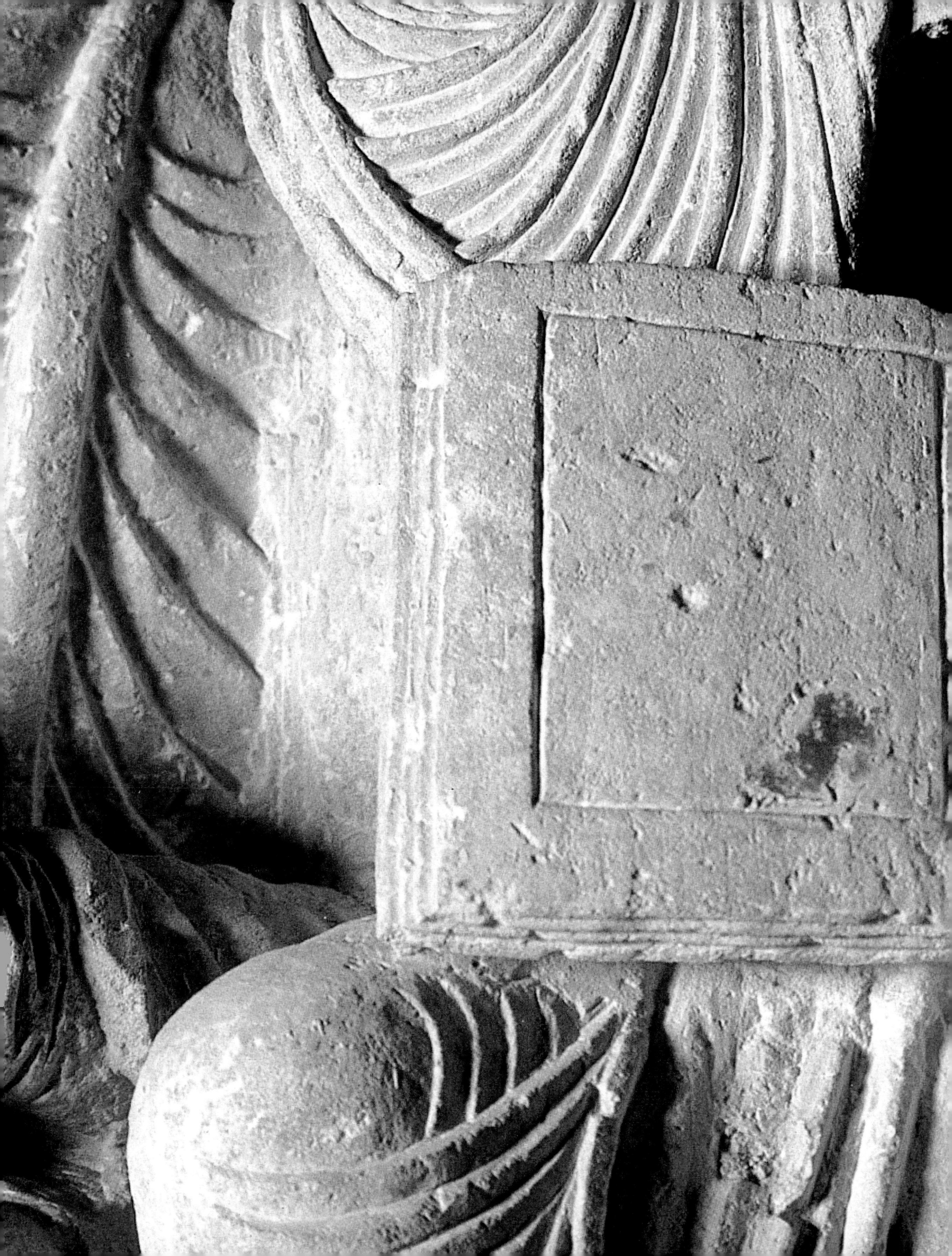

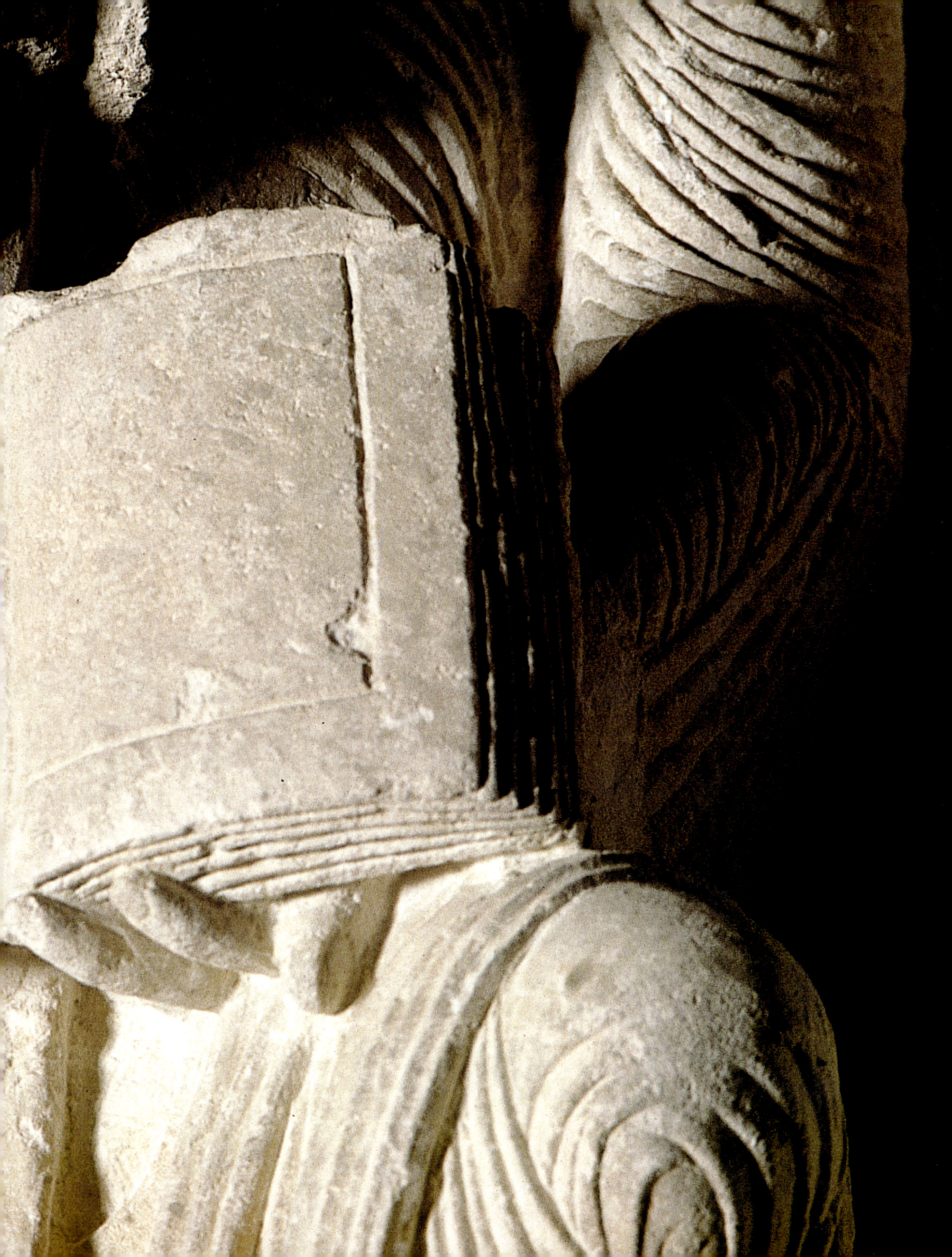

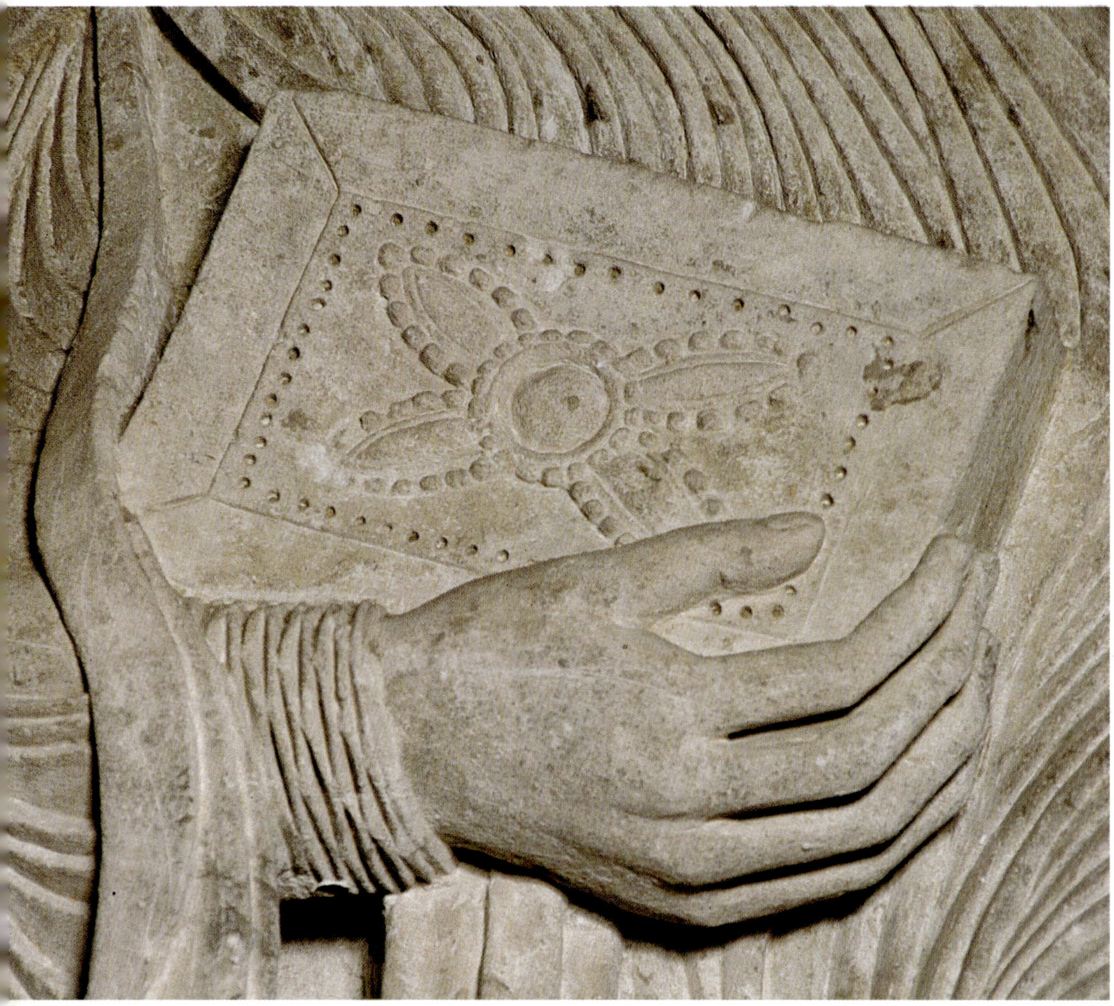

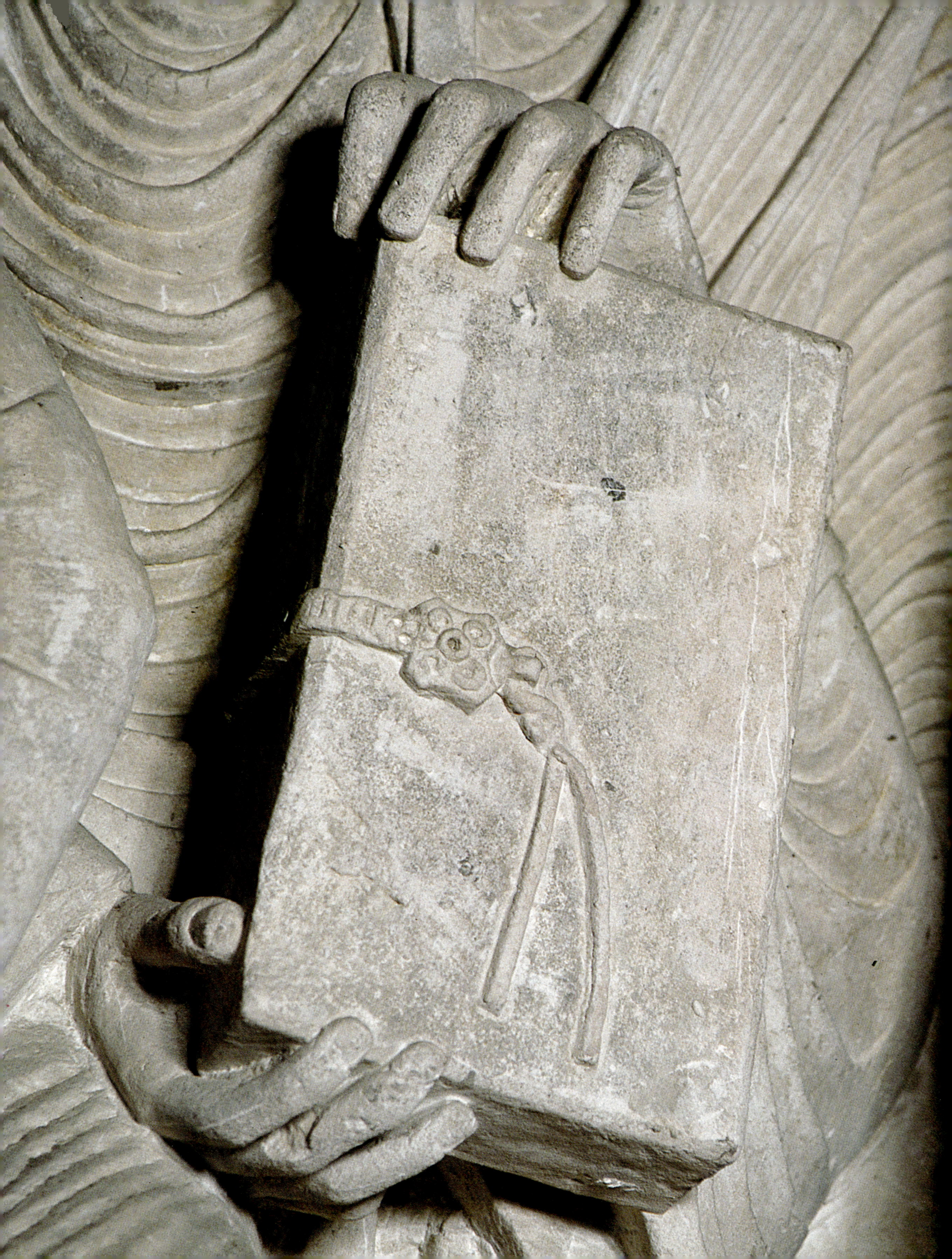

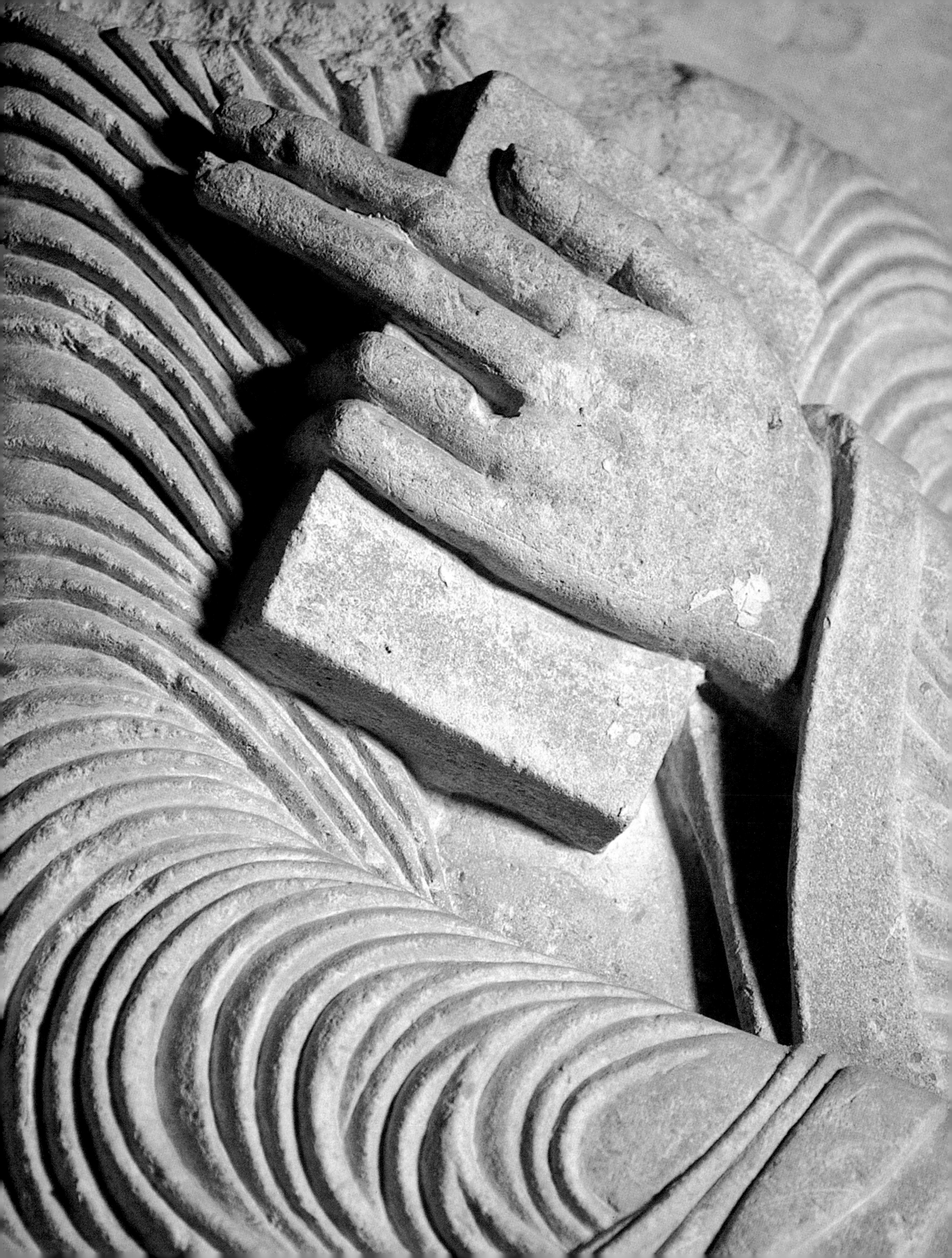

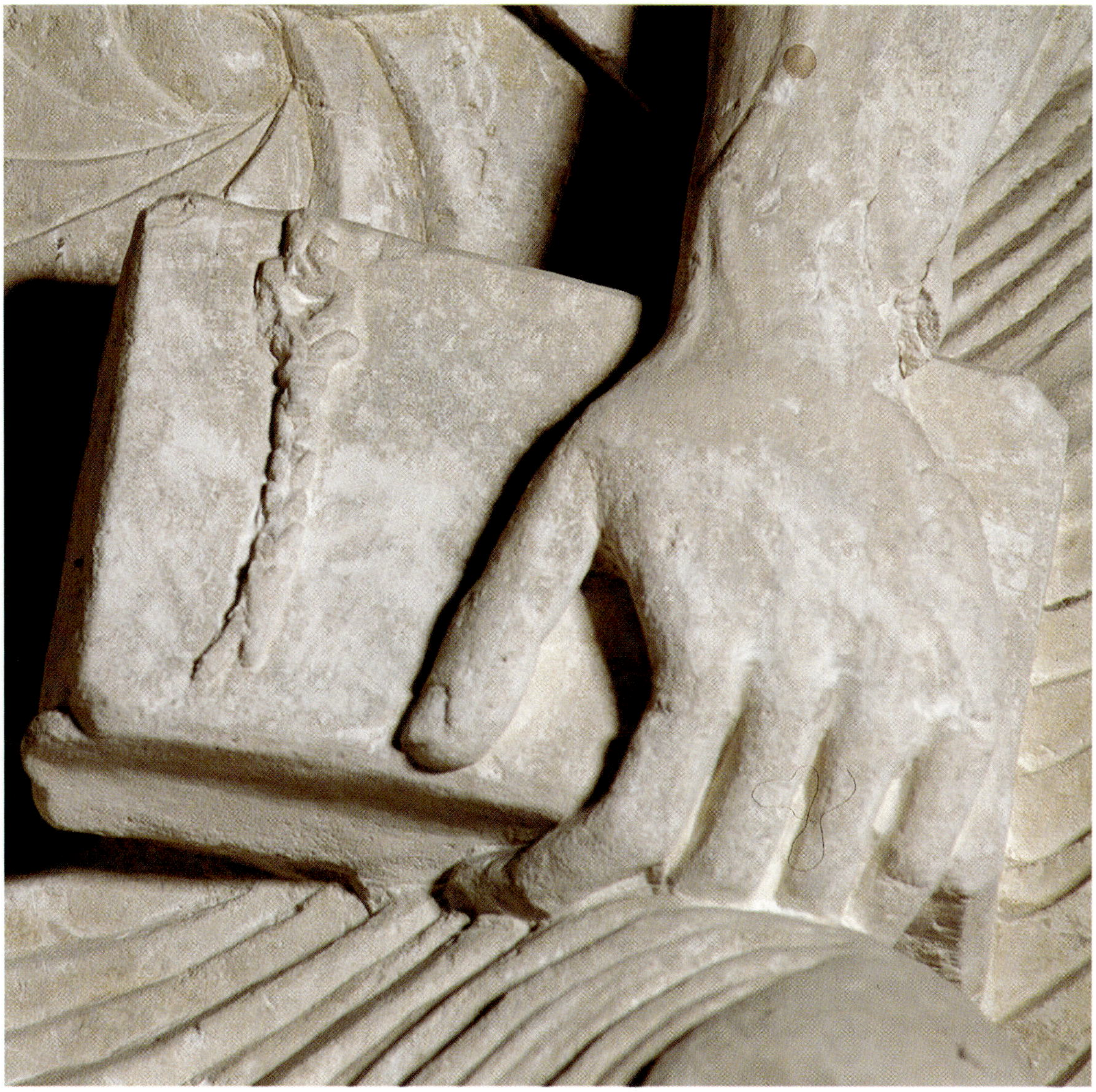

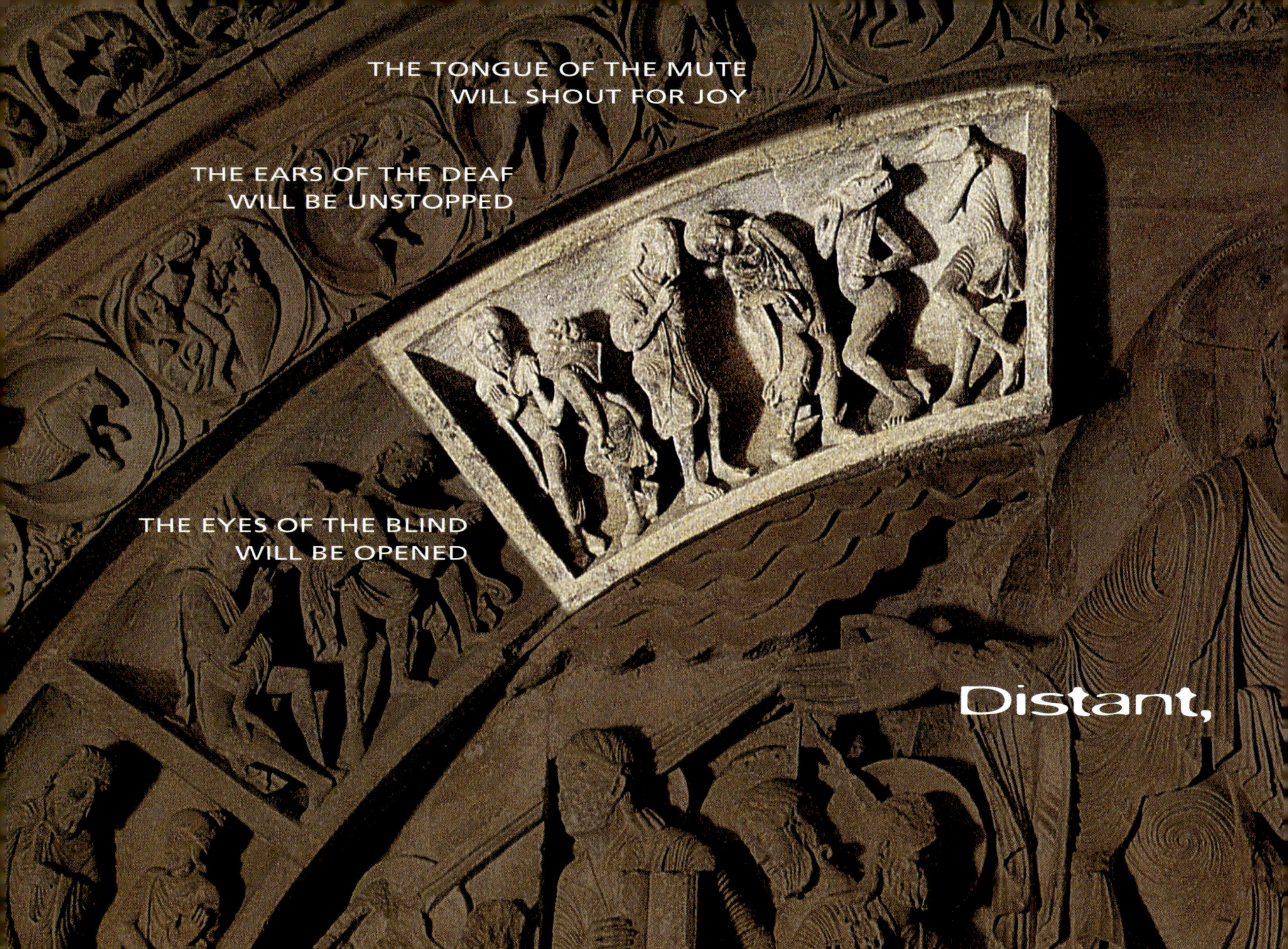

Distant,

TO DRIVE OUT PAIN AND MADNESS

The lintel and the smaller compartments of the tympanum illustrate a fusion of the themes of the Mission of the Apostles and the Pentecost. With a complex richness of feeling, the upper scenes on the tympanum depict a mankind in need of conversion, with ills in need of cure.

CONVERT THE HEART, HEAL THE BODY

Three small episodes are enacted in the first compartment of the tympanum, immediately to the left of the central axis. The first episode shows two men with dog's heads, one clutching his throat as if in pain, the second holding a sword against his throat as if he is in such agony that he wants to put an end to his life. These figures are mutes, who can only bark instead of speaking. According to the writings of the ancient Roman natural historian Pliny the Elder, whose books were well known in medieval Europe, these dog-headed people lived in Cynocephalia ("dog-head-land"), a remote region of India. True children of Adam, and thus capable of salvation, these dog-headed people will one day receive the Gospel, and when they do, a cure for their muteness as well. Immediately to the left, representing deafness (and perhaps another legendary Indian people), a man leans toward the person standing next to him so that he can hear what he is saying. Immediately to the left of these two is a blind man, shown as an old man grasping the arm of the young boy guiding him. With his palm opened broadly in a gesture of denial, the old man seems to be signaling to his companion that his eyes can see nothing. His strange hairstyle—bald at the top of the head, but with a knot of hair wound high on each side—draws a sharp contrast with the boy's opulent curls. Also contrasted are the old man's soft-hooded cape and the

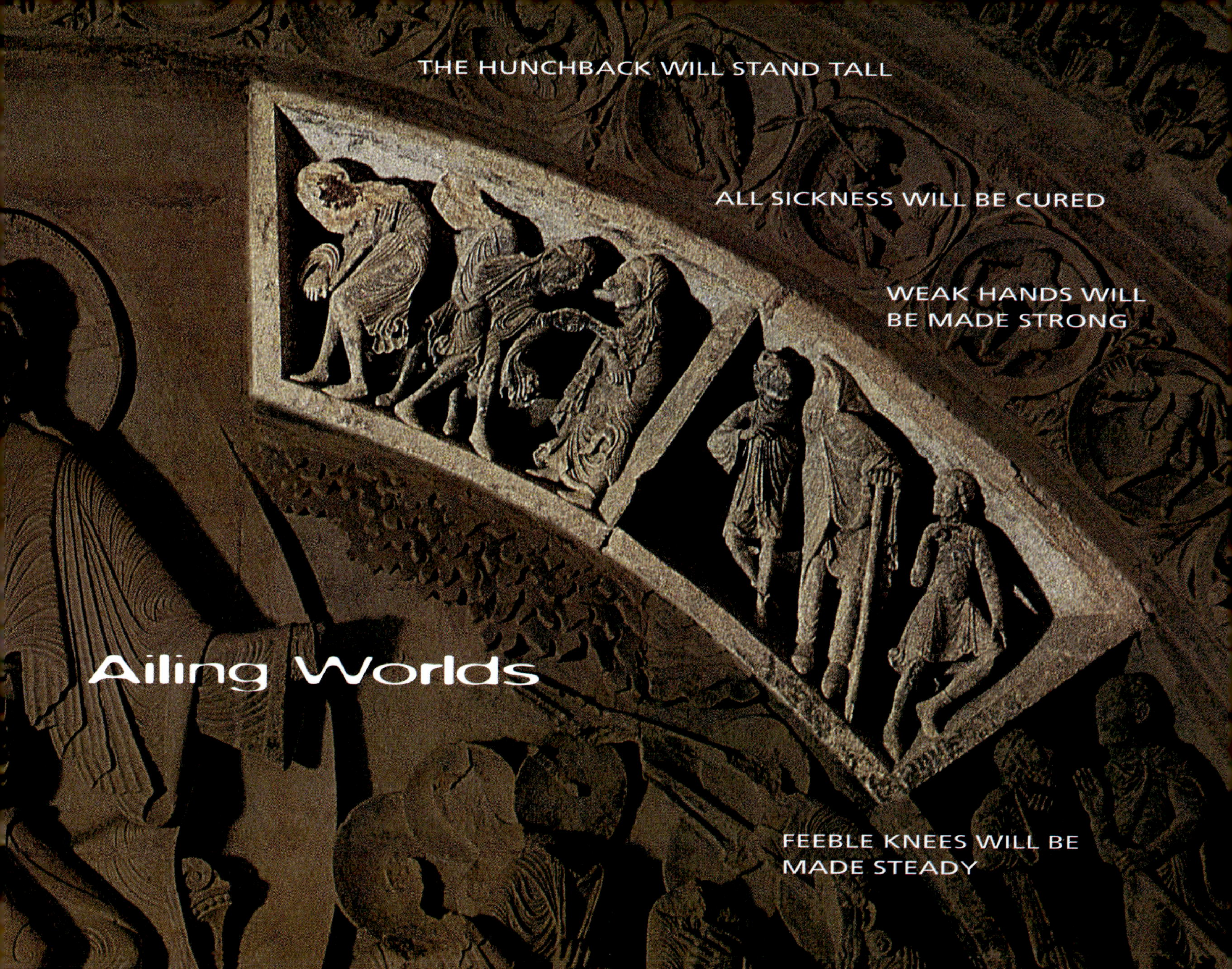

Ailing Worlds

stiff cowl worn by the youth. The national origin of this pair is not clear.

Four figures occupy the compartment immediately across the tympanum, to the right of the central axis. The first two figures were so badly damaged by hammers during the French Revolution that their ethnic origins cannot be deciphered. The silhouettes that are left suggest a bent-over hunchback walking in front of his companion, who is touching his back with compassion, or perhaps for good luck. The couple that follows is a blend of the sublime and the ridiculous. In a magnificently elegant movement, which emphasizes the fine cutting of the drapery, the man gallantly takes the hand of his lady. But, incongruously, set in the center of each lover's face is, not a human nose, but the snout of a pig. Ancient ethnographers believed that Ethiopians had flat noses, which are shown here in what is apparently intended as a humorous caricature. Since the ills of sight and hearing are illustrated elsewhere on the tympanum, these people presumably represent the loss of the sense of smell.

The three figures in the next compartment to the right are suffering from afflictions of the limbs. With his forearm covered by a cloak, the first man protects his withered, lifeless hand. The second man, who is leaning on his cane, has a clubfoot, and the third man suffers from a wounded knee. Details of the dress and other accessories, such as the Phrygian cap worn by the first figure, and the tall crutch held by the central figure, with its elegant scrolled handle in the style of an Ionic capital, suggest that these characters are from Hellenic Asia. Whether mute, blind, or lame, all the actors in the scenes on the tympanum recall that, in the Gospels, the cure of an ailment is often either the cause or the consequence of conversion to Christianity.

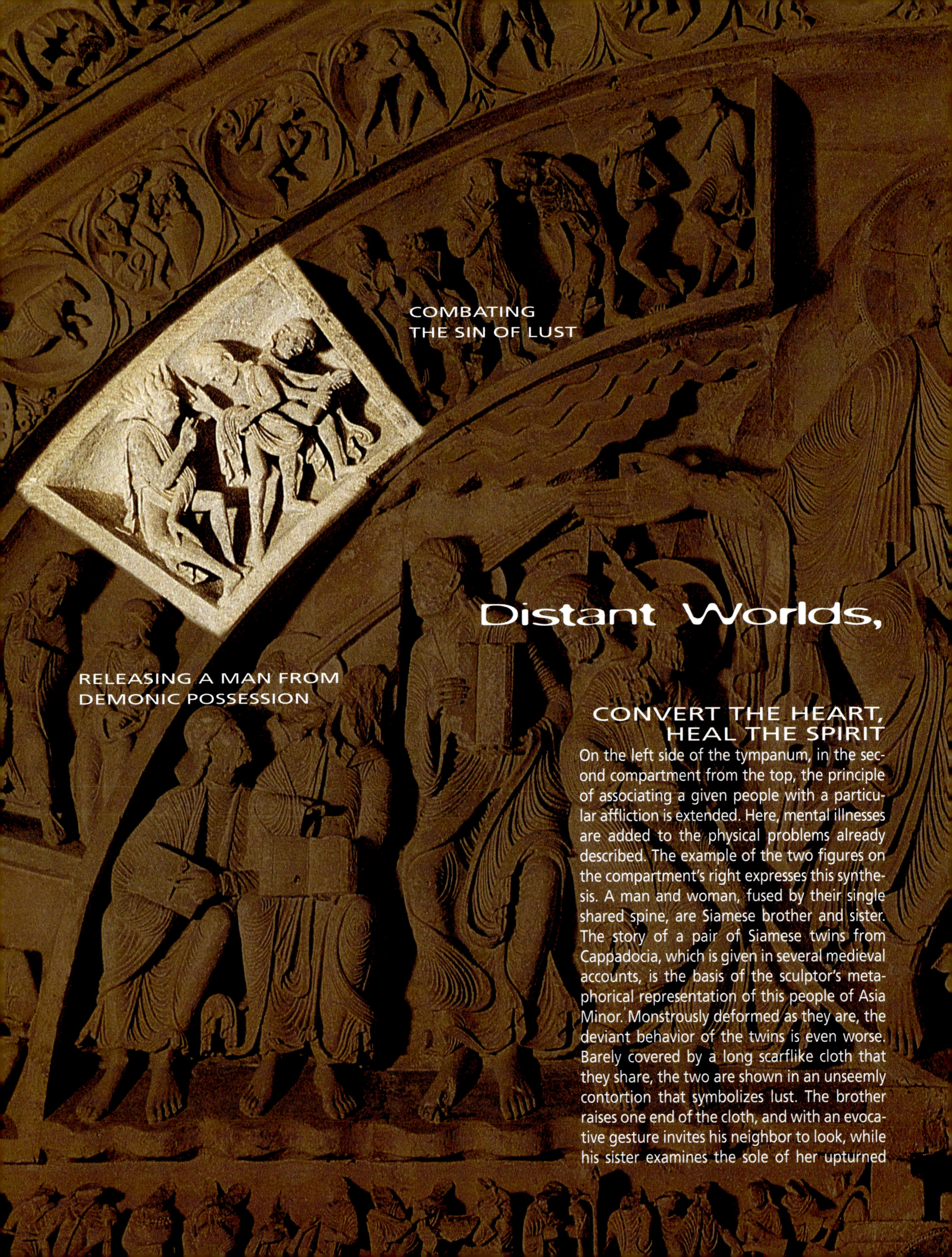

COMBATING
THE SIN OF LUST

RELEASING A MAN FROM
DEMONIC POSSESSION

Distant Worlds,

CONVERT THE HEART, HEAL THE SPIRIT

On the left side of the tympanum, in the second compartment from the top, the principle of associating a given people with a particular affliction is extended. Here, mental illnesses are added to the physical problems already described. The example of the two figures on the compartment's right expresses this synthesis. A man and woman, fused by their single shared spine, are Siamese brother and sister. The story of a pair of Siamese twins from Cappadocia, which is given in several medieval accounts, is the basis of the sculptor's metaphorical representation of this people of Asia Minor. Monstrously deformed as they are, the deviant behavior of the twins is even worse. Barely covered by a long scarflike cloth that they share, the two are shown in an unseemly contortion that symbolizes lust. The brother raises one end of the cloth, and with an evocative gesture invites his neighbor to look, while his sister examines the sole of her upturned

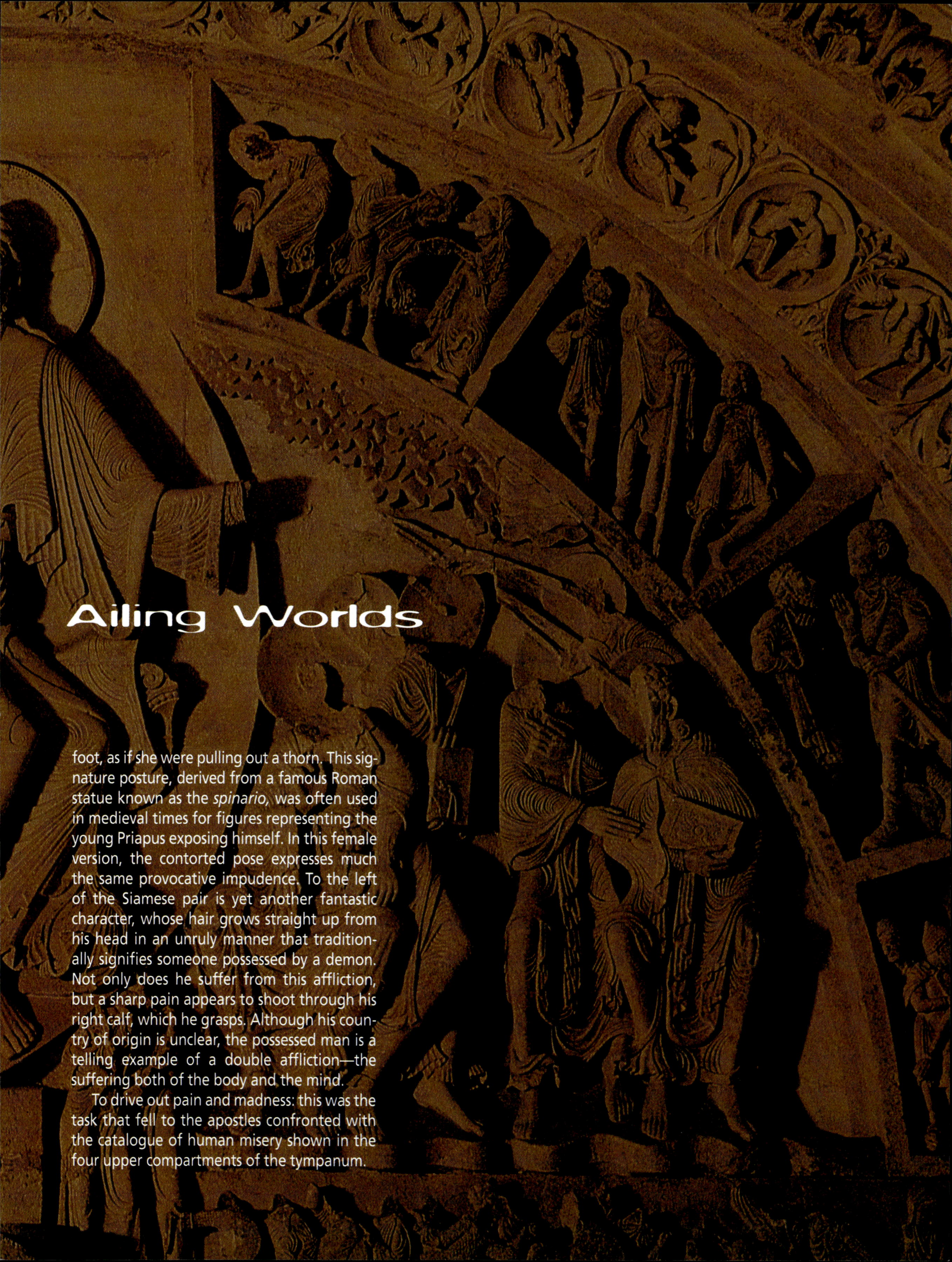

Ailing Worlds

foot, as if she were pulling out a thorn. This signature posture, derived from a famous Roman statue known as the *spinario,* was often used in medieval times for figures representing the young Priapus exposing himself. In this female version, the contorted pose expresses much the same provocative impudence. To the left of the Siamese pair is yet another fantastic character, whose hair grows straight up from his head in an unruly manner that traditionally signifies someone possessed by a demon. Not only does he suffer from this affliction, but a sharp pain appears to shoot through his right calf, which he grasps. Although his country of origin is unclear, the possessed man is a telling example of a double affliction—the suffering both of the body and the mind.

To drive out pain and madness: this was the task that fell to the apostles confronted with the catalogue of human misery shown in the four upper compartments of the tympanum.

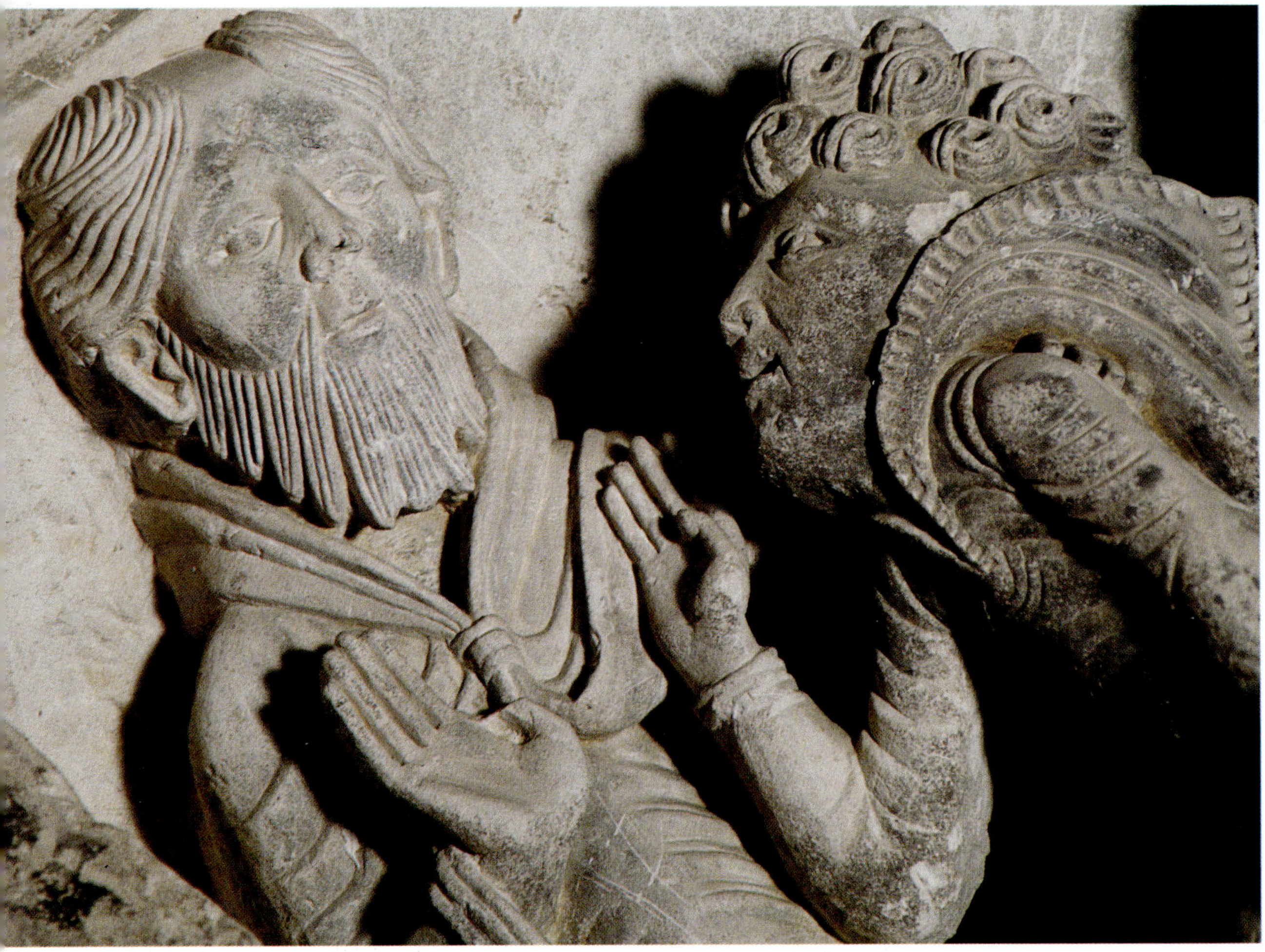

THE BLIND MAN AND HIS YOUNG GUIDE
THE DOG-HEADED MAN CLUTCHING HIS VOICELESS THROAT
THE PIG-SNOUTED ETHIOPIAN COUPLE

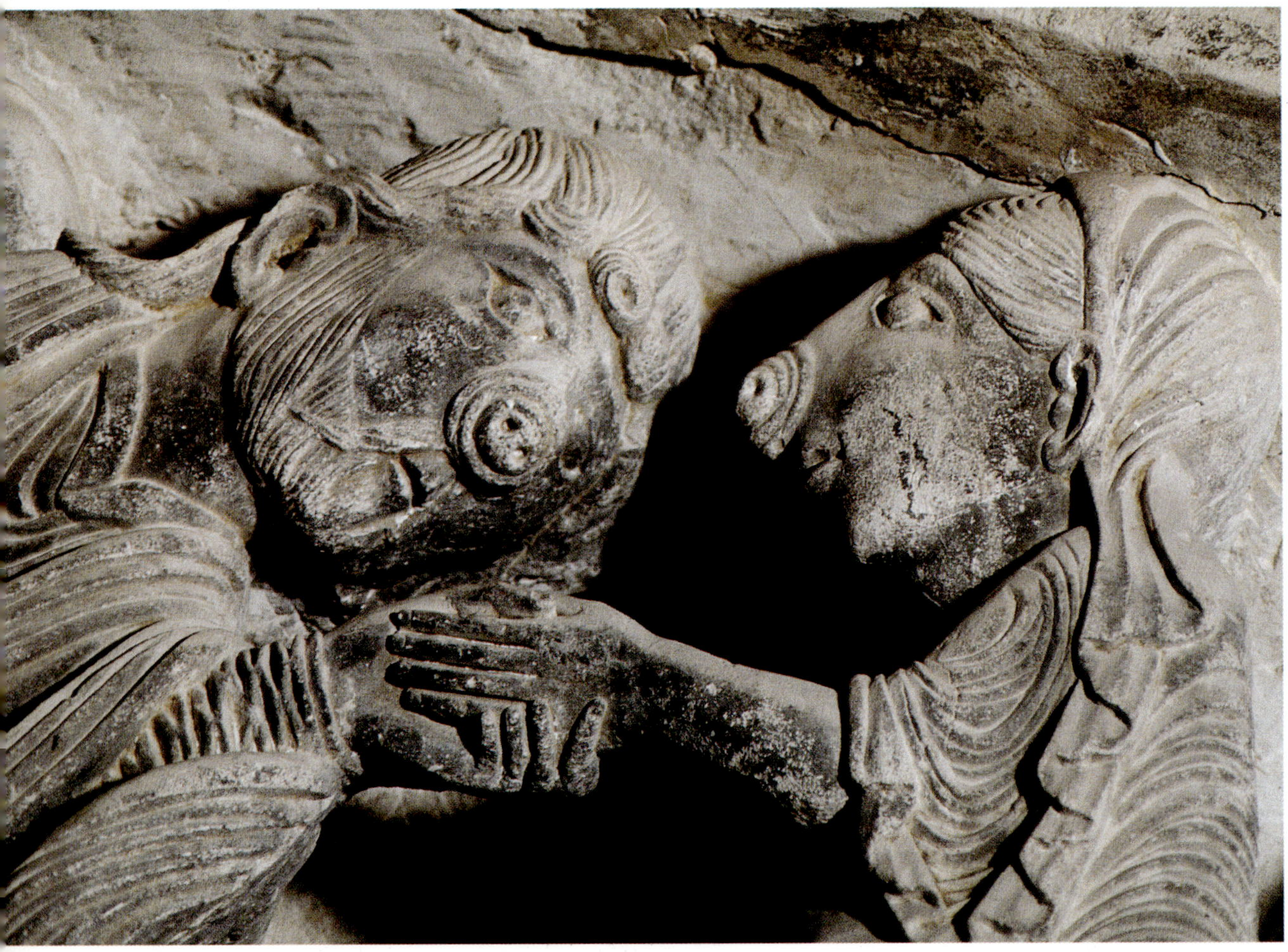

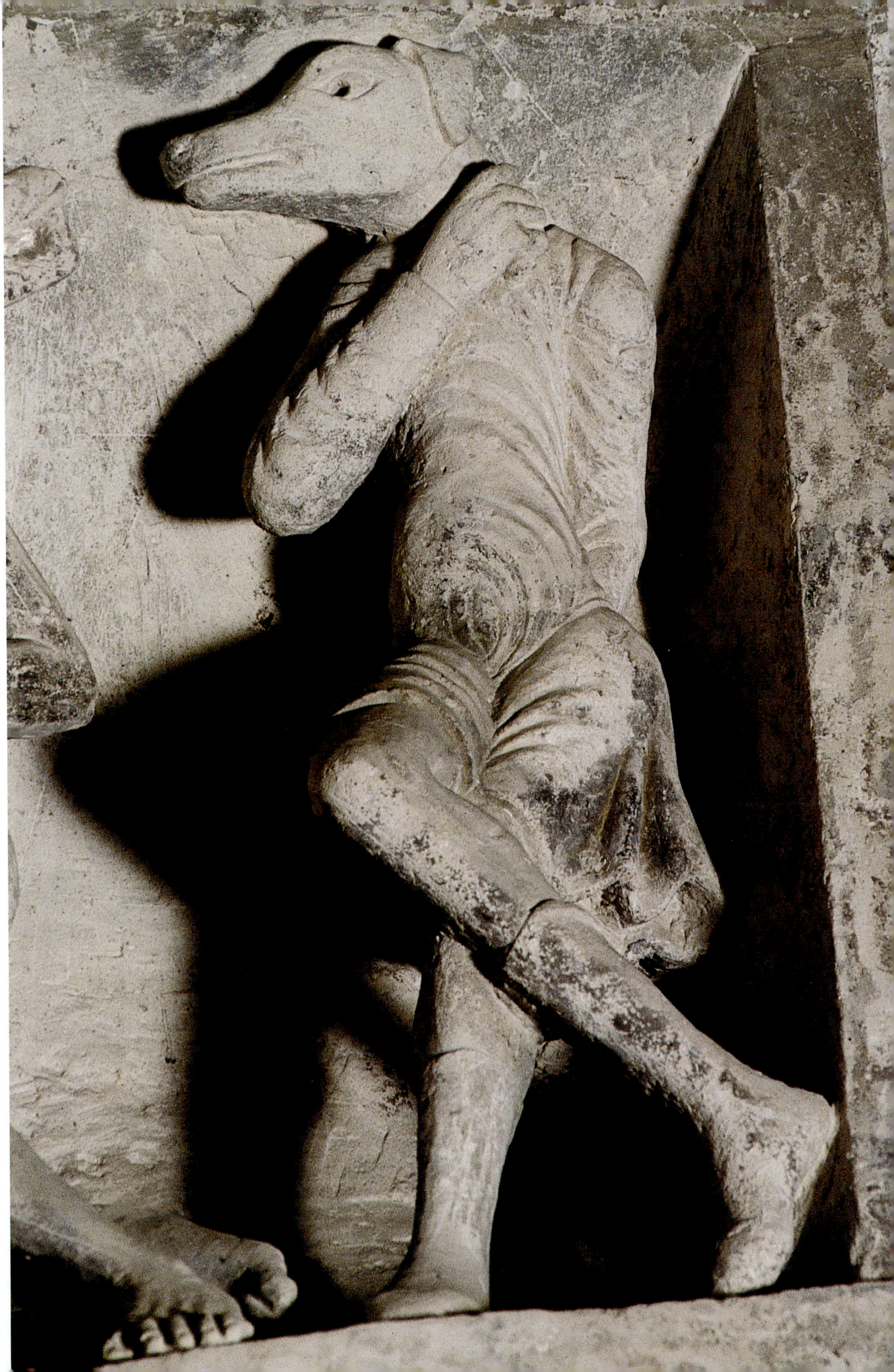

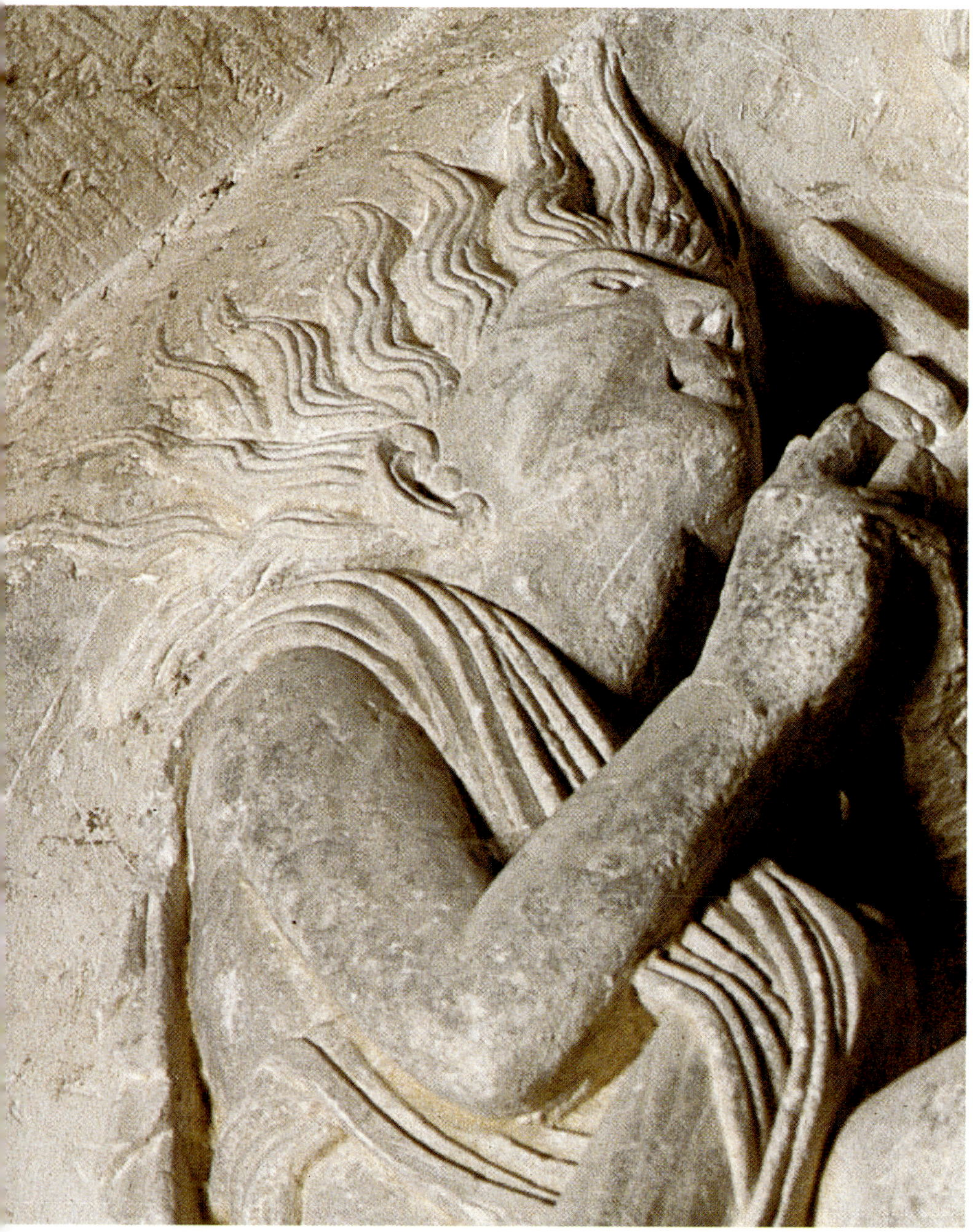

THE FRENZY OF THE
DEMON-POSSESSED MAN

THE SIAMESE TWINS
OF CAPPADOCIA

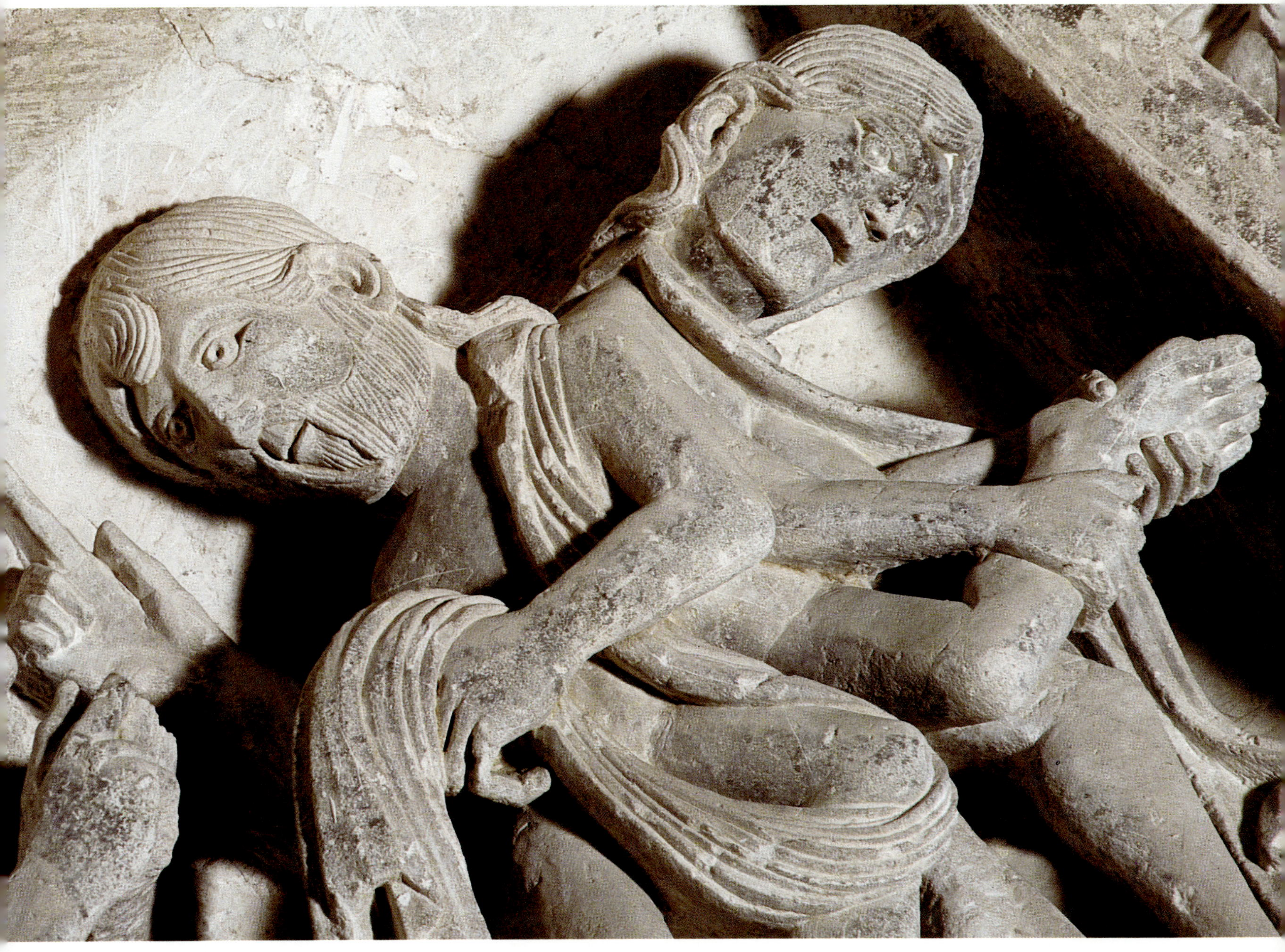

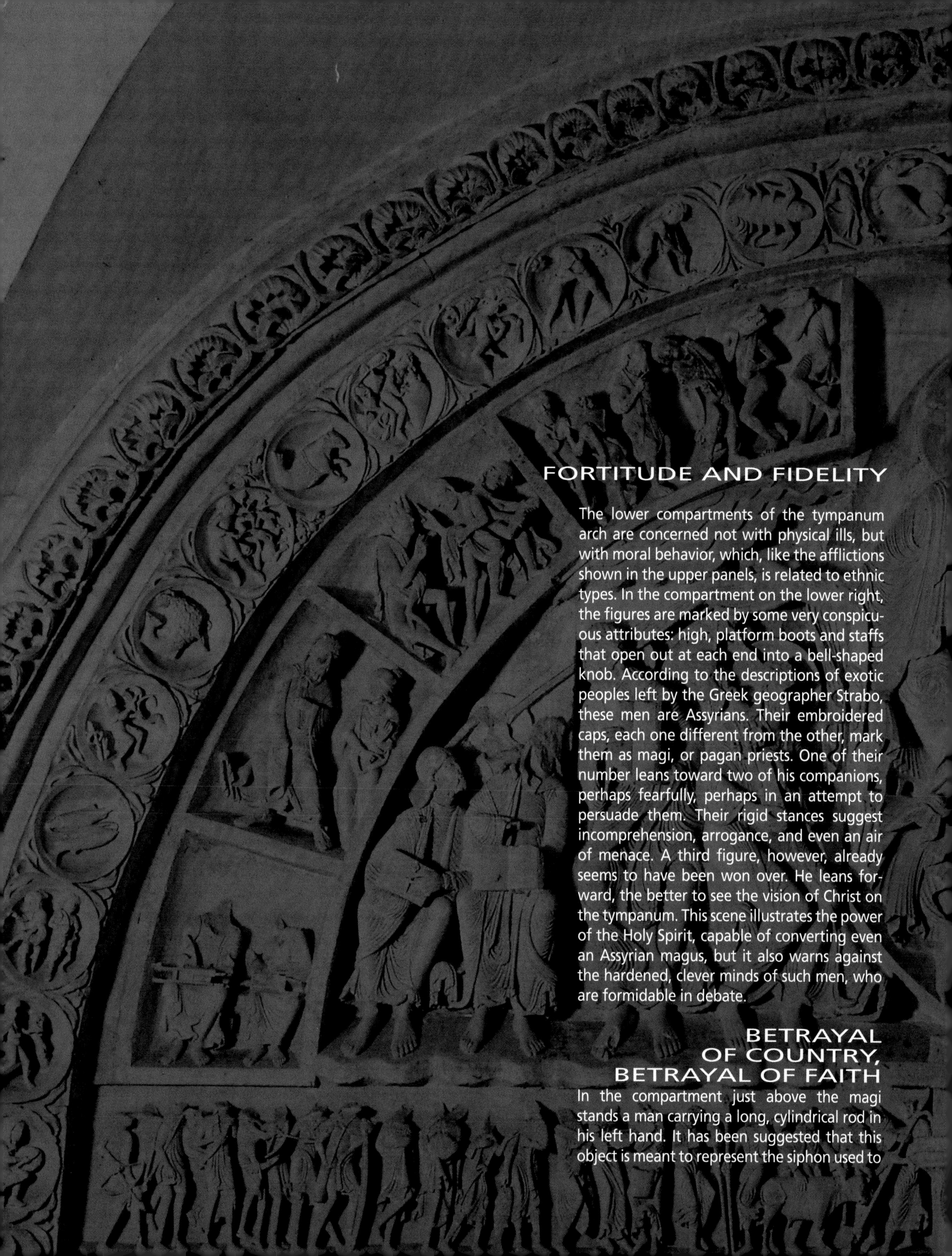

FORTITUDE AND FIDELITY

The lower compartments of the tympanum arch are concerned not with physical ills, but with moral behavior, which, like the afflictions shown in the upper panels, is related to ethnic types. In the compartment on the lower right, the figures are marked by some very conspicuous attributes: high, platform boots and staffs that open out at each end into a bell-shaped knob. According to the descriptions of exotic peoples left by the Greek geographer Strabo, these men are Assyrians. Their embroidered caps, each one different from the other, mark them as magi, or pagan priests. One of their number leans toward two of his companions, perhaps fearfully, perhaps in an attempt to persuade them. Their rigid stances suggest incomprehension, arrogance, and even an air of menace. A third figure, however, already seems to have been won over. He leans forward, the better to see the vision of Christ on the tympanum. This scene illustrates the power of the Holy Spirit, capable of converting even an Assyrian magus, but it also warns against the hardened, clever minds of such men, who are formidable in debate.

BETRAYAL OF COUNTRY, BETRAYAL OF FAITH

In the compartment just above the magi stands a man carrying a long, cylindrical rod in his left hand. It has been suggested that this object is meant to represent the siphon used to

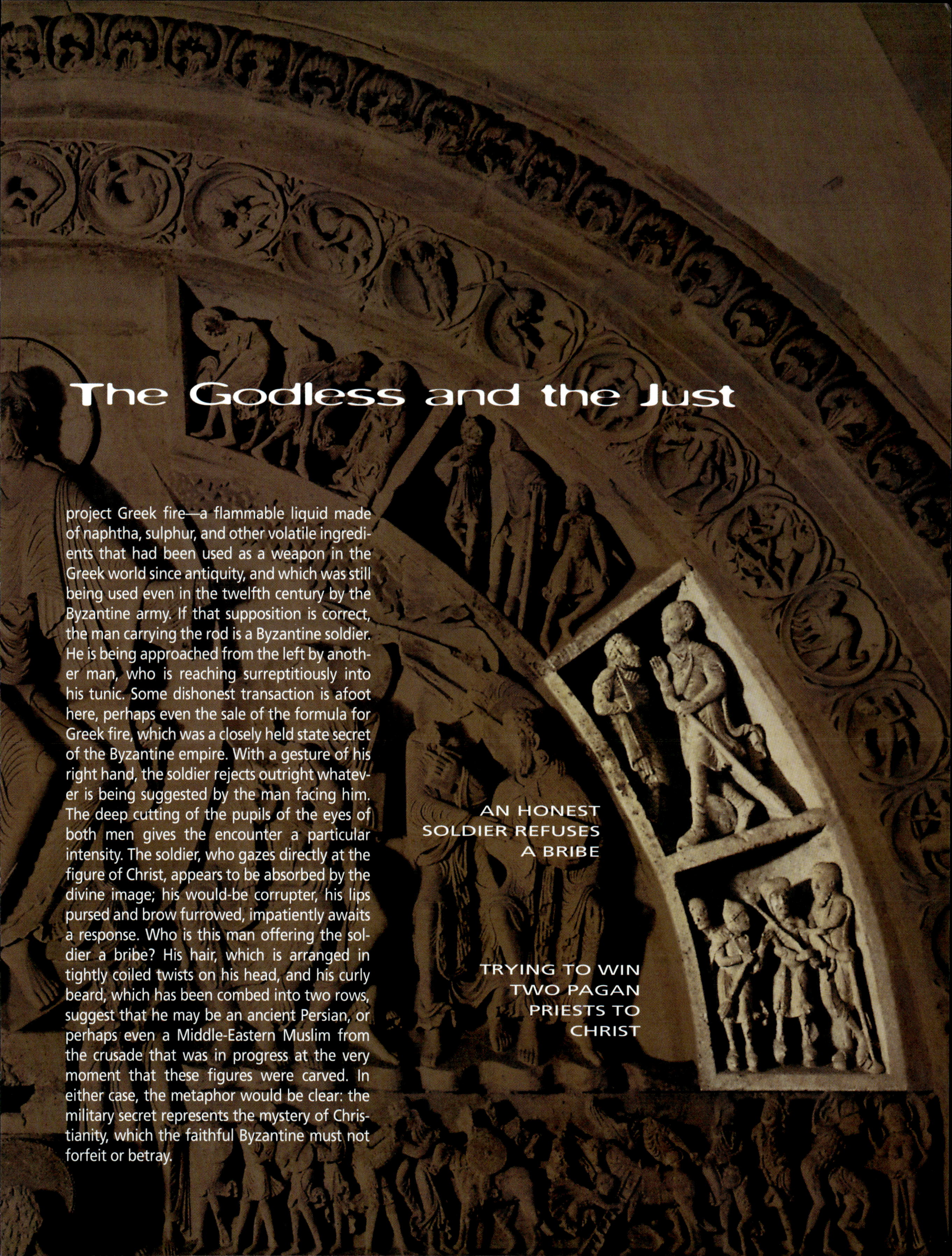

The Godless and the Just

project Greek fire—a flammable liquid made of naphtha, sulphur, and other volatile ingredients that had been used as a weapon in the Greek world since antiquity, and which was still being used even in the twelfth century by the Byzantine army. If that supposition is correct, the man carrying the rod is a Byzantine soldier. He is being approached from the left by another man, who is reaching surreptitiously into his tunic. Some dishonest transaction is afoot here, perhaps even the sale of the formula for Greek fire, which was a closely held state secret of the Byzantine empire. With a gesture of his right hand, the soldier rejects outright whatever is being suggested by the man facing him. The deep cutting of the pupils of the eyes of both men gives the encounter a particular intensity. The soldier, who gazes directly at the figure of Christ, appears to be absorbed by the divine image; his would-be corrupter, his lips pursed and brow furrowed, impatiently awaits a response. Who is this man offering the soldier a bribe? His hair, which is arranged in tightly coiled twists on his head, and his curly beard, which has been combed into two rows, suggest that he may be an ancient Persian, or perhaps even a Middle-Eastern Muslim from the crusade that was in progress at the very moment that these figures were carved. In either case, the metaphor would be clear: the military secret represents the mystery of Christianity, which the faithful Byzantine must not forfeit or betray.

AN HONEST SOLDIER REFUSES A BRIBE

TRYING TO WIN TWO PAGAN PRIESTS TO CHRIST

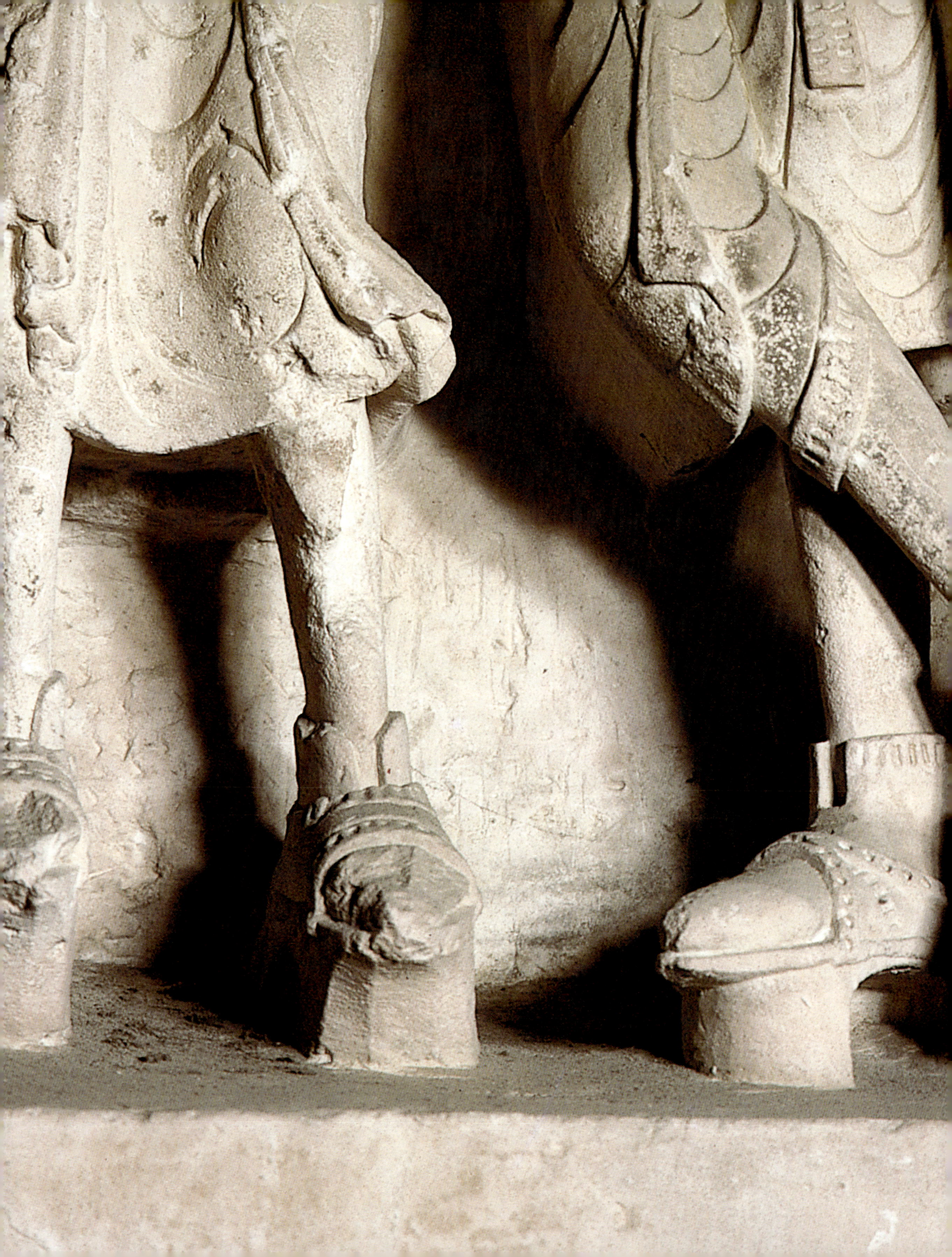

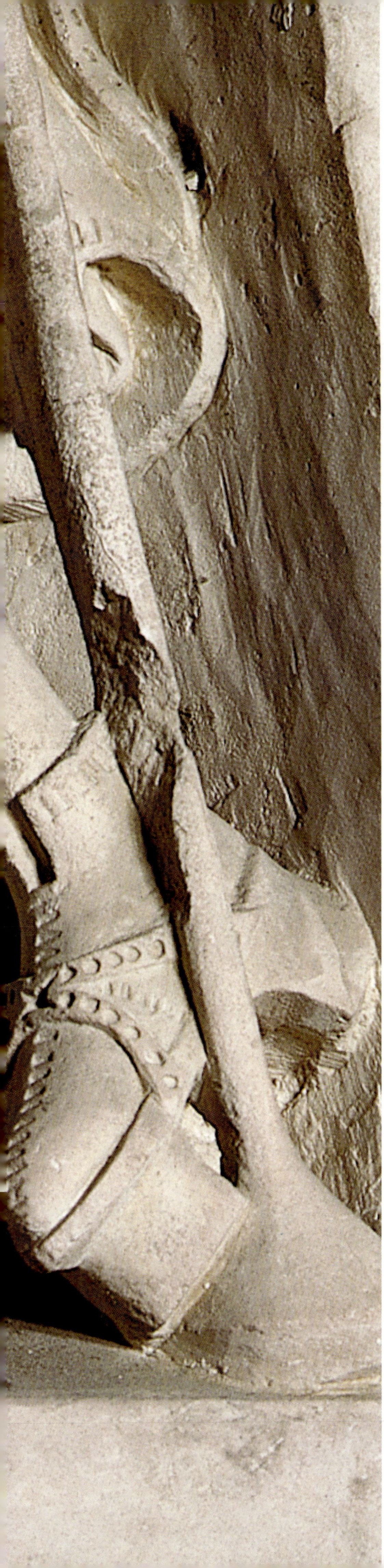

THE PLATFORM BOOTS
OF THE ASSYRIAN MAGI

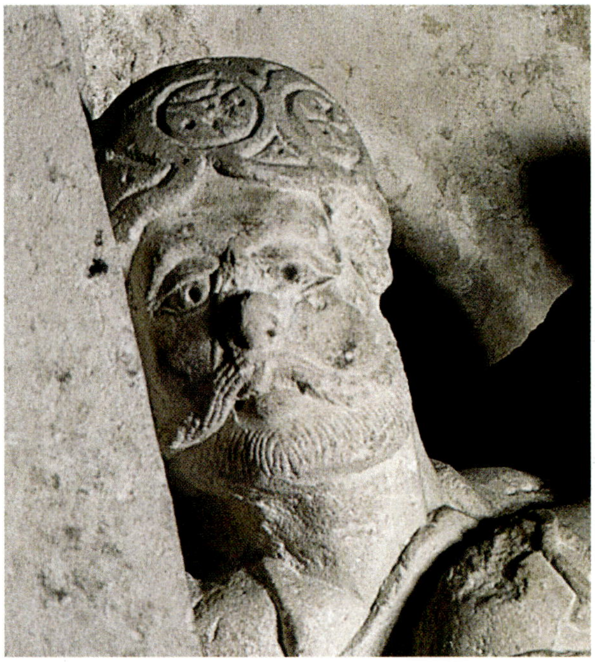

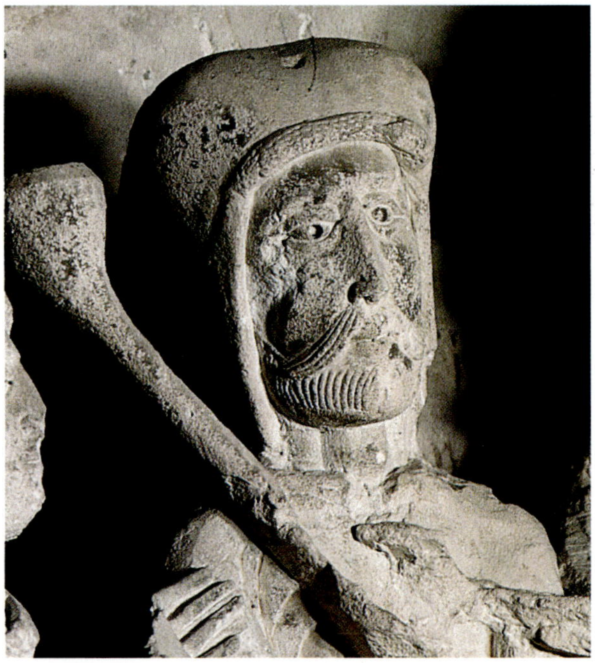

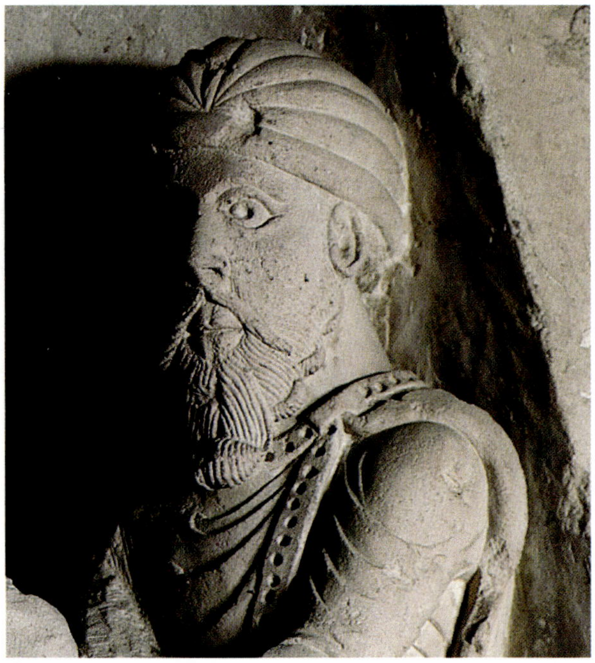

THE IMPIOUS MAGI

THE BRIBER AND THE HONORABLE SOLDIER

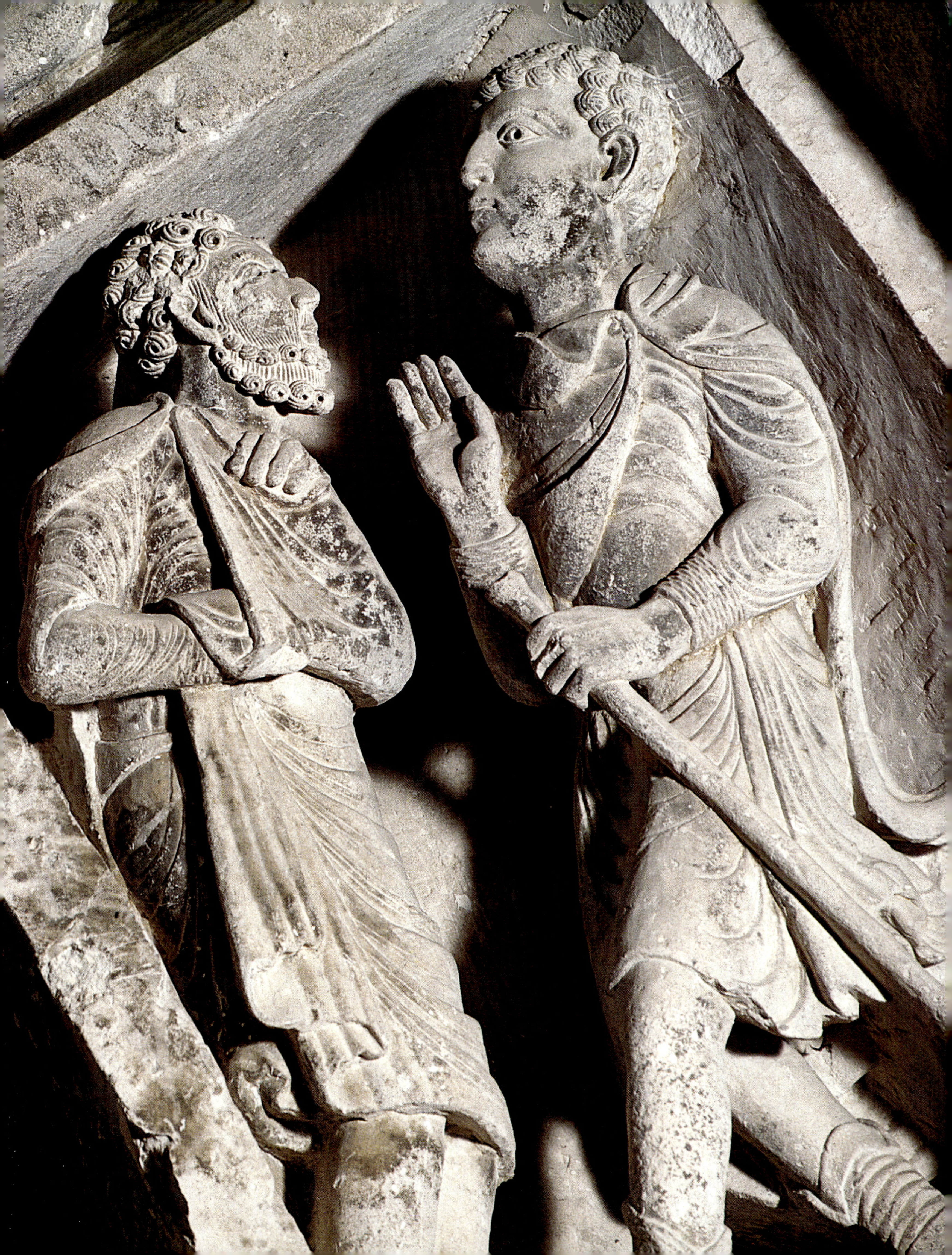

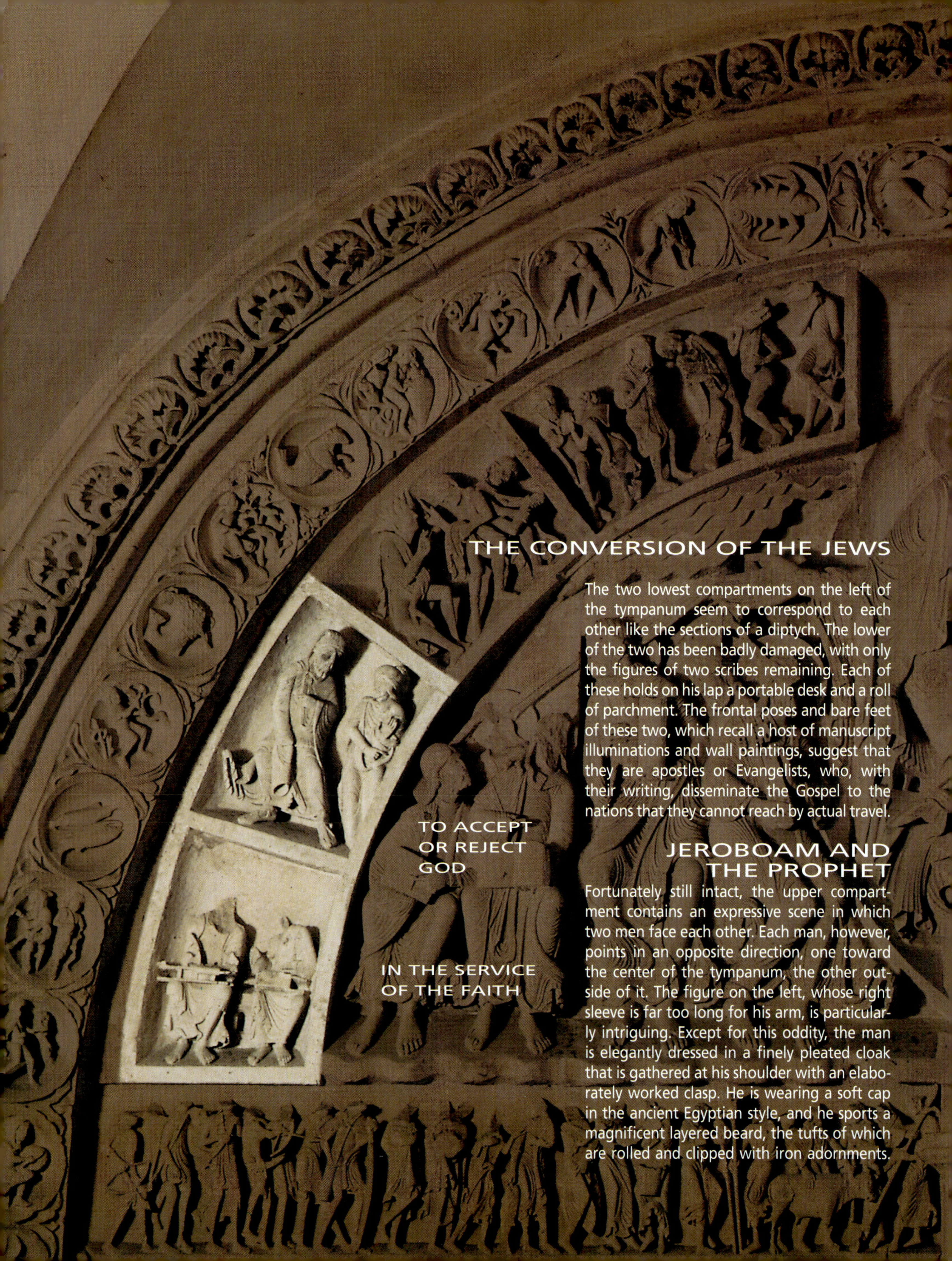

THE CONVERSION OF THE JEWS

The two lowest compartments on the left of the tympanum seem to correspond to each other like the sections of a diptych. The lower of the two has been badly damaged, with only the figures of two scribes remaining. Each of these holds on his lap a portable desk and a roll of parchment. The frontal poses and bare feet of these two, which recall a host of manuscript illuminations and wall paintings, suggest that they are apostles or Evangelists, who, with their writing, disseminate the Gospel to the nations that they cannot reach by actual travel.

JEROBOAM AND THE PROPHET

Fortunately still intact, the upper compartment contains an expressive scene in which two men face each other. Each man, however, points in an opposite direction, one toward the center of the tympanum, the other outside of it. The figure on the left, whose right sleeve is far too long for his arm, is particularly intriguing. Except for this oddity, the man is elegantly dressed in a finely pleated cloak that is gathered at his shoulder with an elaborately worked clasp. He is wearing a soft cap in the ancient Egyptian style, and he sports a magnificent layered beard, the tufts of which are rolled and clipped with iron adornments.

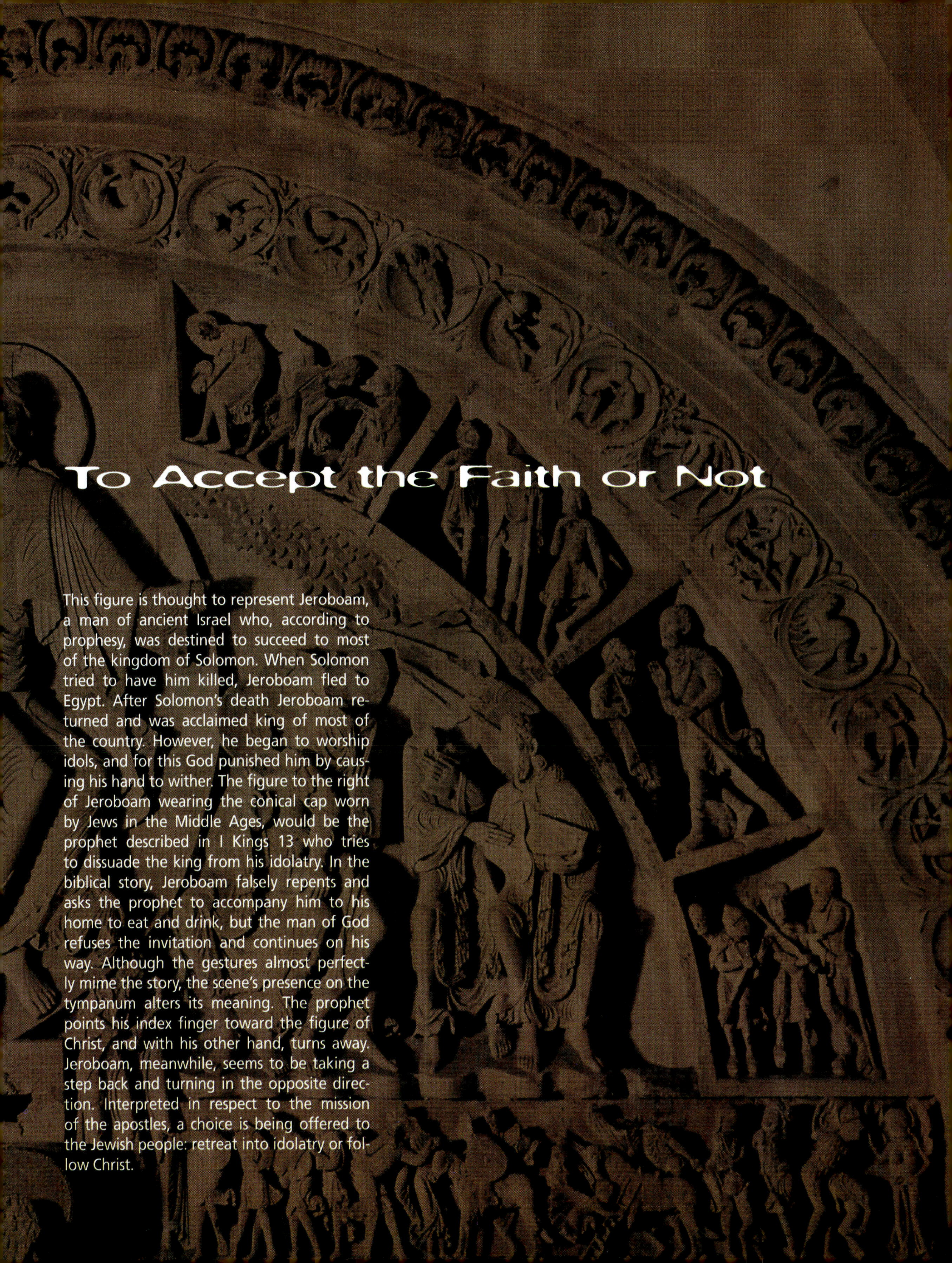

To Accept the Faith or Not

This figure is thought to represent Jeroboam, a man of ancient Israel who, according to prophesy, was destined to succeed to most of the kingdom of Solomon. When Solomon tried to have him killed, Jeroboam fled to Egypt. After Solomon's death Jeroboam returned and was acclaimed king of most of the country. However, he began to worship idols, and for this God punished him by causing his hand to wither. The figure to the right of Jeroboam wearing the conical cap worn by Jews in the Middle Ages, would be the prophet described in I Kings 13 who tries to dissuade the king from his idolatry. In the biblical story, Jeroboam falsely repents and asks the prophet to accompany him to his home to eat and drink, but the man of God refuses the invitation and continues on his way. Although the gestures almost perfectly mime the story, the scene's presence on the tympanum alters its meaning. The prophet points his index finger toward the figure of Christ, and with his other hand, turns away. Jeroboam, meanwhile, seems to be taking a step back and turning in the opposite direction. Interpreted in respect to the mission of the apostles, a choice is being offered to the Jewish people: retreat into idolatry or follow Christ.

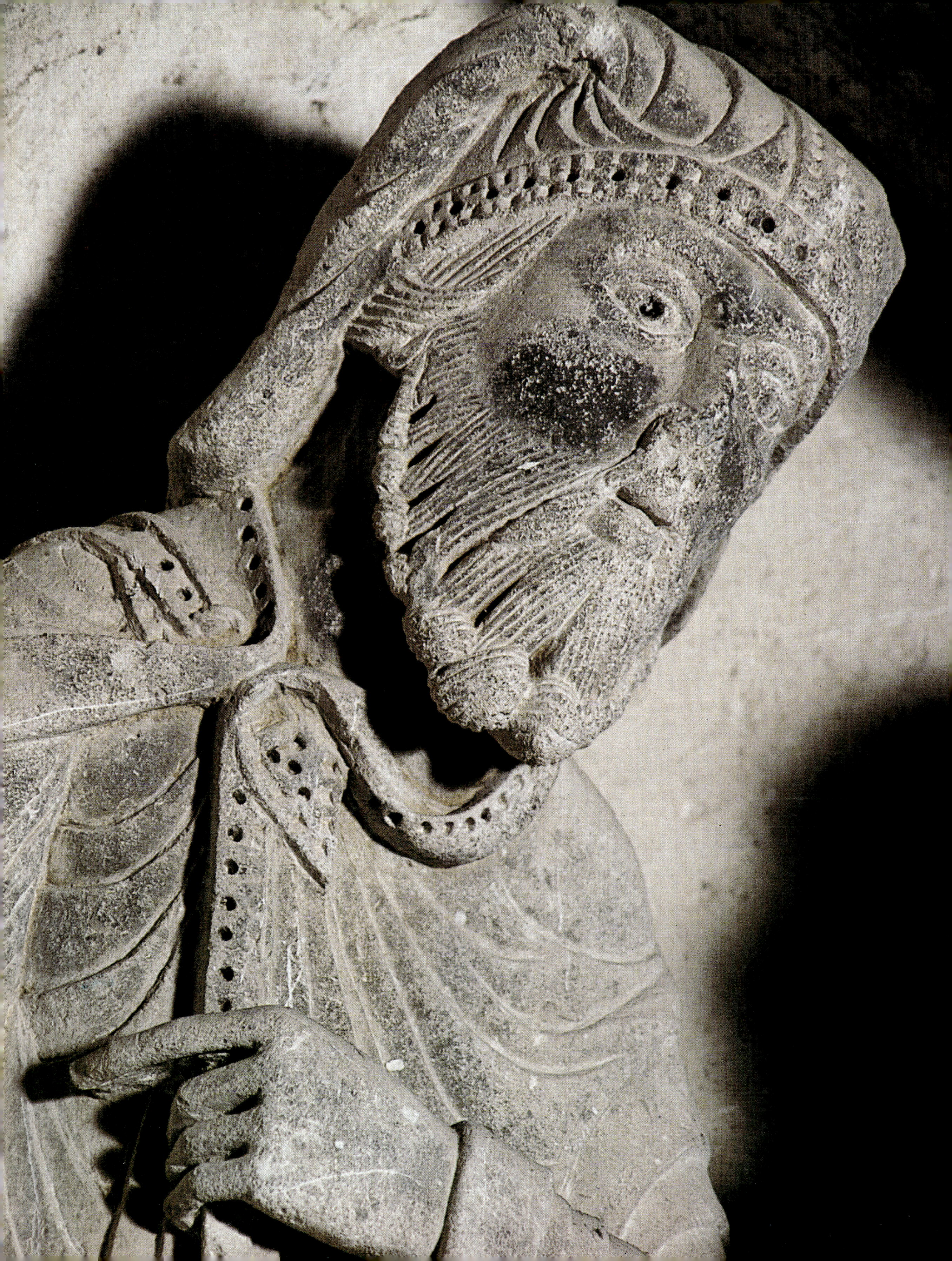

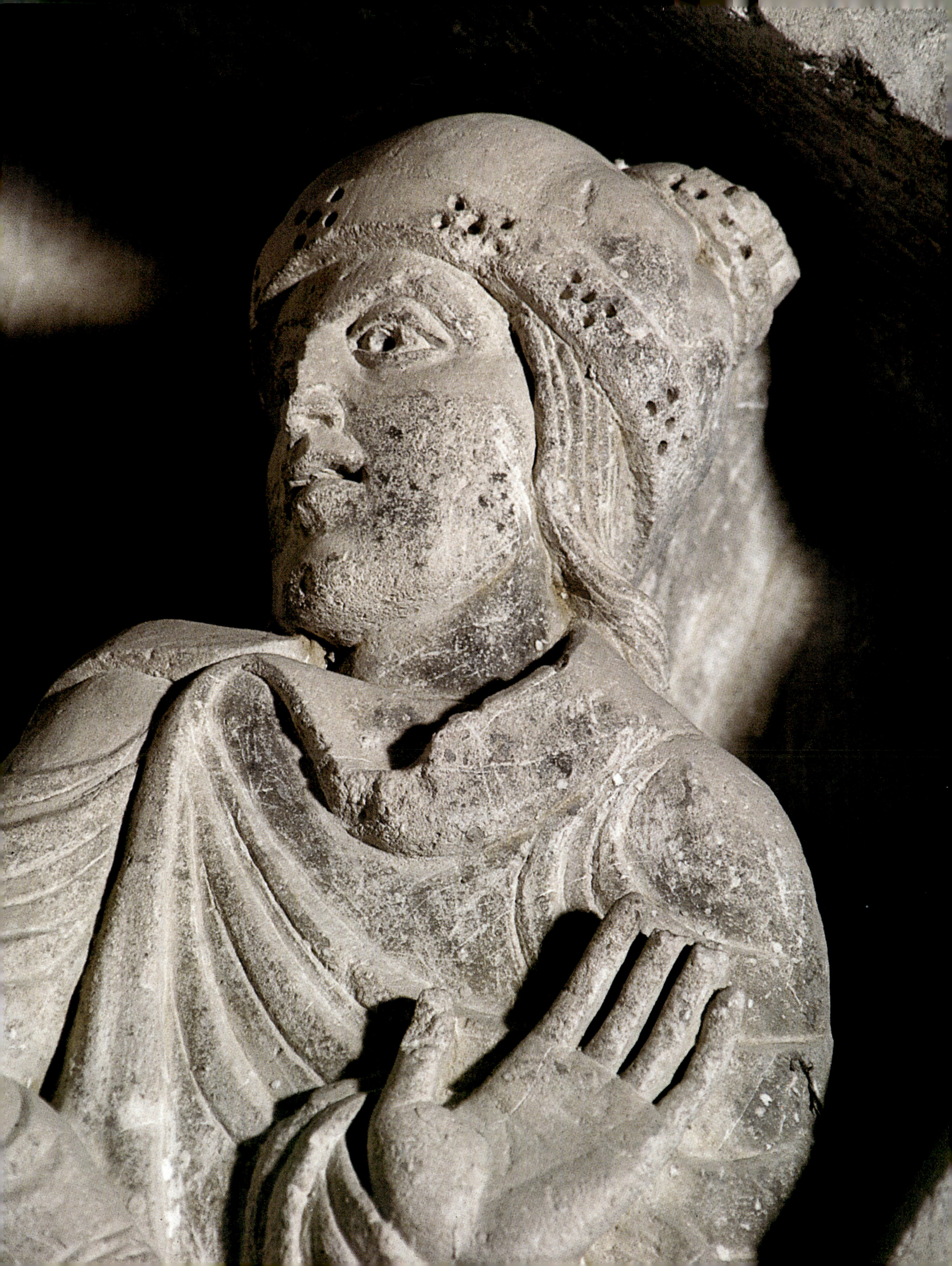

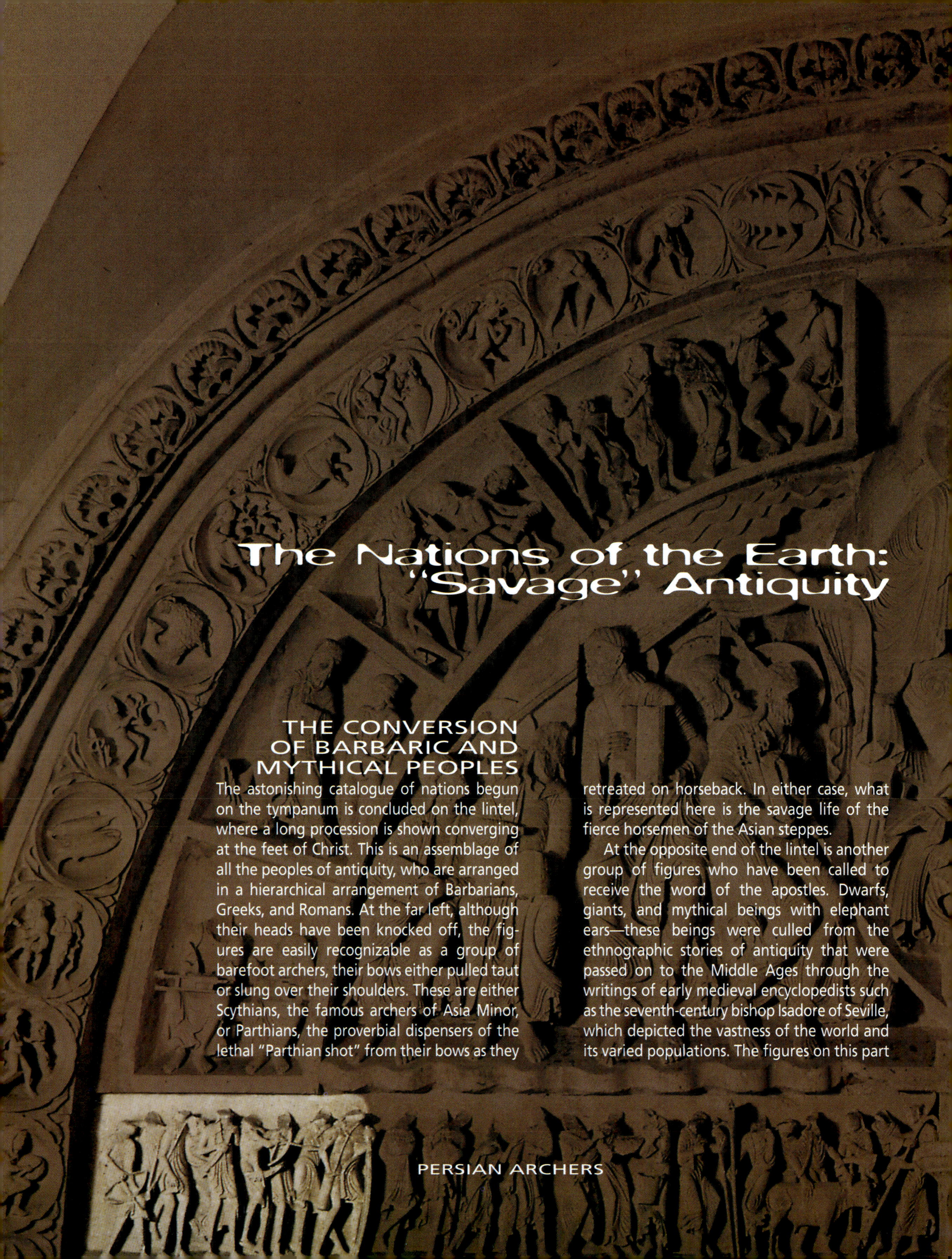

The Nations of the Earth: "Savage" Antiquity

THE CONVERSION OF BARBARIC AND MYTHICAL PEOPLES

The astonishing catalogue of nations begun on the tympanum is concluded on the lintel, where a long procession is shown converging at the feet of Christ. This is an assemblage of all the peoples of antiquity, who are arranged in a hierarchical arrangement of Barbarians, Greeks, and Romans. At the far left, although their heads have been knocked off, the figures are easily recognizable as a group of barefoot archers, their bows either pulled taut or slung over their shoulders. These are either Scythians, the famous archers of Asia Minor, or Parthians, the proverbial dispensers of the lethal "Parthian shot" from their bows as they retreated on horseback. In either case, what is represented here is the savage life of the fierce horsemen of the Asian steppes.

At the opposite end of the lintel is another group of figures who have been called to receive the word of the apostles. Dwarfs, giants, and mythical beings with elephant ears—these beings were culled from the ethnographic stories of antiquity that were passed on to the Middle Ages through the writings of early medieval encyclopedists such as the seventh-century bishop Isadore of Seville, which depicted the vastness of the world and its varied populations. The figures on this part

PERSIAN ARCHERS

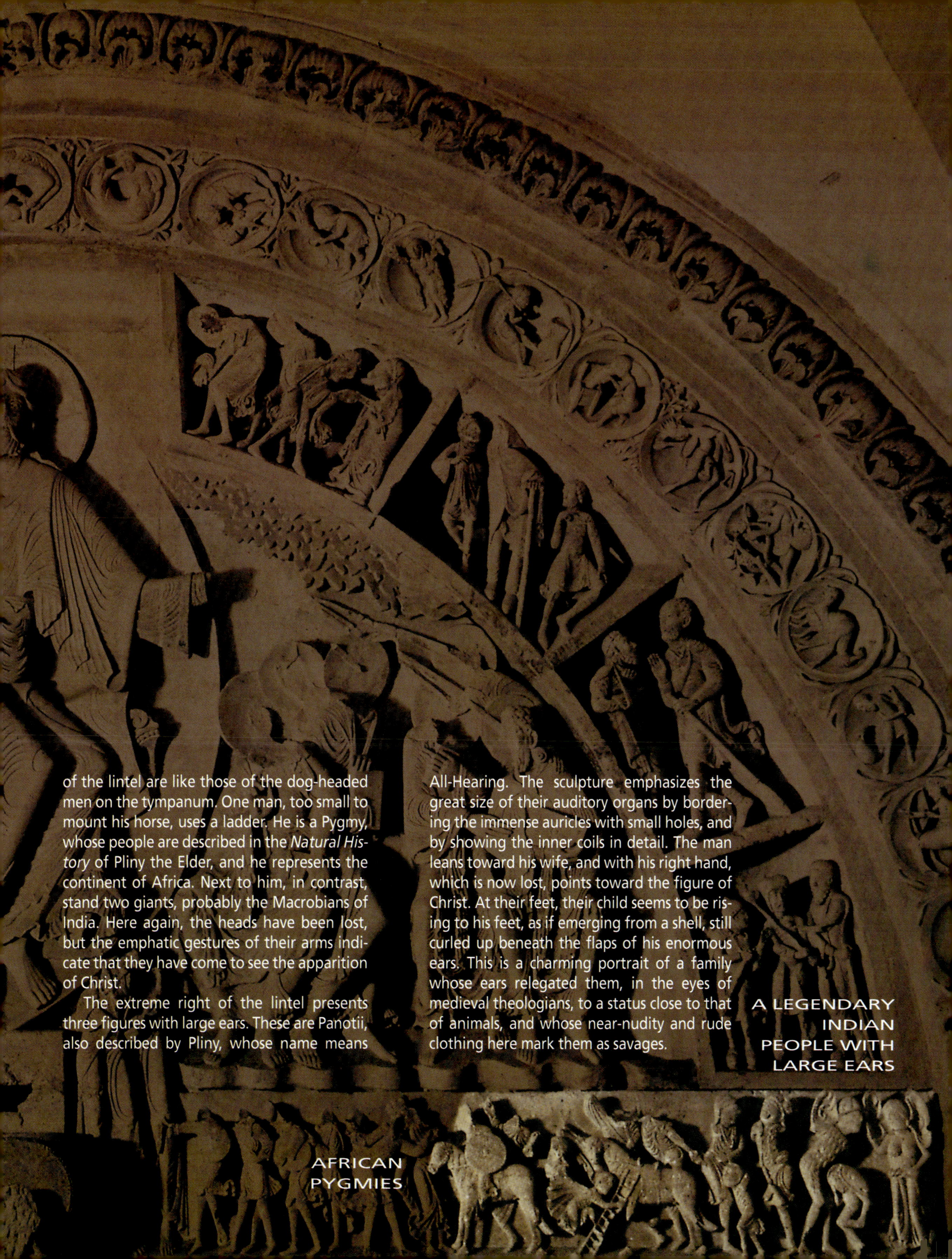

of the lintel are like those of the dog-headed men on the tympanum. One man, too small to mount his horse, uses a ladder. He is a Pygmy, whose people are described in the *Natural History* of Pliny the Elder, and he represents the continent of Africa. Next to him, in contrast, stand two giants, probably the Macrobians of India. Here again, the heads have been lost, but the emphatic gestures of their arms indicate that they have come to see the apparition of Christ.

The extreme right of the lintel presents three figures with large ears. These are Panotii, also described by Pliny, whose name means All-Hearing. The sculpture emphasizes the great size of their auditory organs by bordering the immense auricles with small holes, and by showing the inner coils in detail. The man leans toward his wife, and with his right hand, which is now lost, points toward the figure of Christ. At their feet, their child seems to be rising to his feet, as if emerging from a shell, still curled up beneath the flaps of his enormous ears. This is a charming portrait of a family whose ears relegated them, in the eyes of medieval theologians, to a status close to that of animals, and whose near-nudity and rude clothing here mark them as savages.

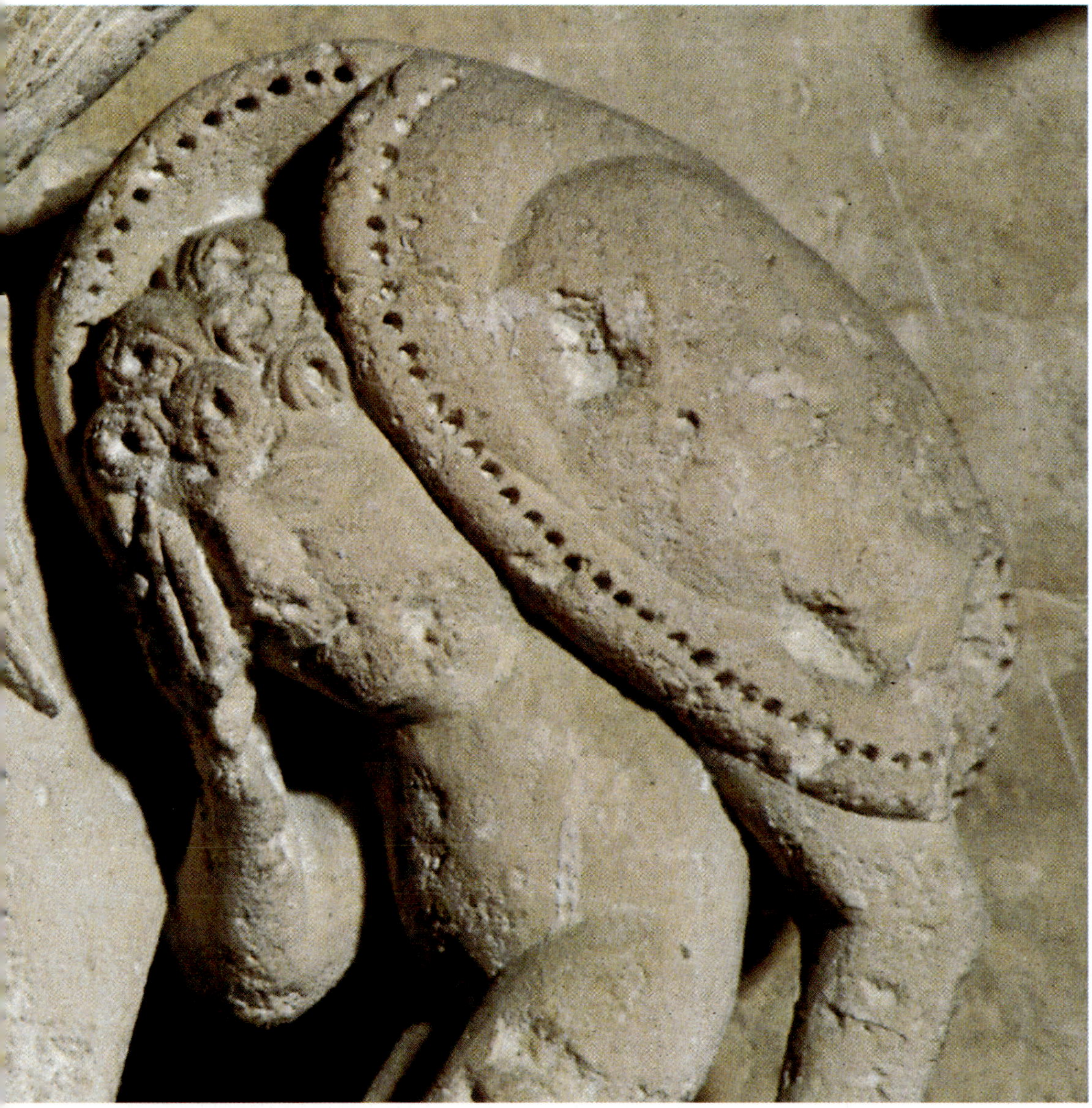

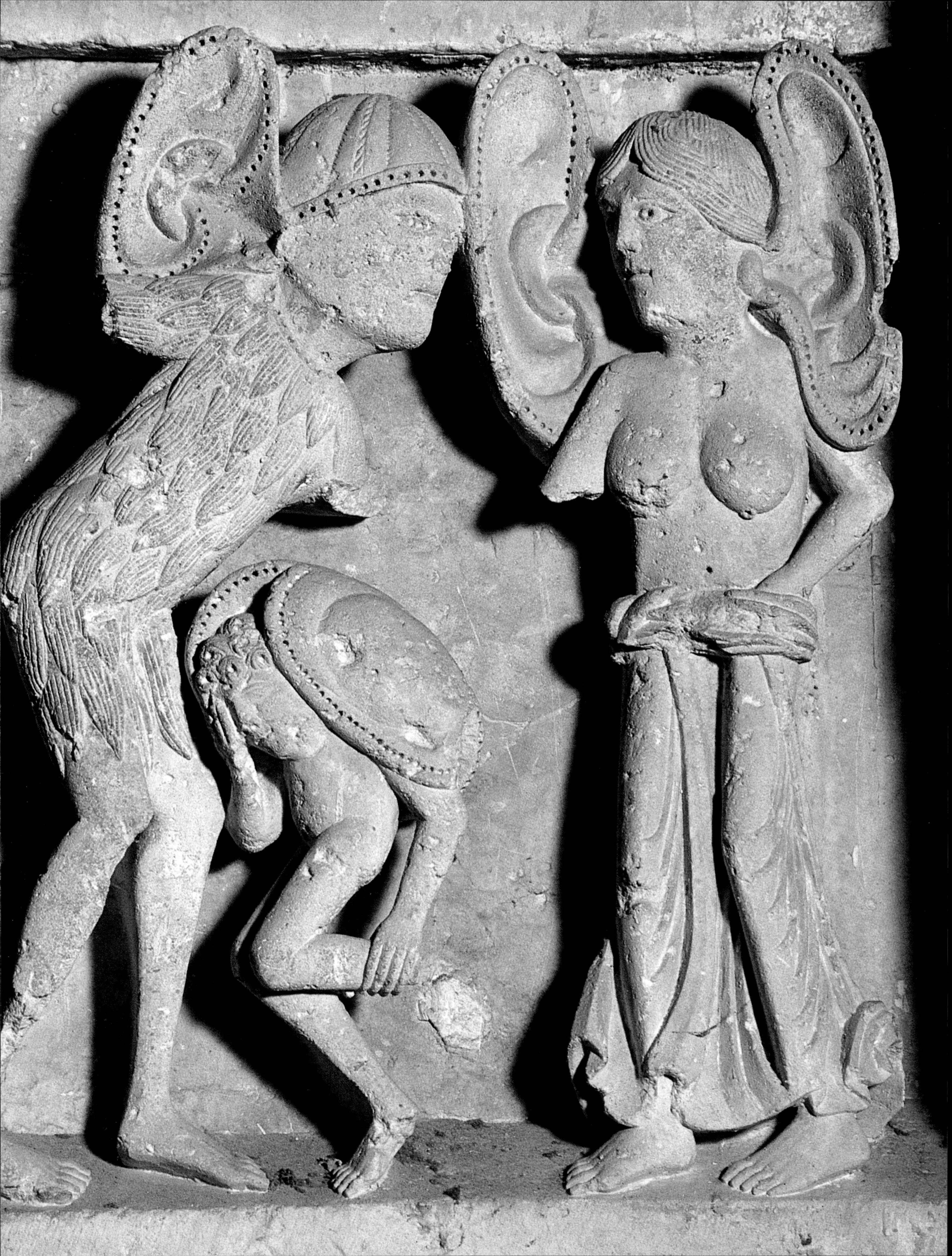

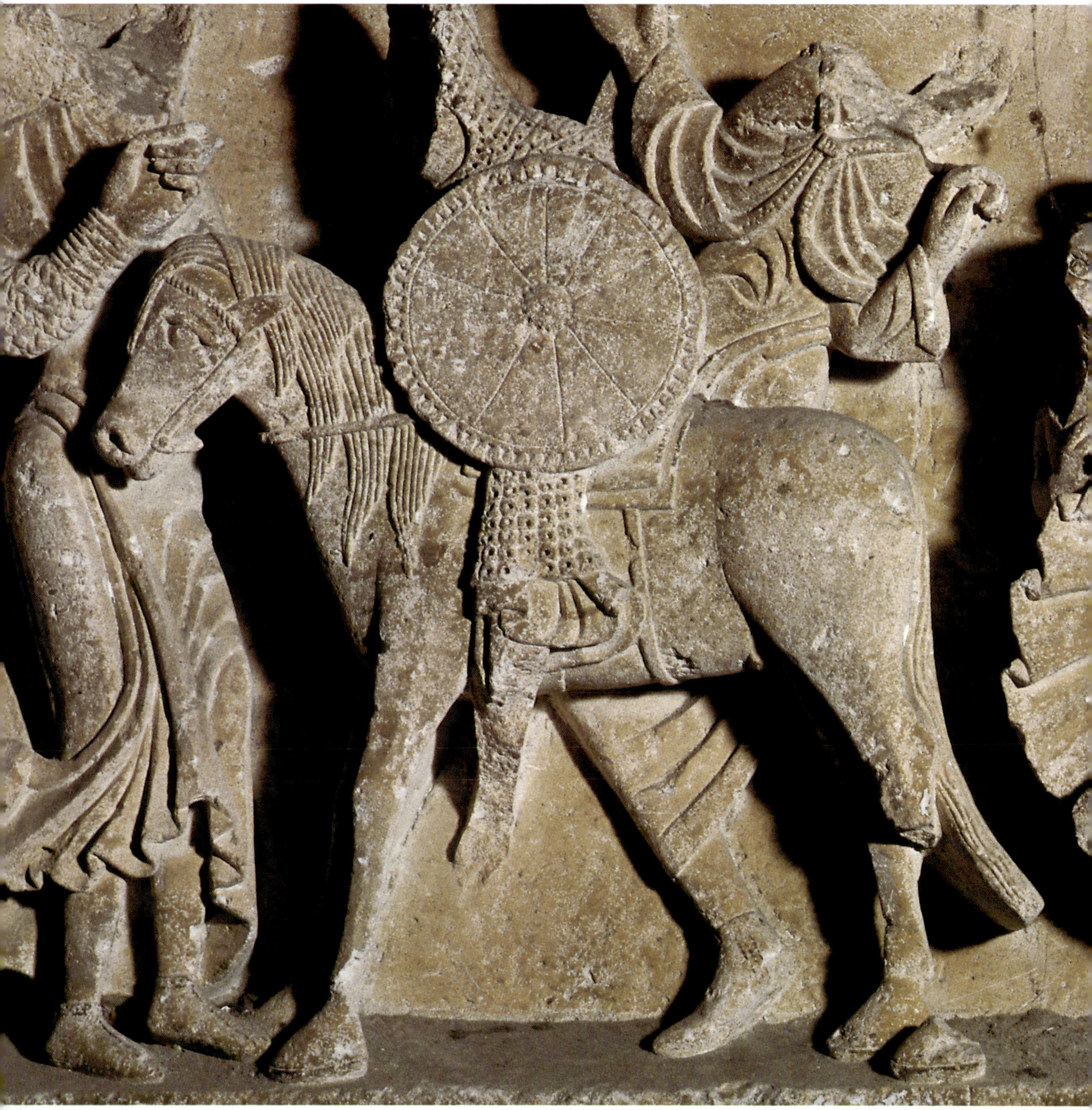

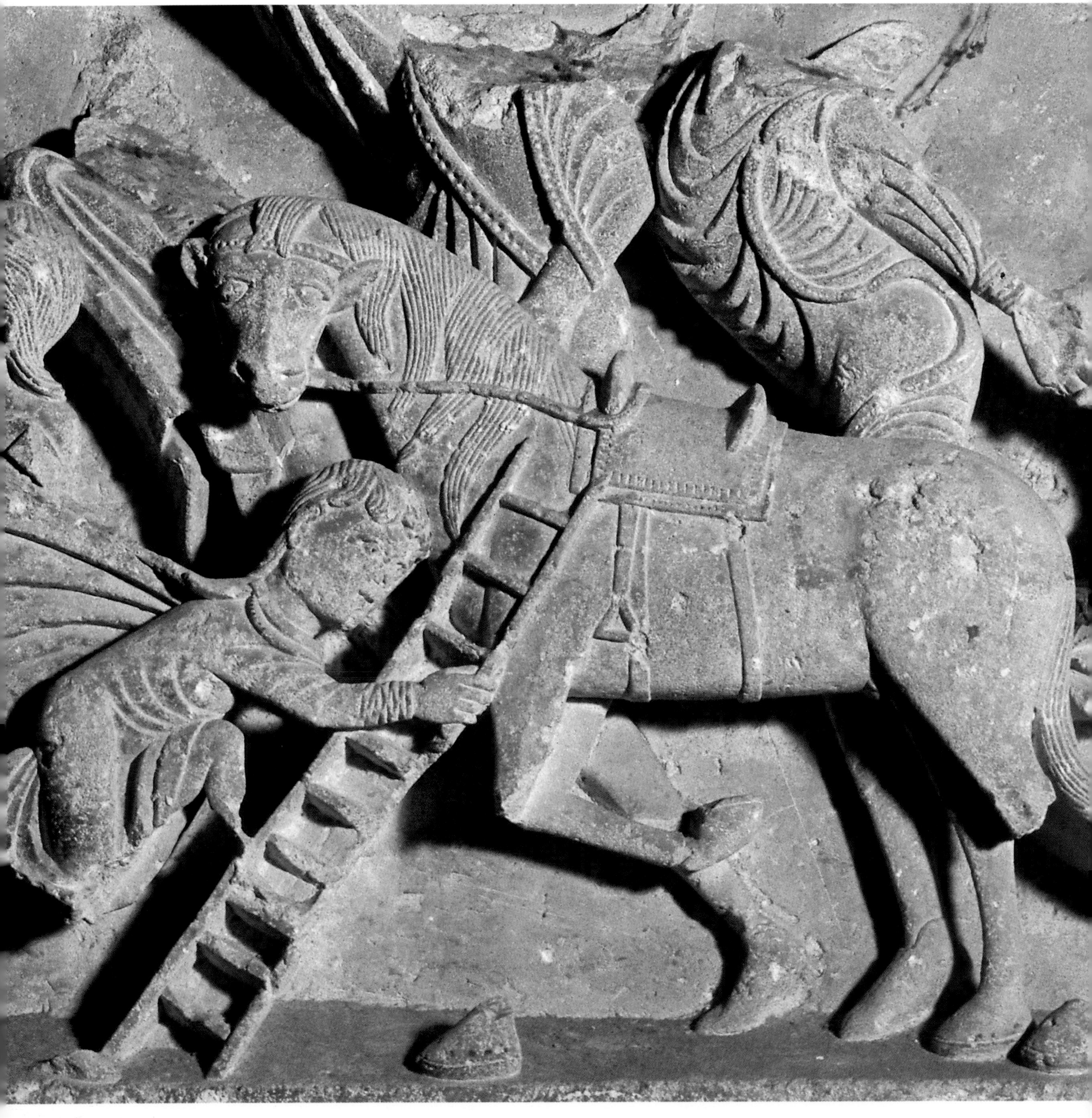

AFRICAN PYGMIES

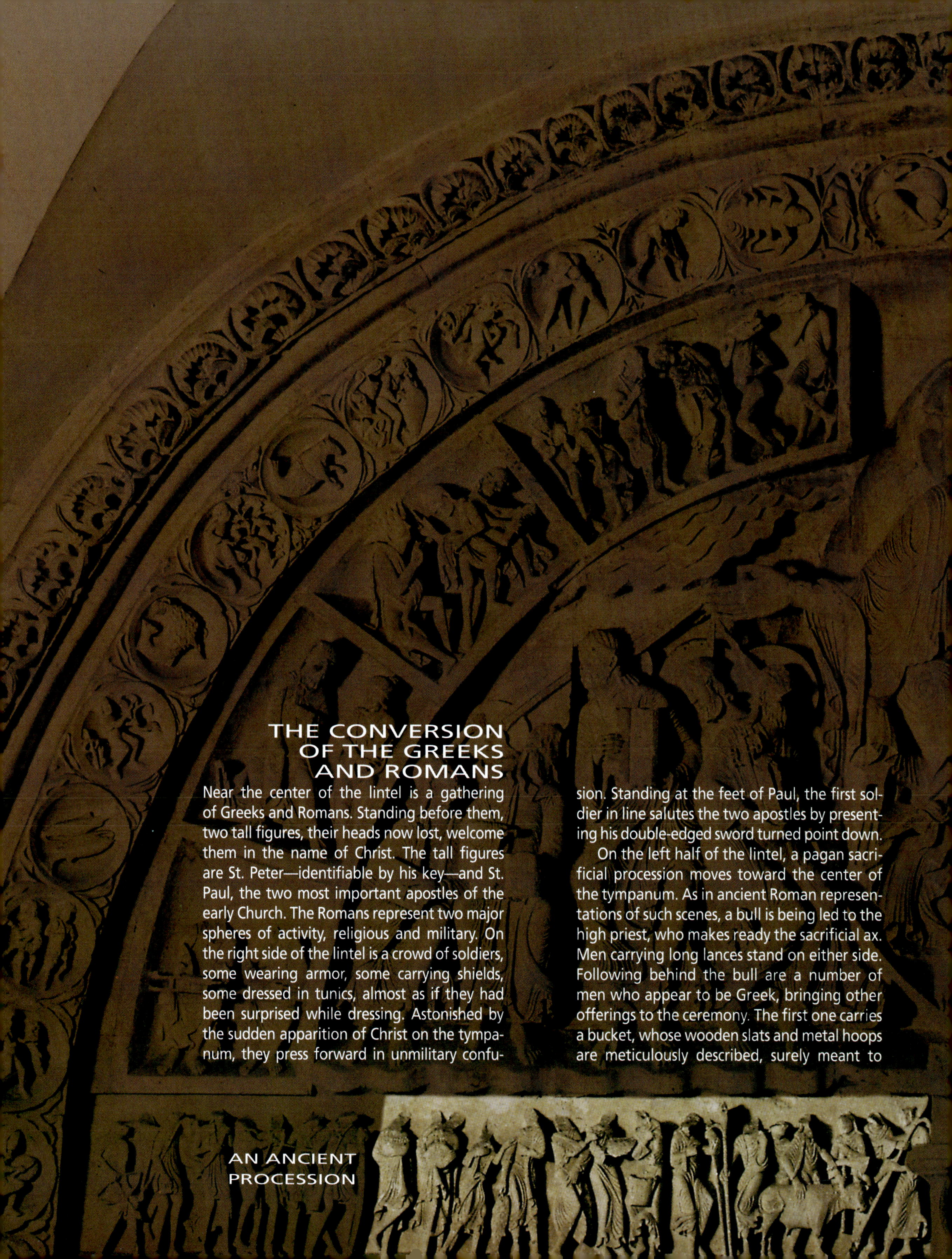

THE CONVERSION OF THE GREEKS AND ROMANS

Near the center of the lintel is a gathering of Greeks and Romans. Standing before them, two tall figures, their heads now lost, welcome them in the name of Christ. The tall figures are St. Peter—identifiable by his key—and St. Paul, the two most important apostles of the early Church. The Romans represent two major spheres of activity, religious and military. On the right side of the lintel is a crowd of soldiers, some wearing armor, some carrying shields, some dressed in tunics, almost as if they had been surprised while dressing. Astonished by the sudden apparition of Christ on the tympanum, they press forward in unmilitary confusion. Standing at the feet of Paul, the first soldier in line salutes the two apostles by presenting his double-edged sword turned point down.

On the left half of the lintel, a pagan sacrificial procession moves toward the center of the tympanum. As in ancient Roman representations of such scenes, a bull is being led to the high priest, who makes ready the sacrificial ax. Men carrying long lances stand on either side. Following behind the bull are a number of men who appear to be Greek, bringing other offerings to the ceremony. The first one carries a bucket, whose wooden slats and metal hoops are meticulously described, surely meant to

AN ANCIENT PROCESSION

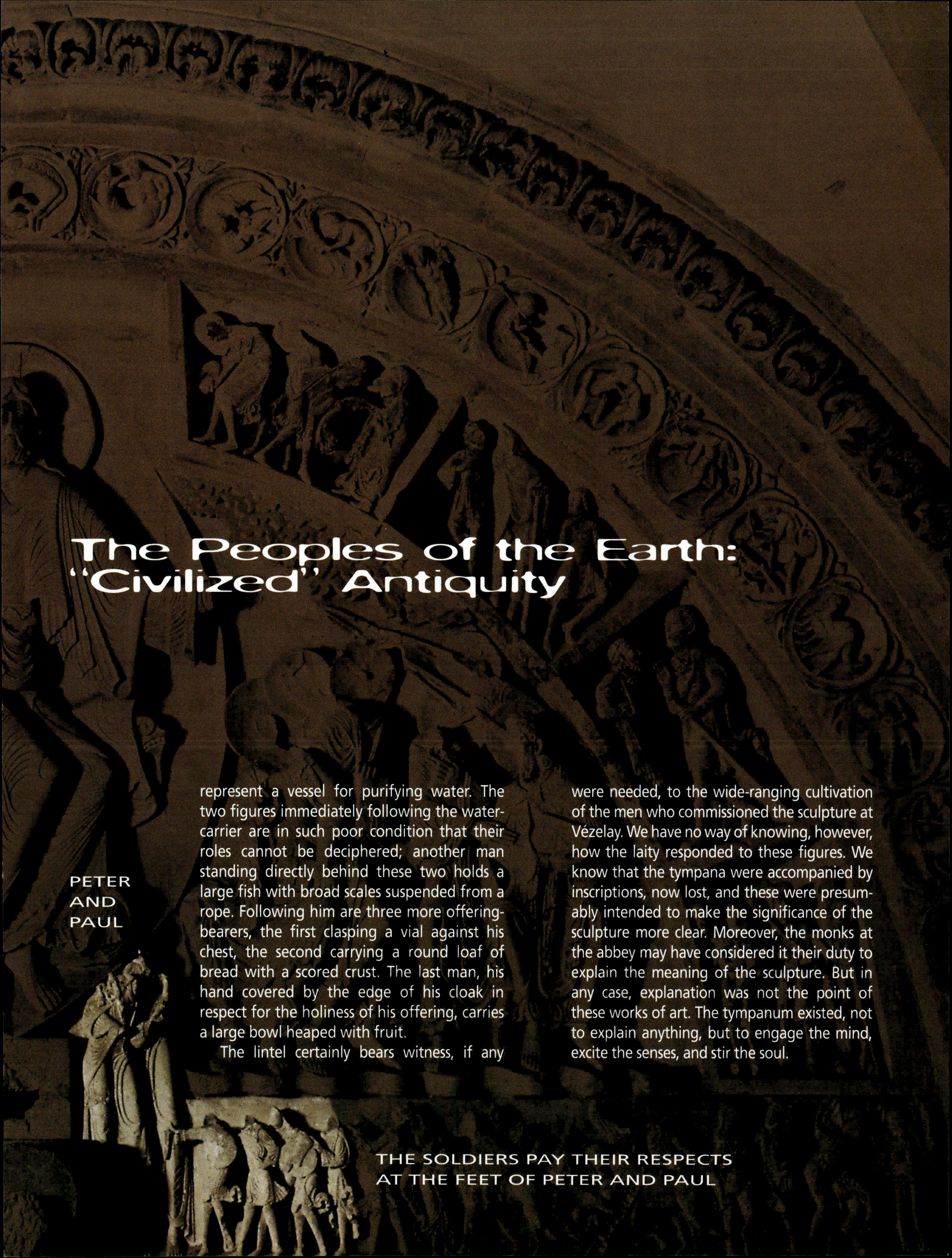

The Peoples of the Earth: "Civilized" Antiquity

PETER AND PAUL

represent a vessel for purifying water. The two figures immediately following the water-carrier are in such poor condition that their roles cannot be deciphered; another man standing directly behind these two holds a large fish with broad scales suspended from a rope. Following him are three more offering-bearers, the first clasping a vial against his chest, the second carrying a round loaf of bread with a scored crust. The last man, his hand covered by the edge of his cloak in respect for the holiness of his offering, carries a large bowl heaped with fruit.

The lintel certainly bears witness, if any were needed, to the wide-ranging cultivation of the men who commissioned the sculpture at Vézelay. We have no way of knowing, however, how the laity responded to these figures. We know that the tympana were accompanied by inscriptions, now lost, and these were presumably intended to make the significance of the sculpture more clear. Moreover, the monks at the abbey may have considered it their duty to explain the meaning of the sculpture. But in any case, explanation was not the point of these works of art. The tympanum existed, not to explain anything, but to engage the mind, excite the senses, and stir the soul.

THE SOLDIERS PAY THEIR RESPECTS AT THE FEET OF PETER AND PAUL

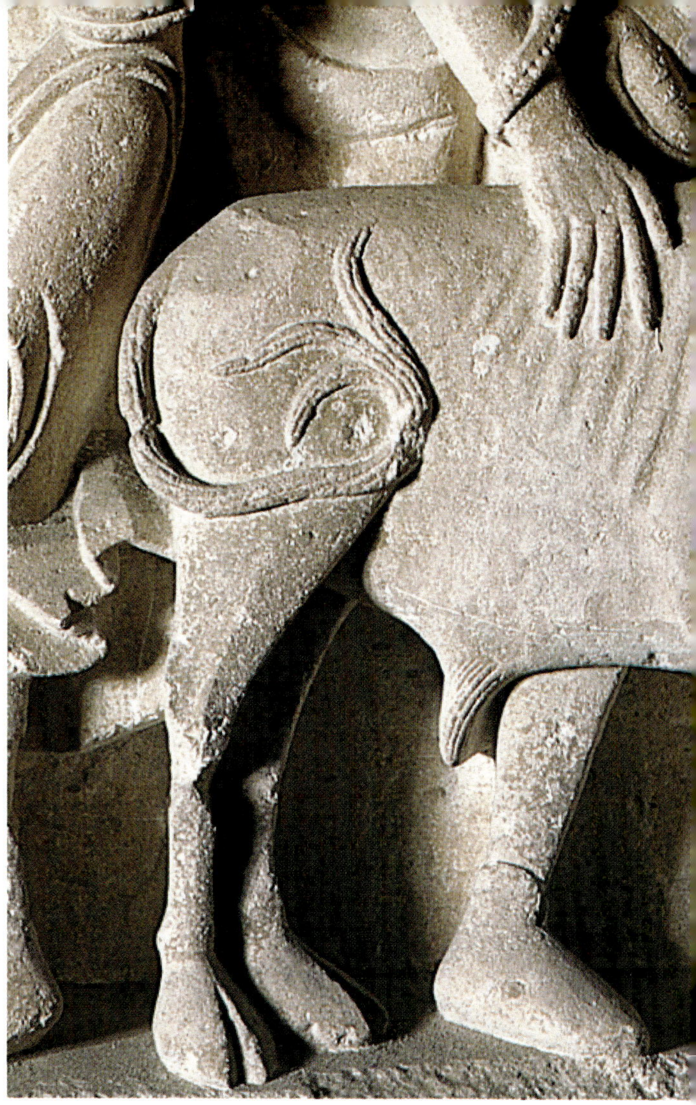

THE BULL LED TO SACRIFICE

GREEKS LADEN WITH OFFERINGS

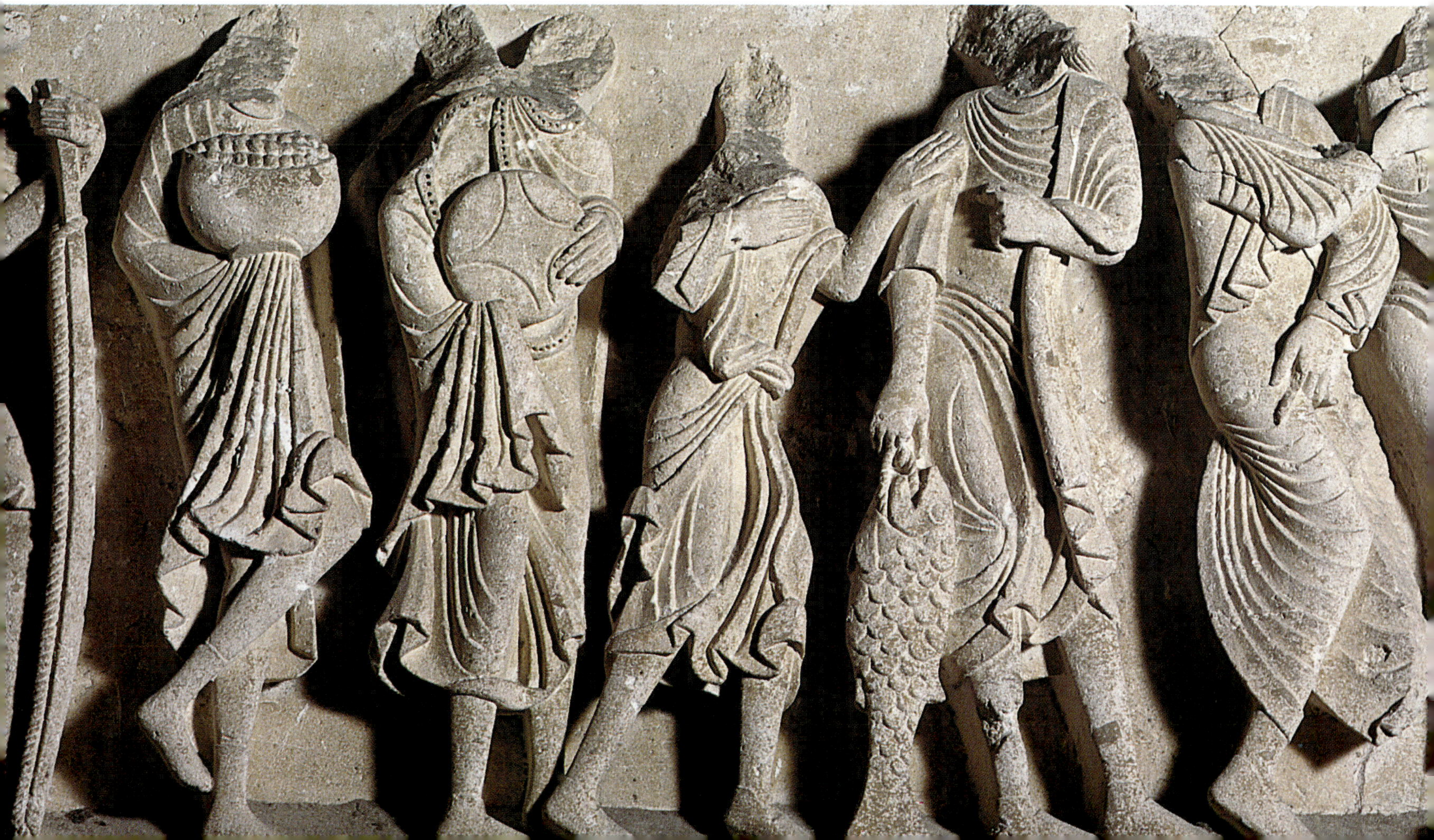

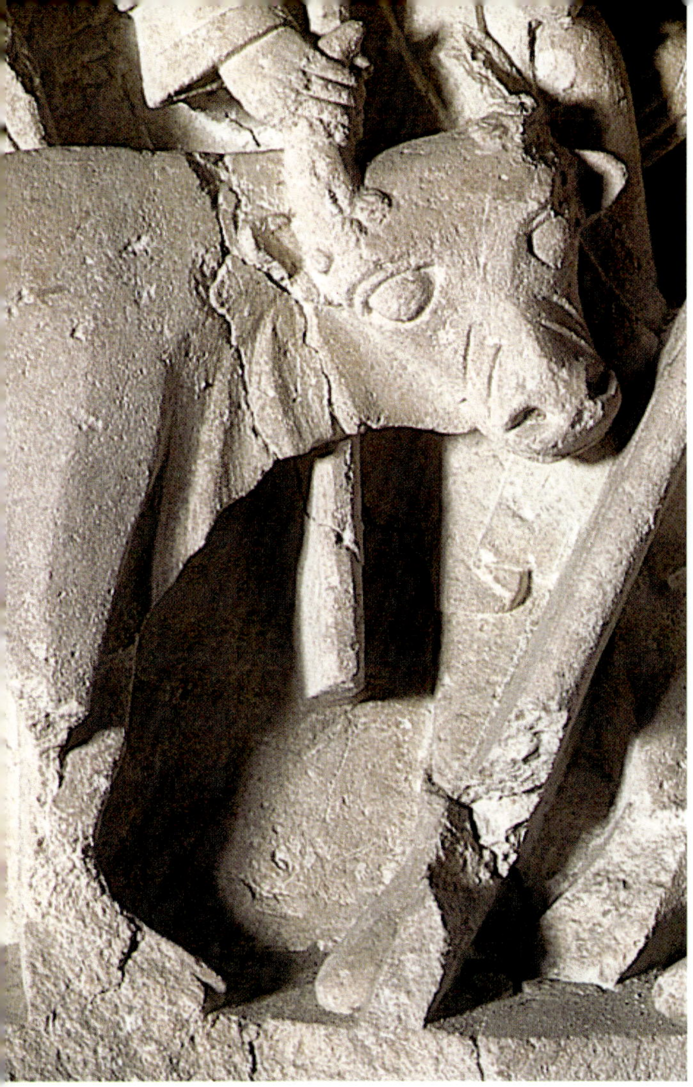

ROMAN SOLDIERS AWESTRUCK
BY THE VISION OF CHRIST

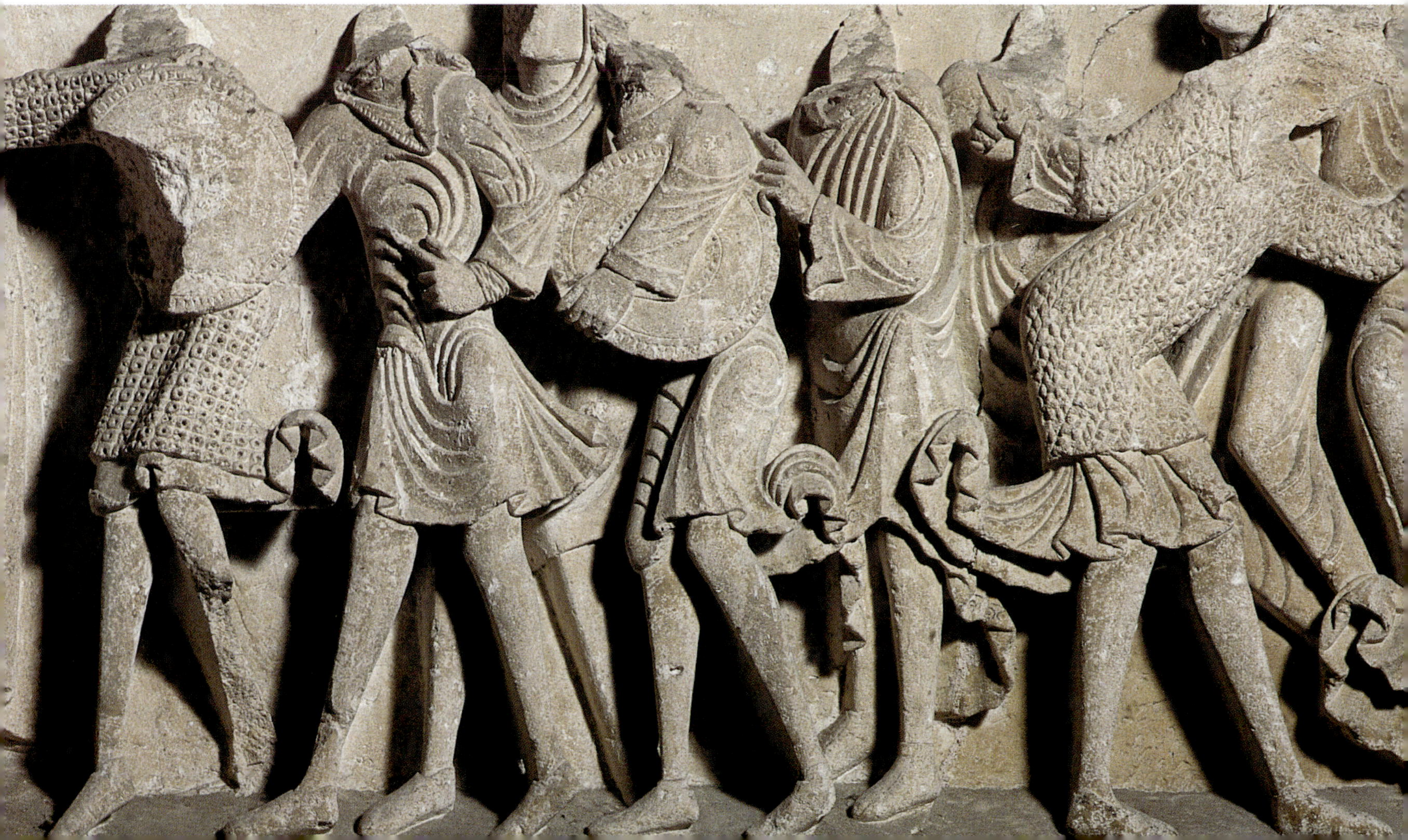

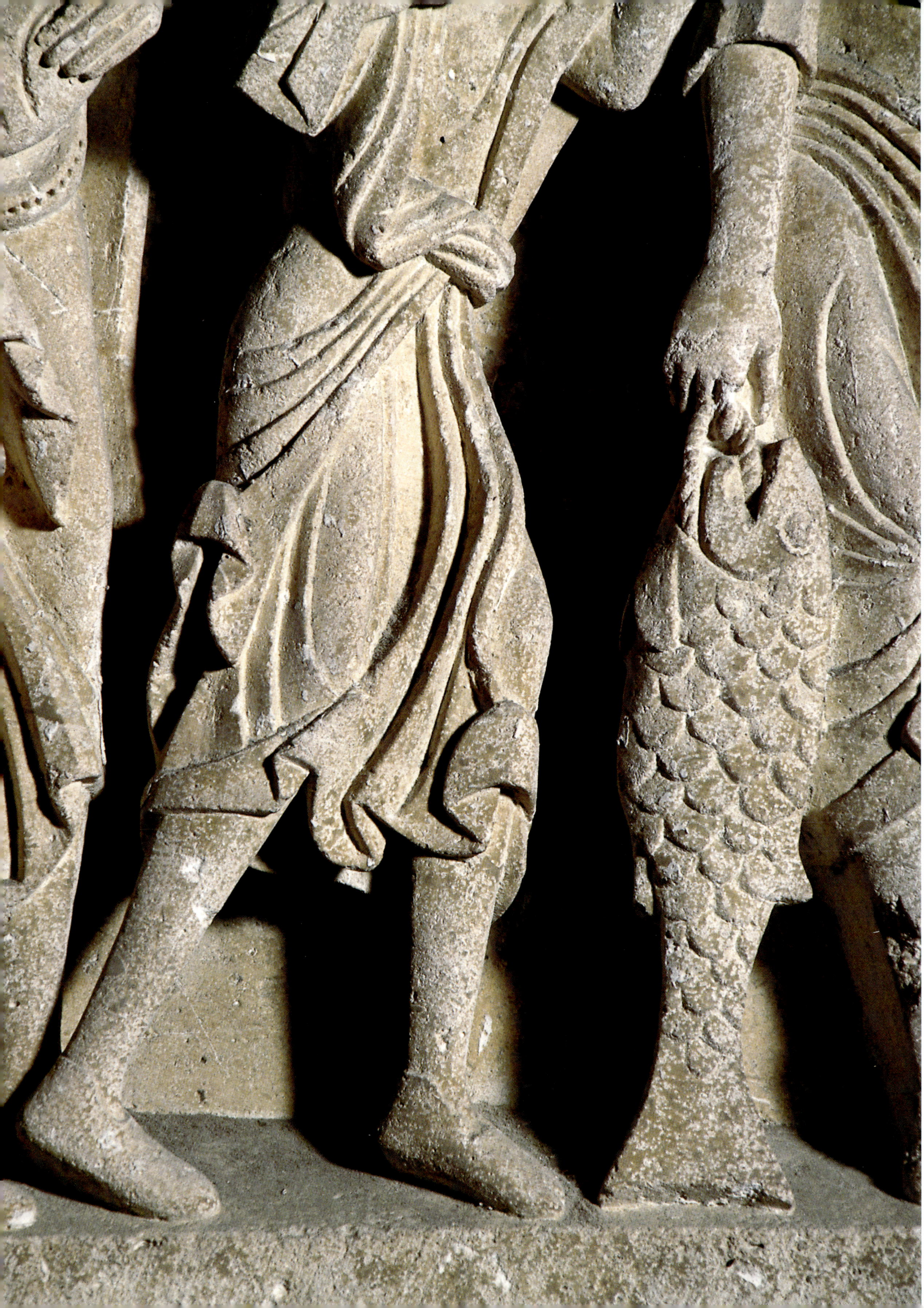

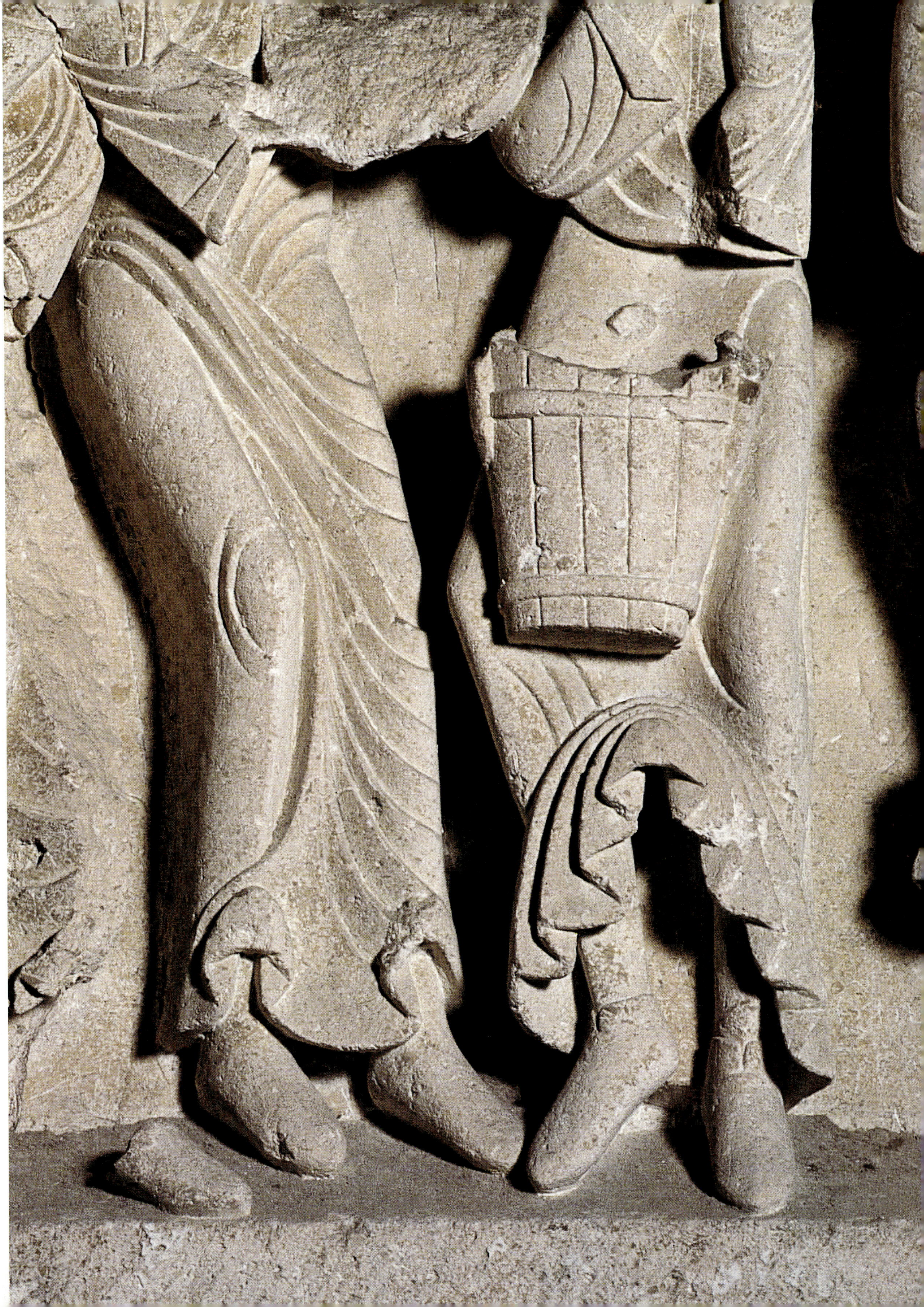

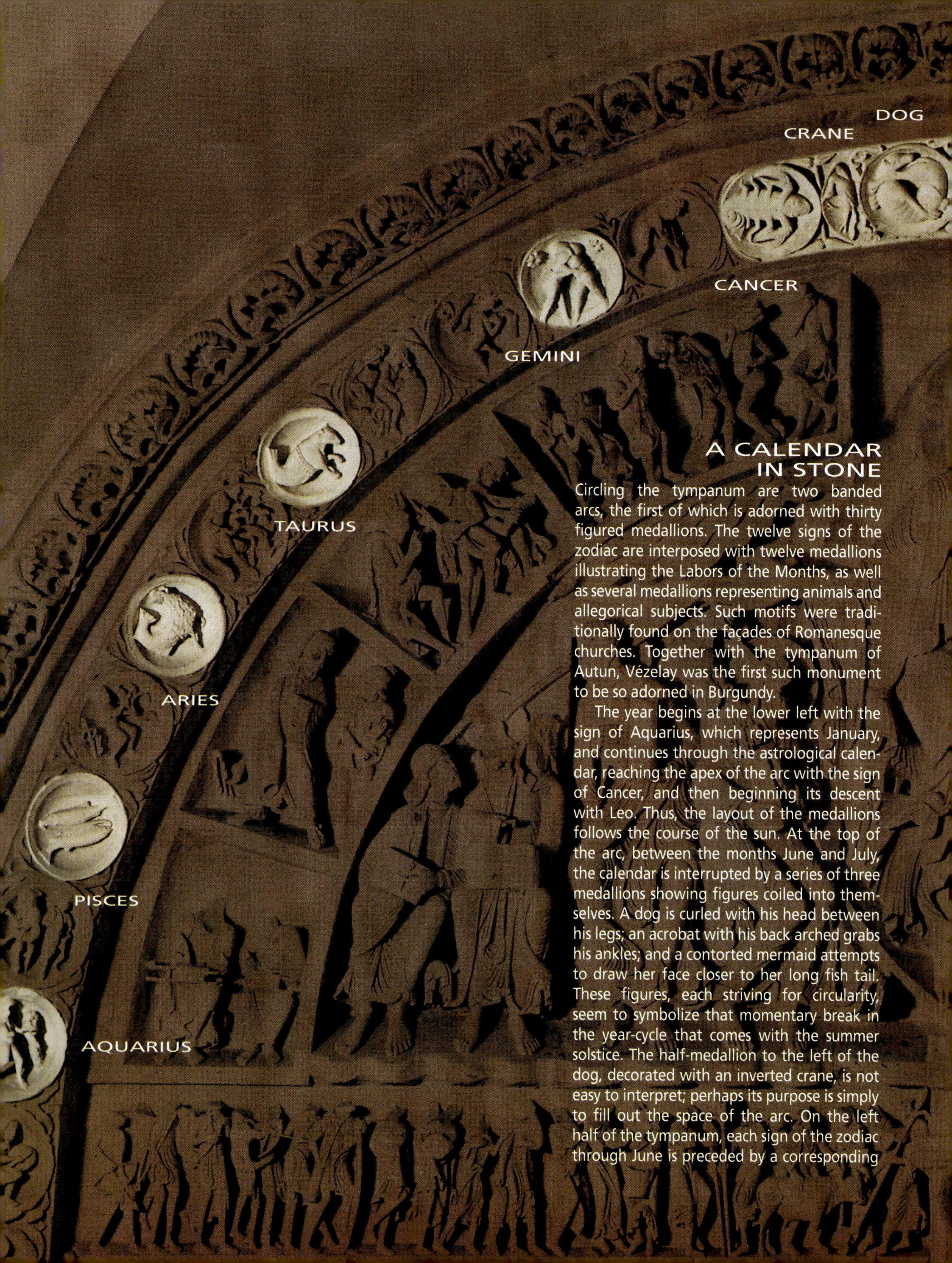

A CALENDAR IN STONE

Circling the tympanum are two banded arcs, the first of which is adorned with thirty figured medallions. The twelve signs of the zodiac are interposed with twelve medallions illustrating the Labors of the Months, as well as several medallions representing animals and allegorical subjects. Such motifs were traditionally found on the façades of Romanesque churches. Together with the tympanum of Autun, Vézelay was the first such monument to be so adorned in Burgundy.

The year begins at the lower left with the sign of Aquarius, which represents January, and continues through the astrological calendar, reaching the apex of the arc with the sign of Cancer, and then beginning its descent with Leo. Thus, the layout of the medallions follows the course of the sun. At the top of the arc, between the months June and July, the calendar is interrupted by a series of three medallions showing figures coiled into themselves. A dog is curled with his head between his legs; an acrobat with his back arched grabs his ankles; and a contorted mermaid attempts to draw her face closer to her long fish tail. These figures, each striving for circularity, seem to symbolize that momentary break in the year-cycle that comes with the summer solstice. The half-medallion to the left of the dog, decorated with an inverted crane, is not easy to interpret; perhaps its purpose is simply to fill out the space of the arc. On the left half of the tympanum, each sign of the zodiac through June is preceded by a corresponding

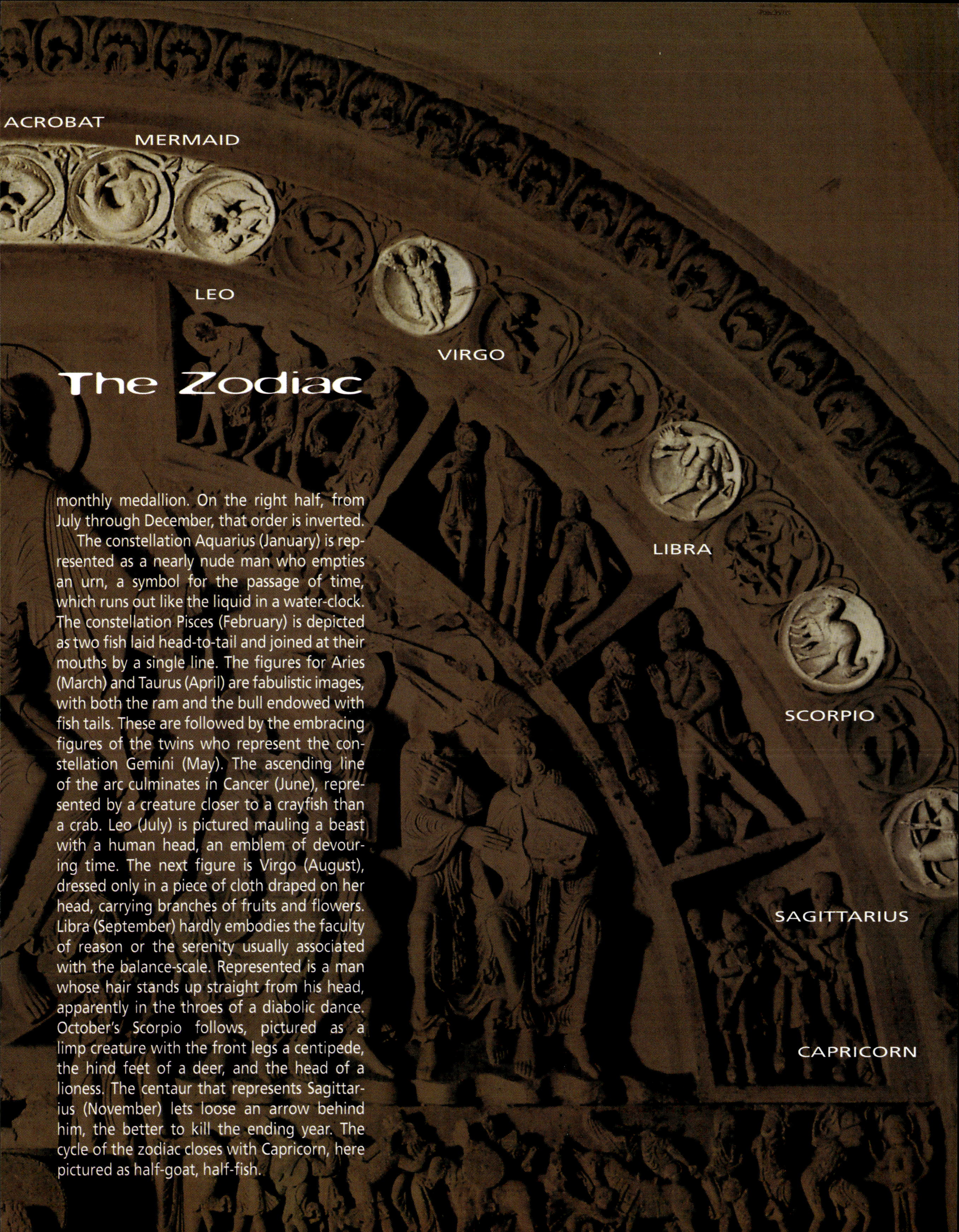

The Zodiac

monthly medallion. On the right half, from July through December, that order is inverted.

The constellation Aquarius (January) is represented as a nearly nude man who empties an urn, a symbol for the passage of time, which runs out like the liquid in a water-clock. The constellation Pisces (February) is depicted as two fish laid head-to-tail and joined at their mouths by a single line. The figures for Aries (March) and Taurus (April) are fabulistic images, with both the ram and the bull endowed with fish tails. These are followed by the embracing figures of the twins who represent the constellation Gemini (May). The ascending line of the arc culminates in Cancer (June), represented by a creature closer to a crayfish than a crab. Leo (July) is pictured mauling a beast with a human head, an emblem of devouring time. The next figure is Virgo (August), dressed only in a piece of cloth draped on her head, carrying branches of fruits and flowers. Libra (September) hardly embodies the faculty of reason or the serenity usually associated with the balance-scale. Represented is a man whose hair stands up straight from his head, apparently in the throes of a diabolic dance. October's Scorpio follows, pictured as a limp creature with the front legs a centipede, the hind feet of a deer, and the head of a lioness. The centaur that represents Sagittarius (November) lets loose an arrow behind him, the better to kill the ending year. The cycle of the zodiac closes with Capricorn, here pictured as half-goat, half-fish.

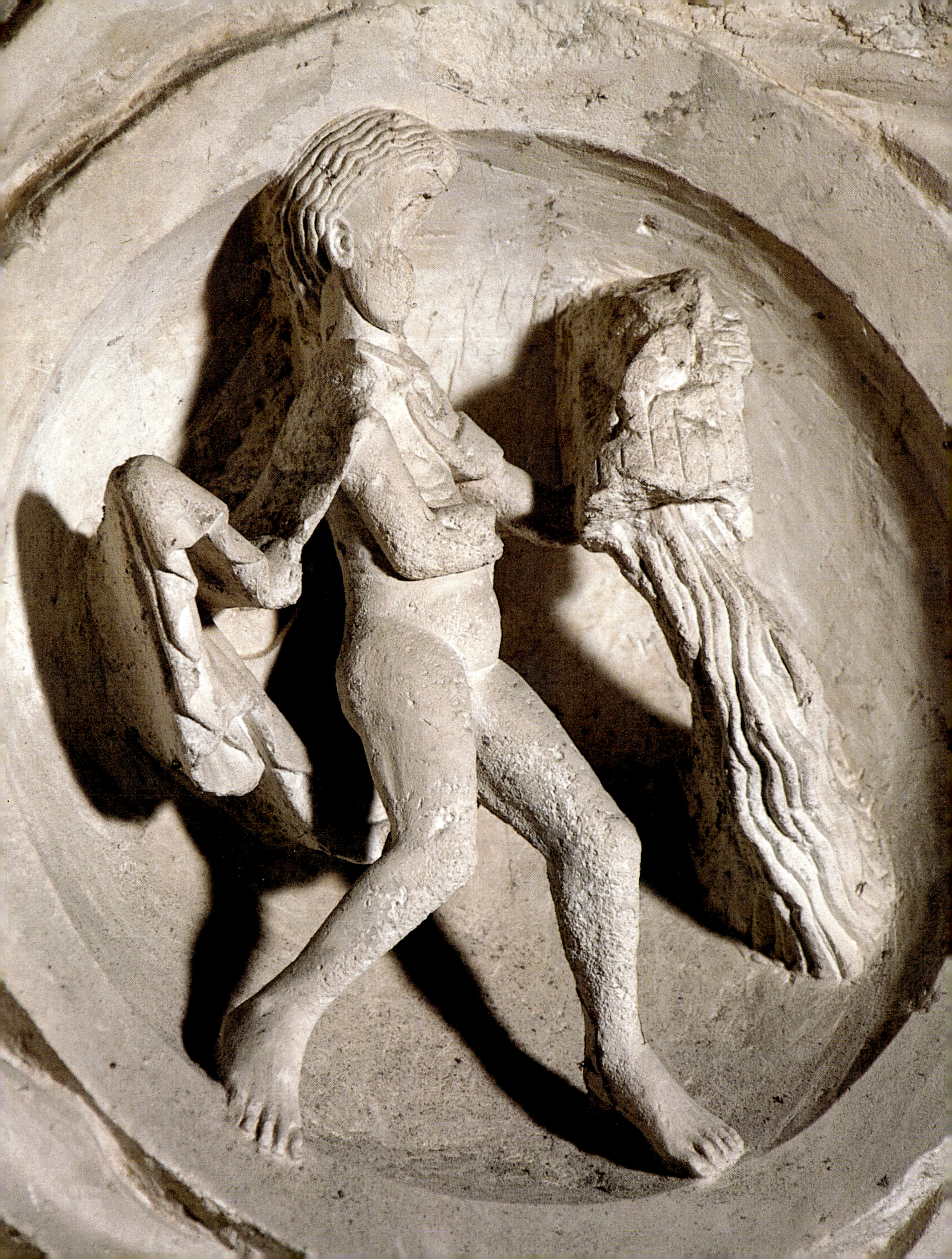

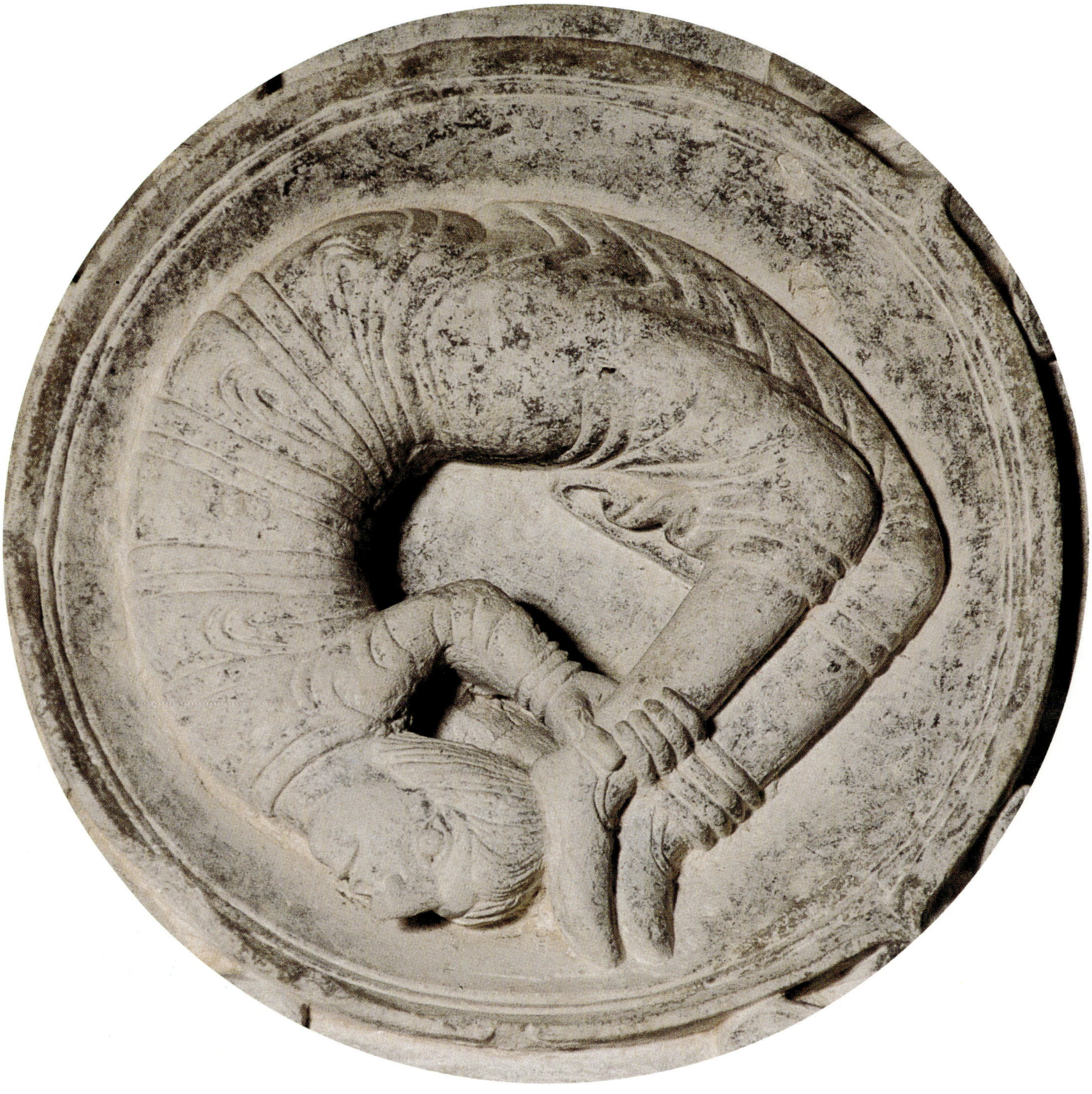

AQUARIUS (JANUARY)

THE ACROBAT

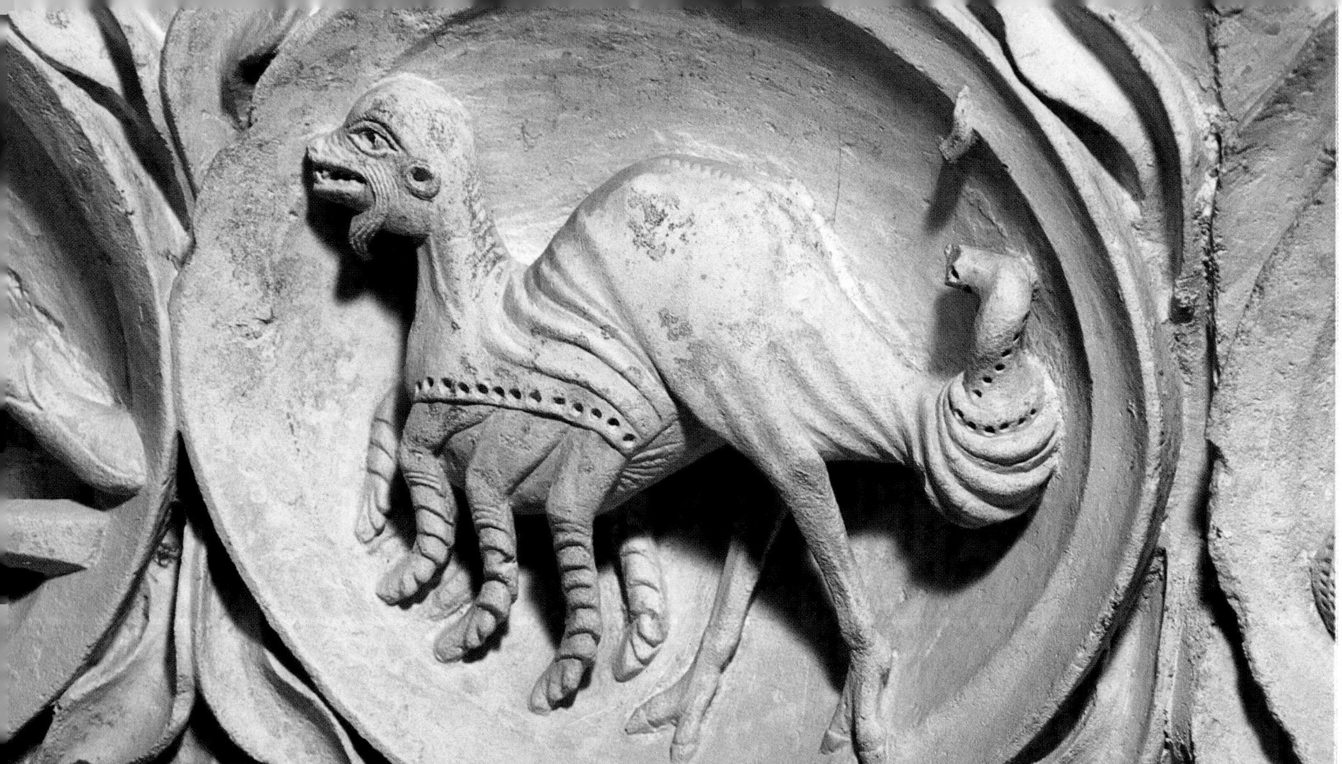

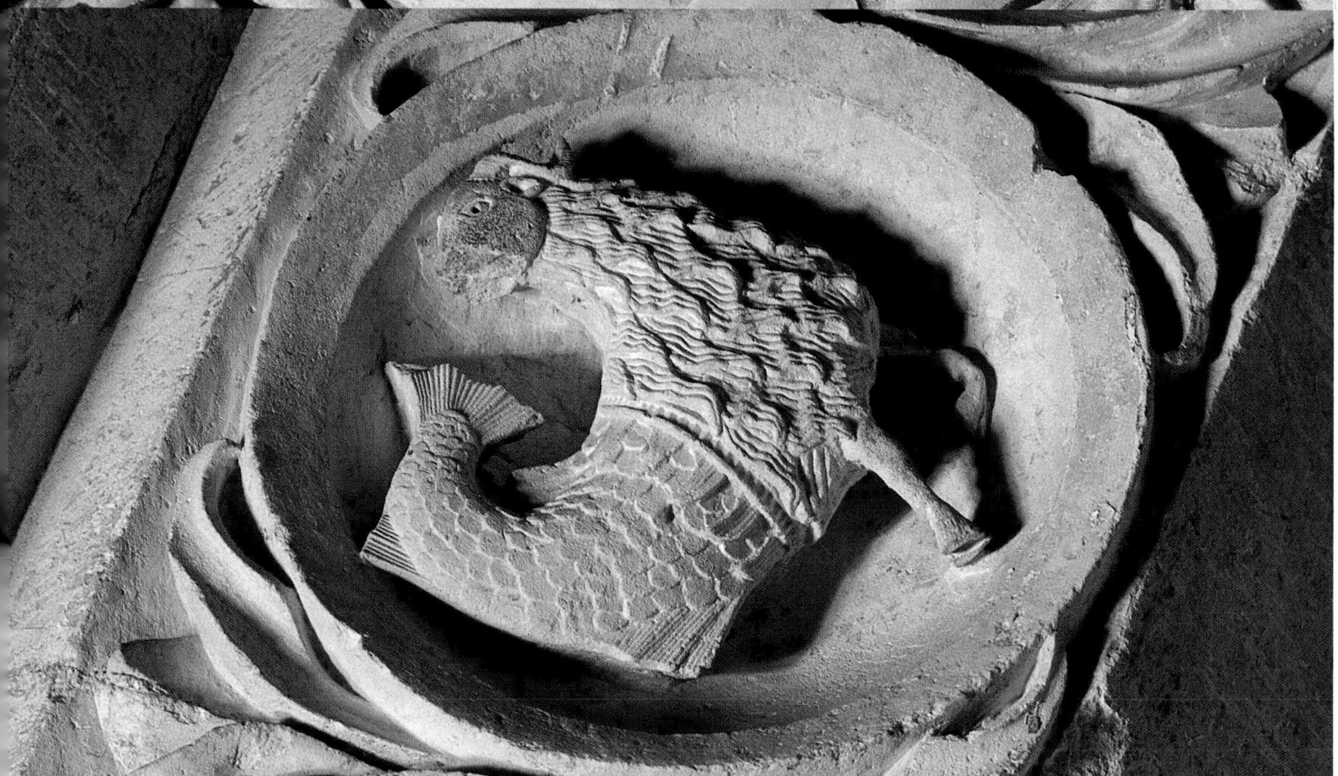

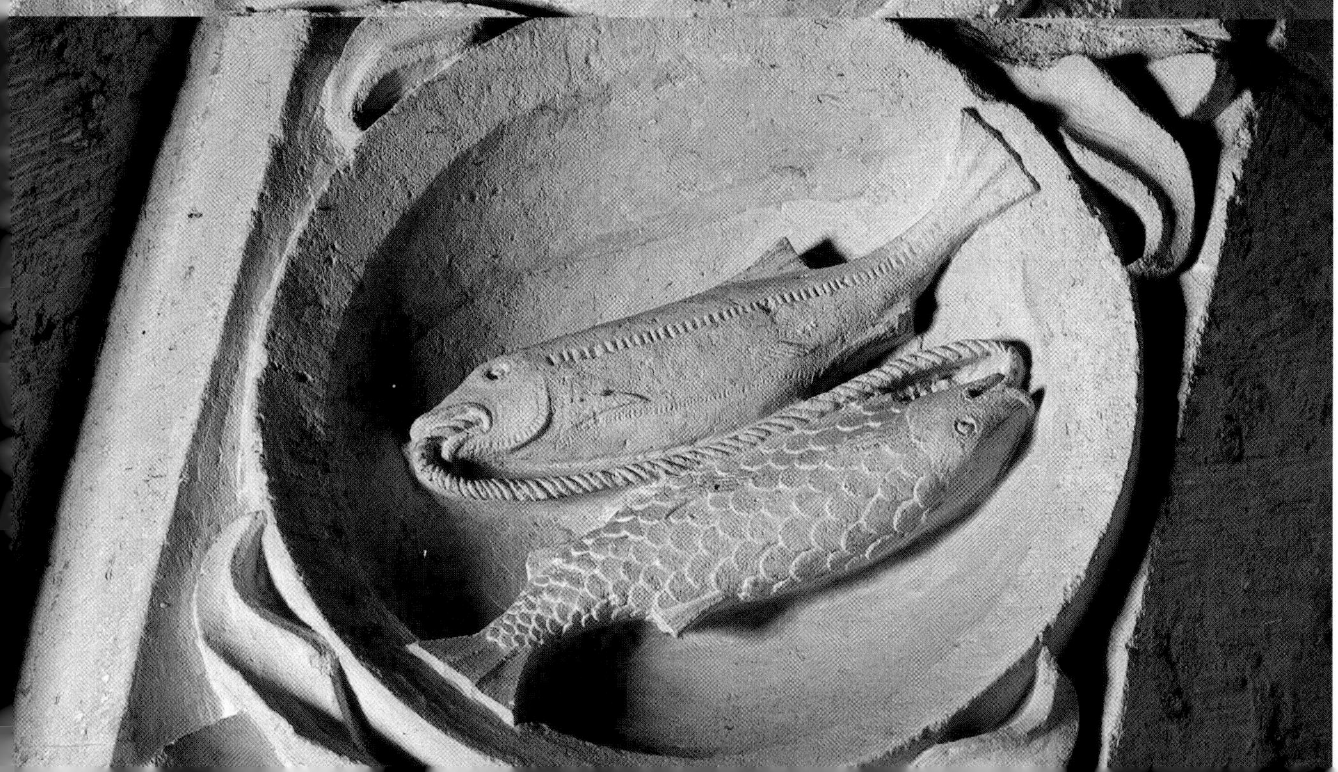

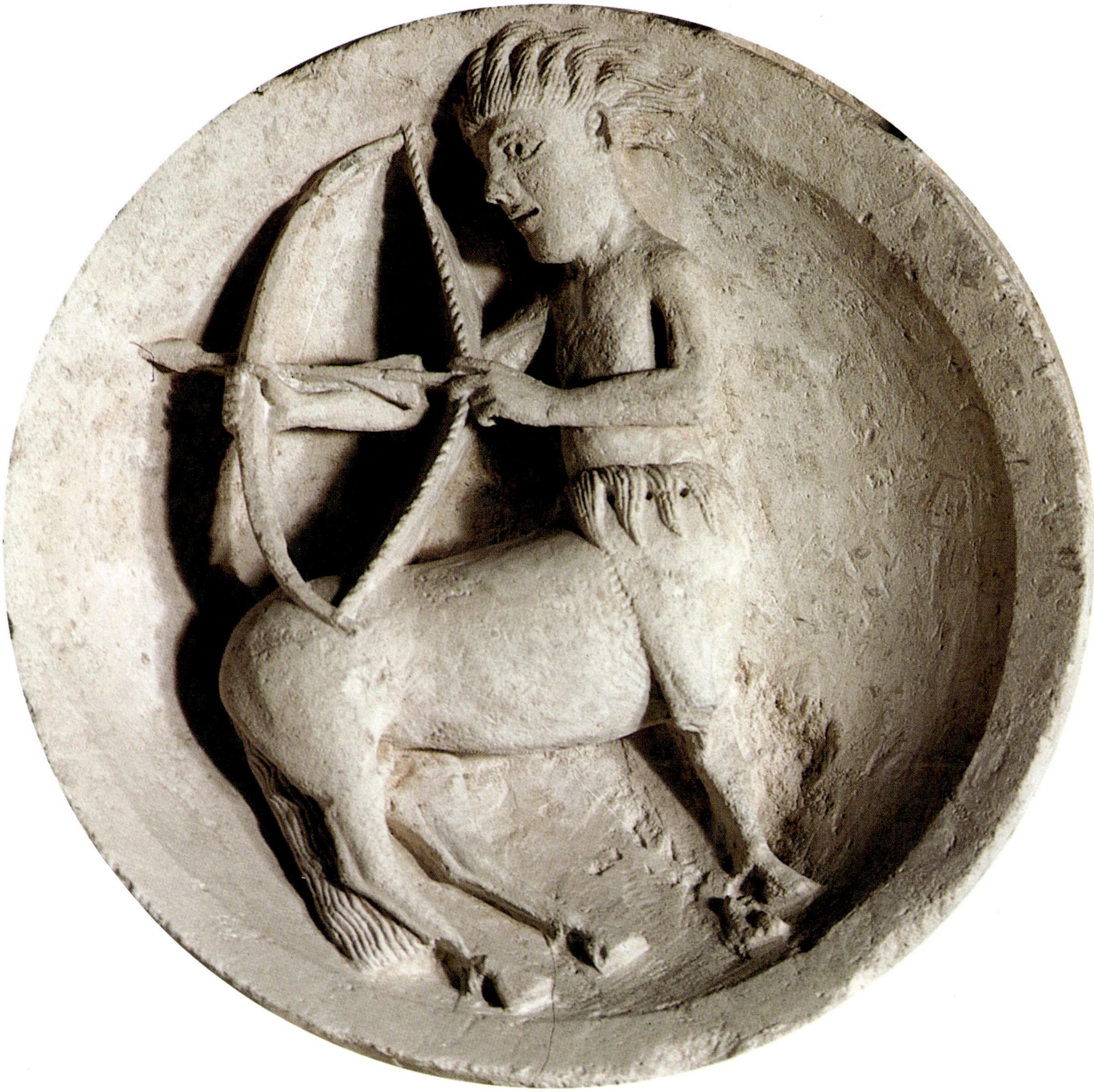

SCORPIO (OCTOBER)
ARIES (MARCH)
PISCES (FEBRUARY)
SAGITTARIUS (NOVEMBER)

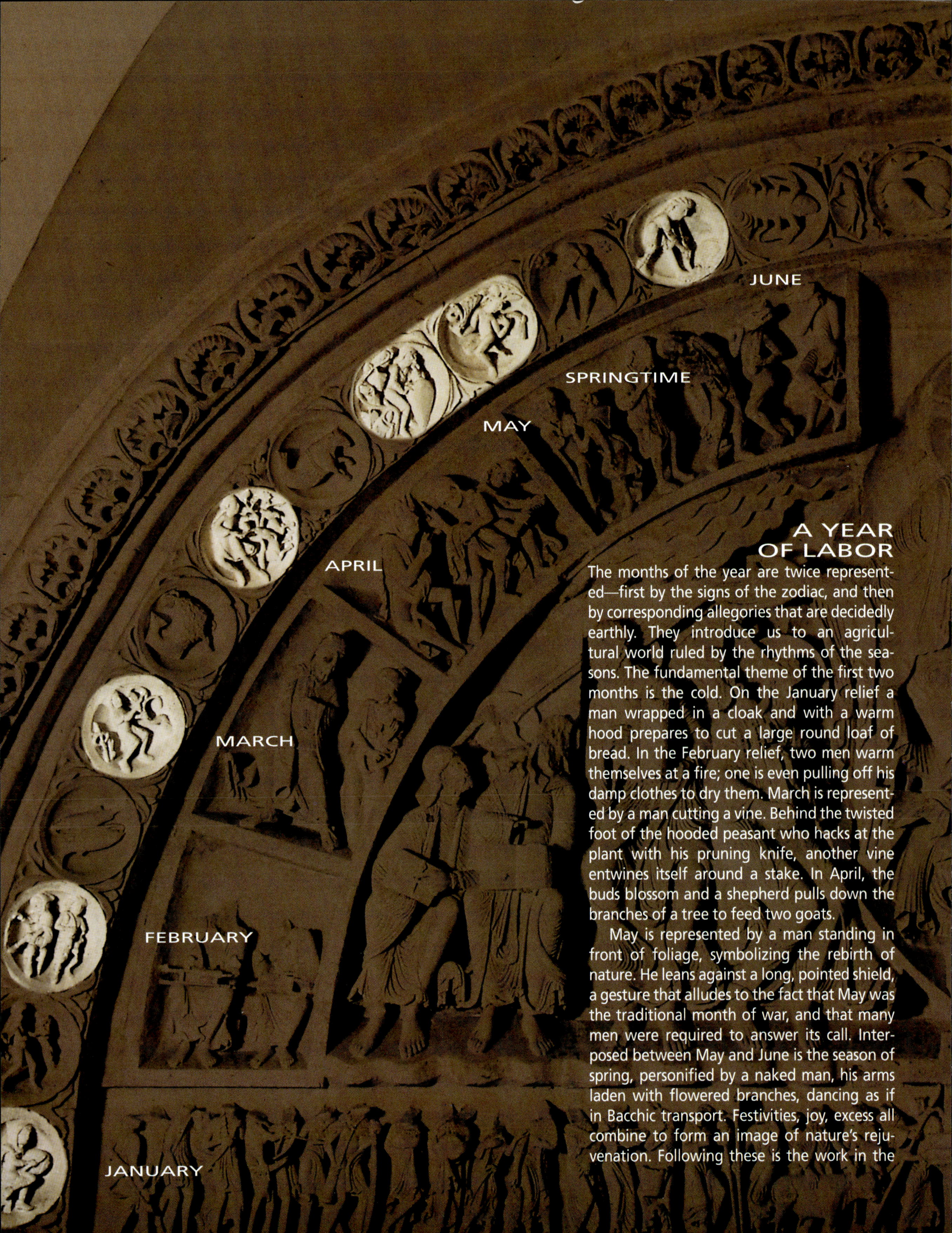

A YEAR OF LABOR

The months of the year are twice represented—first by the signs of the zodiac, and then by corresponding allegories that are decidedly earthly. They introduce us to an agricultural world ruled by the rhythms of the seasons. The fundamental theme of the first two months is the cold. On the January relief a man wrapped in a cloak and with a warm hood prepares to cut a large round loaf of bread. In the February relief, two men warm themselves at a fire; one is even pulling off his damp clothes to dry them. March is represented by a man cutting a vine. Behind the twisted foot of the hooded peasant who hacks at the plant with his pruning knife, another vine entwines itself around a stake. In April, the buds blossom and a shepherd pulls down the branches of a tree to feed two goats.

May is represented by a man standing in front of foliage, symbolizing the rebirth of nature. He leans against a long, pointed shield, a gesture that alludes to the fact that May was the traditional month of war, and that many men were required to answer its call. Interposed between May and June is the season of spring, personified by a naked man, his arms laden with flowered branches, dancing as if in Bacchic transport. Festivities, joy, excess all combine to form an image of nature's rejuvenation. Following these is the work in the

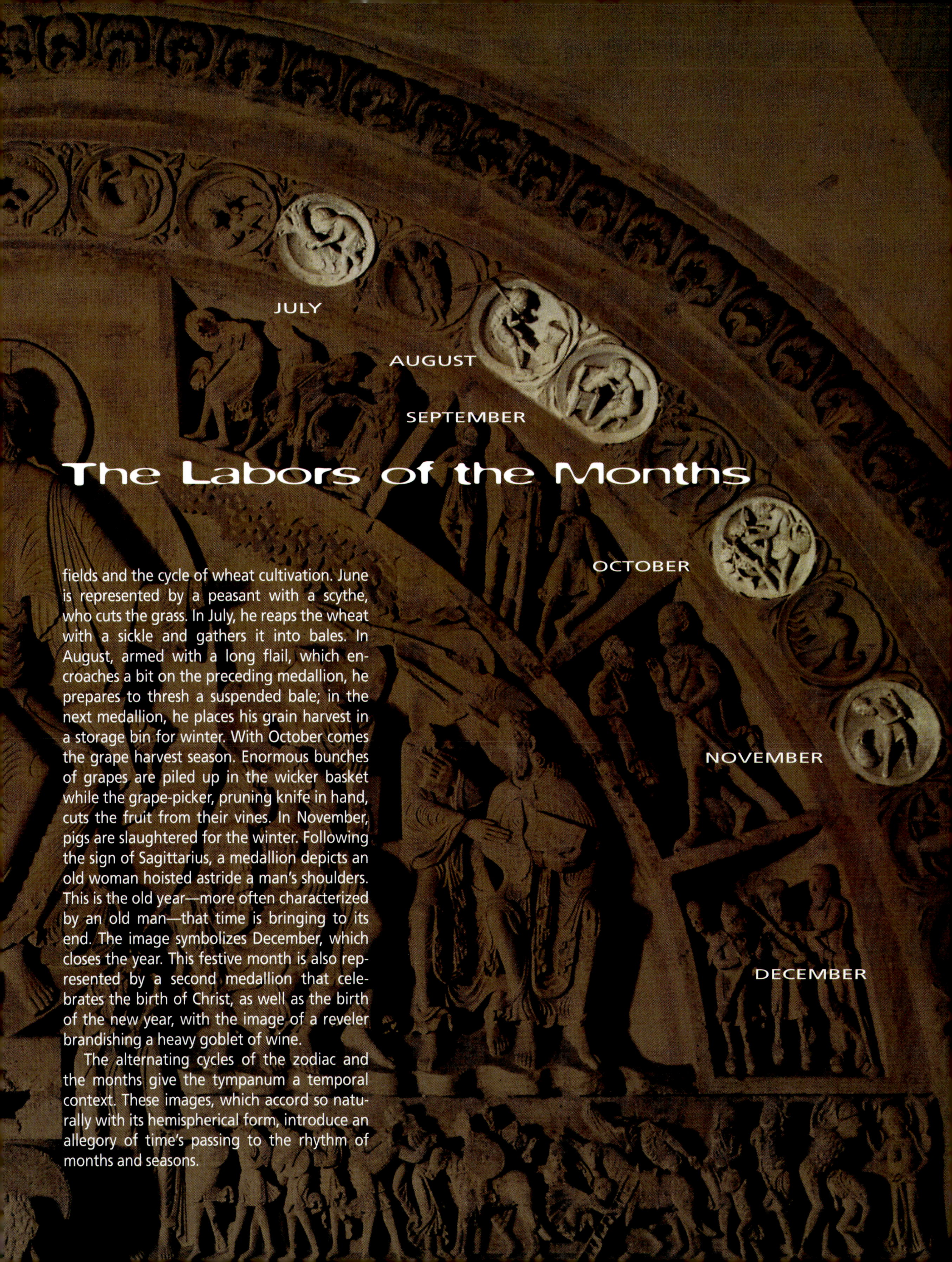

The Labors of the Months

fields and the cycle of wheat cultivation. June is represented by a peasant with a scythe, who cuts the grass. In July, he reaps the wheat with a sickle and gathers it into bales. In August, armed with a long flail, which encroaches a bit on the preceding medallion, he prepares to thresh a suspended bale; in the next medallion, he places his grain harvest in a storage bin for winter. With October comes the grape harvest season. Enormous bunches of grapes are piled up in the wicker basket while the grape-picker, pruning knife in hand, cuts the fruit from their vines. In November, pigs are slaughtered for the winter. Following the sign of Sagittarius, a medallion depicts an old woman hoisted astride a man's shoulders. This is the old year—more often characterized by an old man—that time is bringing to its end. The image symbolizes December, which closes the year. This festive month is also represented by a second medallion that celebrates the birth of Christ, as well as the birth of the new year, with the image of a reveler brandishing a heavy goblet of wine.

The alternating cycles of the zodiac and the months give the tympanum a temporal context. These images, which accord so naturally with its hemispherical form, introduce an allegory of time's passing to the rhythm of months and seasons.

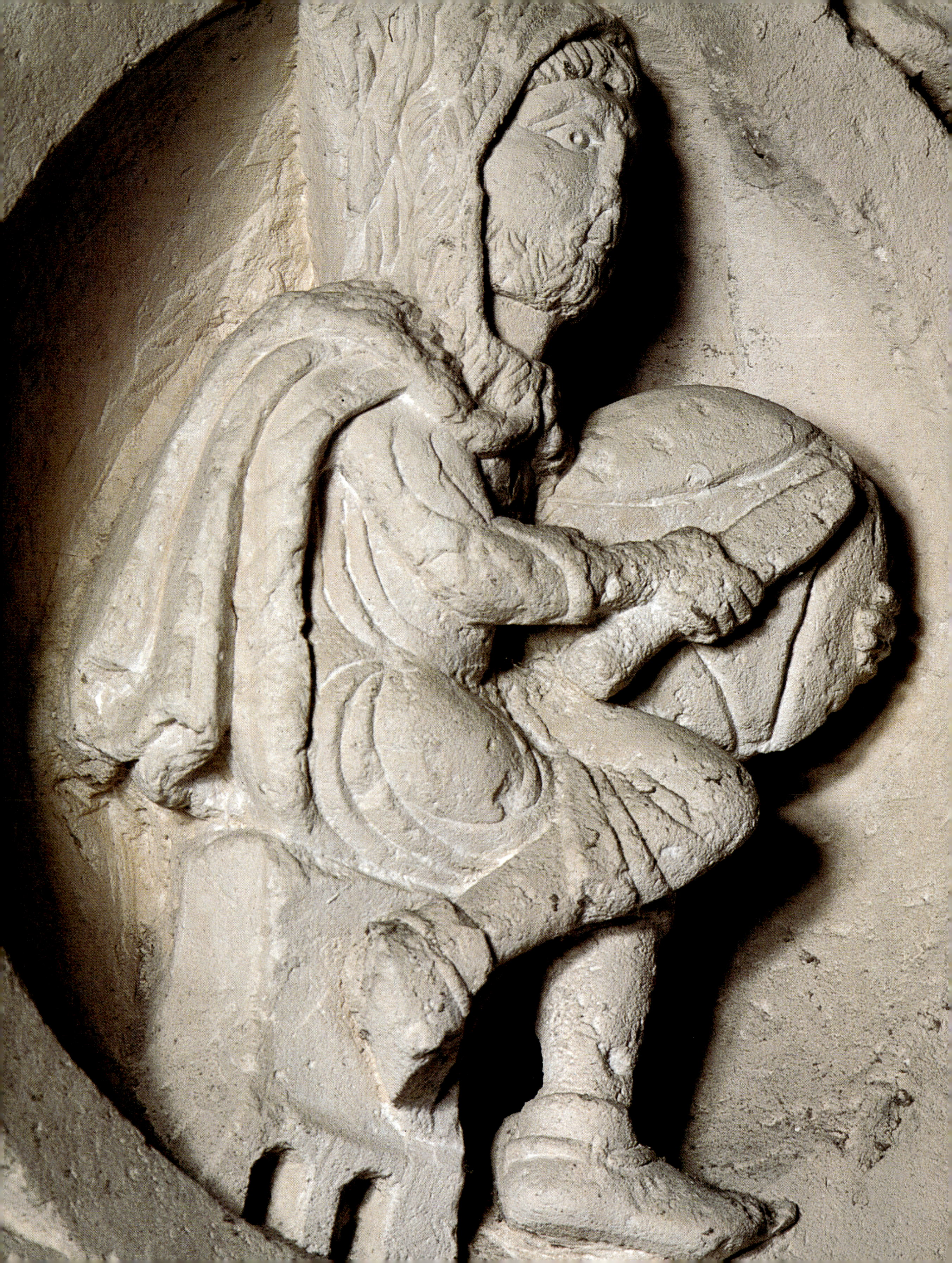

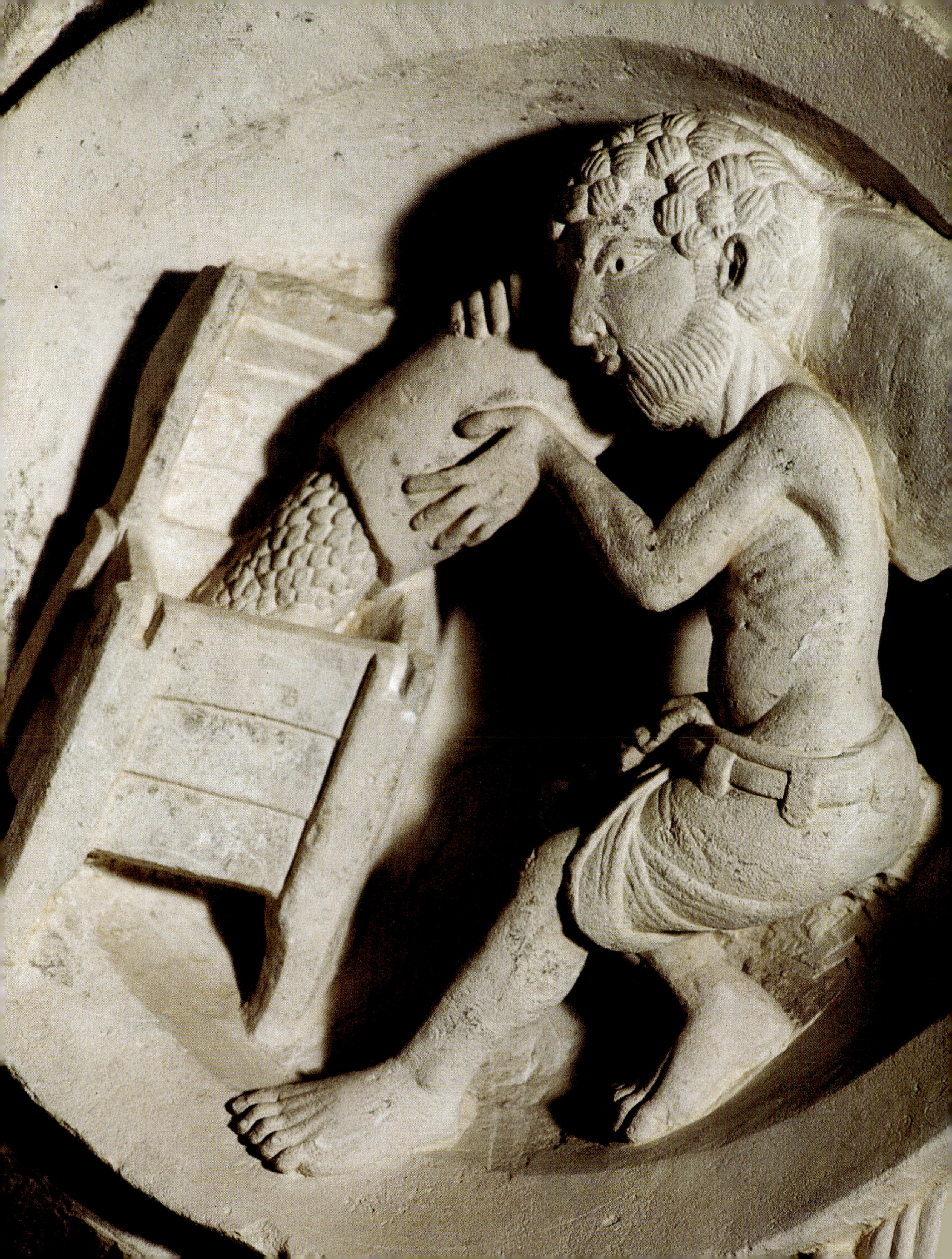

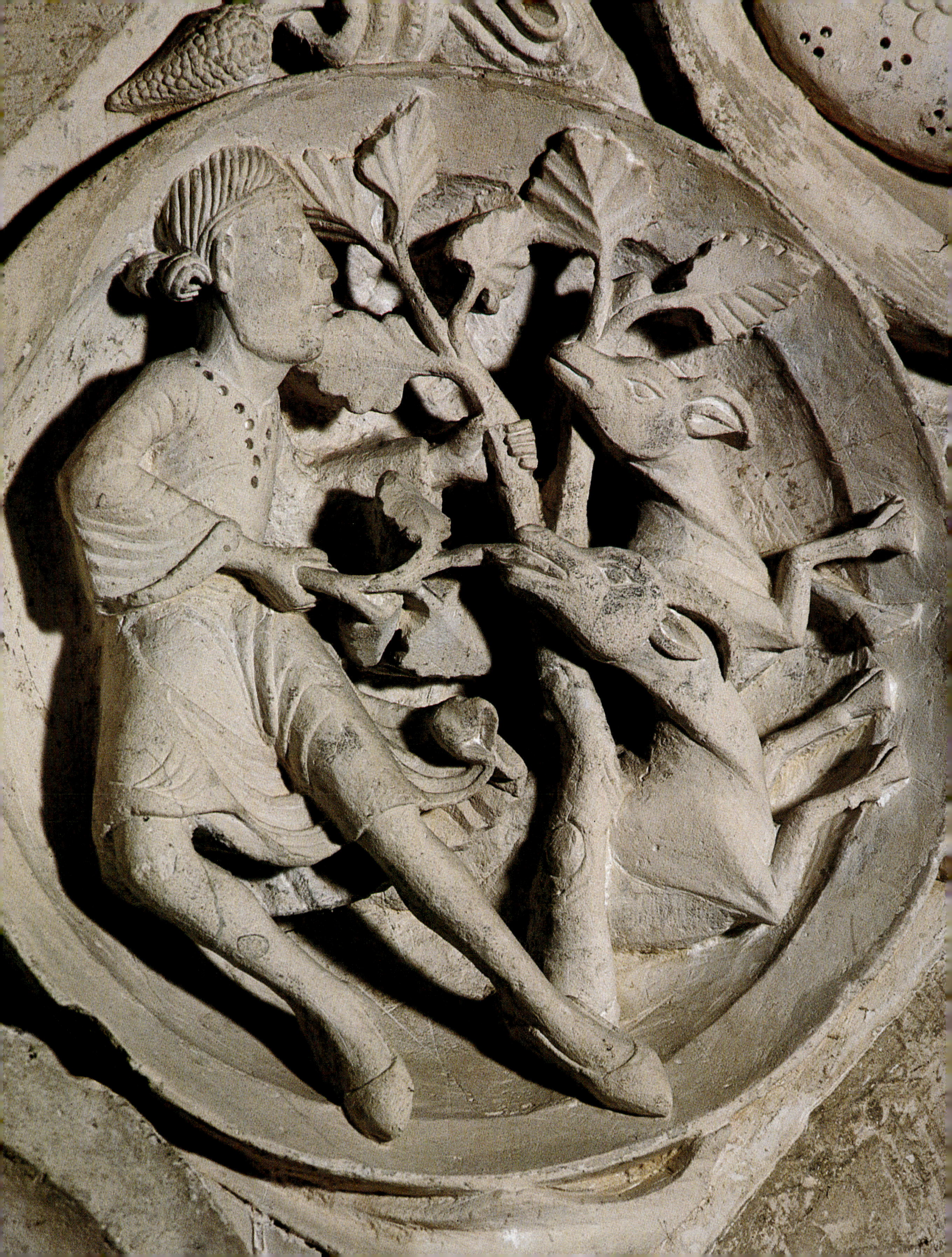

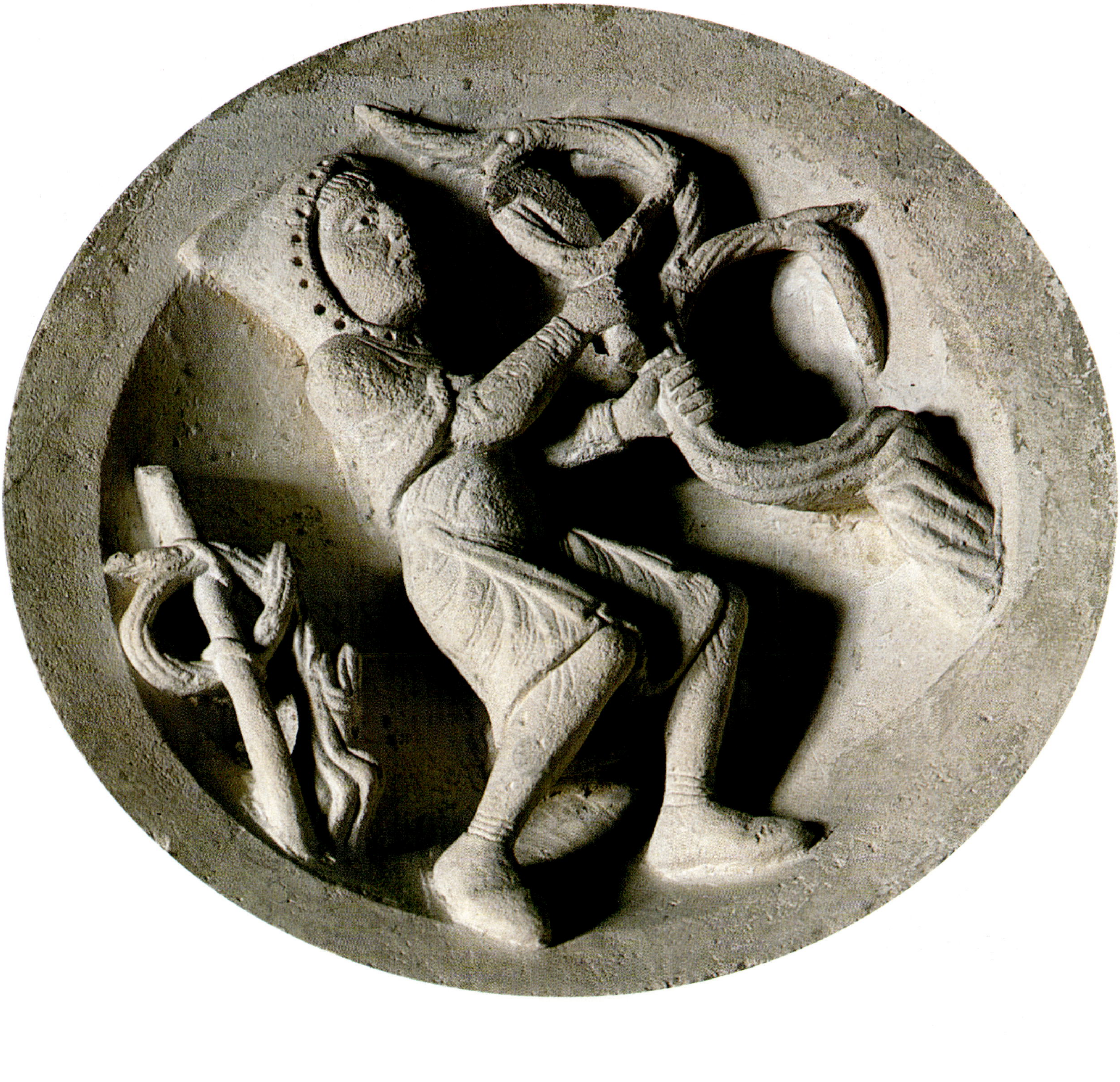

THE FIRST BUDS OF APRIL

MARCH: CUTTING THE VINES

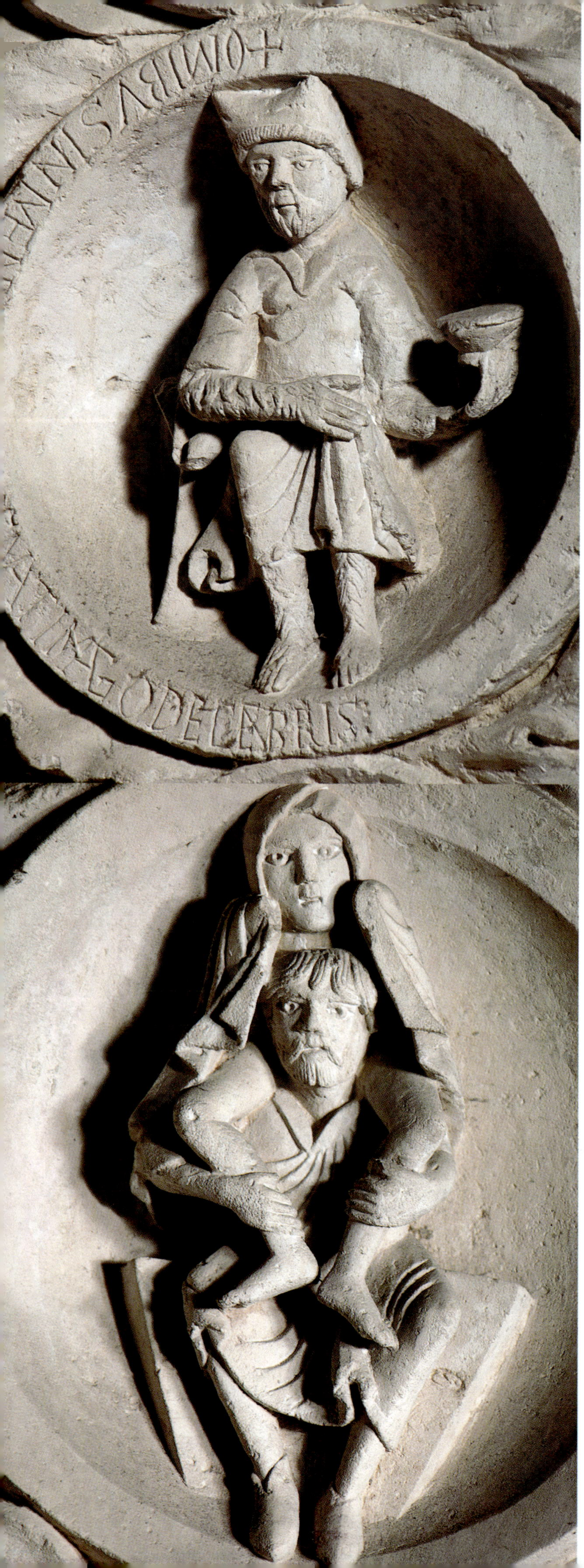

THE FESTIVITIES OF DECEMBER
THE OLD YEAR PASSES AWAY
OCTOBER: PICKING GRAPES

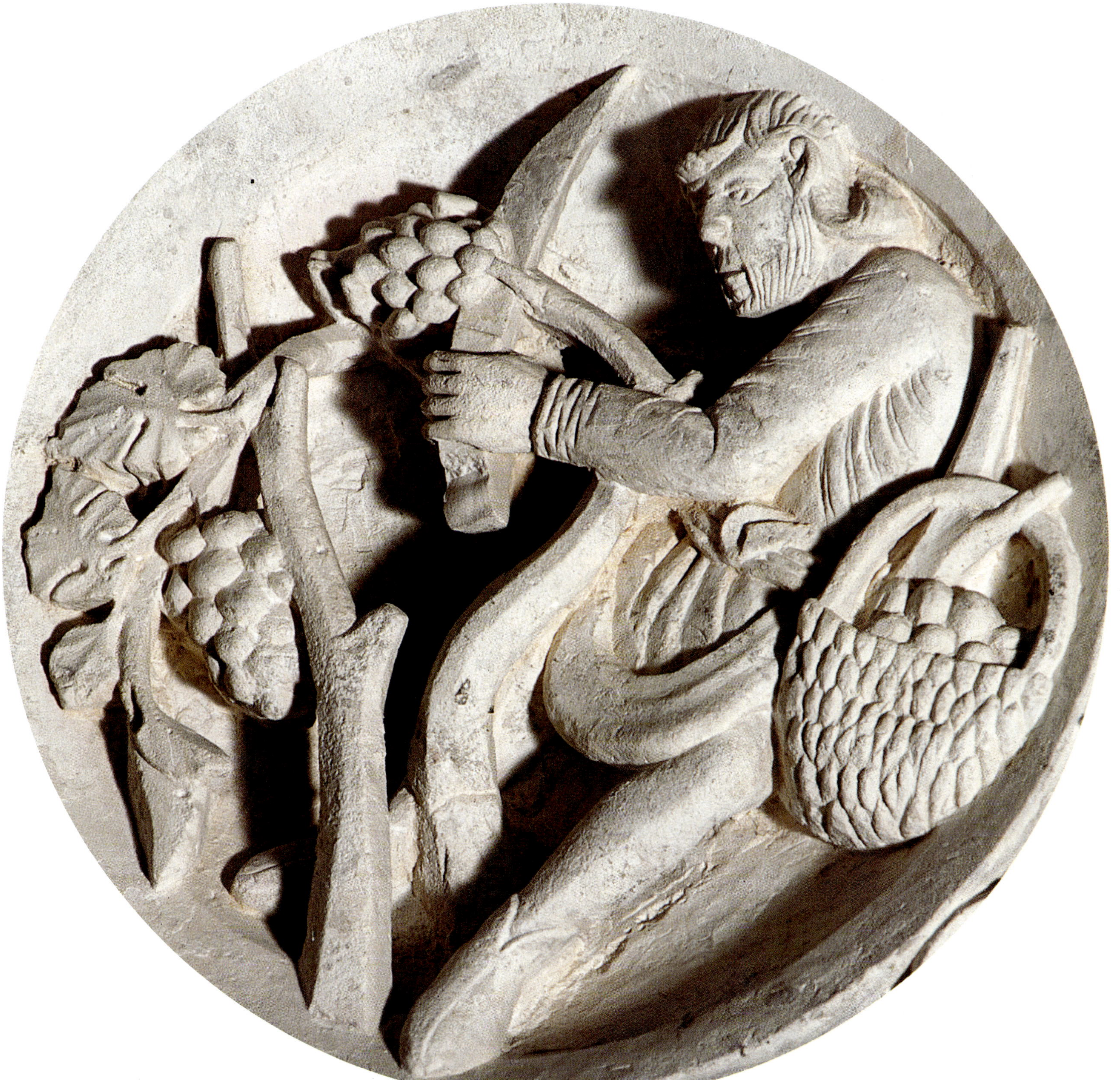

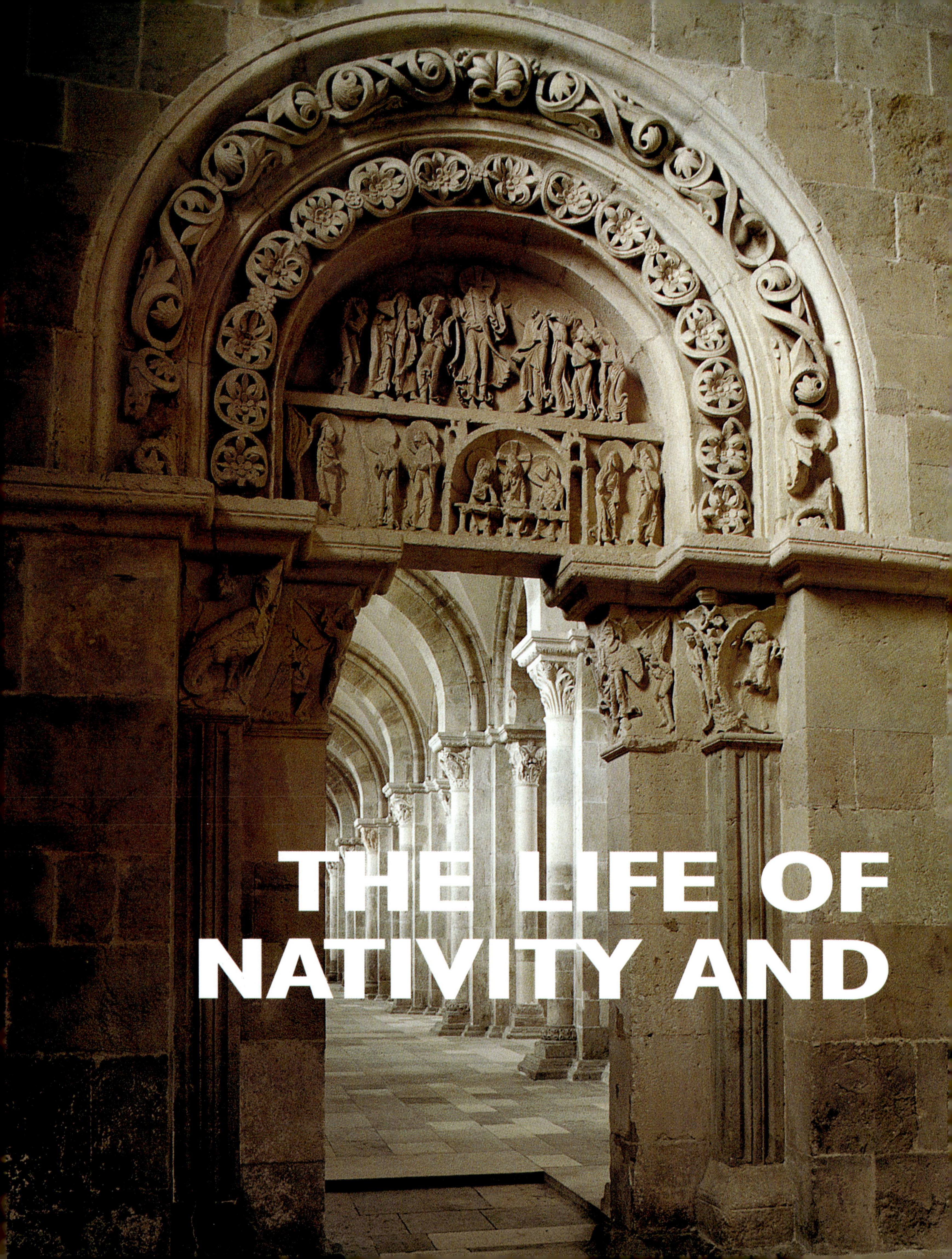

THE LIFE OF NATIVITY AND

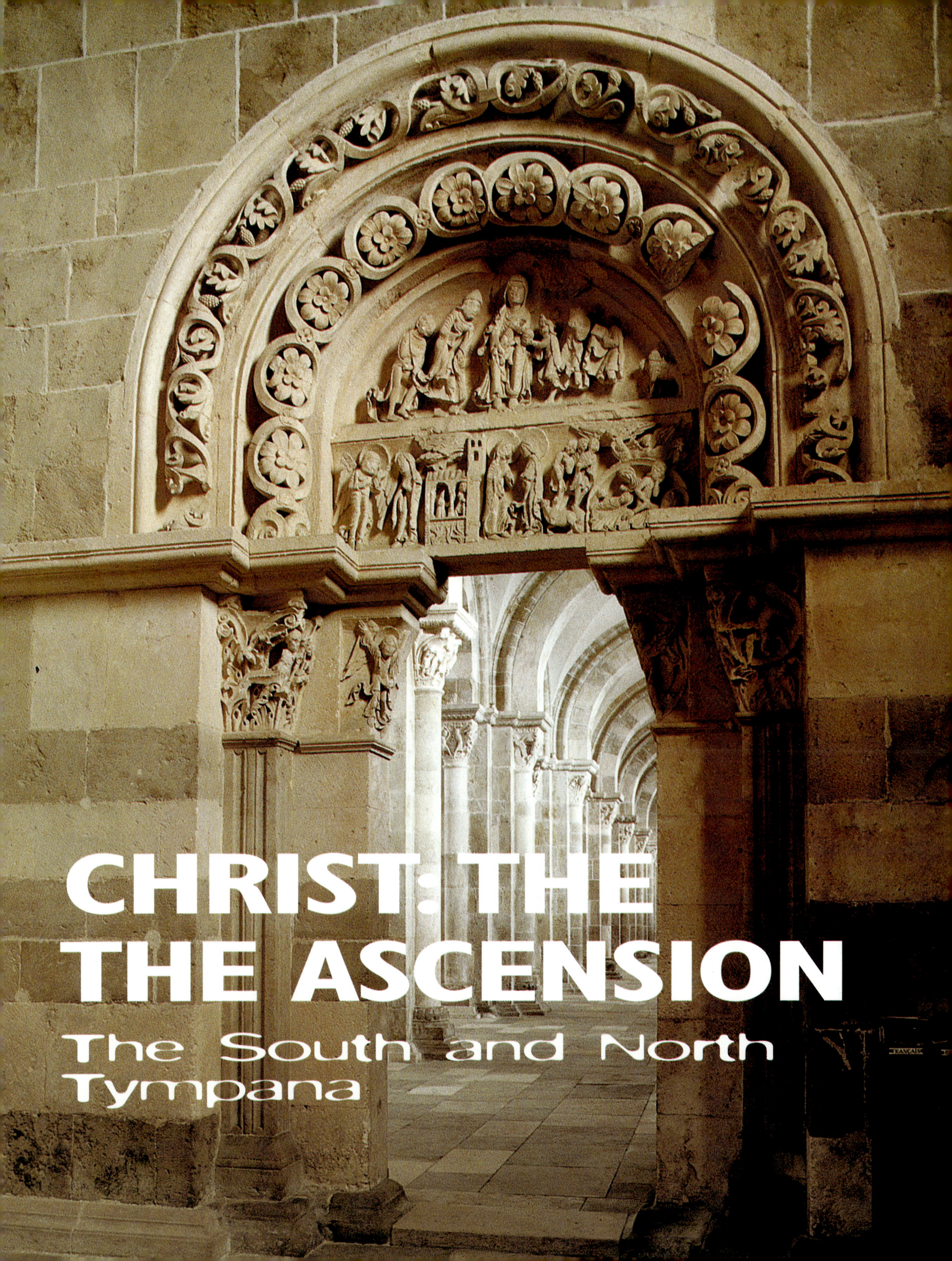

CHRIST: THE
THE ASCENSION

The South and North Tympana

The Childhood of Christ

THE SOUTH TYMPANUM

Vézelay's importance as a center of great art is due not only to the large tympanum of the central portal, but also to the smaller tympana over the two lateral doors that flank it. As if in response to the vision of divinity over the central door, these two side tympana recount scenes from the life of Christ. One depicts his early life, and the other, his final moments on earth.

The south tympanum is dedicated to the infant Jesus, and thus also to the Virgin Mary. The first scene shows the Annunciation and the Incarnation of Christ. At the lower left, the angel Gabriel approaches Mary, who shows her astonishment at his sudden appearance with a gesture of her hand. Above her shoulder, clouds surround the figure of a dove, the symbol of the Holy Spirit, who comes to envelop Mary in shadow as the infant is conceived. Separating this scene from the next one, the Visitation, is a house. Within its open arcade are two small figures, which undoubtedly represent St. Elizabeth and her husband Zacharias. On the house's threshold at the right, the figure of St. Elizabeth appears again (now much larger), to welcome her cousin Mary. Each woman is pregnant with a miraculously conceived child, for Elizabeth, the older of the two, had thought that she was unable to conceive, and Mary is still a virgin. Thus their two divinely chosen sons, John the Baptist and Jesus, meet for the first time. At the far right is a scene of the Nativity, in which Mary is shown lying down, her body covering the entire width of the tiny, semicircular cave of Bethlehem. The swaddled infant Jesus is close by, watched over by two figures drawn from the Apocrypha. One is the midwife Salome, who, at

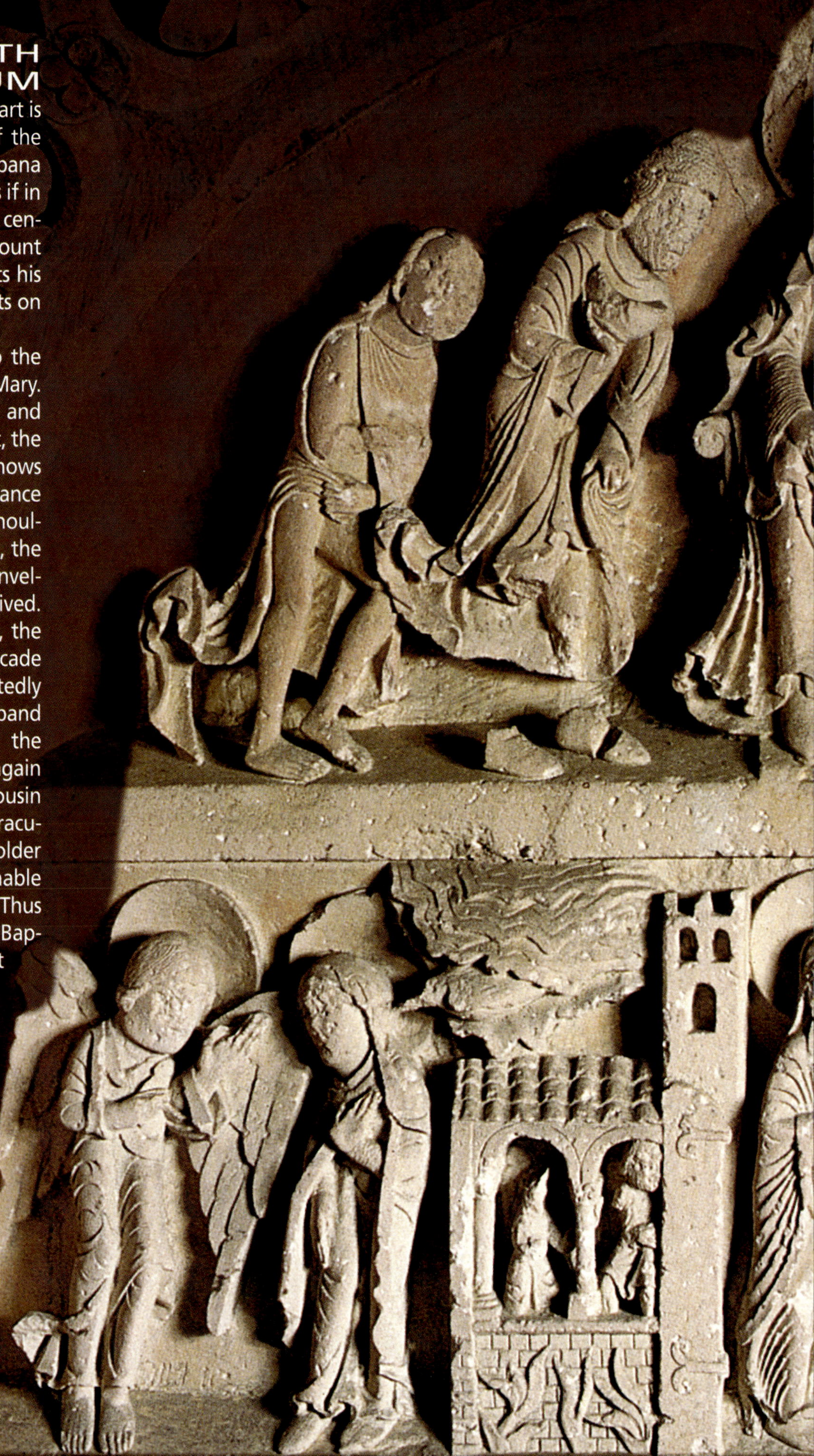

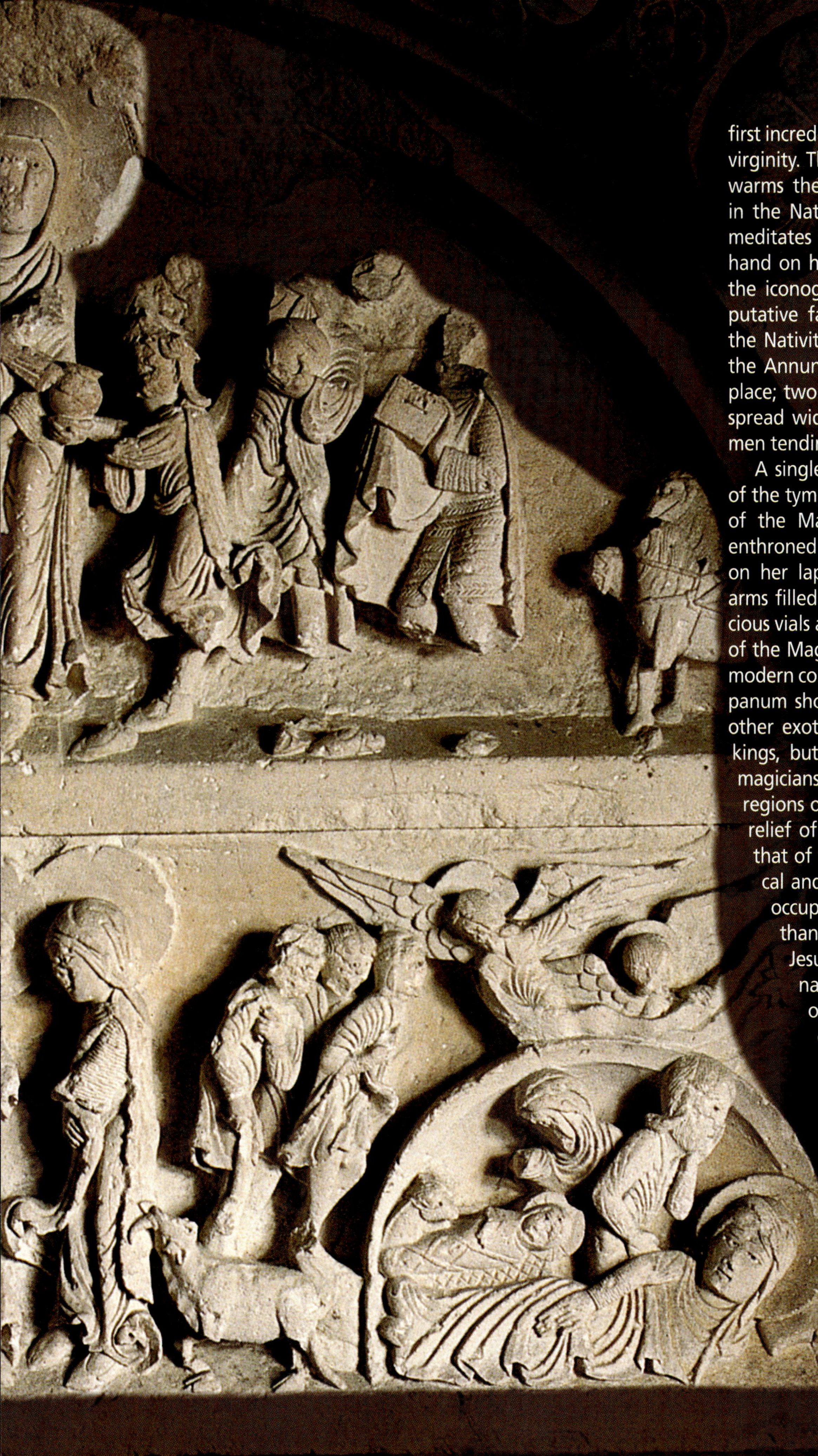

first incredulous, was then convinced of Mary's virginity. The other is the peaceable bull, who warms the infant with his breath. As often in the Nativity scenes of this period, Joseph meditates in the corner, his back turned, his hand on his cheek in a sign of distress. Thus the iconography conveys the turmoil of the putative father described in the account of the Nativity in the Gospels. Behind the cave, the Annunciation to the Shepherds is taking place; two angels, with their wings and arms spread wide, bring the news to three herdsmen tending their flocks.

A single scene occupies the upper portion of the tympanum: the Epiphany, or Adoration of the Magi. In the center the Virgin sits enthroned in majesty, holding the infant Jesus on her lap. The Magi surround them, their arms filled with gifts: purses, chests, and precious vials and vases. At this point, the number of the Magi was still not fixed; instead of the modern conventional three wise men, the tympanum shows five. Wearing conical caps and other exotic headdresses, these men are not kings, but rather, as in the Gospel account, magicians and astrologers from the distant regions of Asia Minor. The placement of the relief of the Adoration of the Magi above that of the Nativity expresses the theological and liturgical belief that the Epiphany occupies a status of greater importance than Christmas, as it is the moment when Jesus was first revealed as God Incarnate and received the homage of all of humanity, whose representatives came from the ends of the earth to worship him. With this majestic Epiphany, the tympanum marks the first stage of the revelation of the divinity of Christ.

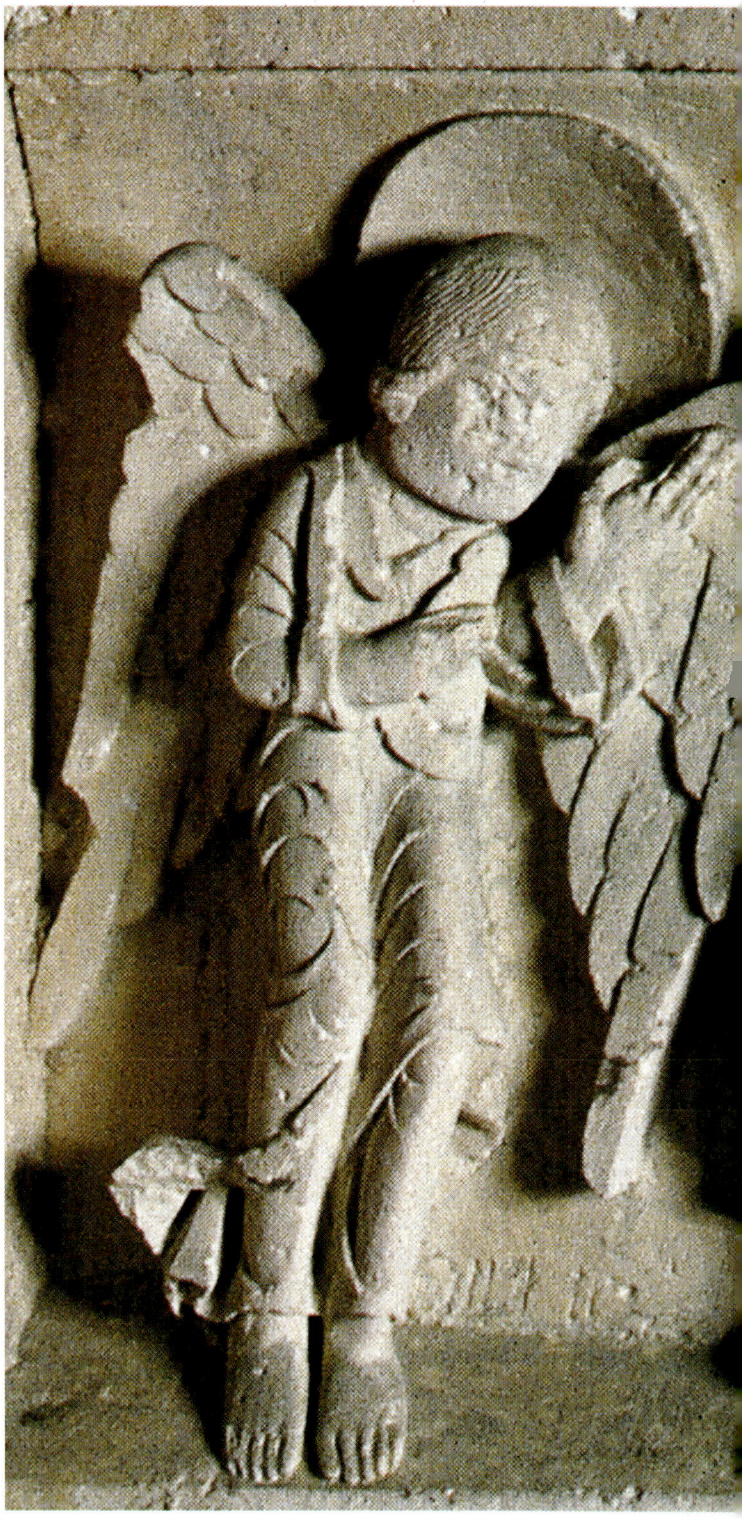

THE ANNUNCIATION AND THE VISITATION:
THE VIRGIN MARY WITH THE ANGEL GABRIEL,
THEN MEETING ST. ELIZABETH

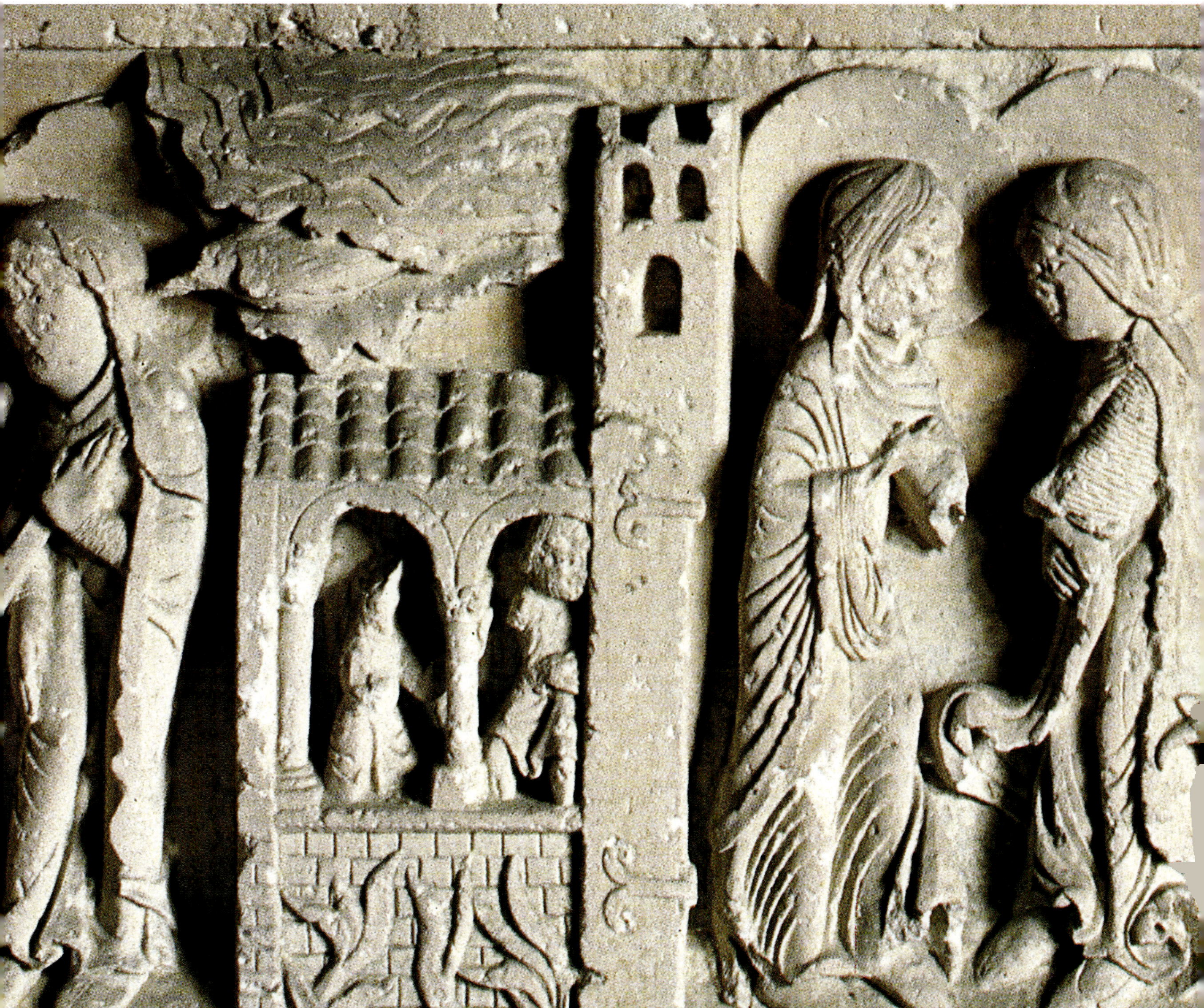

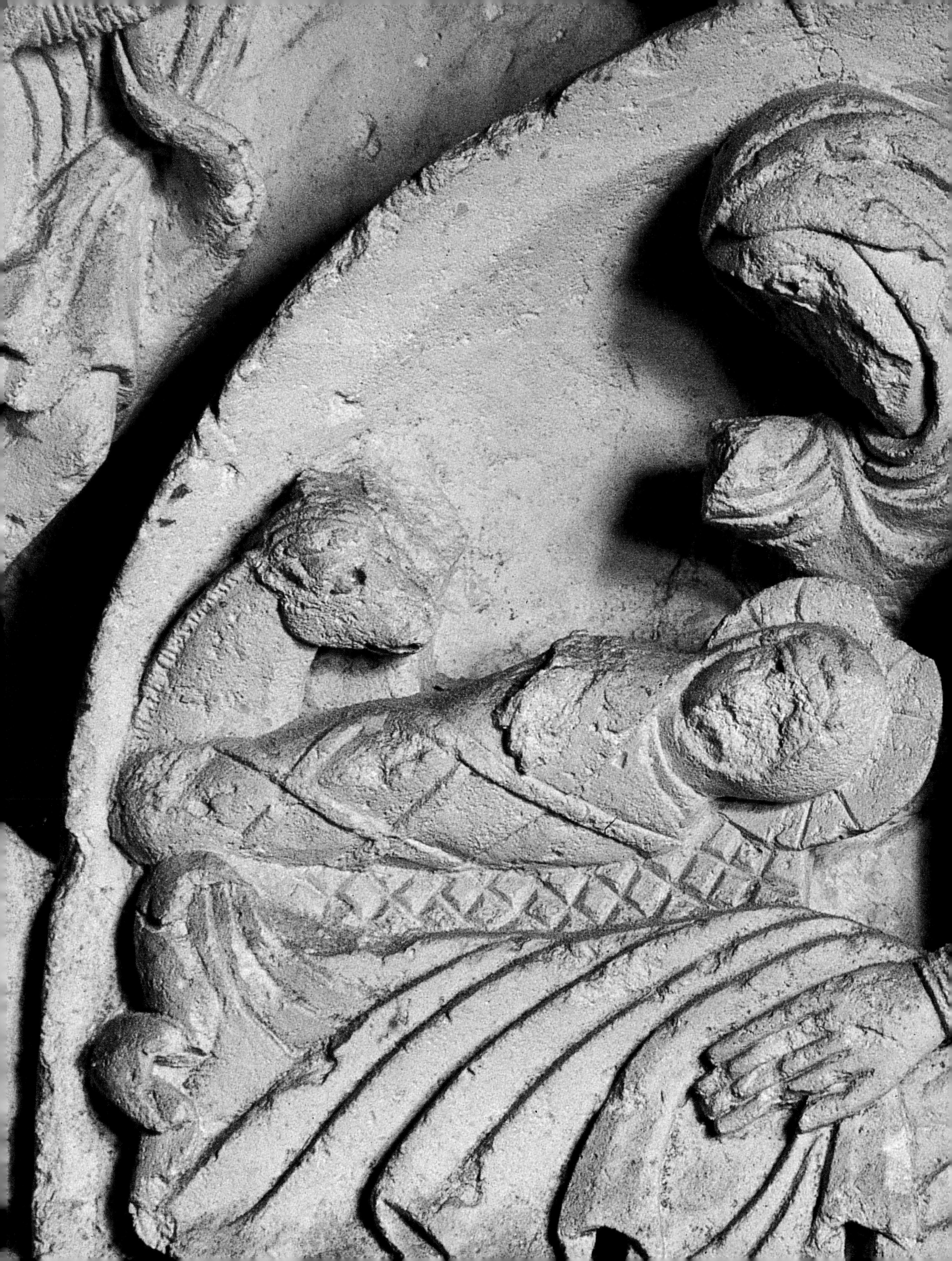

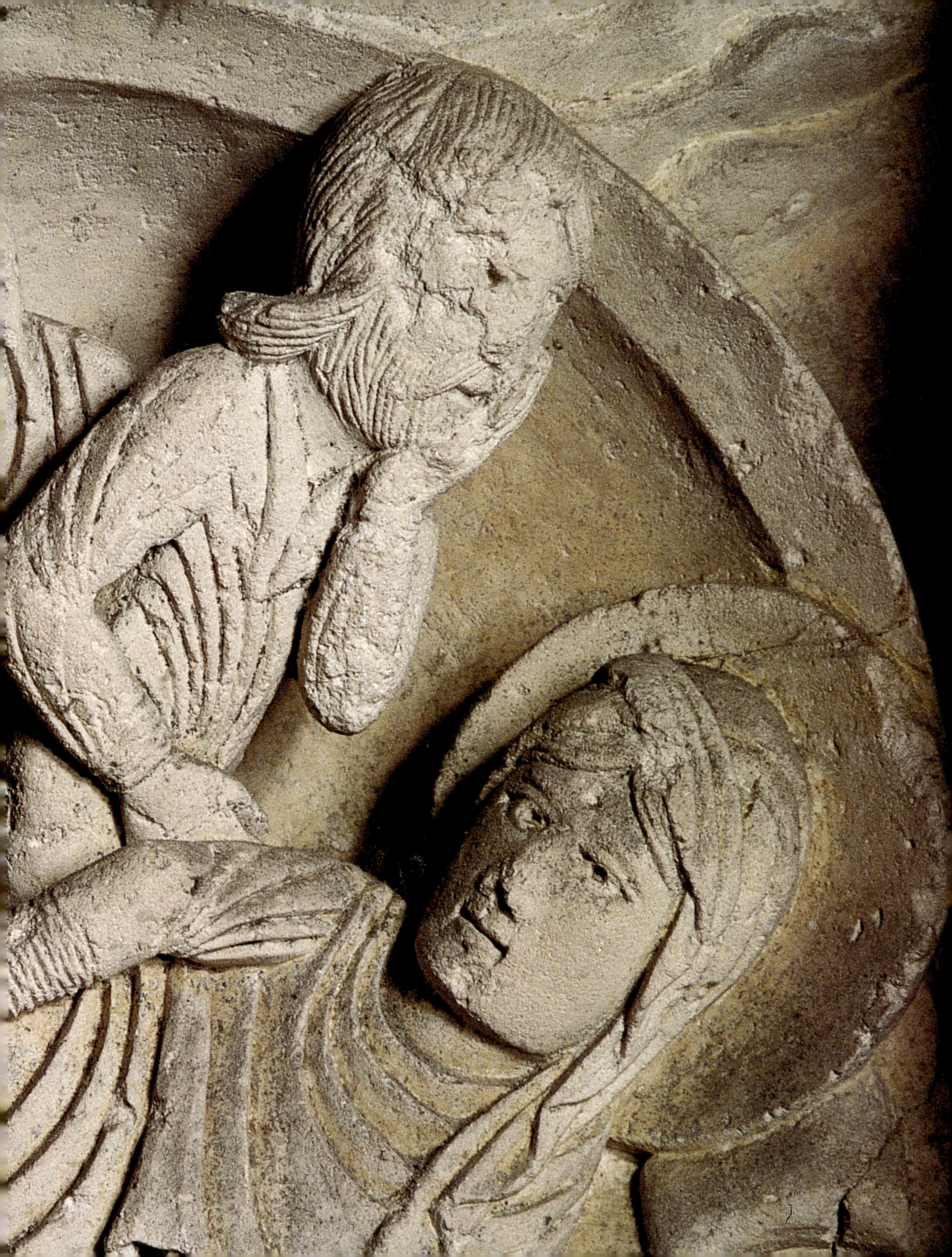

THE NORTH TYMPANUM

Although the north portal is stylistically very close to the south portal and is laid out in much the same pattern, the hand of the sculptor here seems to have been more skilled. This can be appreciated in the crisp carving of the two surrounding arcs of foliage, as well as on the entablature that rests on the capitals of the piers. The portal opens through a narrow door on the south aisle of the nave; the tympanum is divided into two registers.

The lower register represents the story of the Supper at Emmaus (Luke 24:13–31). A domed building, whose semicircular cut-away form echoes that of the cave of Bethlehem on the south portal, divides this register almost perfectly in half. To the left, as the story in the Gospel relates, the resurrected Christ meets two of his disciples, who do not recognize him, on a road outside of Jerusalem. The three continue walking to the village of Emmaus, discussing the scriptures. The dome at the center represents the inn where Christ and his companions have stopped to eat. Christ, shown with a cross-halo, is seated at a table between his two disciples. At the moment that Christ blesses and breaks the bread, the disciples realize who he is, after which he immediately vanishes. The composition is intentionally borrowed from the iconography of the Last Supper, to emphasize the moment of the breaking of bread, when the disciples recognize their companion. In the last scene at the right, Christ has disappeared, and the disciples

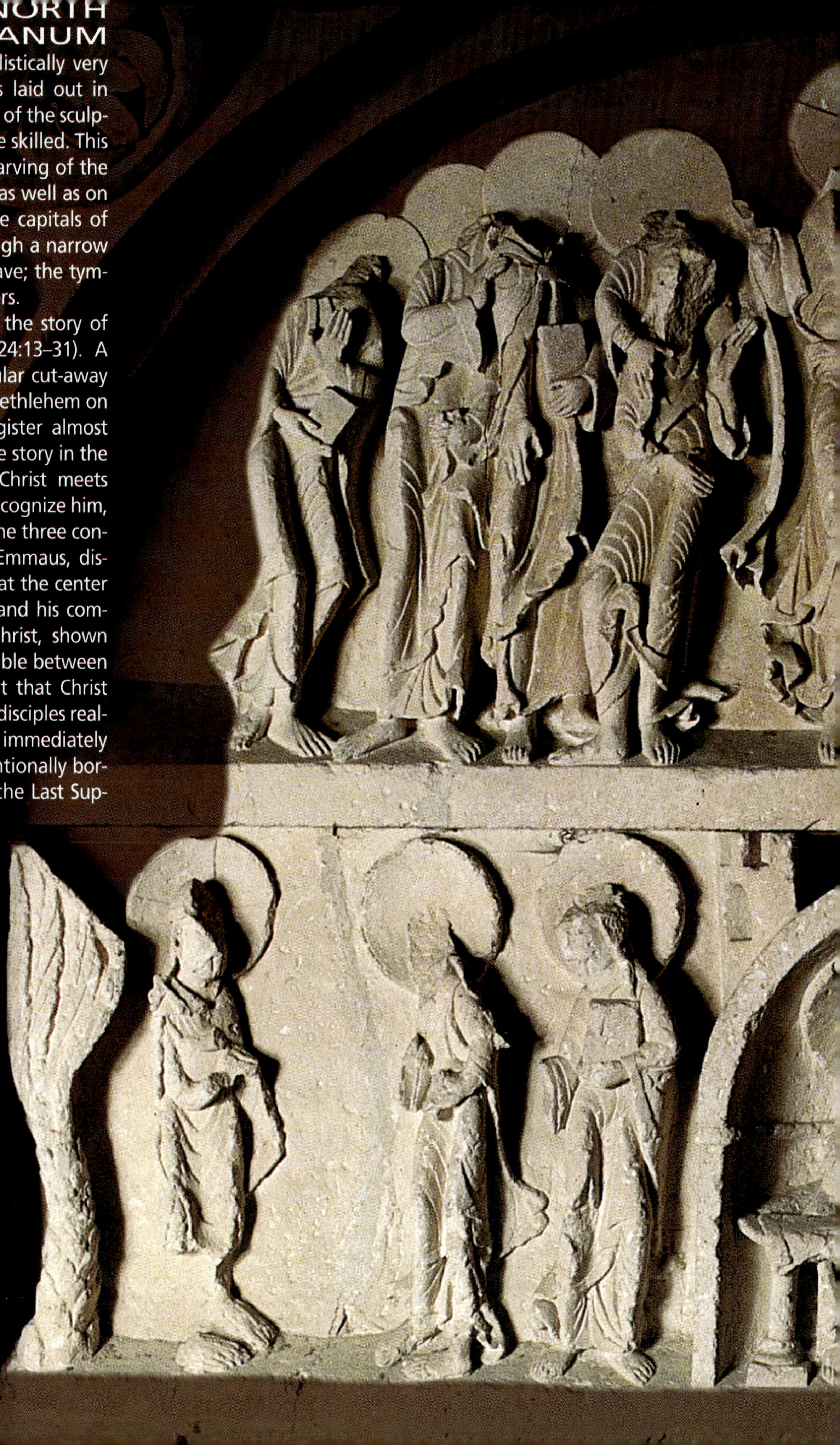

The Last Moments Before Ascension of Christ

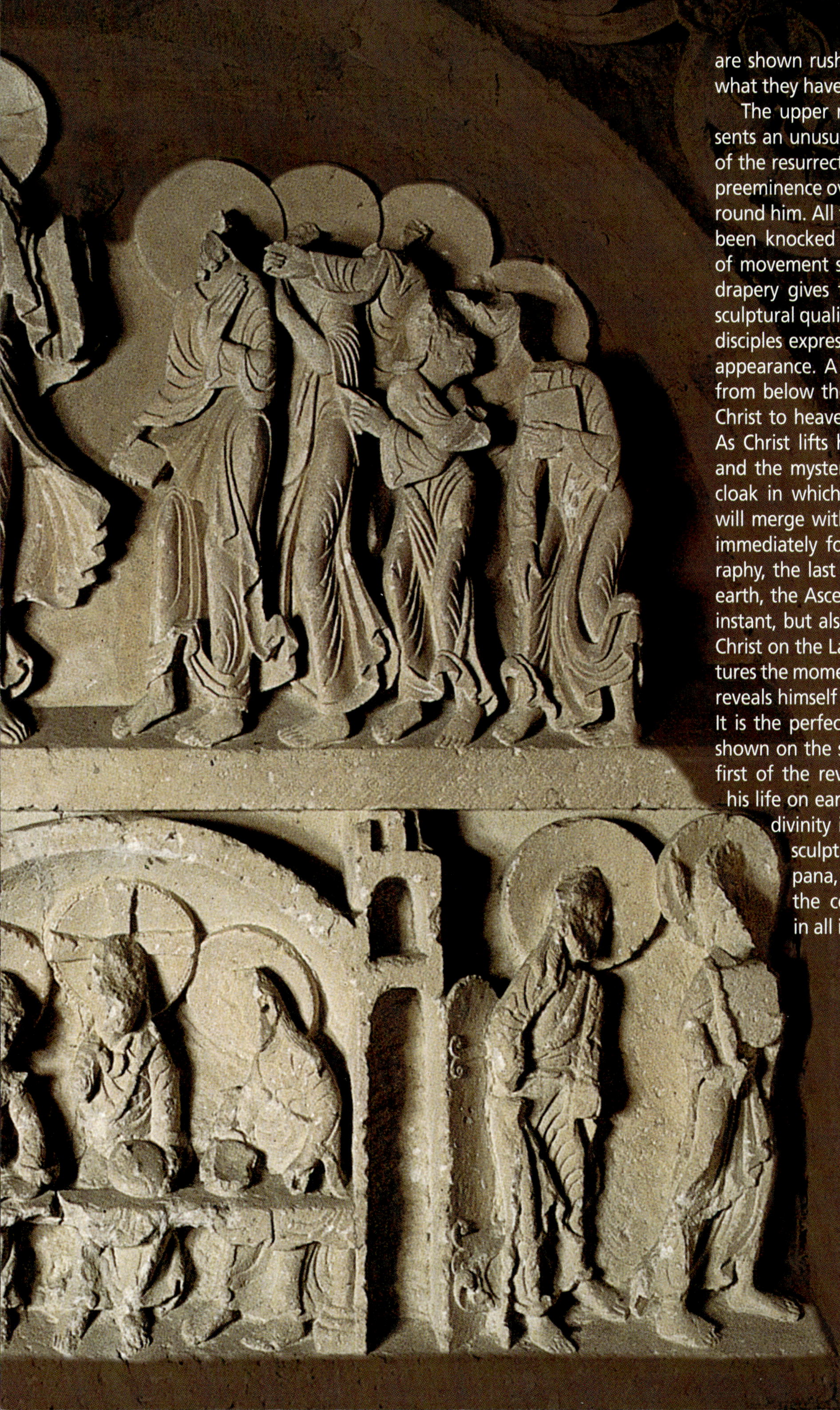

are shown rushing off to Jerusalem to report what they have seen to the other apostles.

The upper register of the tympanum presents an unusual theme, the final appearance of the resurrected Christ. His stature marks his preeminence over the eleven apostles who surround him. All the heads of these figures have been knocked off, but the fascinating sense of movement suggested by the folds of their drapery gives these figures an extraordinary sculptural quality. The vivacious gestures of the disciples express their astonishment at Christ's appearance. A breeze, which seems to come from below the figures and will shortly carry Christ to heaven, rushes through their tunics. As Christ lifts his right heel, his hands open, and the mysterious wind rushes through the cloak in which he is wrapped. This moment will merge with that of the Ascension, which immediately follows. In Romanesque iconography, the last moment of God's presence on earth, the Ascension, represents not only that instant, but also the promise of the return of Christ on the Last Day. The sculpture thus captures the moment in the narration when Christ reveals himself in the glory of his resurrection. It is the perfect counterpart to the Epiphany shown on the south portal, which depicts the first of the revelations of his divinity during his life on earth. As the revelation of Christ's divinity is enacted, step by step, in the sculptures of the two lateral tympana, the theophany represented on the central tympanum shines forth in all its splendor.

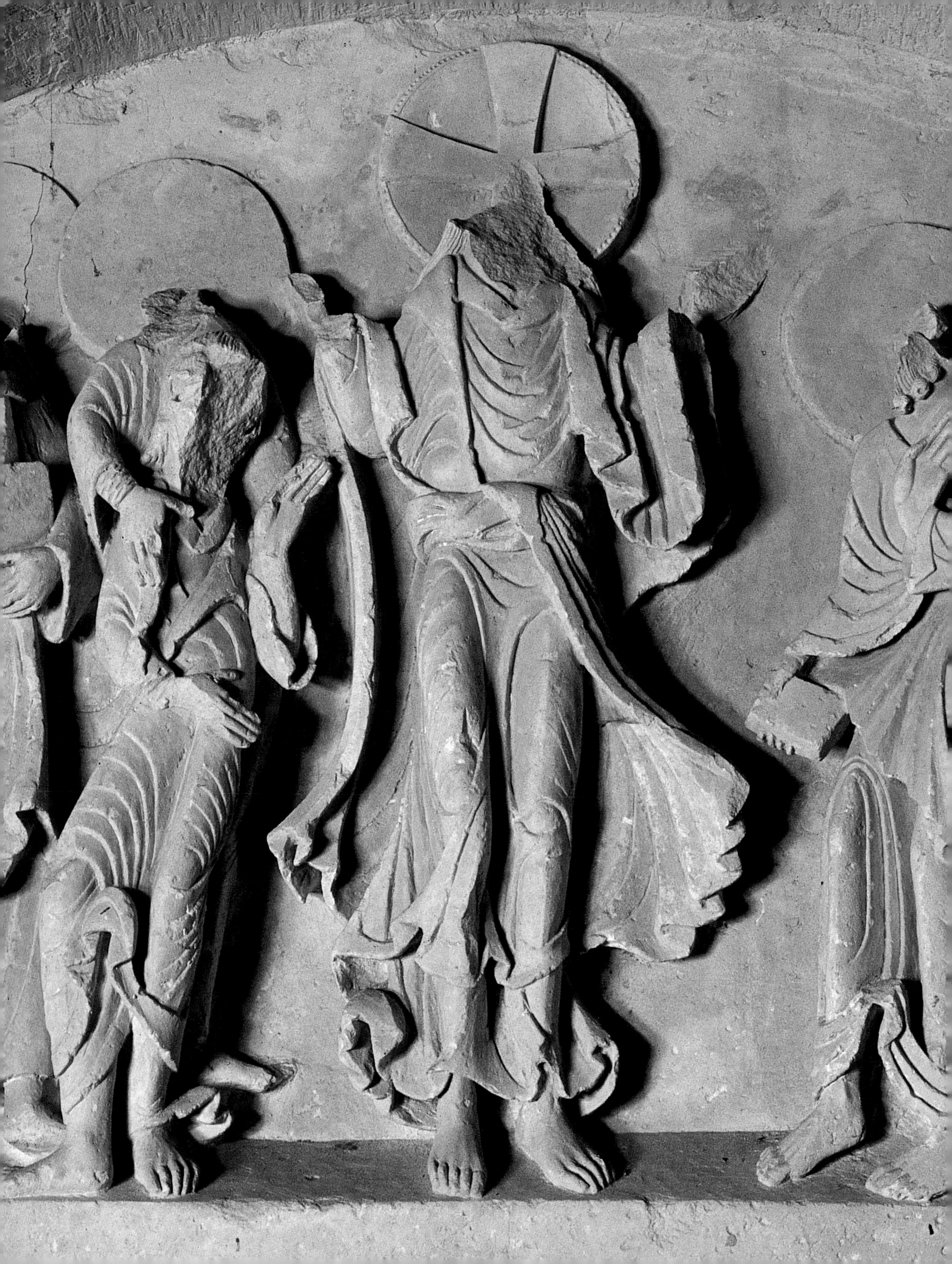

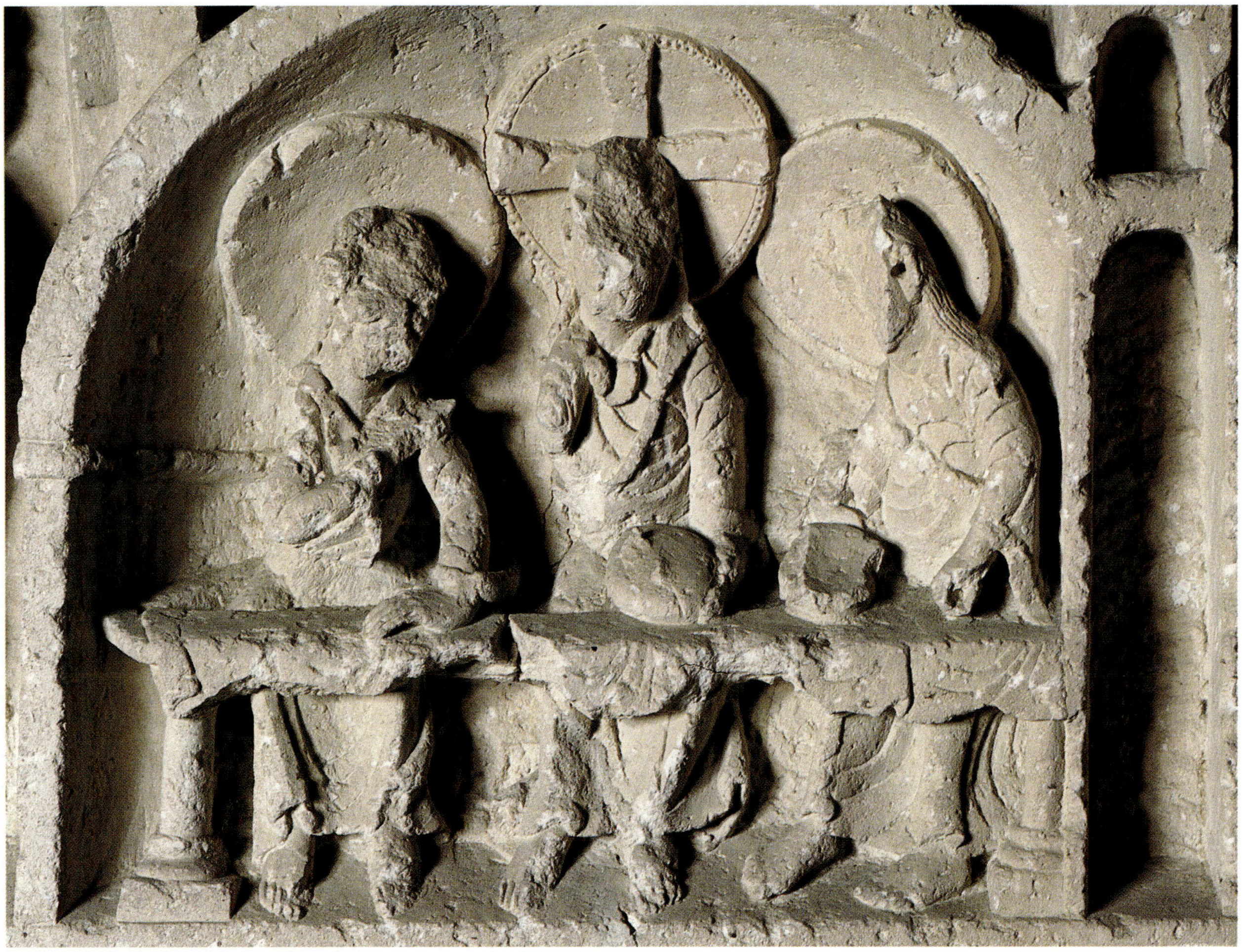

THE RESURRECTED CHRIST
APPEARS TO HIS APOSTLES

THE SUPPER AT EMMAUS

THE BASILICA

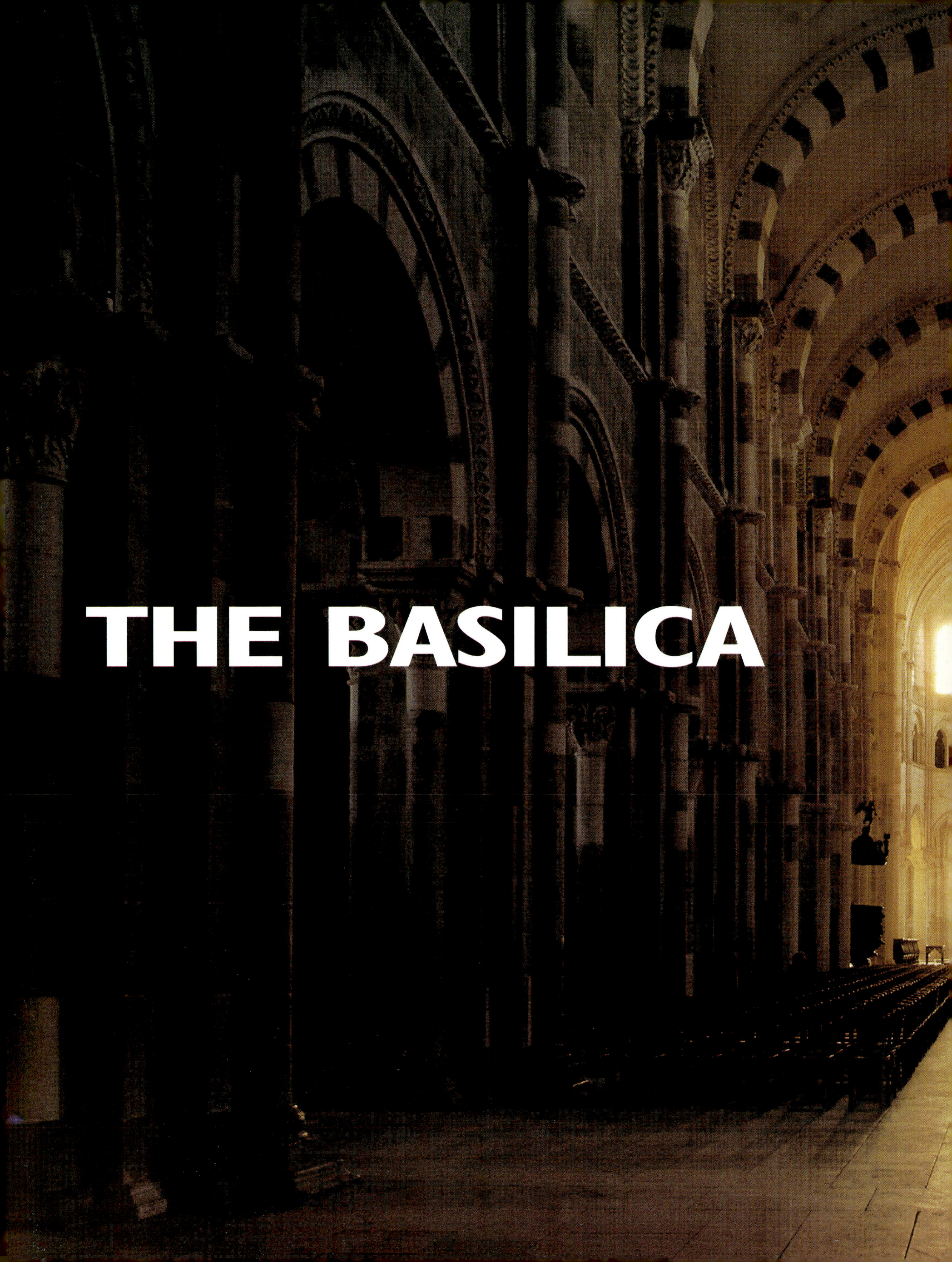

Realm of Light and Shadow

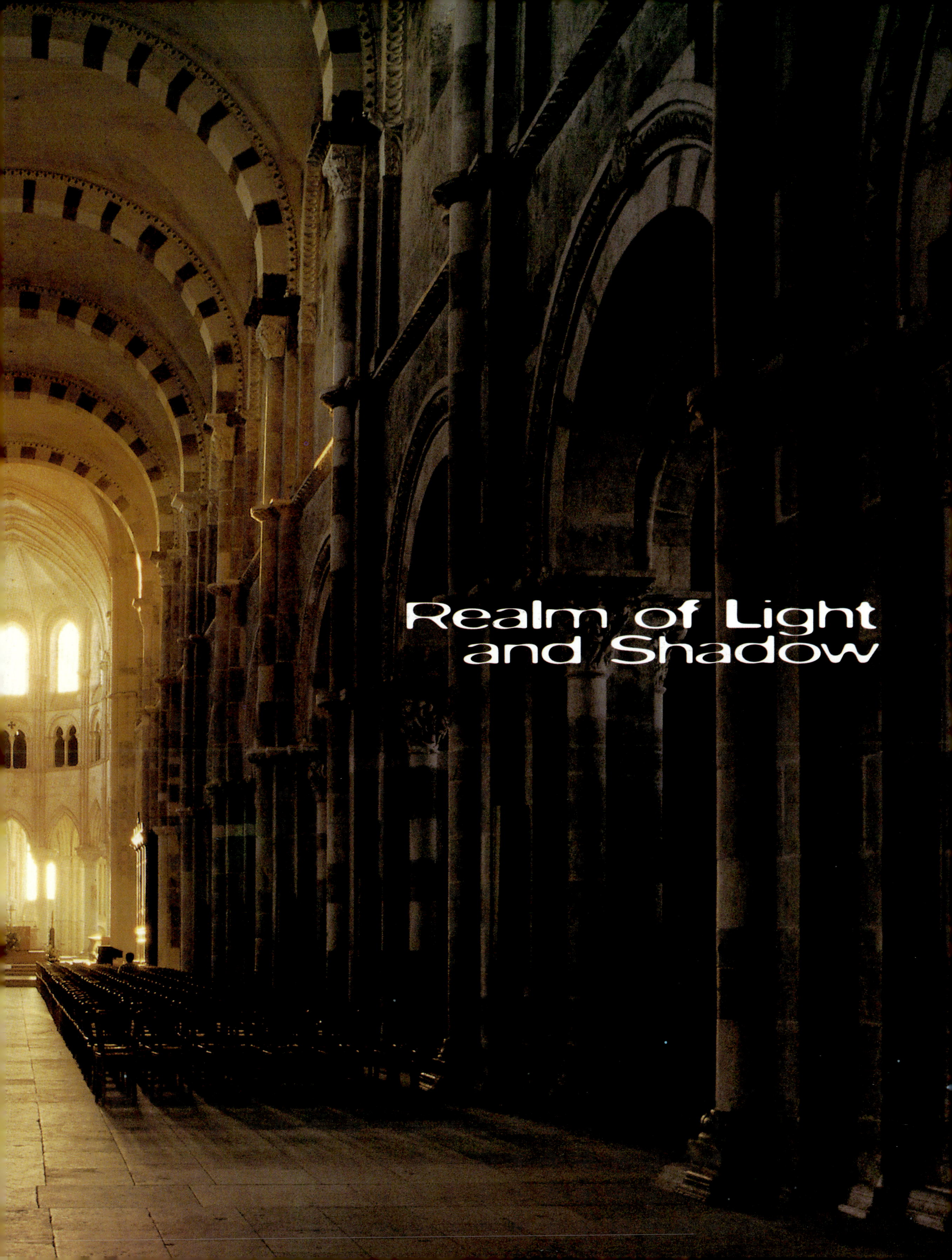

THE BASILICA, Realm of

At Vézelay, stone assumes multiple roles: stone-carved text on the tympana, purity and warmth in elevation of the nave. Once having entered the narthex, the visitor can see, through the open doors of the central portal, the bright width of the nave with its double arcade of alternating white and brown stone. The nave extends for ten long bays to the transept, where the Gothic choir begins. Approximately seventy years—from 1120 to 1190—separate the two building periods. The semicircular barrel vault of the nave is clearly Romanesque, while the choir is in a style inspired by the early Gothic architecture that flourished throughout the Ile-de-France in the late twelfth century. The contrast of the two styles is also apparent in their coloration. The limestone of the Romanesque nave is pink, white, and brown, while in the Gothic choir it is bluish and light gray. Nevertheless, the two styles are aesthetically complementary. The unornamented forms of the choir draw their elegance from the nave, and the focused light that bathes the central space emanates from the lancet windows in the choir.

The architecture of the nave is one of unity and simplicity. The central aisle, which traverses the church's east-west axis, is flanked on the north and south by side aisles. The elevation rises in two levels, with a massive arcade below and windows set high on the wall of the second story, which is supported by cruciform piers. Each of the piers is flanked by four engaged columns, one on each side, the one facing the nave rising to the springing of the vault. At the height of the capitals of the shorter engaged columns is a plain molding, which matches the archivolts of the great arches of the central nave. A second, elaborately carved molding, runs around the entire nave above the arcade. The geometric forms of the decoration both define and complement the architecture; the alternating carved stones that make up the double arcade are repeated on the great arches of the central vault. The arches along the walls of the upper story are adorned with carved moldings that resemble long ribbons folded into loops.

Rising a few steps higher than the nave, the choir comprises three levels: on the first story, the arcade, with arches that are Gothic, but of a somewhat Moorish shape; on the second story a triforium gallery with double Gothic windows; on the third, a tall clerestory. This elevation was surely inspired by that of the cathedral at Sens. The choir's floor plan, however, recalls that at Saint-Denis, with an ambulatory opening into intercommunicating, radiating chapels. Unlike at Saint-Denis, however, the chapels are not completely enclosed; instead the walls that separate them rise only two and a half meters and, for the

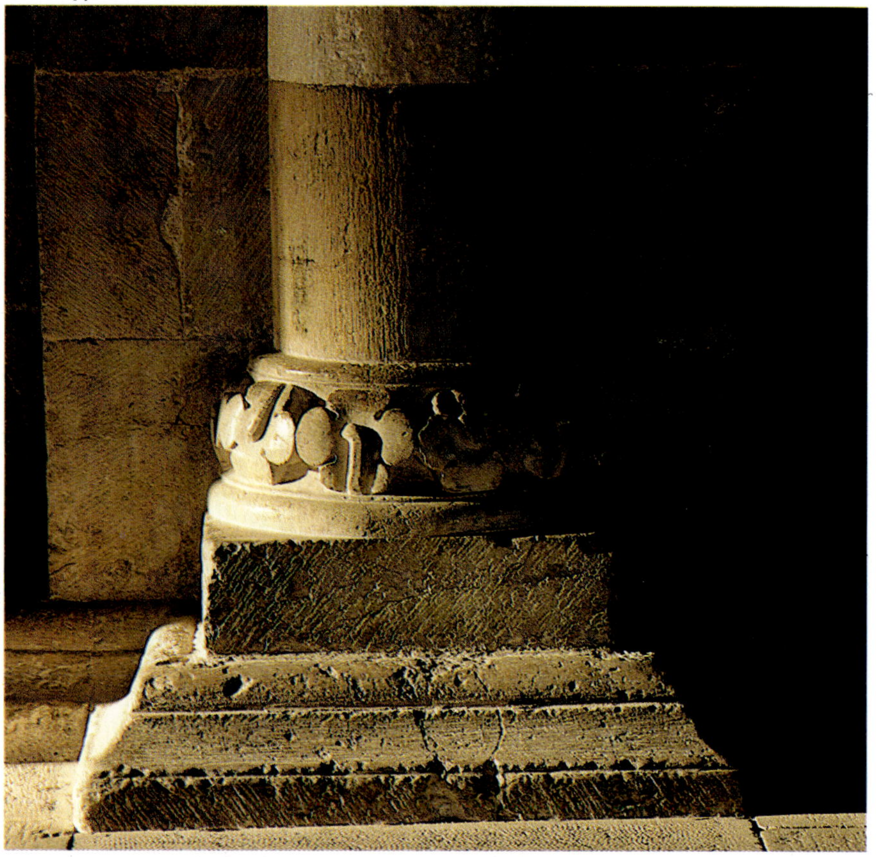

most part, stop beneath the windows. The choir appears to be ringed by a double ambulatory that is filled with light. The transept, which was built after the choir, is irregular and clumsy. Constructed in angles, it is divided into numerous unequal sections. It seems to have suffered, during the course of construction, from a change in architectural planning. The Gothic sector of the construction is believed to have been completed not long before 1215.

Solid and rather sturdy, the basilica at Vézelay does not at all resemble a thirteenth-century church. In the middle of the nineteenth century, the writer Prosper Mérimée, who was then Inspector General of historic monuments in France, engaged a young architect, Eugène Viollet-le-Duc, to restore the basilica. Viollet-le-Duc reinforced the Romanesque arches of the nave, which had been slowly crumbling, and thus saved the Madeleine from complete collapse.

Viollet-le-Duc also repaired the four final sections of the nave vault that preceded the transept, restoring three of the sections to their original Romanesque appearance; ribbed Gothic

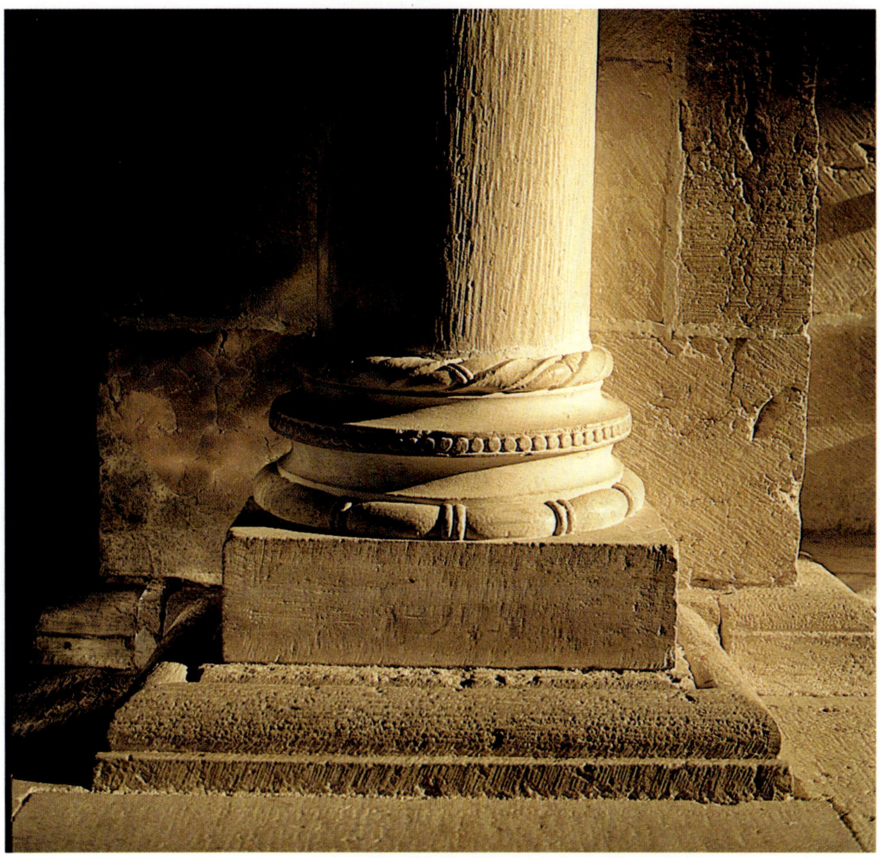

vaulting had been substituted for the original forms at the time that the Gothic choir was built. Only the last section remains in the Gothic style, left as a testimony to that period of the building's history. Unfortunately, in the restoration of the double arcade, the architect used paint to simulate the alternating brown and white stones, rather than colored limestone. The restoration of the sculpture of the church, undertaken by the sculptor Pascal at the same time that the architectural work was done by Viollet-le-Duc, also leaves something to be desired. This is particularly true of the tympanum on the façade and several of the capitals.

Despite its somewhat crude execution, the result of the restoration that began in 1120 following the fire that destroyed the old Carolingian nave, the Romanesque nave does lend itself to contemplation. The team of architects who began their work in 1120 remained faithful to the building's past, rejecting the look of the then-fashionable style of the monastery at Cluny (this period of which architectural historians call Cluny III). This conservative approach was clearly deliberate, as Renaud de Semur, at one time a Cluniac monk and the nephew of the abbot Hugues de Cluny (d. 1109), was then abbot of Vézelay. While not far away, other churches were beginning to tower to imposing heights and the Gothic arch was to be found everywhere, the nave at Vézelay was built in the Romanesque style, to the relatively modest height of 18.5 meters, and it continued the use of the round arch. Only the galleried narthex, a traditional feature in Burgundy, here constructed around 1140, recalls the forms of Cluny III. At Vézelay the plan is somewhat elongated, and the nave is only three aisles wide; the contemporary nave at Cluny is five aisles wide, and there the Gothic arch was already in use.

The church at Vézelay is not a daring design, although nineteenth-century restoration did reveal the great technical virtuosity of its architects. Ten meters in width and not supported by the side aisles, which are half its height, the central nave would pose serious problems when it came to building the vault. A number of ingenious devices were used to lighten the weight of the roof and to maintain its trajectory. Thus, the lower portions of each section of the vault are made of horizontally laid stone corbels. Toward the center of each section, these corbels are replaced by concentric rows of stones that are built up to form a sort of dome. In addition, materials specifically designed to lighten their weight were used in the construction of the apex of the vaultings.

The architecture of Vézelay gives testimony to a true inventiveness, used with discretion to produce a refined result that breathes with balance and serenity.

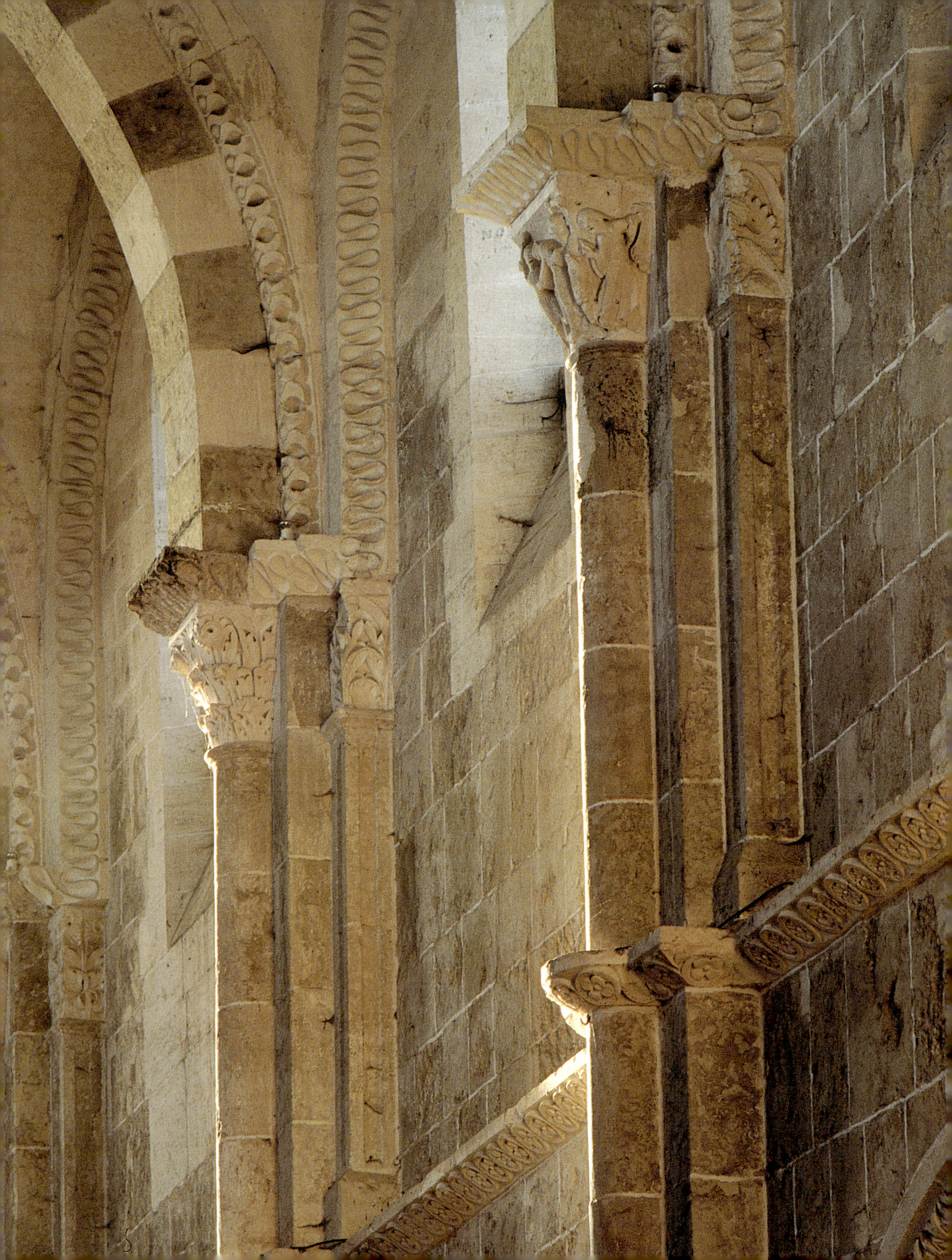

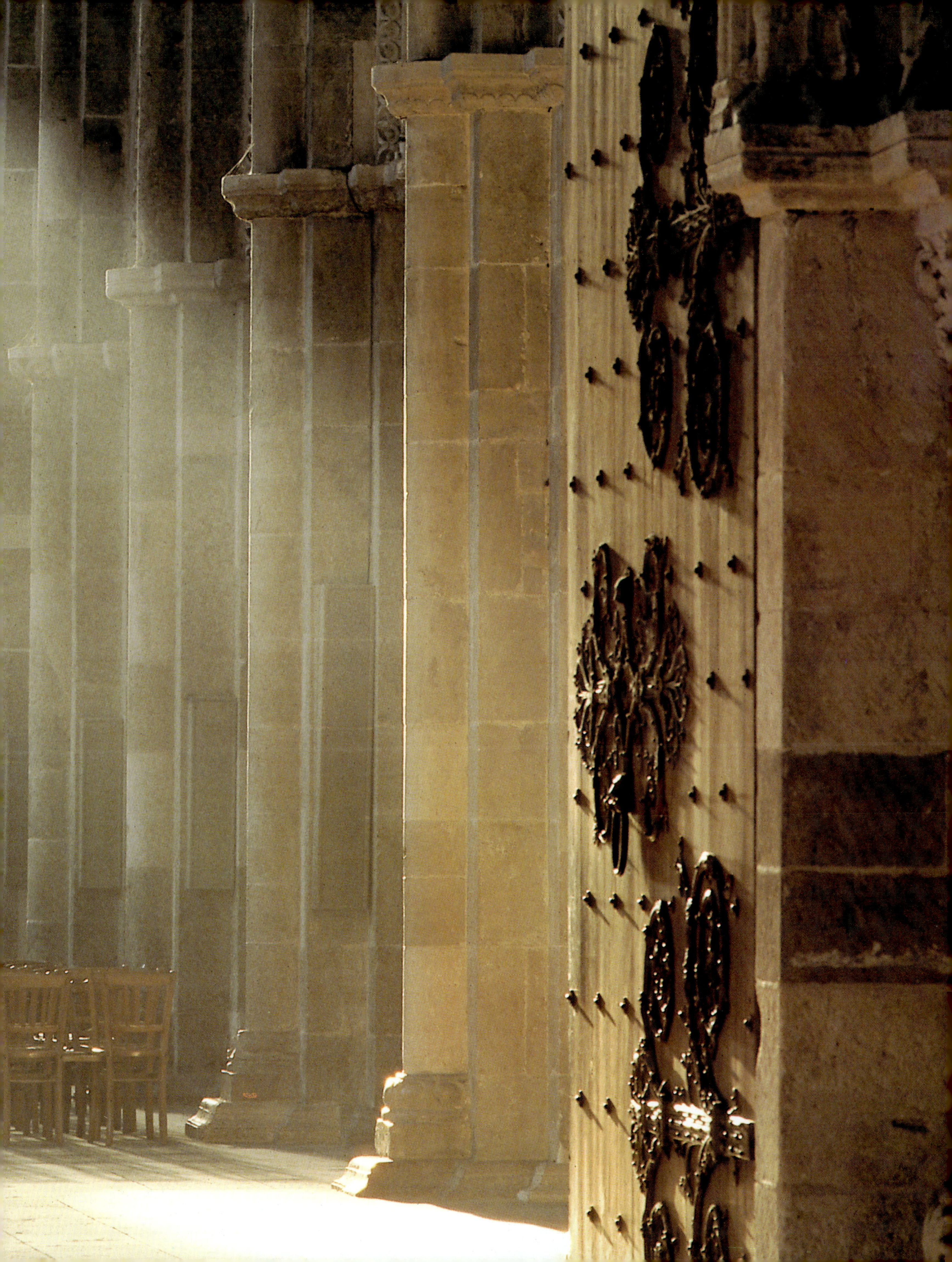

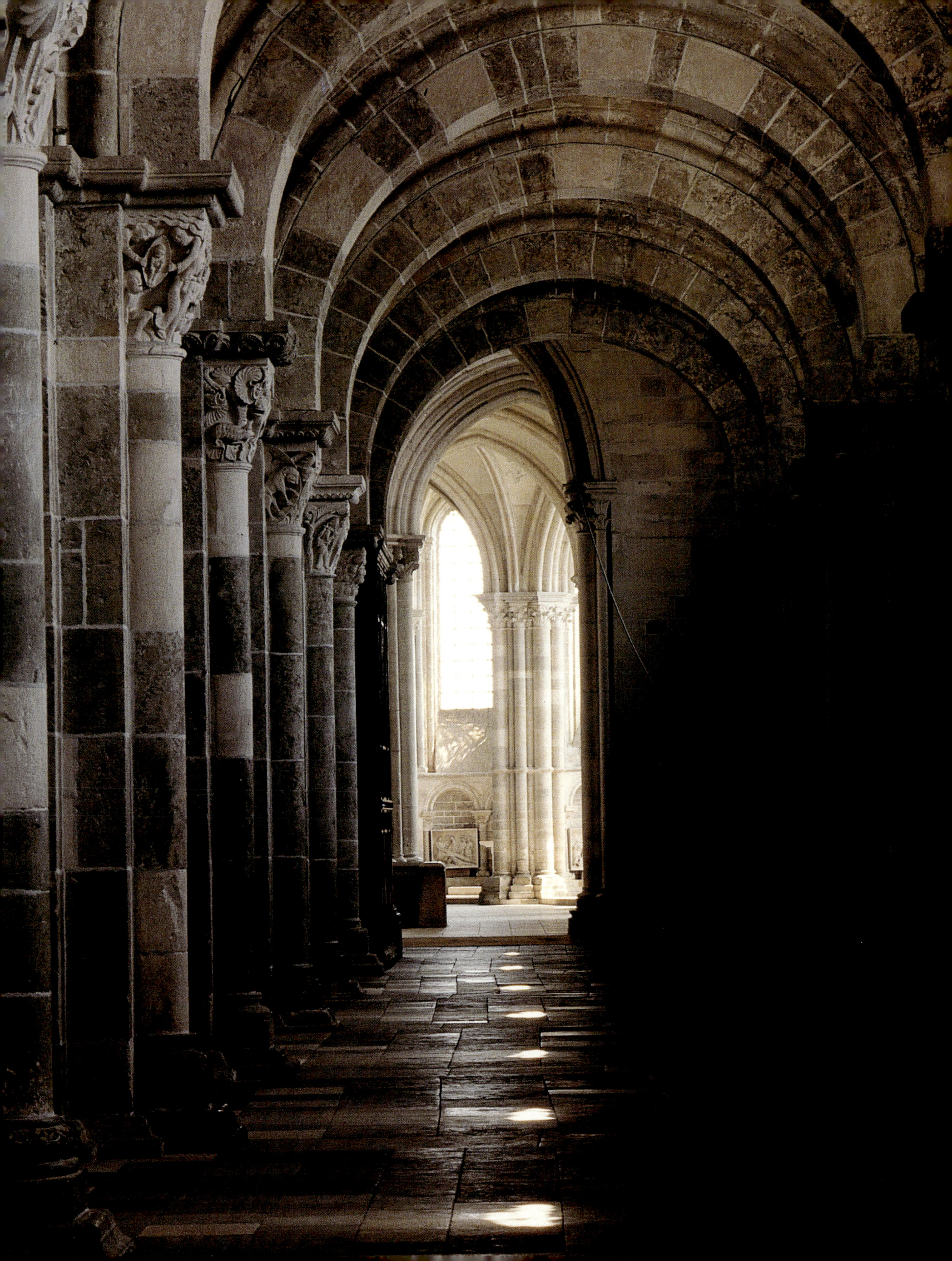

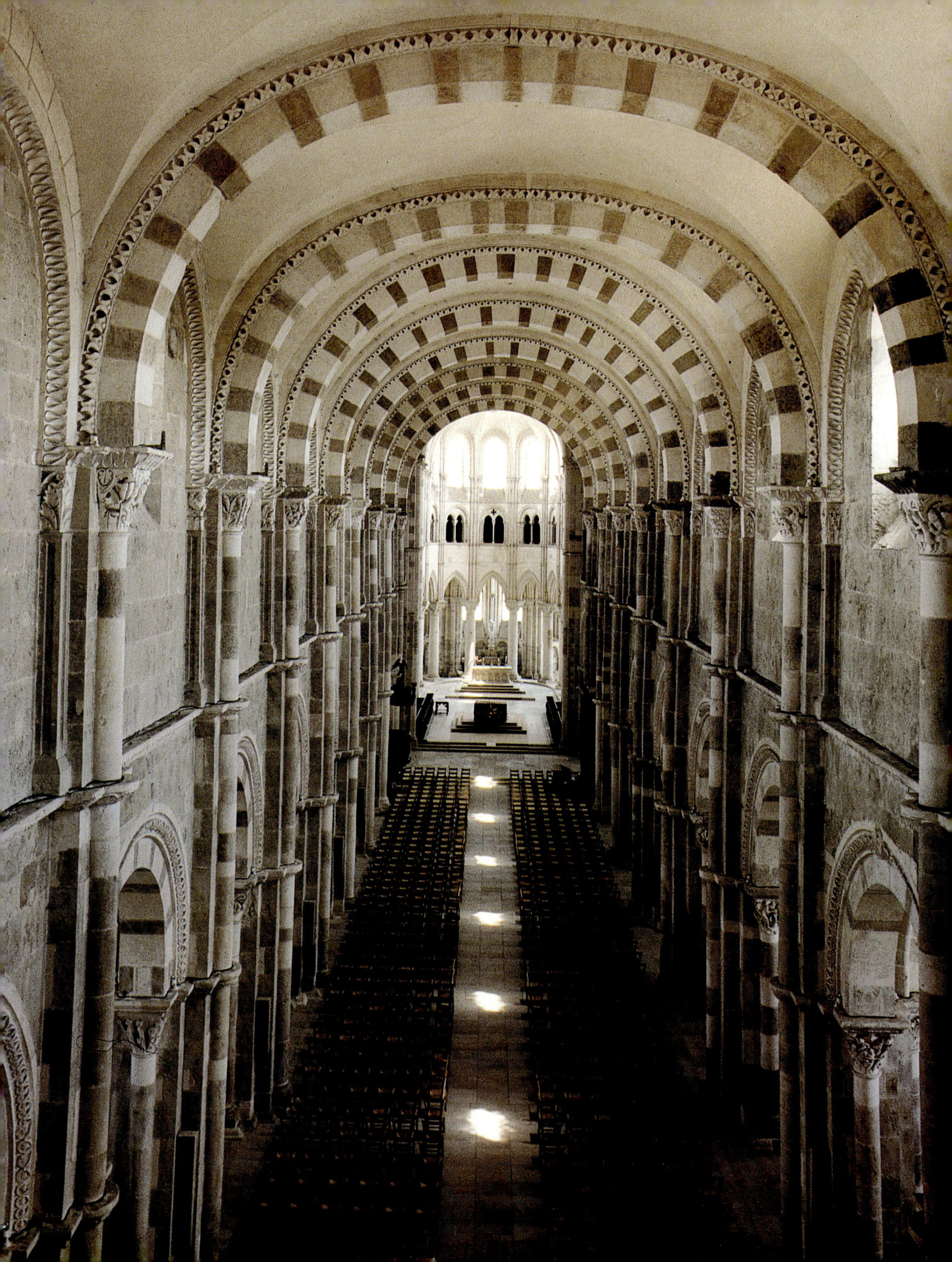

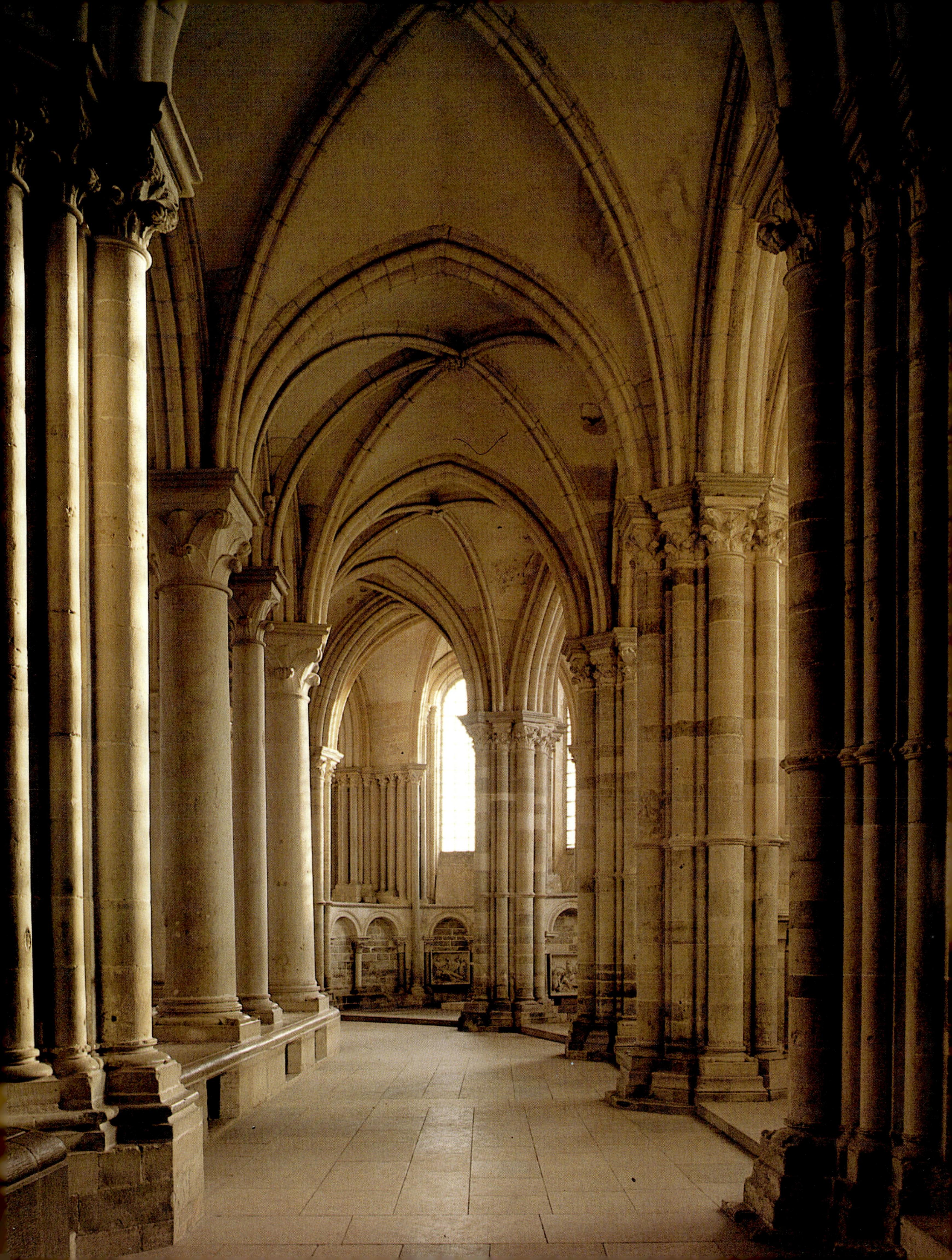

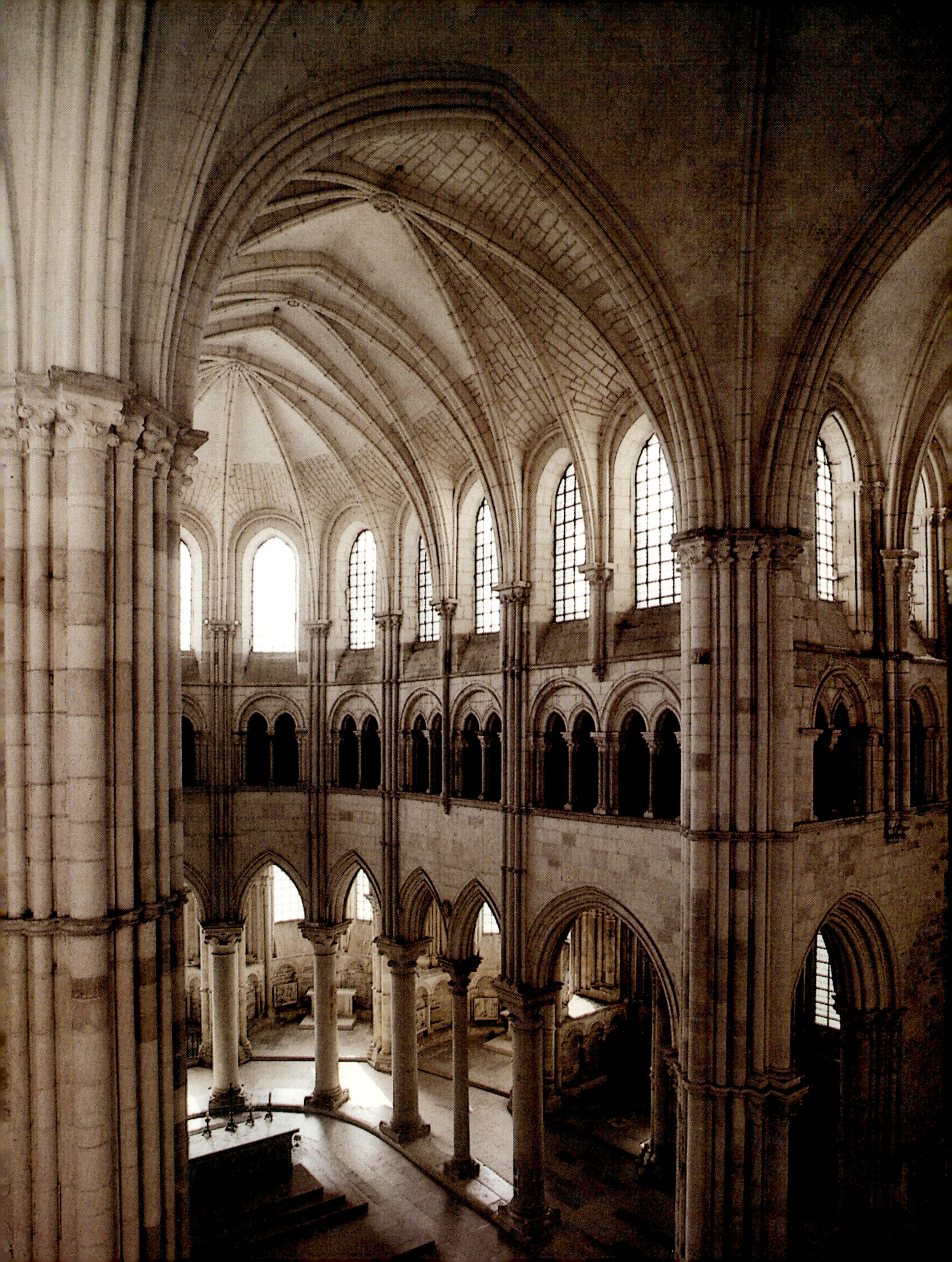

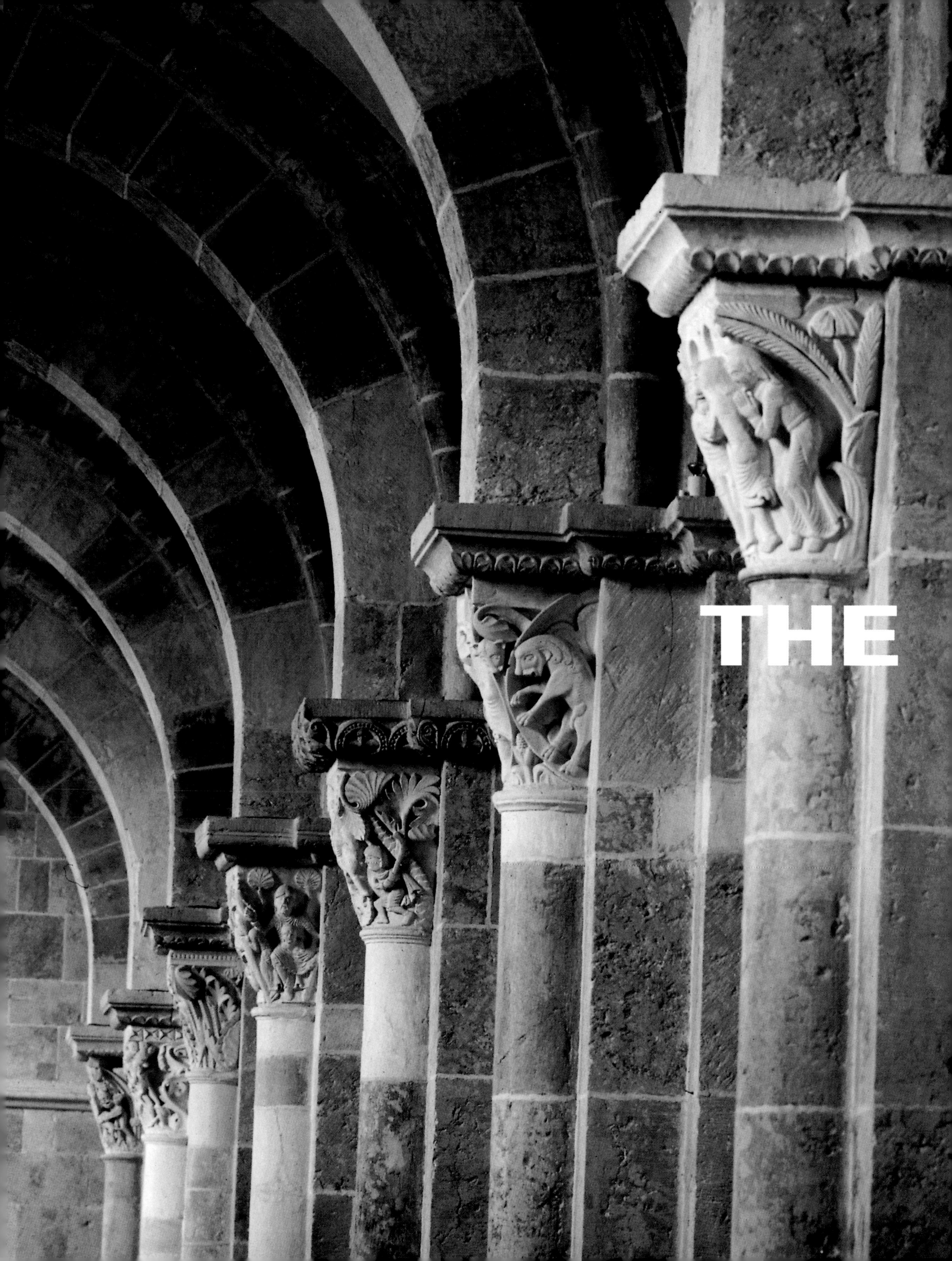

THE

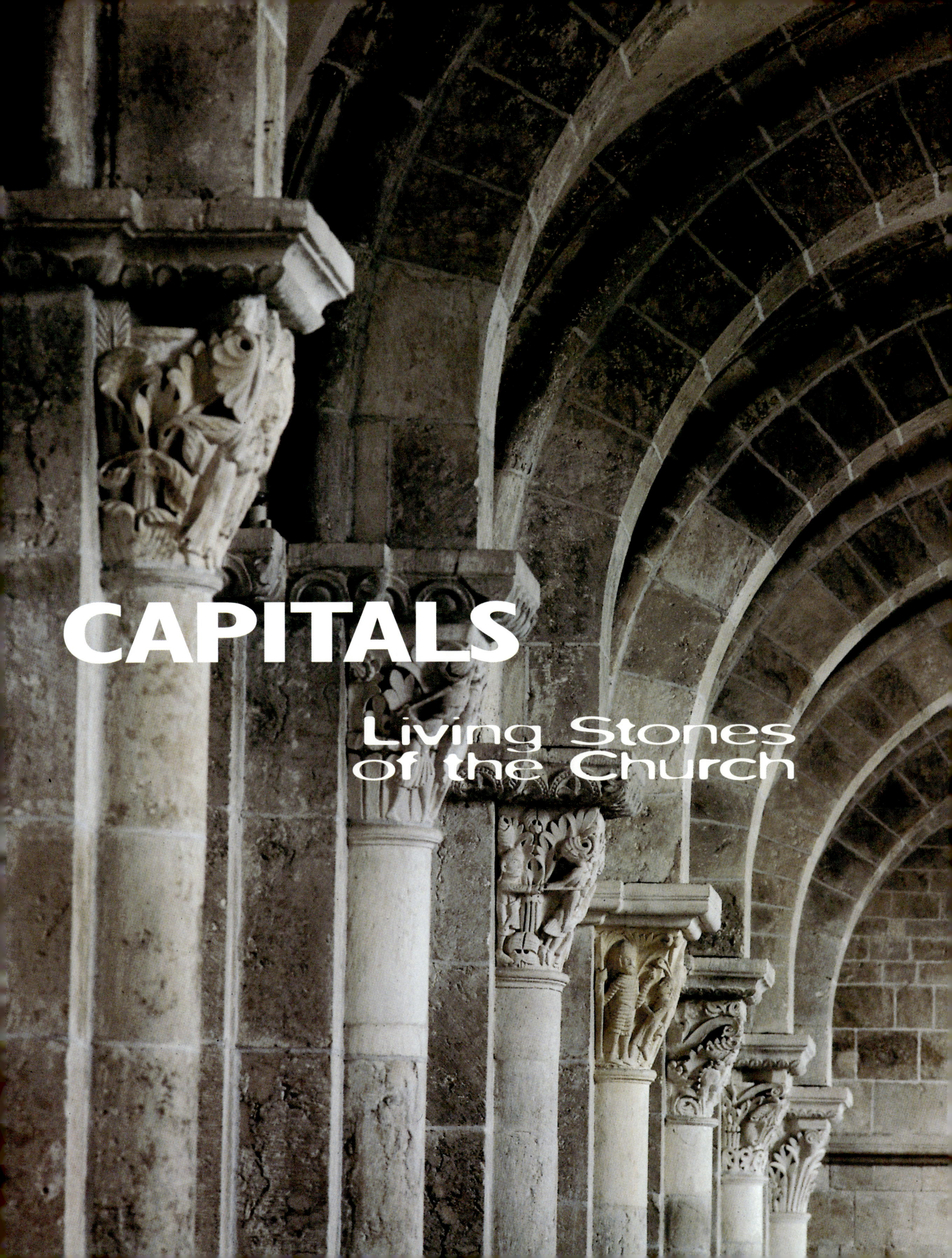
CAPITALS
Living Stones
of the Church

THE CAPITALS

In addition to the sculpture on the tympana, the engaged columns lining the walls and surrounding the piers of the narthex and the nave are surmounted by nearly two hundred capitals carved with foliage and figural scenes. Dating from the 1120s, these capitals are a veritable book in stone. Together they present a rich decorative program that encompasses the piers of the three tympana over the doors to the nave, the columns attached to the piers of the narthex

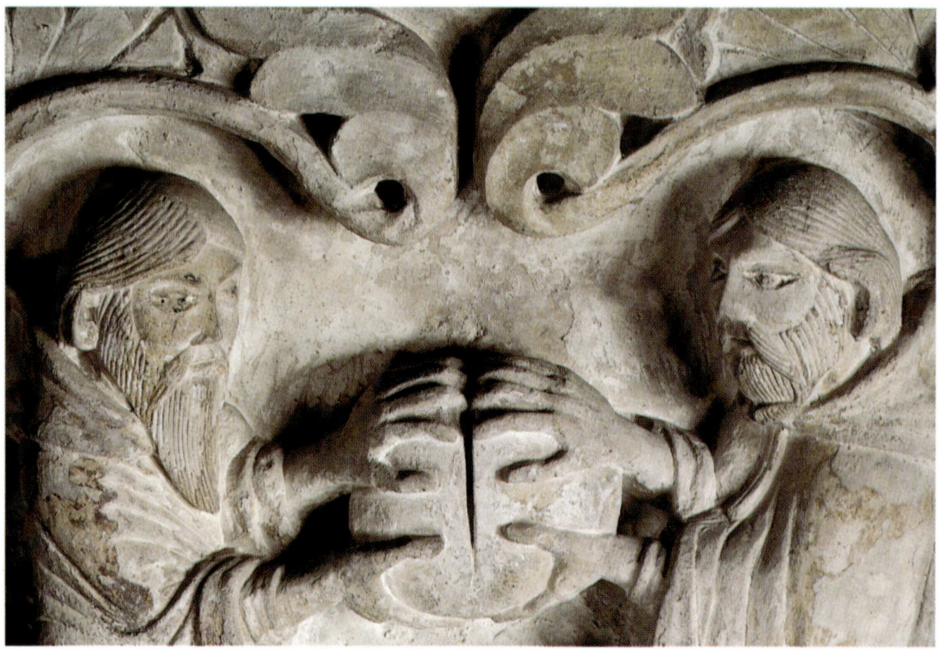

ABOVE: ST. PAUL AND ST. ANTHONY BREAKING BREAD

OPPOSITE: THE MYSTIC MILL (SEE PP. 152–53)

and the nave, and the columns along the walls that demarcate the thirteen Romanesque bays of the nave and the narthex. On the cruciform piers of the nave, the capitals of these engaged columns are set at two different levels; the columns that face the central aisle extend all the way to the top of the wall. Their capitals are placed just below the springing of the vault. On the other three sides of the piers, however, the capitals are set much lower, at the height of the springing of the arches of the arcade. The only exception to this pattern is to be found in the second bay of the narthex, where the four columns attached to the piers are all of the same height. The fact that the capitals of the columns facing the central aisle of the nave are placed so high is puzzling, since a viewer standing on the ground cannot possibly see them clearly. Apparently these capitals are meant to be decorative rather than didactic.

A BEAUTIFUL DISORDER

Whether in the narthex or the nave, whether set along the outside wall or on the piers, the lower capitals abound with imagery. Almost one-third are decorated with a variety of foliage; a dozen

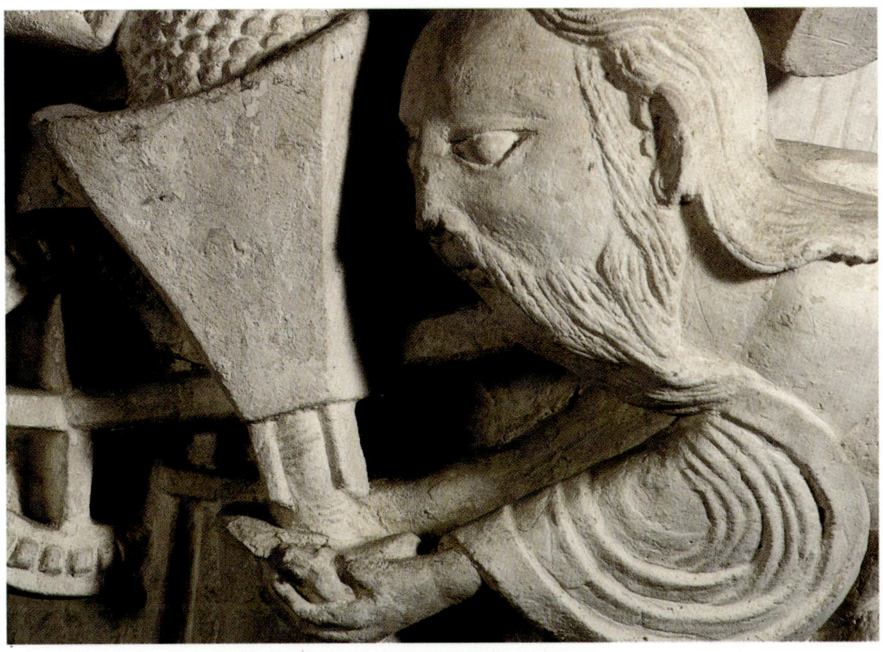

or so others date only to the nineteenth century. The remaining capitals are narrative, depicting an array of stories, some from the Bible, some from the legends of the early Church fathers. Others are derived from mythology, or are based on allegorical allusions. The question arises whether a systematic iconographic program can be discerned in these capitals, as it can on the tympana of the doors. Although there are many sources of inspiration for the capitals, the Old Testament is clearly a predominant one. Stories drawn from Genesis are often represented, with depictions of Adam and Eve, the death of their son Cain, and two episodes from the life of Jacob, the grandson of Abraham. Related through their shared textual origin and narrative order, these capitals, nevertheless, are largely autonomous works of art, often set far apart from one another. For example, the capital showing the Fall of Adam and Eve is on the north pier of the ninth bay of the nave, whereas the capital illustrating the story of Cain is shown on the south pier of the fourth bay. Only the two scenes involving Jacob, one depicting him receiving the blessing of his father Isaac, the other showing him wrestling with the angel, are found on a single pier on the south side of the seventh bay. Several capitals relate the stories of David recorded in the books of Samuel: David as a young shepherd; David overpowering a lion that is attacking his herd; David killing the giant Goliath. Later we see David again, now as king, decreeing the execution of the murderer of his predecessor, Saul. We also see him being reprimanded by the prophet Nathan for having seduced Bathsheba and then arranging for the death of her husband; still later we see David's dead son Absalom, hanging by his thick hair from an oak tree. The representations of these stories are scattered throughout the nave. The capital depicting Nathan's rebuke (p. 130), for example, is found in the narthex, at the north side of the second bay. The other stories from the life of David are to be found on the capitals in the fourth, fifth, and seventh bays of the nave, either on the north or south side.

NARRATION AND ALLEGORY

There is no apparent system organizing the capitals of the columns in the church. Thus, the modern viewer must put aside contemporary expectations, developed during the Renaissance, of symmetry, rationality, and order. In order to understand the conceptions that unite these images, we must first examine their great variety. The most famous capital at Vézelay, the image of the Mystic Mill (left, and pp. 152, 154–55), offers a key. On this capital, a prophet, probably Moses, leans over a miniature mill, pouring grains of wheat into its funnel. St. Paul, who is shown below, collects the flour in a sack. Between the coarse, unmilled grain that streams through Moses' fingers and the refined powder that St. Paul receives, there is no direct continuity. The substance of the grain and the flour is the divine word, offered first in the ancient Law of Moses, and then in the new Law dispensed to Paul. Between the two, the mystical mill that refines the raw material, is Christ. Other symbolic meanings can be read into this image as well. For example, Christ is not only the mill, but also its ultimate product, the mystical bread of the

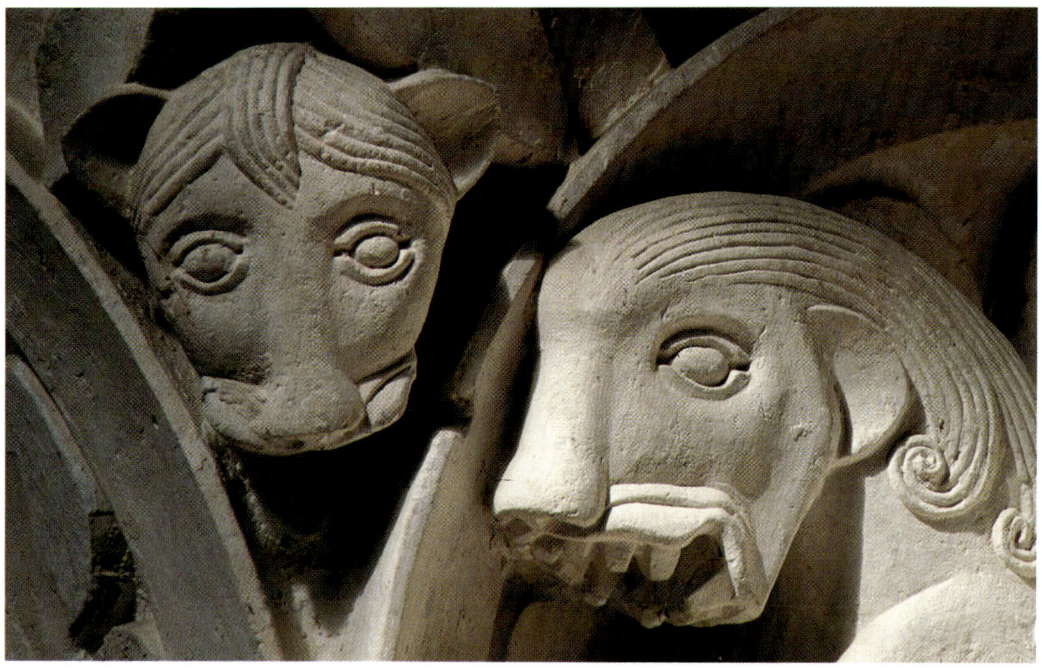

ABOVE: THE LIONS' DEN (SEE PP. 122–23)

OPPOSITE: A FEMALE DEMON (SEE P. 117)

SECOND OVERLEAF: TWO DEMONS

Eucharist. The Mystic Mill thus exemplifies the Romanesque consciousness, and more broadly, the medieval consciousness, in its view of the relationship between the Old and New Testaments. In medieval thinking, the incidents of the Old Testament are interpreted, not simply as events in themselves, but as prefigurations of the events of the New Testament, or as allegories, such as this one of the flour of the Law becoming divine nourishment. Thus, any given capital lends itself to a number of interpretations. The battle between David and the lion represents King David's rule over the people of Judah, who are traditionally represented by this beast, and also the victory of justice over evil. In this light, the Abduction of Ganymede (pp. 144, 151), which is depicted on the first capital in the south aisle of the church, no longer seems out of place in this sacred context. Here, the boy is represented neither as the beloved of Zeus, nor as the cupbearer of the gods; instead he is snatched from his father by an eagle and carried off screaming in terror as a demon shrieks with joy. In a Christian rereading of the myth that draws on iconographic similarities, the scene is transformed into the terrible ordeal of a soul seized by the Devil.

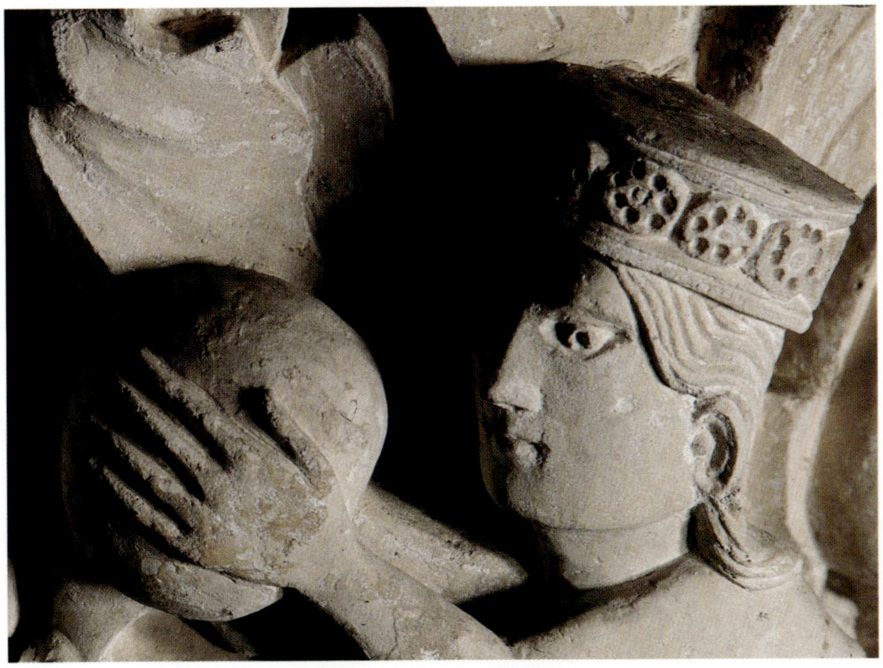

GOOD AND EVIL

To better understand the assortment of themes depicted, one must also take into consideration what is not shown. Whereas the tympana are exclusively dedicated to Christ, the capitals illustrate only a few themes from the New Testament, and Christ is never the actual subject. Instead, for example, we find the apostle Peter being led out of prison by an angel (pp. 123, 124–5); or one of Christ's parables, such as that of Lazarus and Rich Man (Luke 16:19–31; p. 150); or the decapitation of John the Baptist (p. 140). After the books of the Old Testament, the primary sources of the images on the capitals are the legendary lives of the saints. An episode from the life of St. Eustace, a Roman general in the reign of the emperor Hadrian who converted to Christianity and was then martyred, is depicted (pp. 127, 131). We also find a scene from the legend of St. Eugenia, the daughter of a prefect of Alexandria, who disguised herself as a man in order to enter a monastery, and later rose to become its abbot (p. 127). A prominent place is reserved for the early Christian monastics, from both the Eastern and Western churches. The legendary St. Paul the Hermit, credited by his biographer St. Jerome with being the first Christian anchorite, is shown breaking bread with the Egyptian hermit St. Anthony of Egypt (pp. 112, 152–53), famous for his visions of demonic torment. St. Martin, here dressed as an abbot, is depicted rooting out paganism among the peasants by chopping down a tree that had been the object of a cult (pp. 134, 136, 138–39). St. Benedict, whose Rule—a system of regulations for monastic life—has served since the sixth century AD as the basis for all Western monasticism, is also represented. The two capitals devoted to him show his attempted deception by a demon, whose blandishments he overcomes with asceticism and prayer (p. 116).

The lives of the early Church Fathers are presented as examples of the pinnacle of Christian life, to be honored and emulated. The underlying meaning that unites all of these hagiographic themes is the search for goodness, and the battle of virtue. Contrasting to them are the capitals that depict fantastic and demonic figures, who, through their opposition, evoke the stakes of the struggle. Devils, monsters, and mythological beings that peopled the Roman imagination are all to be found at Vézelay, sometimes as vile as evil, at other times as delightful as temptation.

These scenes, whether from Genesis or the life of King David, whether mythological, demonic, or monastic, seem unlikely cohabitants of a single iconography. Nevertheless, in the eyes of the faithful they weave a tissue of symbols in which the forces of good and evil are in constant conflict, and are emblematic of the eternal battle of man against himself.

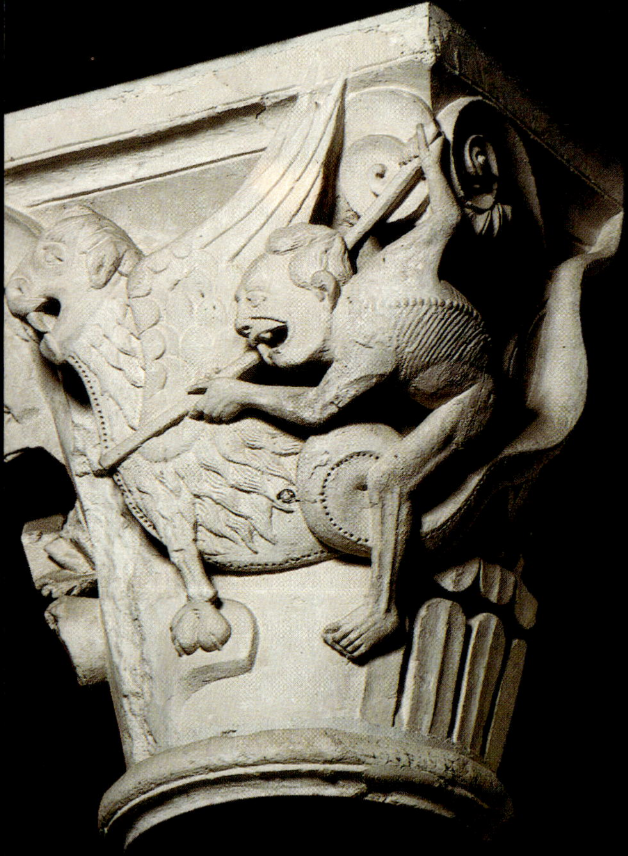

1

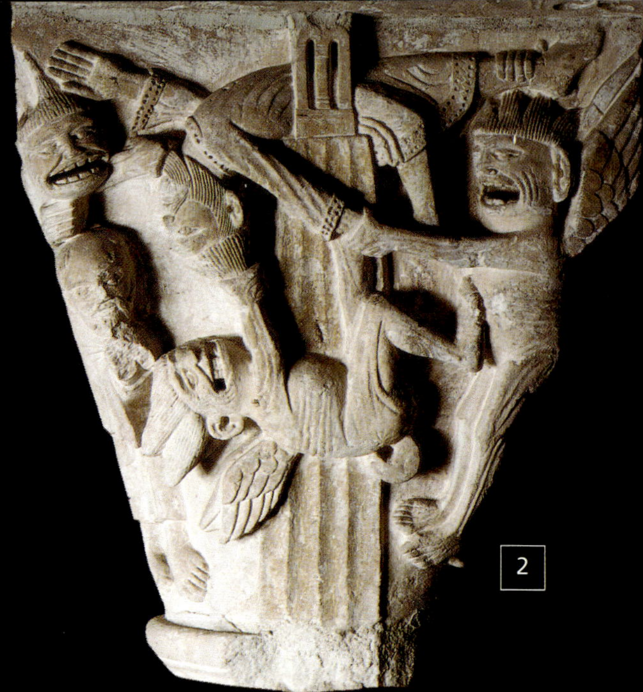

2

BATTLES AND TEMPTATIONS

Scattered throughout the narthex and the nave are capitals teeming with imps and evil animals.

These beings can be divided into two categories: those that torment humanity and those that live far from the human world and fight among themselves. On the north capital of the sixth bay of the nave, a monstrous demon attempts to ram one of his fellow creatures (above, no. 1). He rides a winged dragon, who has the head and body of a lion, and whose long tail wraps around the entire capital. Echoing the expression of his mount, the demon opens his large mouth to reveal two sharp fangs. A similar winged dragon is found once again on the south capital of the first bay. A goblin in a conical cap is seated on the beast's folded wings (p. 120). At first glance, the goblin's body appears human, but, looked at more carefully, its smooth flesh and nimble joints suggest some sort of frog or toad. Behind his back, the goblin holds an enormous ball, which he is about to hurl at an adversary, who lies in wait on the adjoining side of the capital. This adversary is a female demon, half-cow and half-serpent, wearing a heavy, ornate crown (opposite, no. 3; p. 115). Not in the least intimidated by the dragon's roaring mouth, she also brandishes a deadly ball.

Demonic

4 THE TEMPTATION OF ST. BENEDICT

3 A BATTLE OF MYTHICAL CREATURES

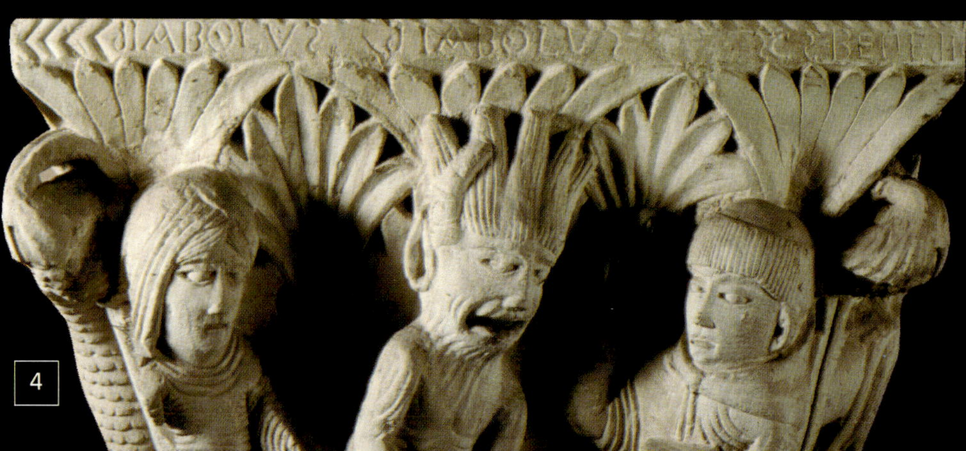

4

This evil world, in which everything is in discord, insinuates itself into the human world, which it works to corrupt. The same theme is also expounded on the lower wall of the sixth bay, where a lascivious demon assists in the seductive action of a profane song. On one side of the capital a minstrel, identifiable by the stringed instrument he carries at his side, inflates his cheeks to blows through a pipe (p. 117, no. 5). The demon, his hideous face with twisted mouth and sideways gaze, turns toward the minstrel, while his hand, which extends onto the next adjoining face of the capital, fondles a nude woman who has been seduced by the music. Through this inspired artistic arrangement, the victim, not seeing the ugliness of her seducer, abandons herself to the beauty of the sound.

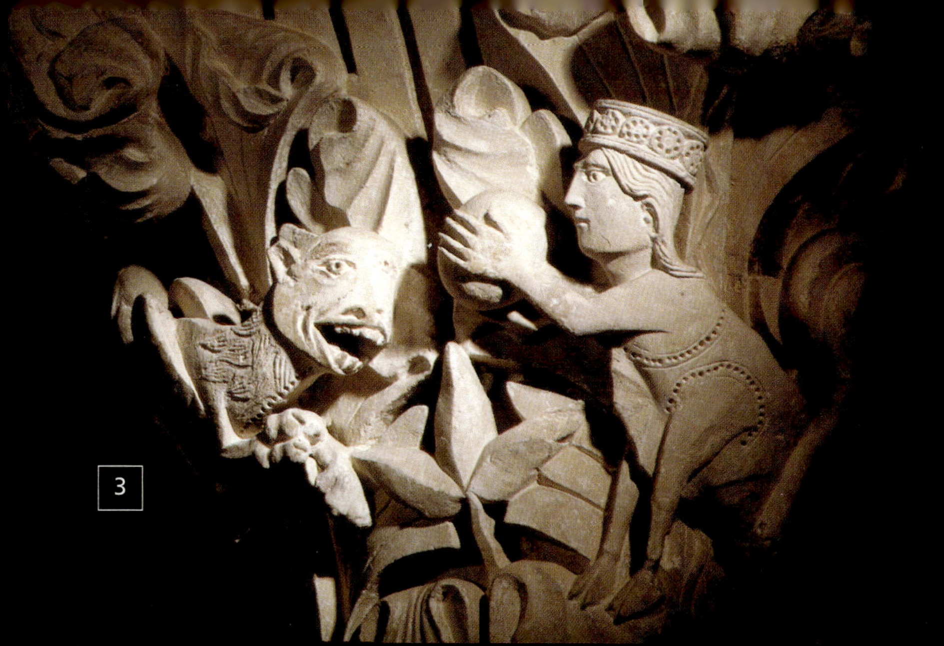

3

A BATTLE OF DEMONS

1

2

THE VISION OF ST. ANTHONY

Variations

5

MUSIC AND IMPURITY

Two capitals depict the temptations of St. Anthony and St. Benedict. In a horrific vision, Anthony is confronted by the sight of a man suspended upside-down on a sort of gallows as he is being tortured by demons (p. 116, no. 2). One of the demons hangs with all his weight from the man's shoulders, while another pulls at the man's beard; a third draws the man in the opposite direction. St. Benedict's demon is more cunning. Instead of terrifying the saint, the demon attempts to charm him by leading forward a woman, whom he grasps tightly by the wrist (p. 116, no. 4). The monk, however, faithful to his vows, represented by the book he carries, rejects this temptation with a gesture of benediction.

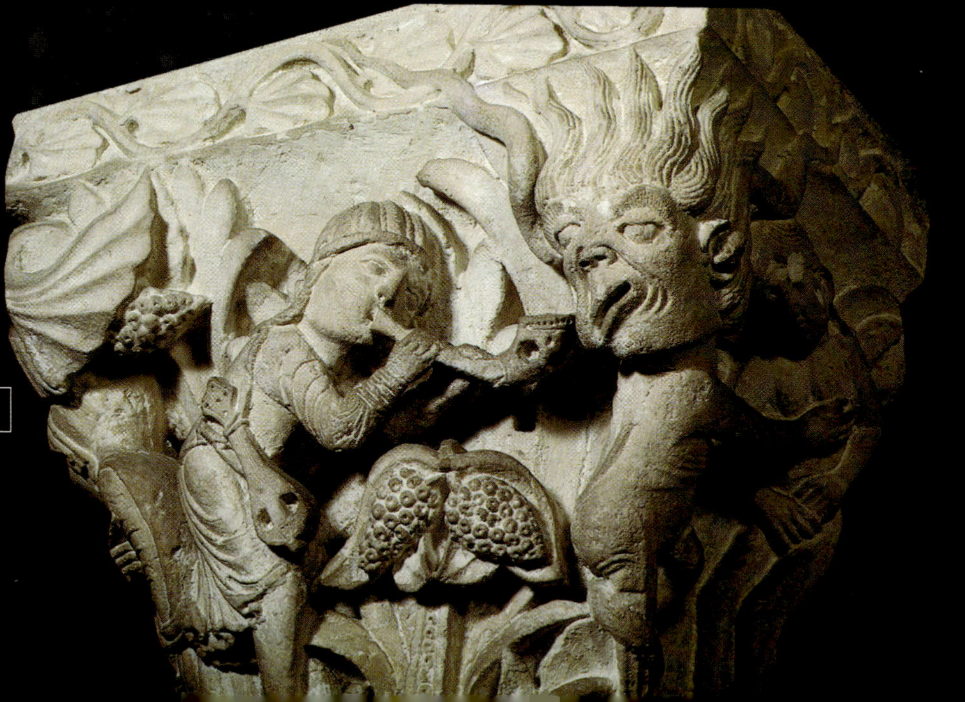

5

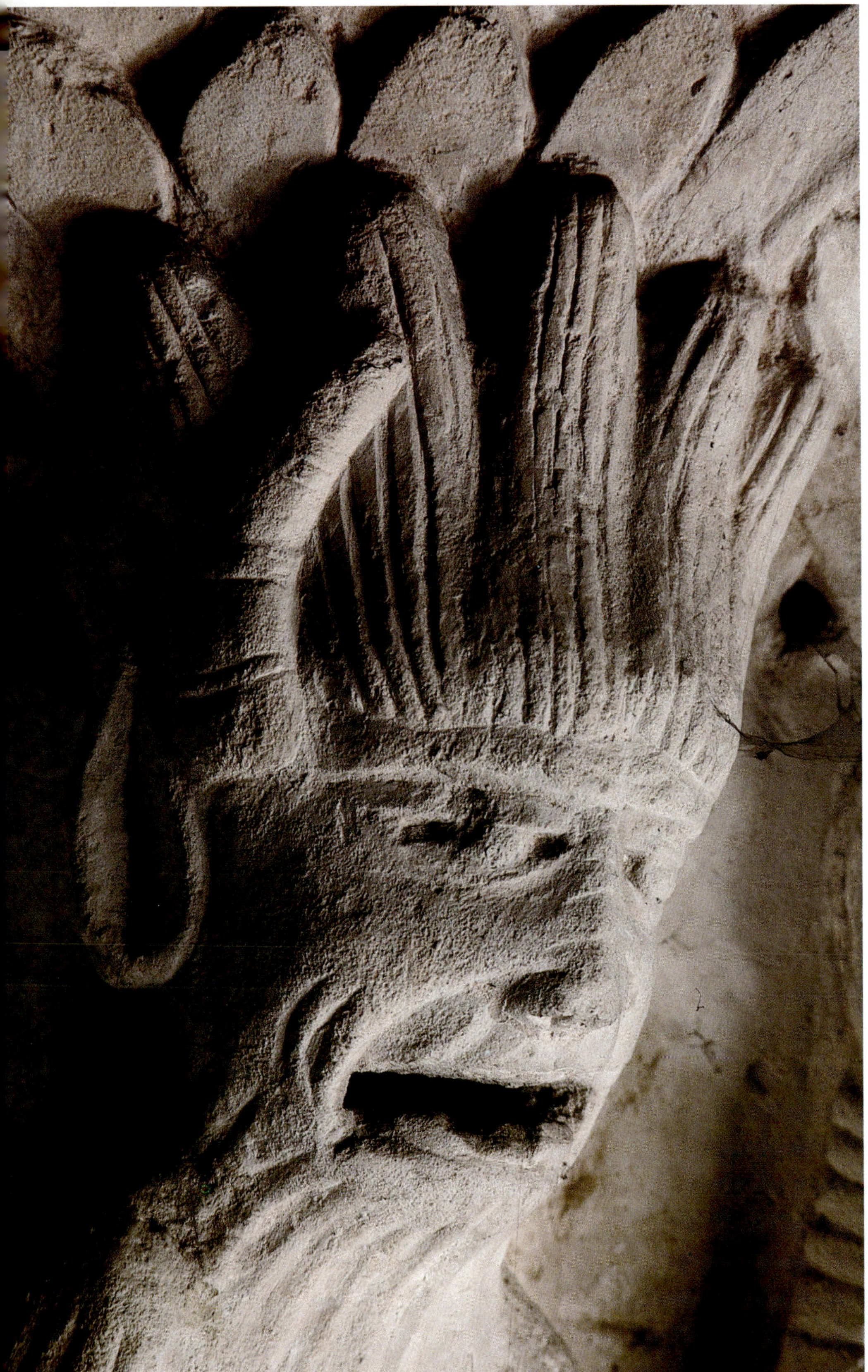

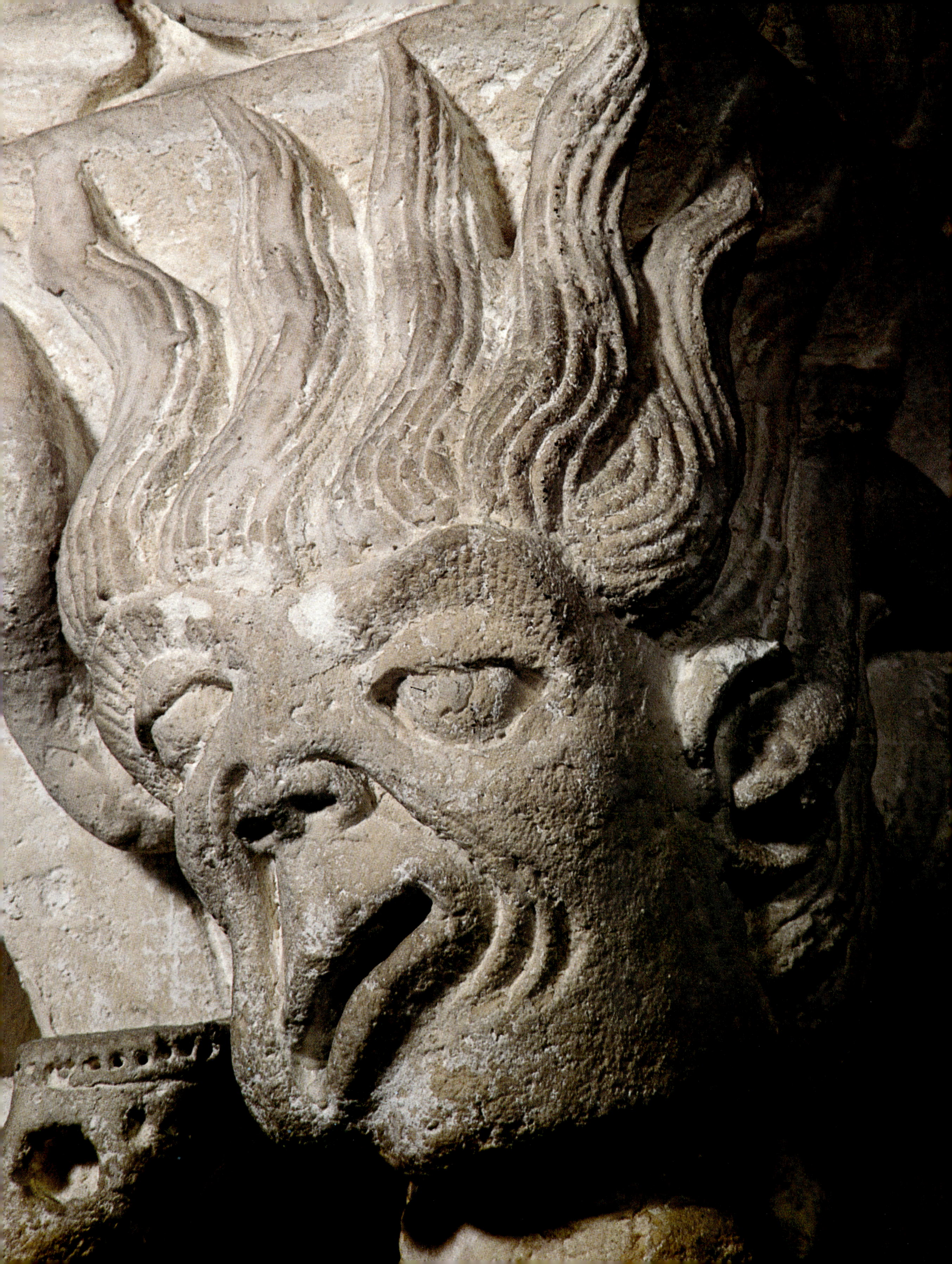

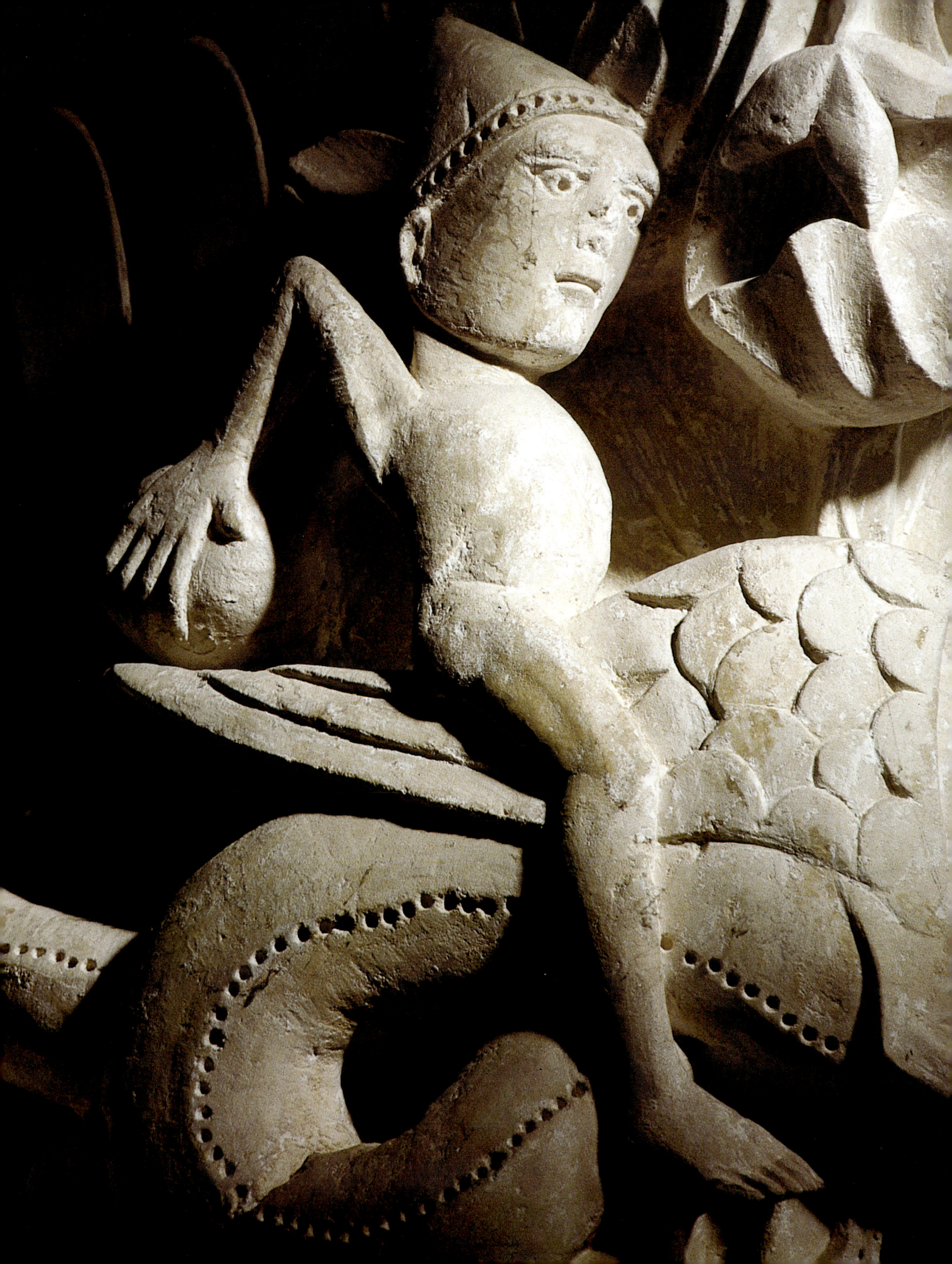

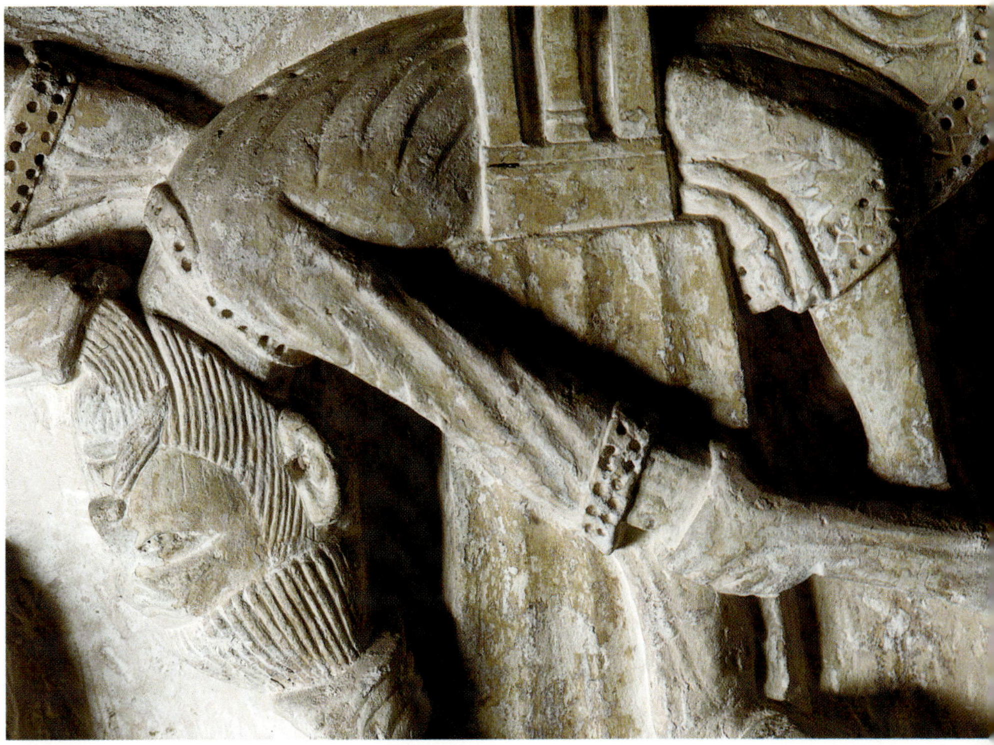

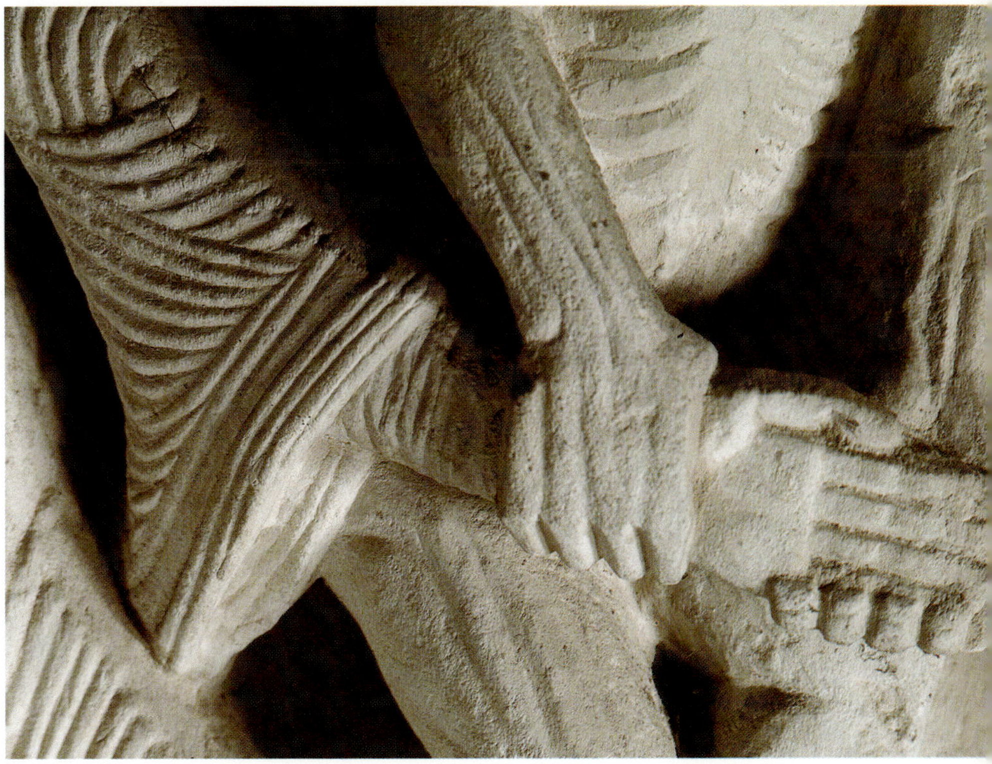

LEFT: A BATTLE OF MYTHICAL BEASTS

UPPER RIGHT: THE VISION OF ST. ANTHONY

RIGHT: THE TEMPTATION OF ST. BENEDICT

SECOND OVERLEAF: THE LIBERATION OF ST. PETER

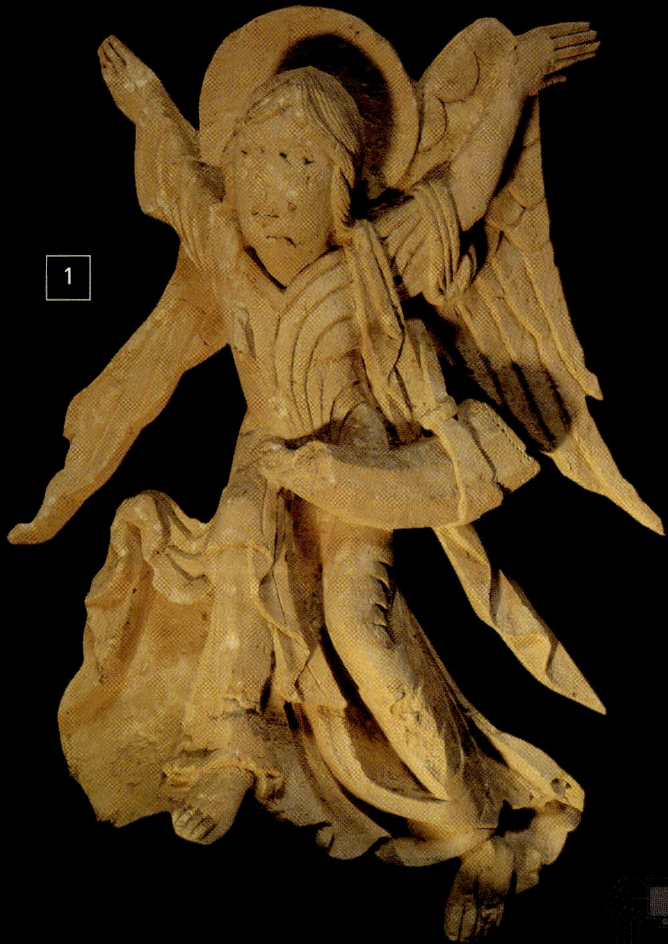

1

DIVINE FORCE

It is easier to depict beings seized by demonic forces in sculpture than those possessed by divine ones. The Vézelay artists seem always to have tempered their lively imaginations with a certain decorous restraint, invariably depicting the force of the divine with symbolic actors, such as David or Daniel. These two, who are brought together at the fifth and sixth south bays of the nave, are both shown as victorious over lions. The young David, still a shepherd, has jumped on the animal's back and is breaking his jaw (opposite). His cloak, as if echoing the energy of the struggle, billows in the wind, rising from his back like a corolla. The depiction of Daniel in the lions' den, however, shows the prophet wrapped in his cloak and circled within a mandorla (below, left), his hand on his chest, in prayer. Here the

The Arm of God

1

THE ANGEL OF THE LAST JUDGMENT

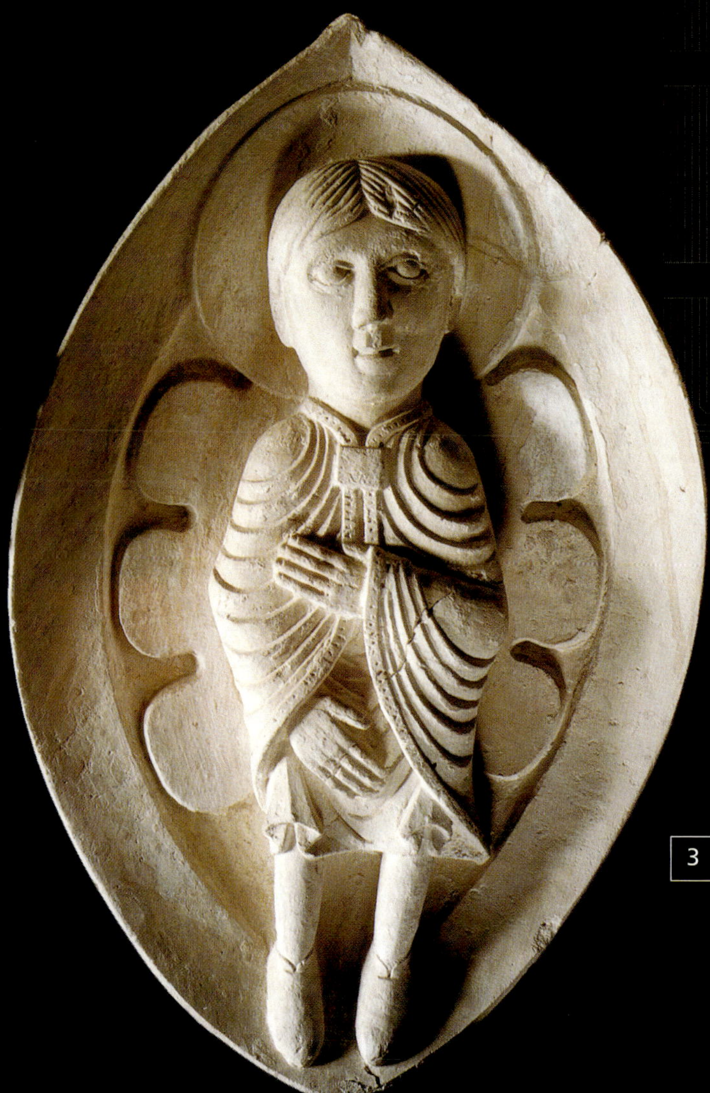

3

wild cats, whose heads are shown pressing forward from behind dense foliage (p. 114), are stopped in their tracks. Passionate faith and serenity, when they emanate from God, can dominate the forces of wild nature.

Angels, the messengers of God, are to be found on several capitals. In the narthex, on one of the piers of the south tympanum, an angel lifts his arms behind him in an elegant gesture that mirrors the shape of his wings (above, no. 1). The ivory horn he carries suspended from his shoulder underscores the meaning of this movement, the duty of the angelic host to summon humanity to the Last Judgment. Floating in his light clothing, which swirls about him, he flies far from the mortal world. But elsewhere, for example in the scenes of the liberation of St. Peter from prison and Jacob wrestling with his angelic adversary, men and angels come into vigorous contact. The tenth, and last, capital on the north side of the church shows the miraculous deliverance of Peter, shown here with shaved head of a monk (below, and overleaf). According to the biblical account (Acts 12:6–11), the apostle thought that he was dreaming. Extending his right hand in front of him, he gropes, while his angelic guide firmly grasps his left wrist. On the adjoining side of the capital, soldiers fall into a deep sleep as the apostle makes his escape. Depicted on the south column of the seventh pier of the nave is Jacob, seizing his angelic adversary by the tunic. This somewhat alarming story, which appears in Genesis 32:24–30, has long been

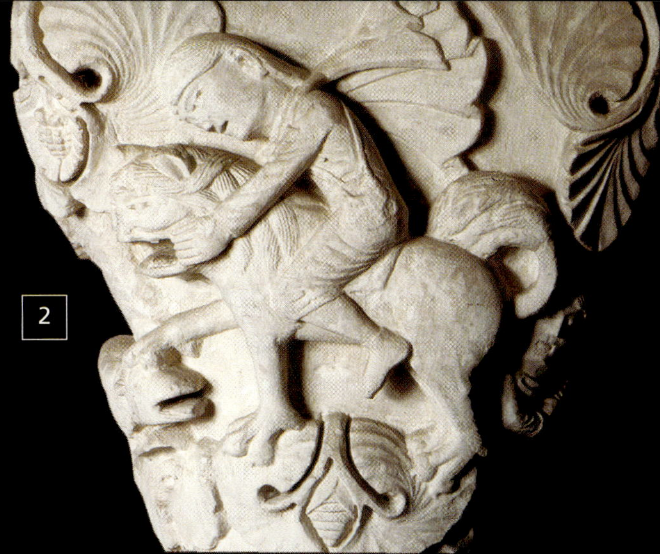

2

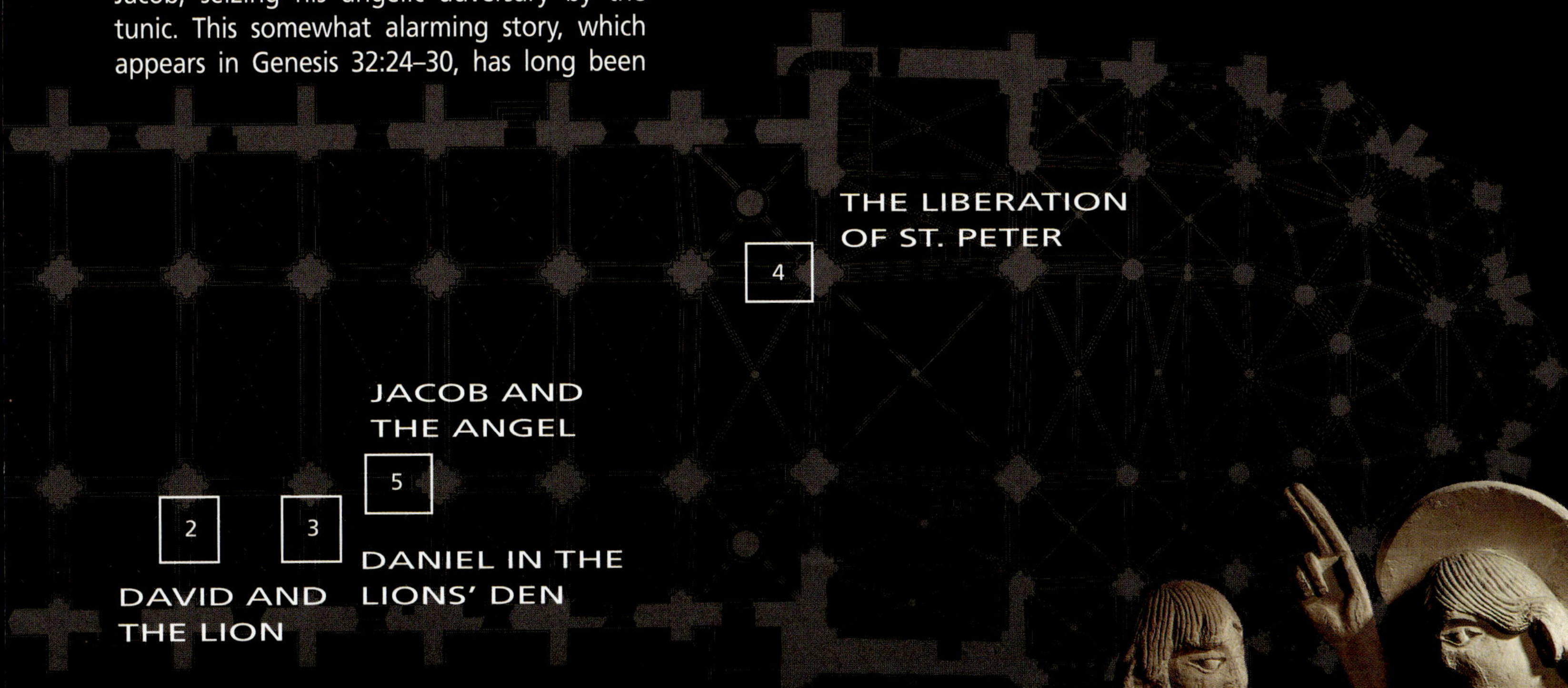

the subject of theological debate. According to the account, Jacob wrestled for an entire night with an unknown "man"—usually interpreted by commentators as an angel, and sometimes as God himself. At the break of day, Jacob is blessed by his unknown adversary, who then takes his leave. The moment shown here is the end of the story, when the angel, with Jacob still clutching his cloak, gives Jacob his blessing, with a grand and serene gesture.

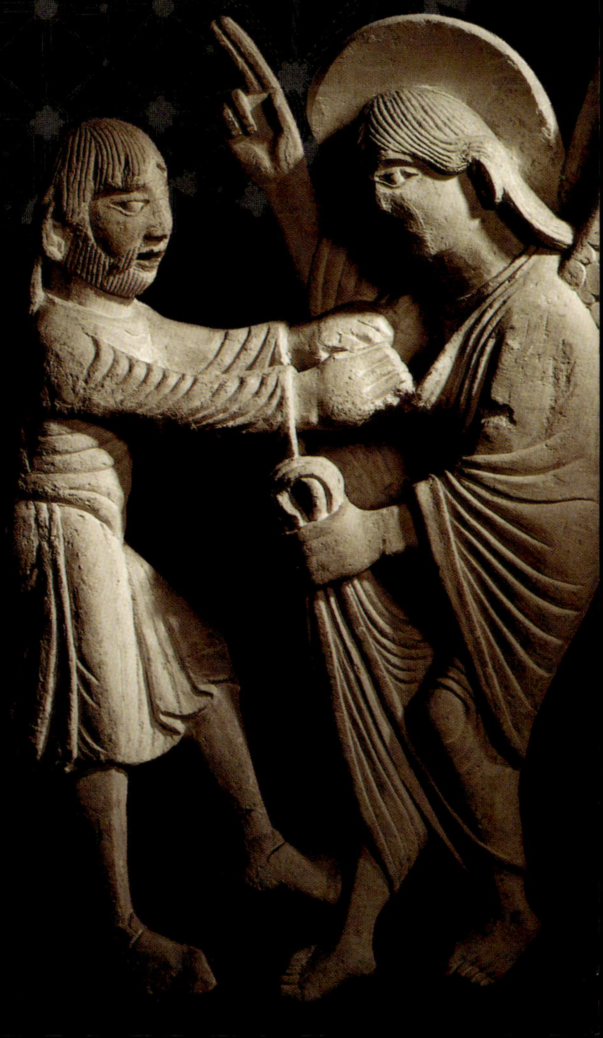

5

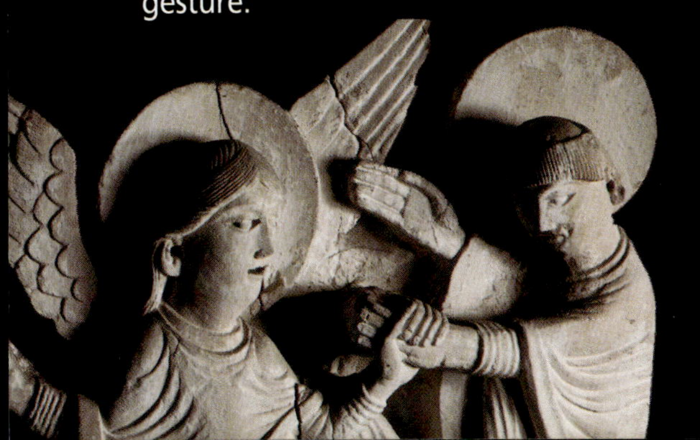

4

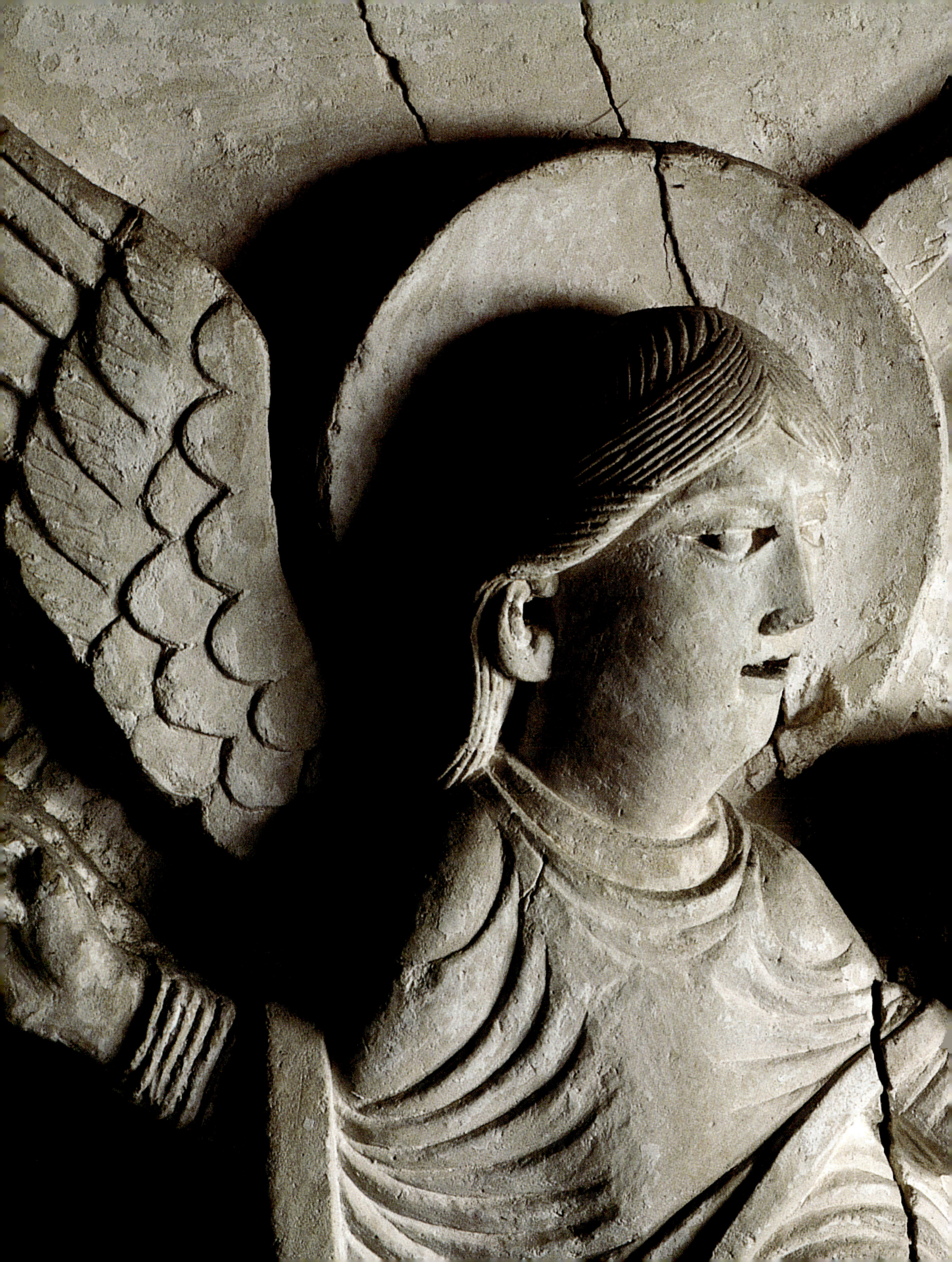

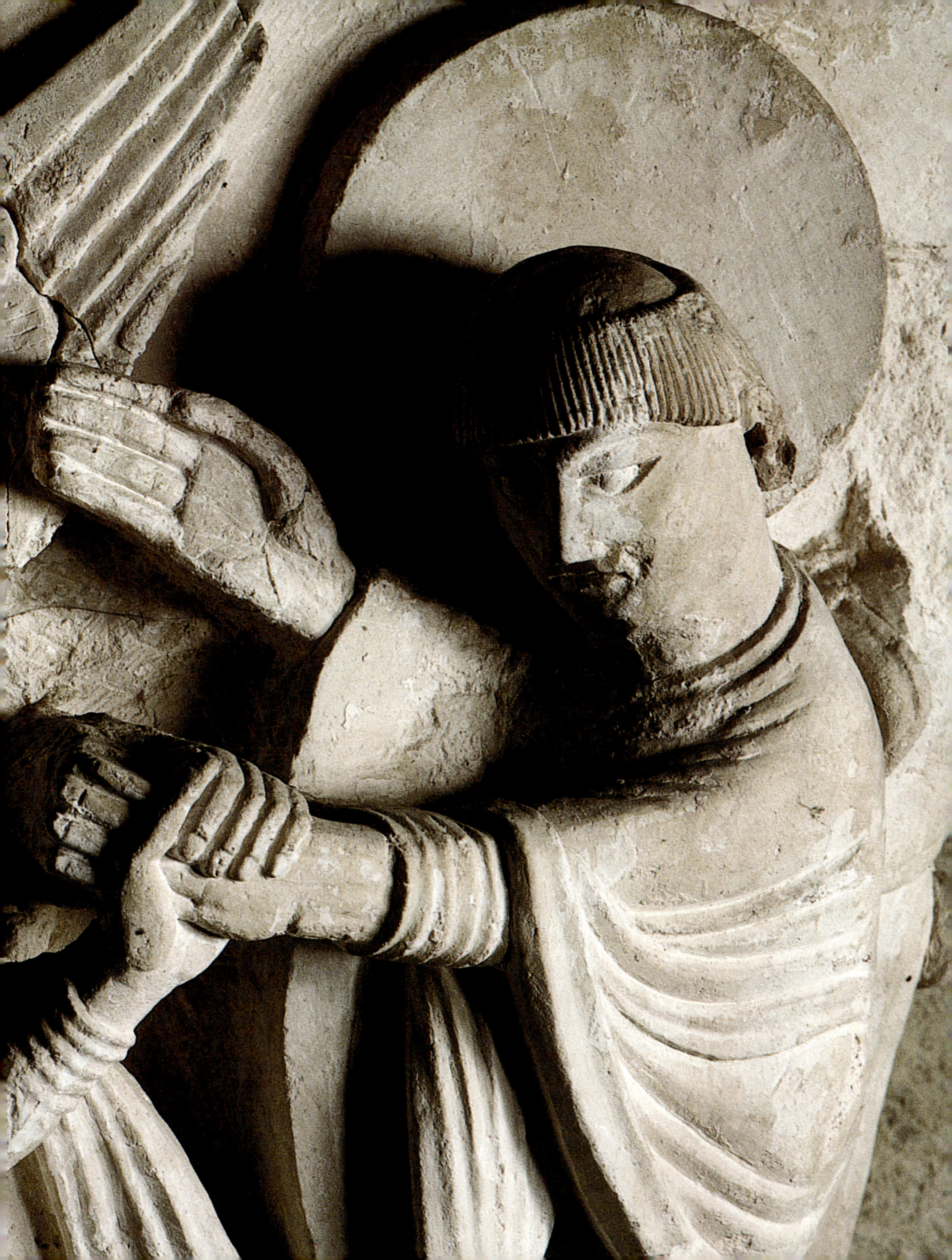

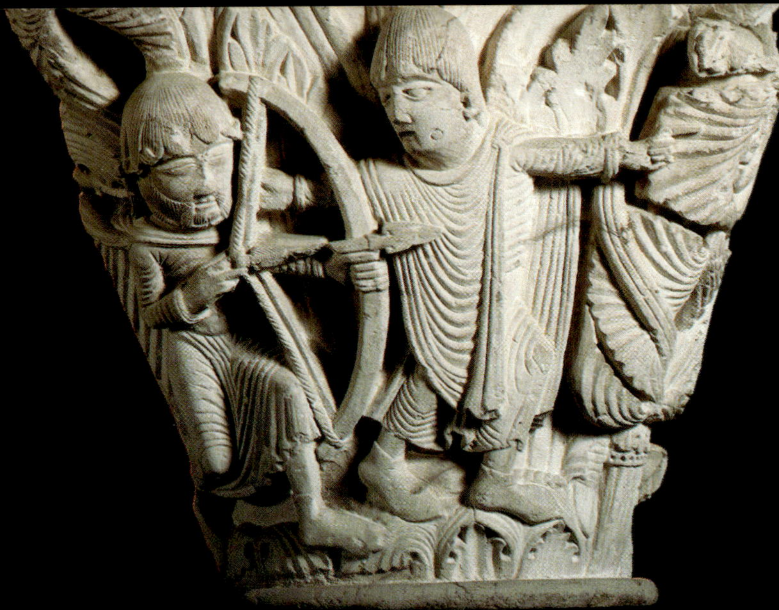

1

"THE WAYS OF GOD ARE INSCRUTABLE"

The justice of God and humanity are sometimes in accord, but often they are not. The justice of God is at times difficult to understand. The just, like all people, may succumb to sin, and evil may arise even from something that seems fundamentally good. Perhaps this perplexing matter is the subject of the capital of the fourth column of the south wall, where a group of men are gathered, as if in counsel (lower left, no. 3; pp. 132–33). The two capitals dedicated to the death of Cain, one in the nave and one in the narthex, serve to illustrate the occasional ambivalence of good and evil. According to the Bible, after Cain murdered his brother Abel, God cursed Cain. But God also forbade anyone to kill him, upon pain of terrible retribution (Genesis 4:11–15). Here the biblical account is unclear, but according

Human Justice,

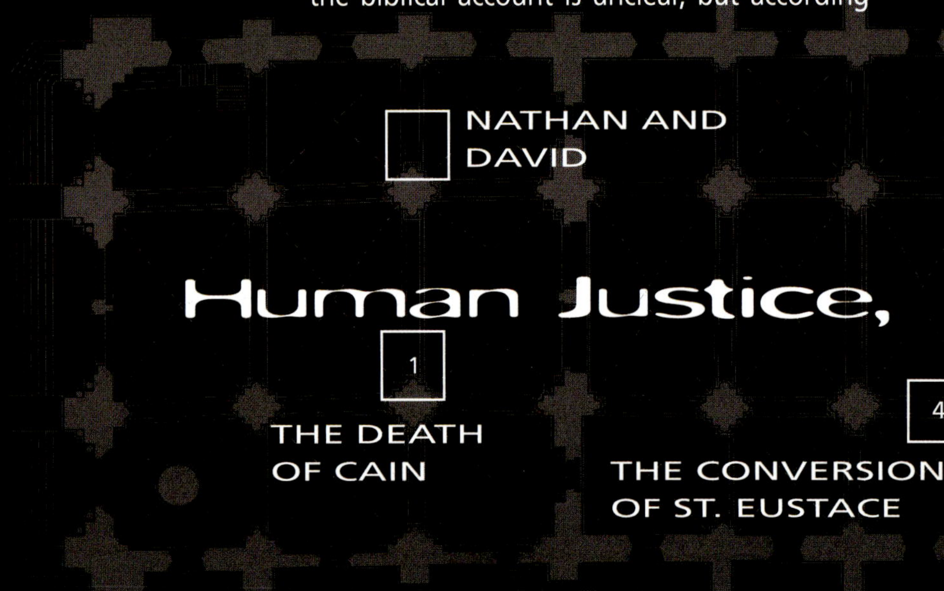

to legend, it was finally Lamech, Cain's own descendant, who brought about his death. Here Lamech is shown as a blind man, his thick eyelids barely open in two slits. Guided by his son Tubalcain, on one side of the capital Lamech points his bow at Cain, who, represented with the antlers of a deer, hides behind the foliage on the adjoining side. Thus Cain was killed, hunted like an animal. When justice was finally attained, it was a blind justice, redeeming fratricide with patricide.

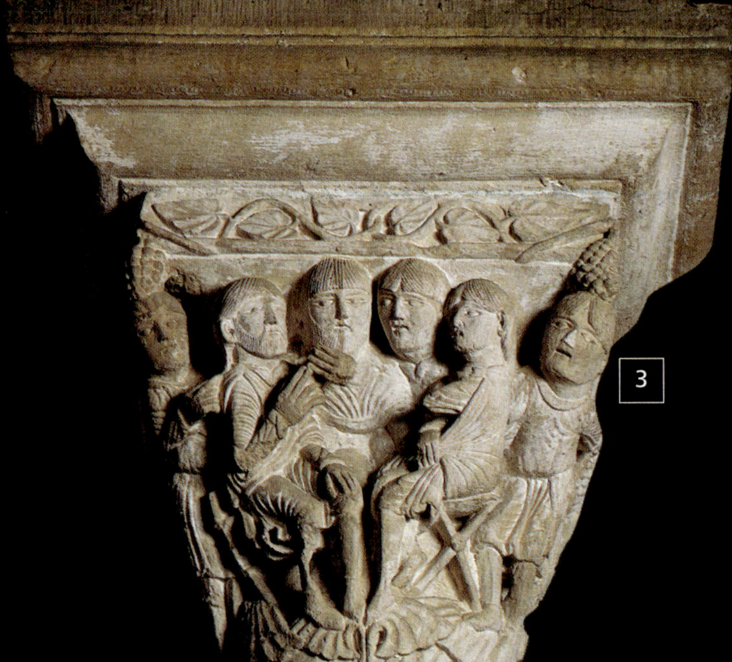

3

David is the just man *par excellence,* who embodies both good and evil. He committed a double offense: adultery with Bathsheba, who became pregnant, and the murder of her husband Uriah, whom he intentionally sent into the front lines of battle. A capital in the narthex recounts this story. On the left face of the capital, the prophet Nathan arrives at

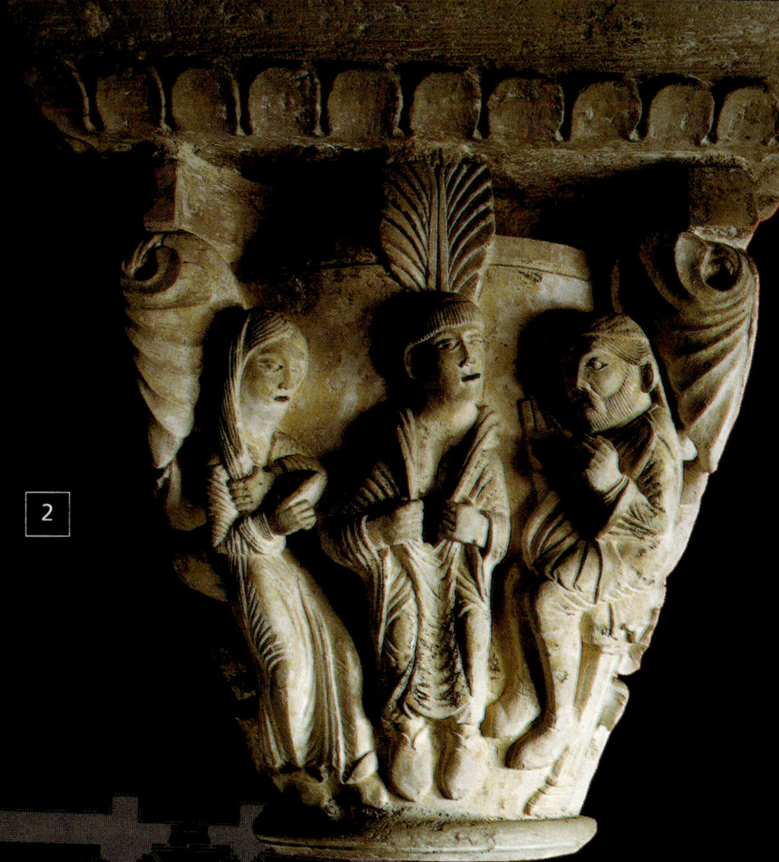

2

the home of the king. Feigning to be judging another man, he reveals to David the crimes that he, David, has actually committed (II Samuel, 12). In the face of these misdeeds that he wants to punish, David loses his temper. But as the prophet reveals, it is he, David, who is guilty of the crimes. The king openly repents, while Bathsheba, on the right face of the capital, makes a fearful gesture. The punishment of God looms over them; Bathsheba's first child will die. But their next child will be Solomon, beloved by God.

The legend of St. Eugenia, shown on the south side of the seventh bay, also evokes the mysteries of justice. A monk, with his head tonsured, is shown tearing his cloak down to the waist. This is St. Eugenia, who had disguised herself as a man so that she could enter

2 THE ABBOT EUGENIA

Divine Justice

THE DEATH OF CAIN

3 MEN IN COUNSEL

a monastery with her two brothers. In anger, a rejected woman, a lady who had been infatuated by the false monk, feigns a rape. Her hair still falling loose, the woman comes before a judge to accuse the monk. Eugenia is thus forced to reveal her breasts in order to exonerate herself. The seated judge, clearly astounded, is none other than the prefect of Alexandria, Eugenia's own father, who earlier had opposed her conversion to the faith. The final reversal comes when the father himself converts to Christianity and suffers martyrdom. Thus, evil can be transformed into good in an instant. Indeed, an instant was all that was needed for the Roman general Placidius to be converted. While out hunting, Placidius saw a vision of Christ between the antlers of a stag that he was about to kill. Converted on the spot, he took the name of Eustace.

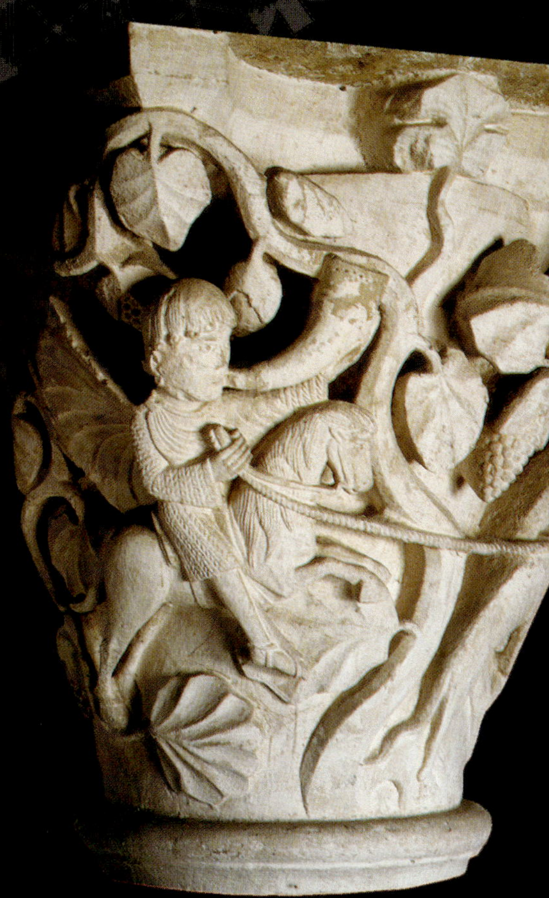

4

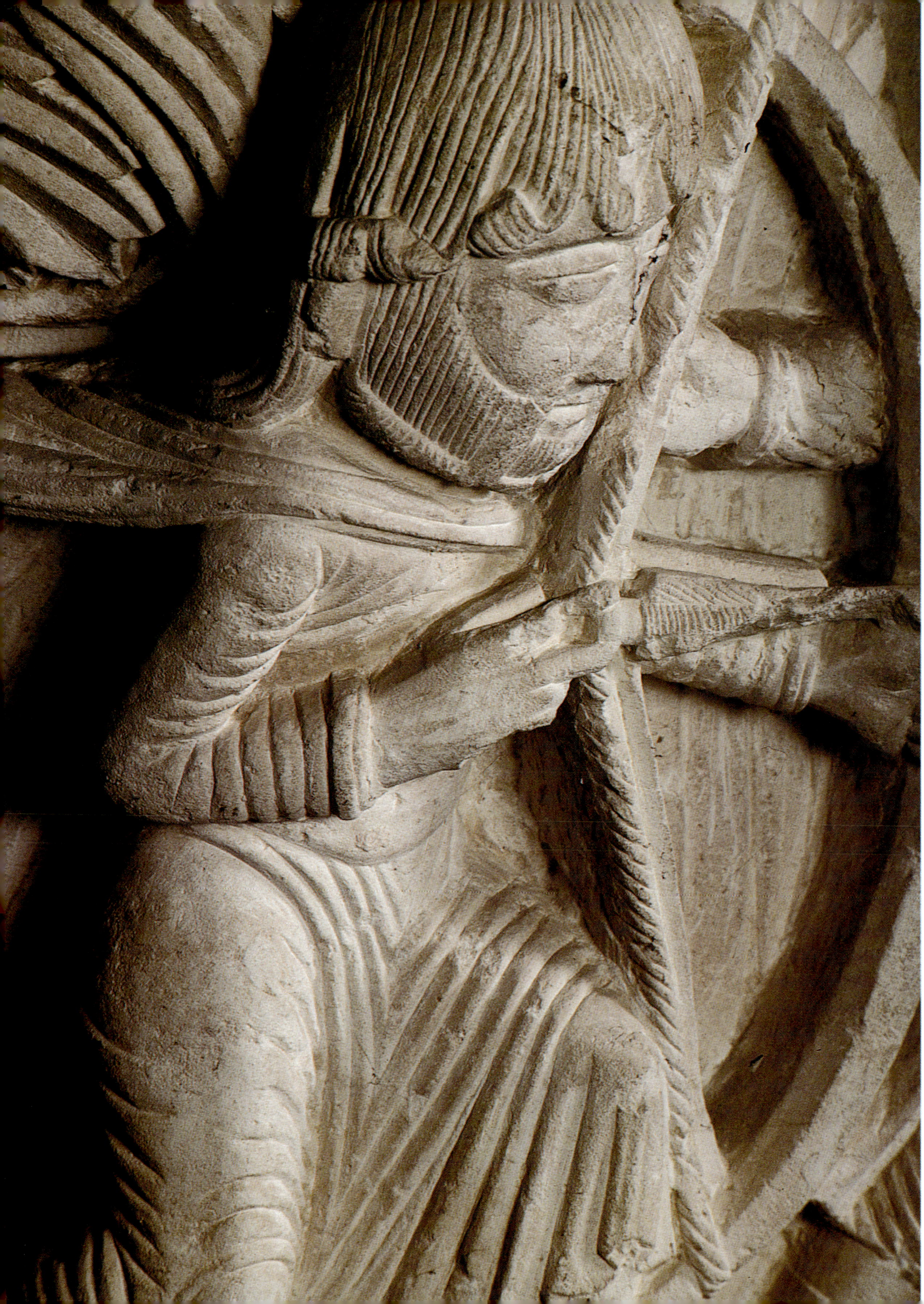

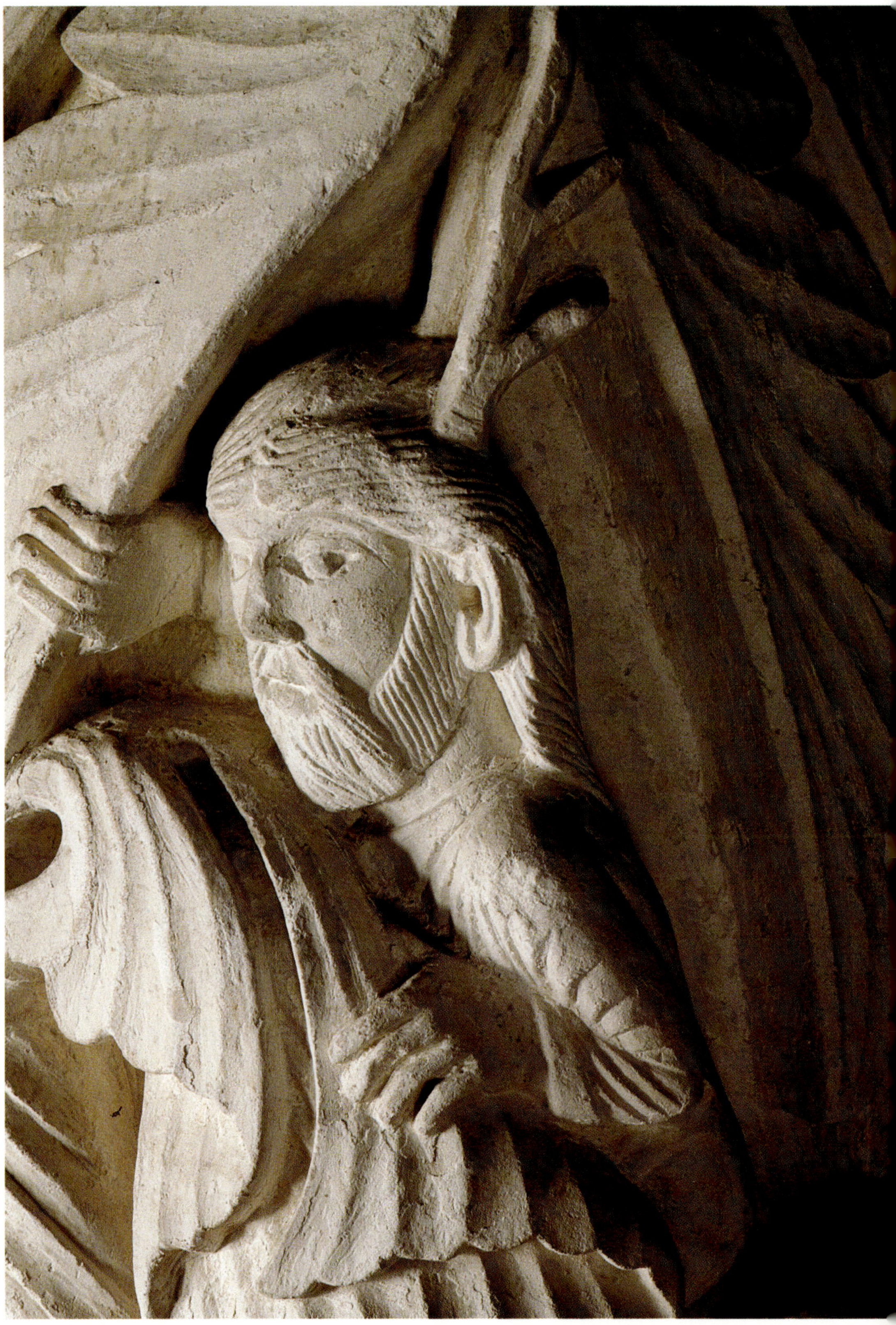

LAMECH (LEFT), THE BLIND ARCHER,
SHOOTS HIS ARROW AT CAIN (RIGHT)

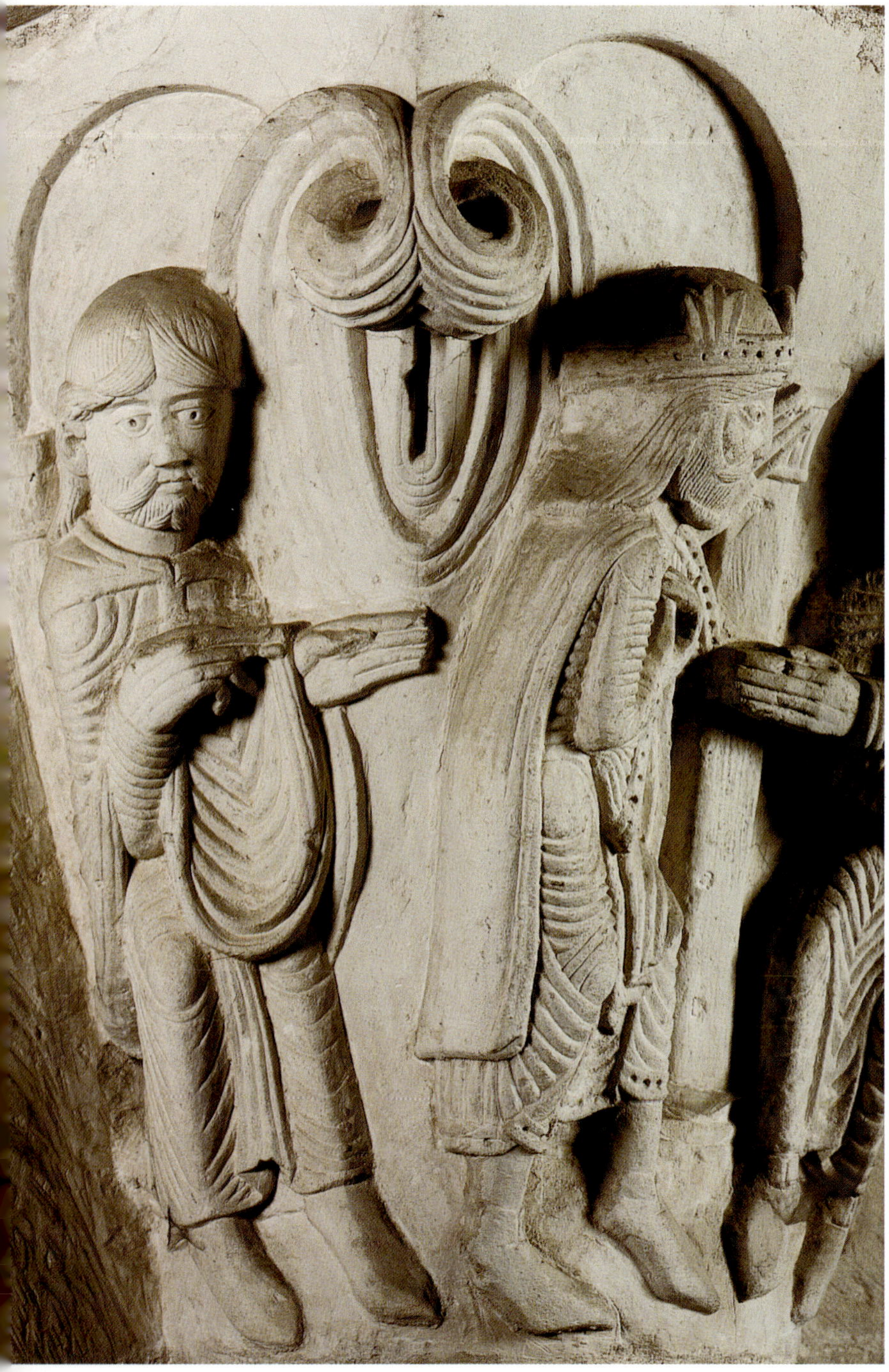

LEFT: NATHAN REBUKES DAVID

RIGHT: THE CONVERSION
OF ST. EUSTACE

OVERLEAF: A COUNSEL

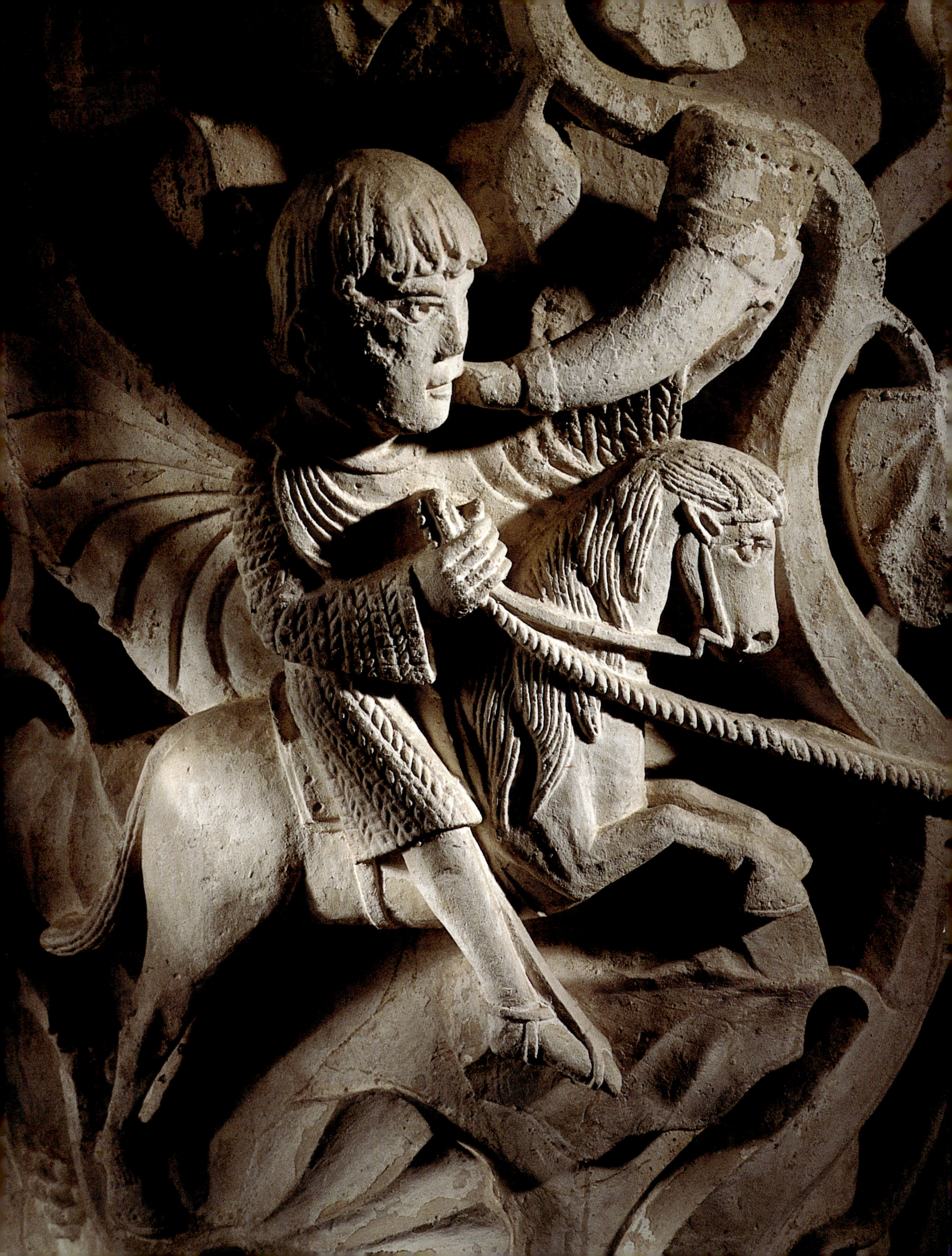

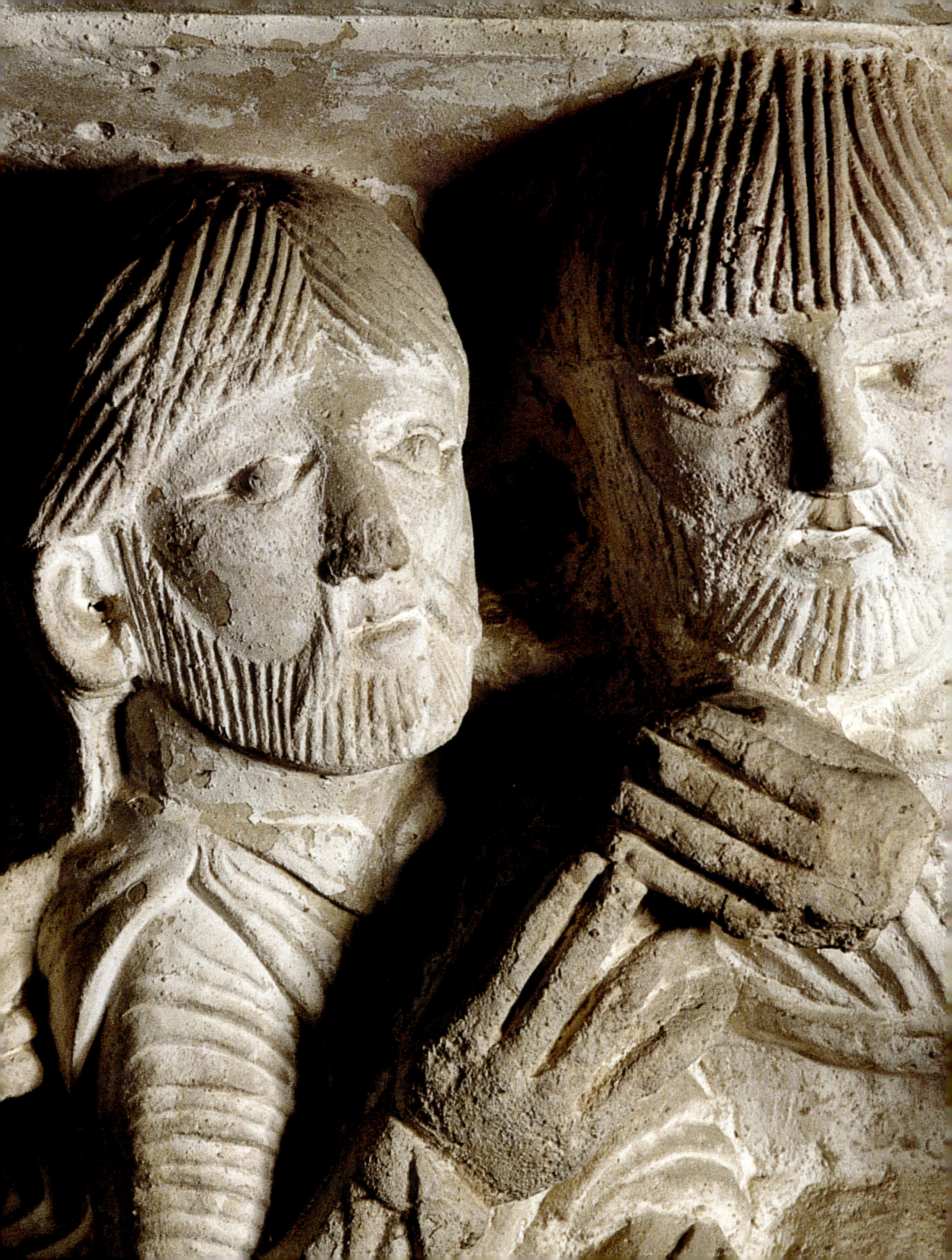

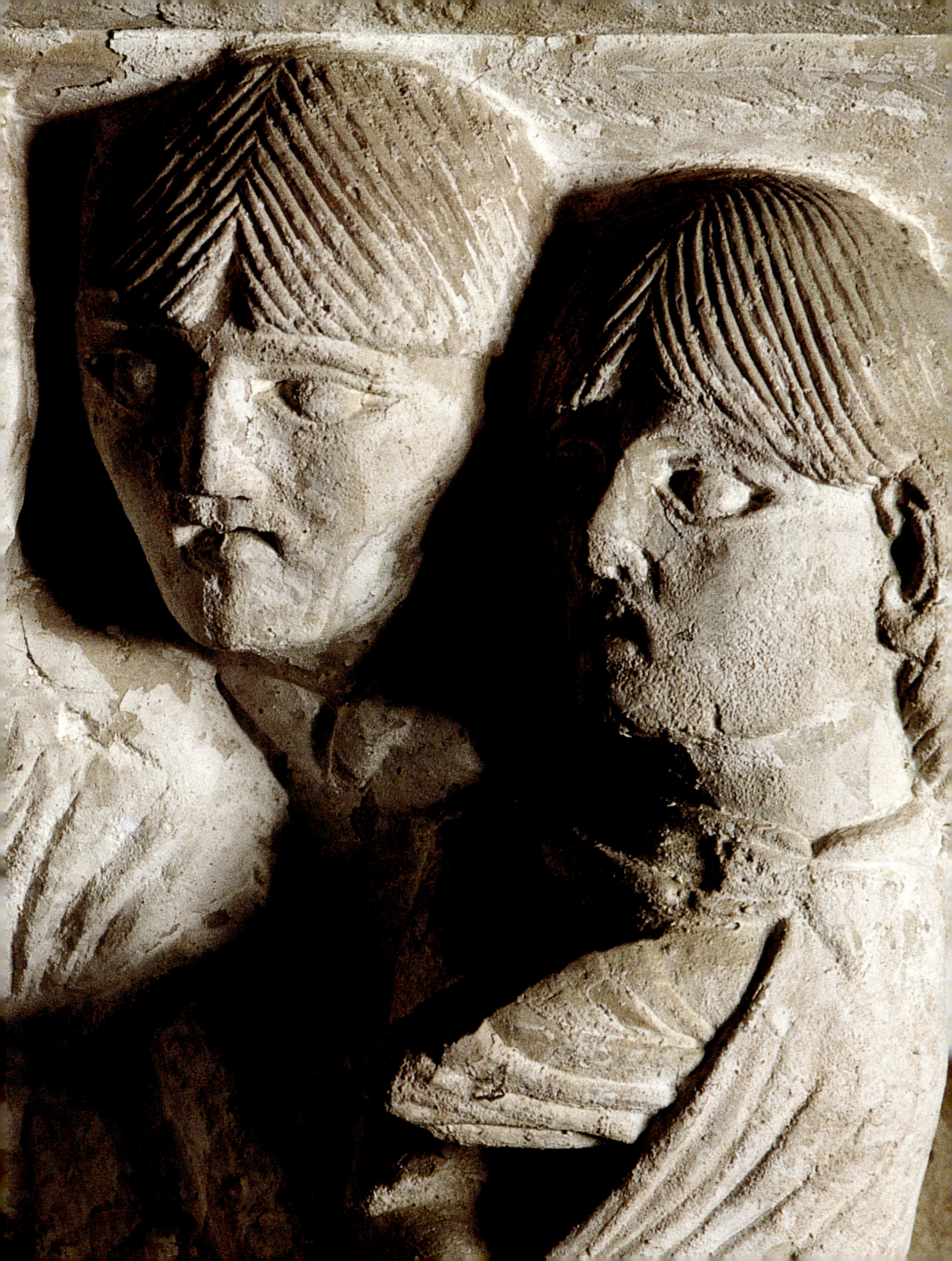

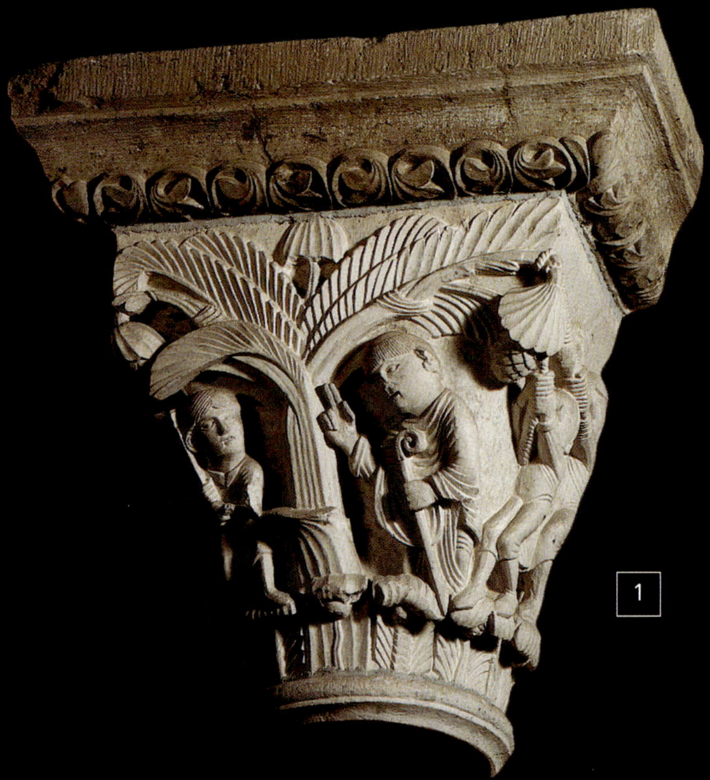

1

THE TRUE GOD AND THE FALSE GODS

According to the Old Testament, the worst sin in all of Israel was idolatry, which embodied the two sins of infidelity and pride. The story of the Golden Calf, which is shown on the sixth pier of the north aisle of the church, illustrates the sin of idolatry better than any other. Moses, on the left, has just come down from Mount Sinai to find his people worshiping a golden calf. He carries the two Tablets of the Law, which he will soon destroy in anger (Exodus, 32). Confronting Moses at the same height as the divine tablets, and in sharp contrast to them, is a griffinlike devil with spiky hair. He springs from the mouth of the golden calf and mocks Moses with a contemptuous gesture. With an arrogant grimace that etches deep wrinkles around the corners of his mouth,

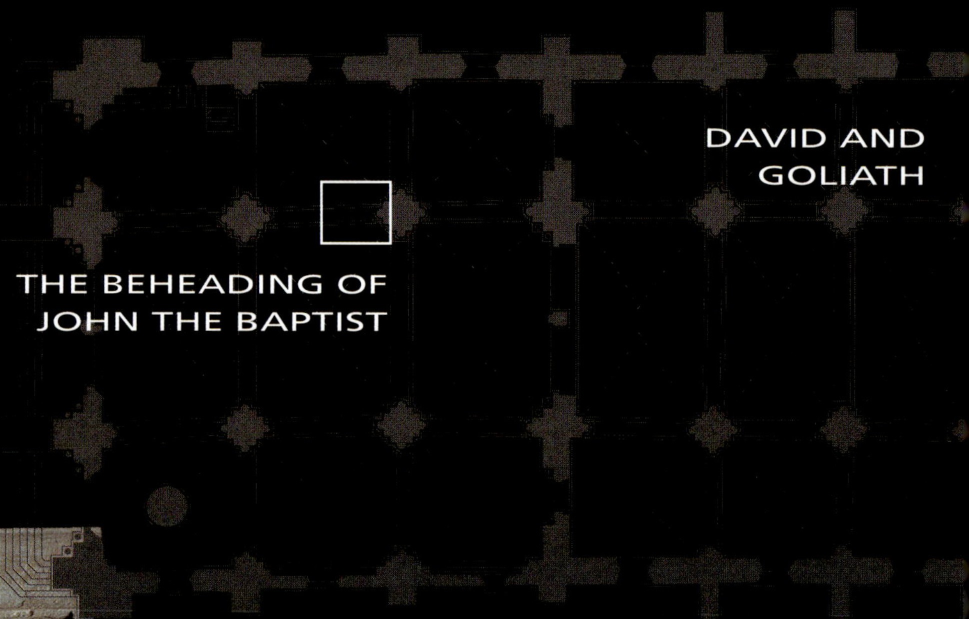

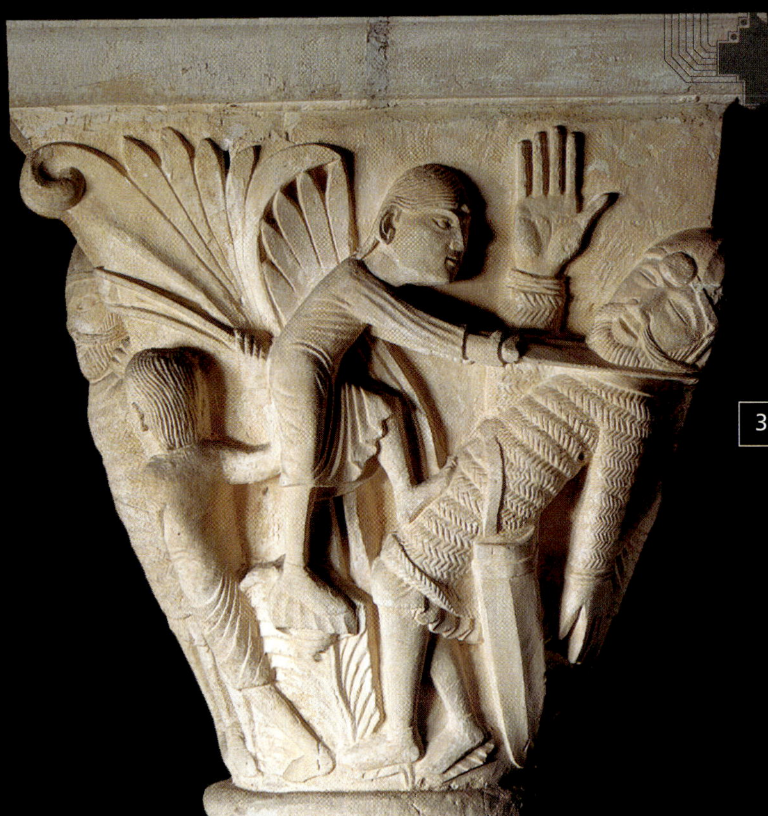

3

he and the gaping-mouthed idol seem to be twin monstrosities.

Religious sacrilege is the theme of other capitals, as well. The giant Goliath, the champion of the Philistines, not only defeated the army of the Israelites, but the Israelites' God. On the left face of the capital, which is modern, the giant awaits David, armed only with his slingshot. On the center face, Goliath, who has been struck on the forehead by a stone, falls backward. The small figure of David is shown climbing a tree, leaning over the giant's body, and pulling his sword from its sheath to cut off his head (I Samuel, 17).

The story of the execution of the murderer of King Saul, depicted at the seventh bay of the north side of the nave, presents a second example. King David has ordered the death of an Amalekite, an idolater, as punishment for the murder of his predecessor, Saul. This was considered a crime of sacrilege, as Saul had been anointed king by God. Leaning forward, with his two hands the condemned man grips the tunic of his executioner, who raises his sword to strike. A similar scheme is used in the depiction of the beheading of John the Baptist found in the narthex, in which the executioner, armed with a thin cutlass, seizes the saint by the hair. Here, the condemned man is the martyr and the judge ungodly. Like the Amalekite, the Baptist takes hold of his executioner's cloak, creating a pocket that will shortly receive his decapitated head (p. 140).

Paganism, another form of idolatry, was brought down under the onslaught of early

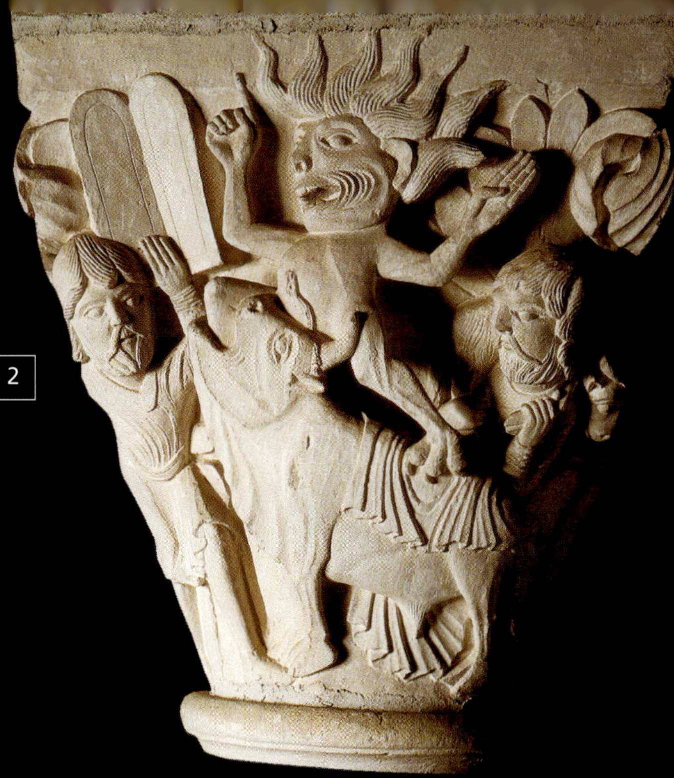

2

Idolatries

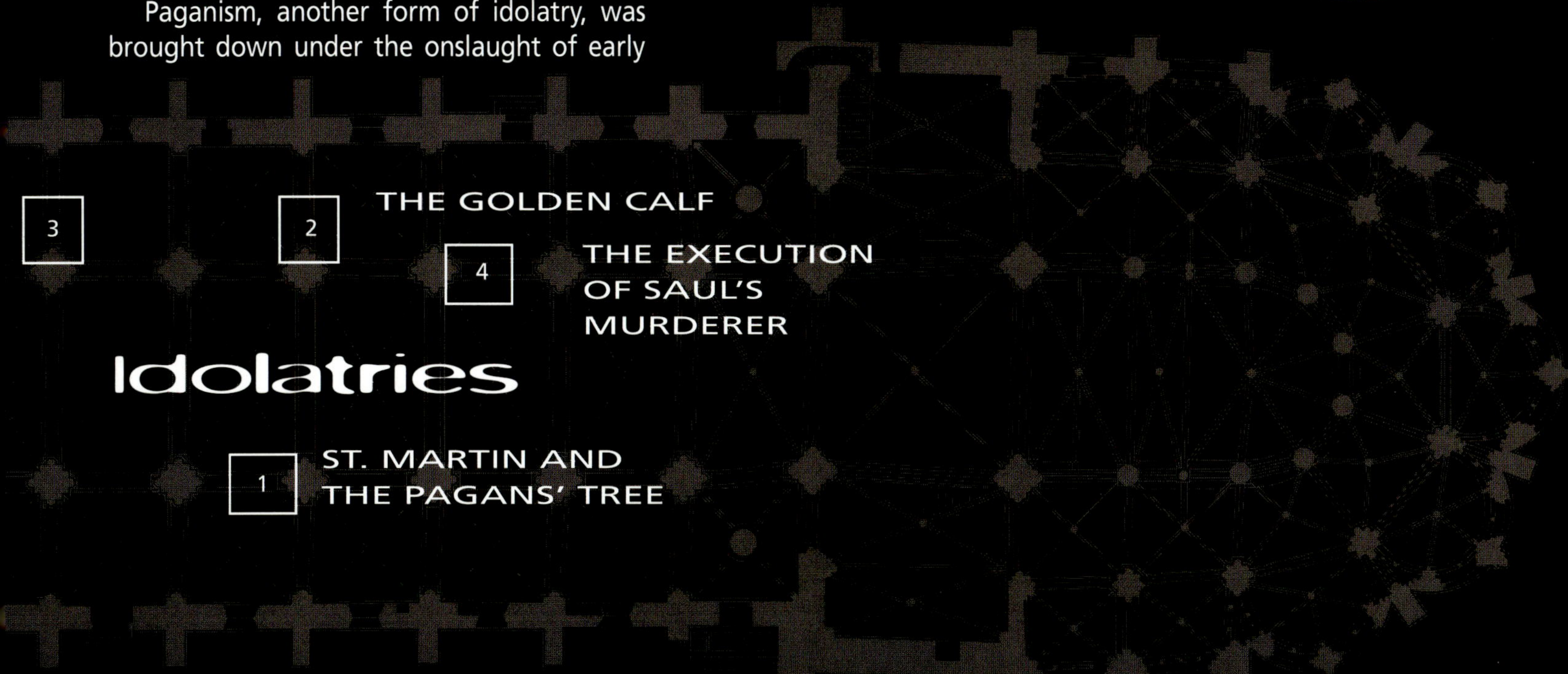

Christianity. On the sixth pier on the south side of the nave, St. Martin, who is depicted as an abbot in a clerical vestment, his head tonsured and carrying a crosier, decides to chop down a tree thought by the pagans to be sacred. The artist has depicted the tree as an elegant palm from an exotic country, with heavy leaves fanned out and laden with blossoms. At St. Martin's order, a woodsman begins to hack at the trunk. On the left, two men bearing offerings are shocked at the scene. On the right side of the capital, other pagans are shown pulling as hard on their ropes as they can, in an effort to make the tree fall on the saint. However, the palm tree will actually fall in the opposite direction, conquering pagan superstition and allowing the true faith to triumph.

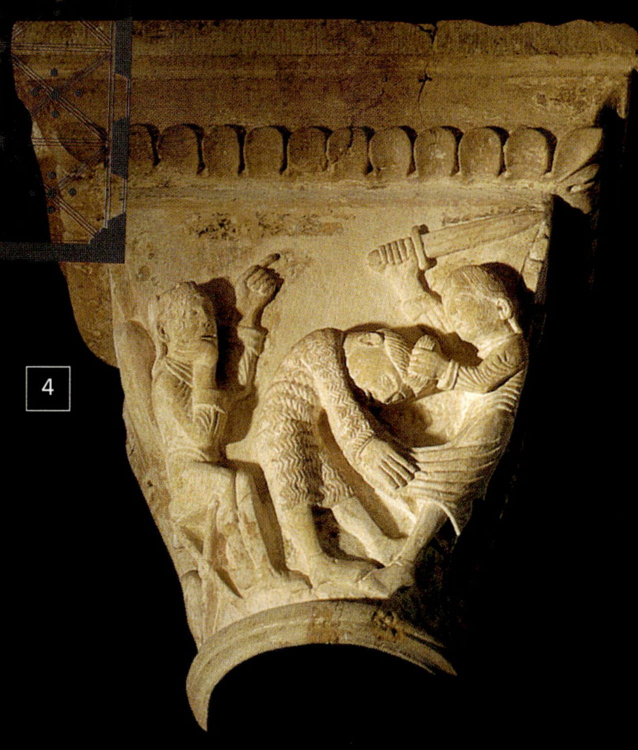

4

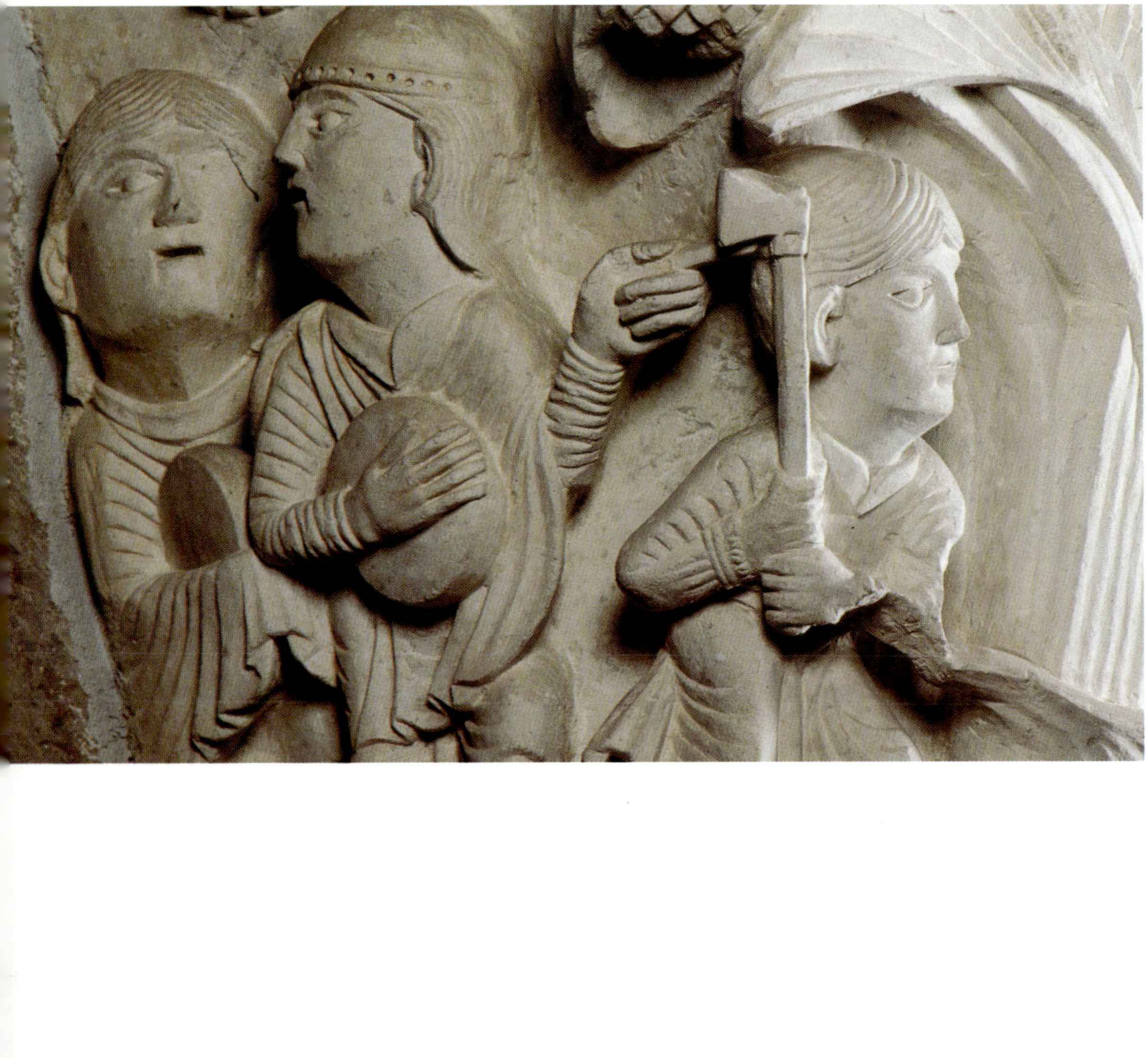

LEFT: ST. MARTIN AND THE PALM TREE: THE WOODSMAN, AND OFFERING-BEARERS

RIGHT: THE CAPITAL OF THE GOLDEN CALF: A COWHERD

OVERLEAF: ST. MARTIN AND THE PALM TREE

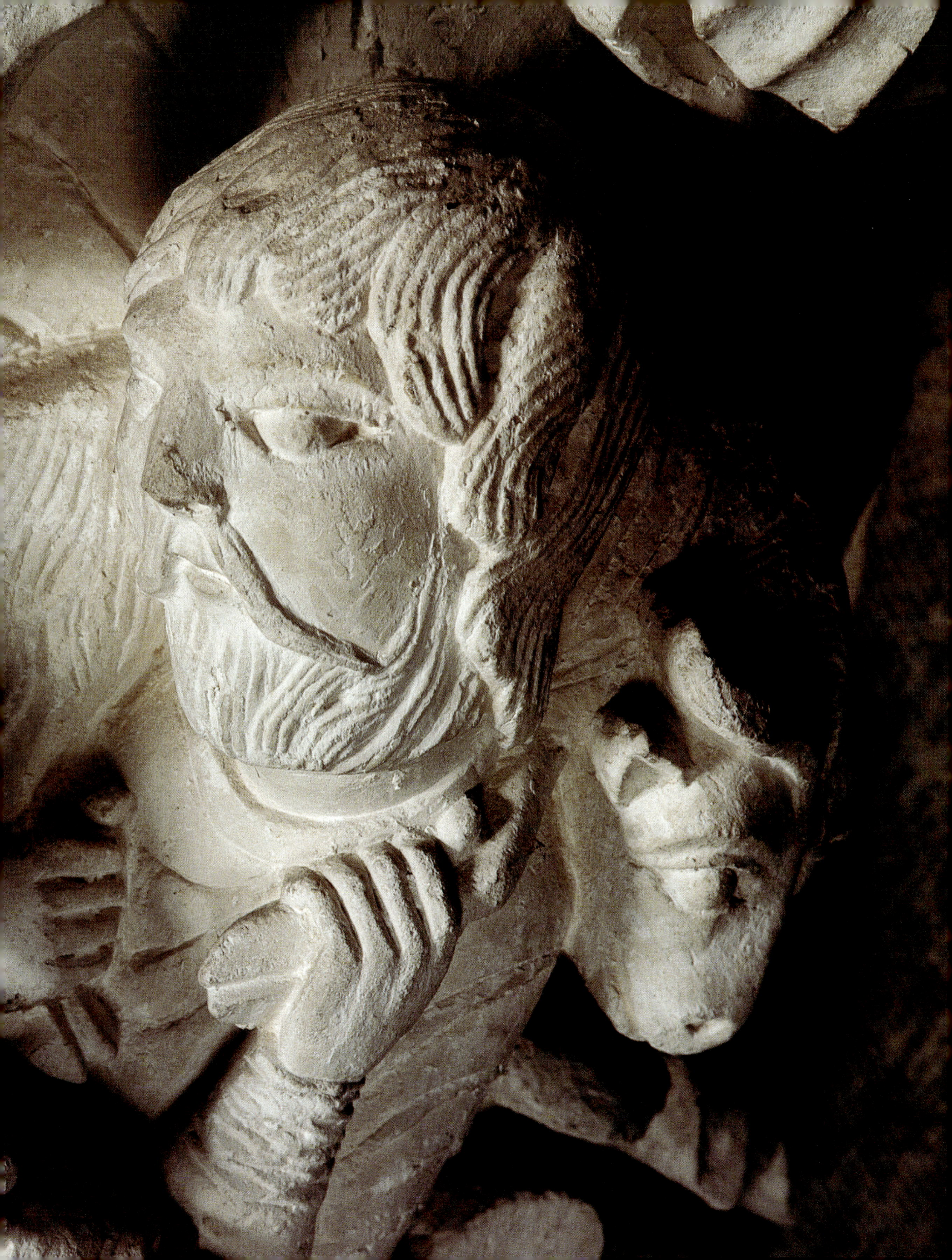

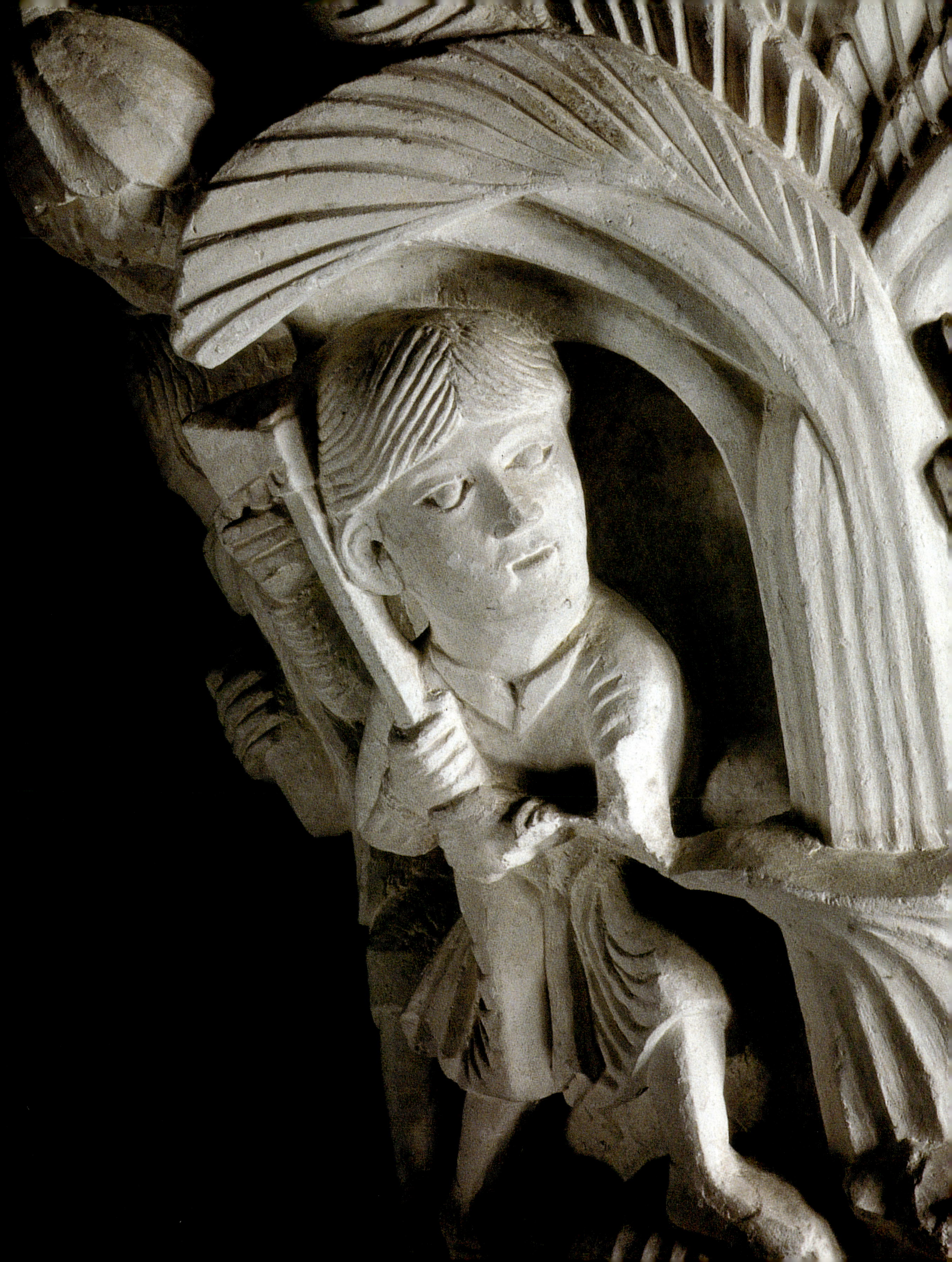

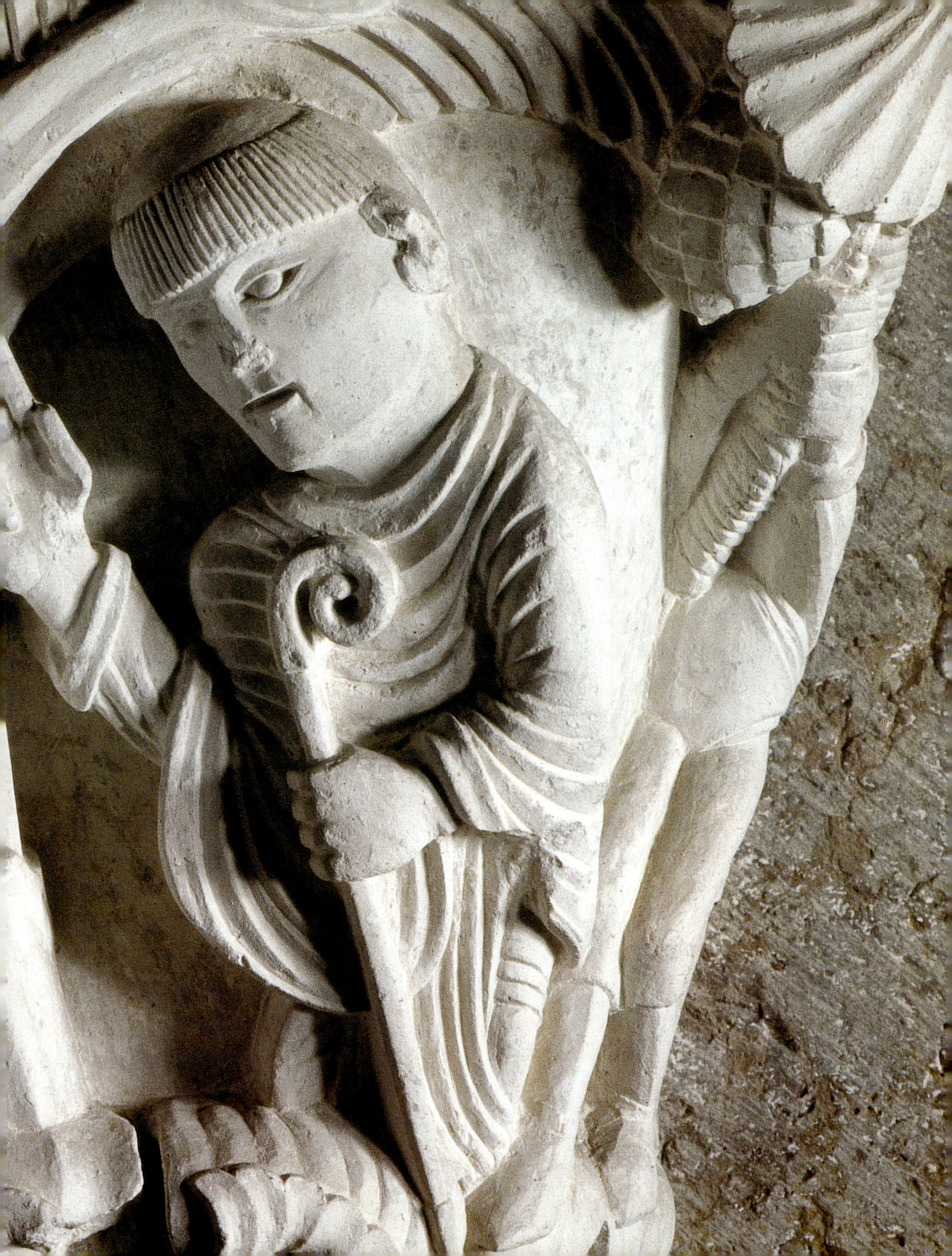

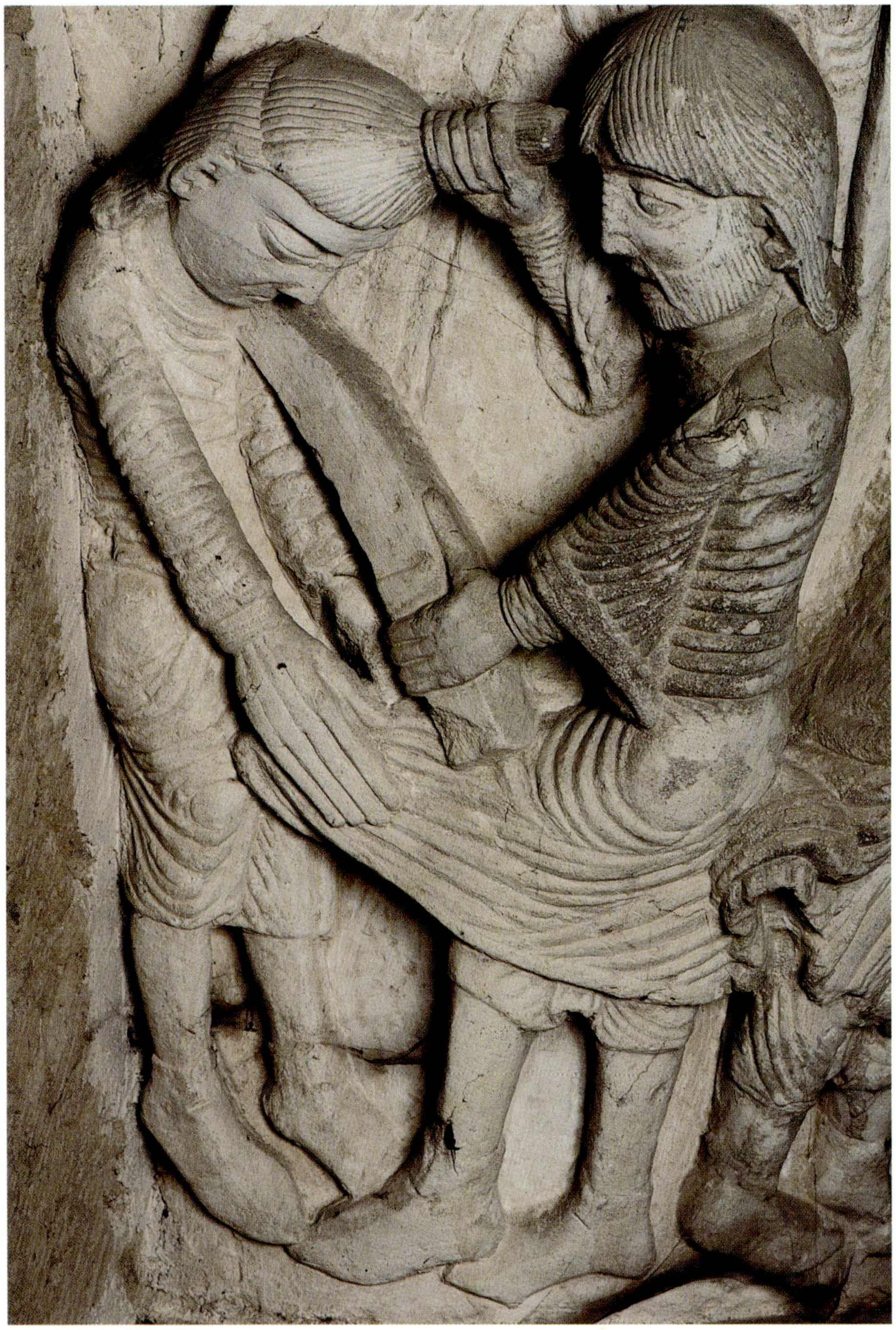

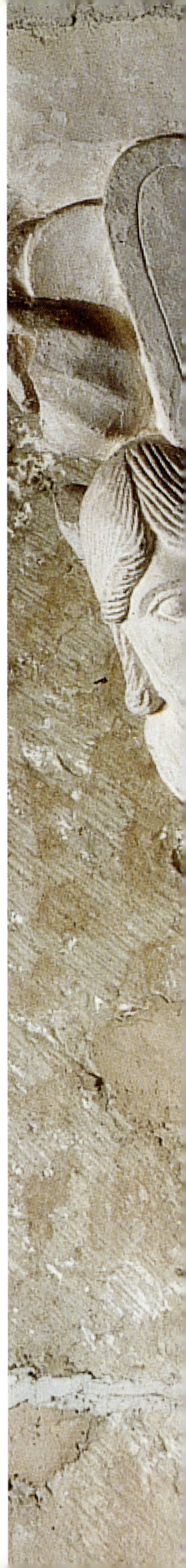

ABOVE: THE BEHEADING
OF JOHN THE BAPTIST

RIGHT: MOSES AND
THE GOLDEN CALF

OVERLEAF: ST. MARTIN AND
THE PALM TREE: PAGANS
PULLING ON THE ROPES

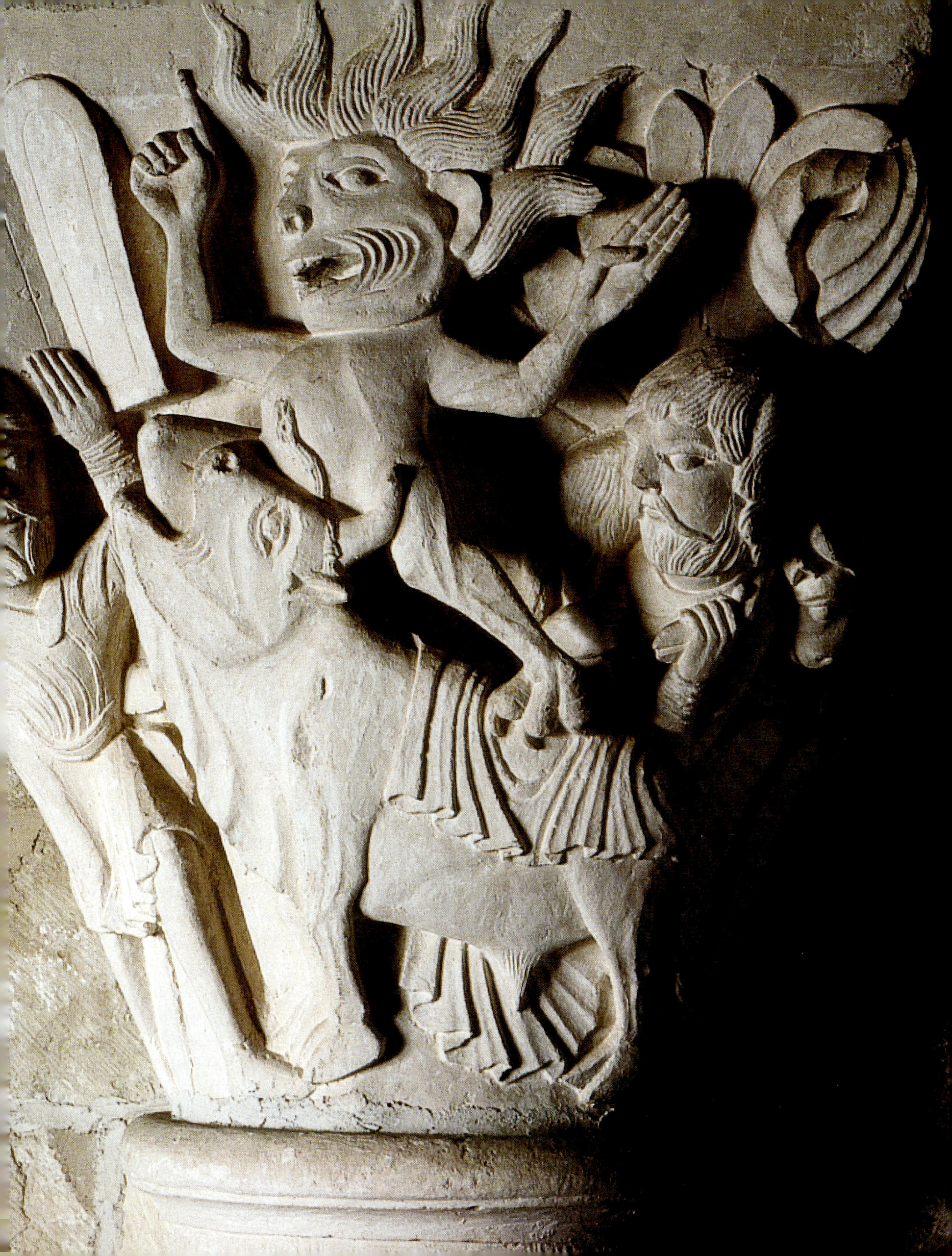

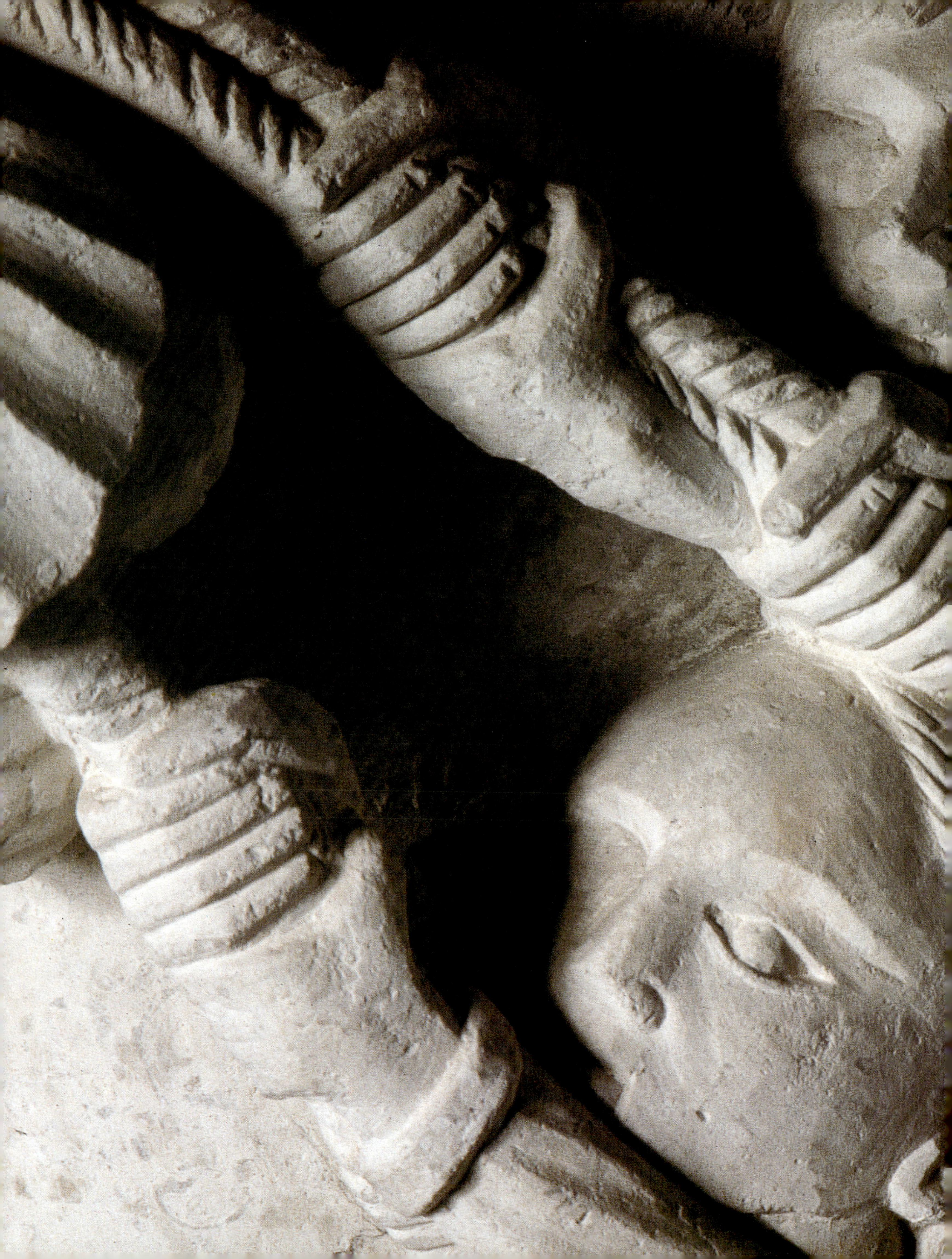

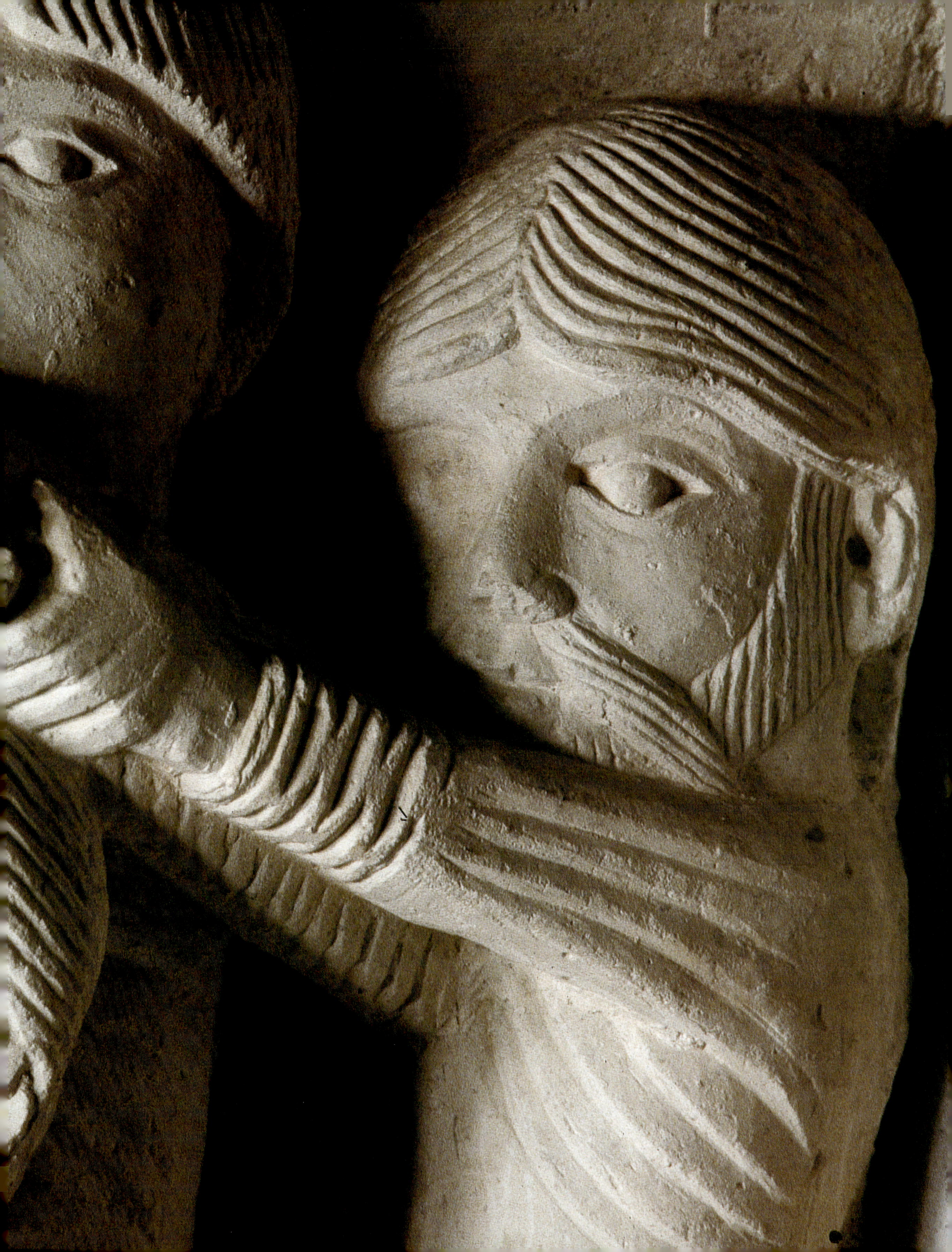

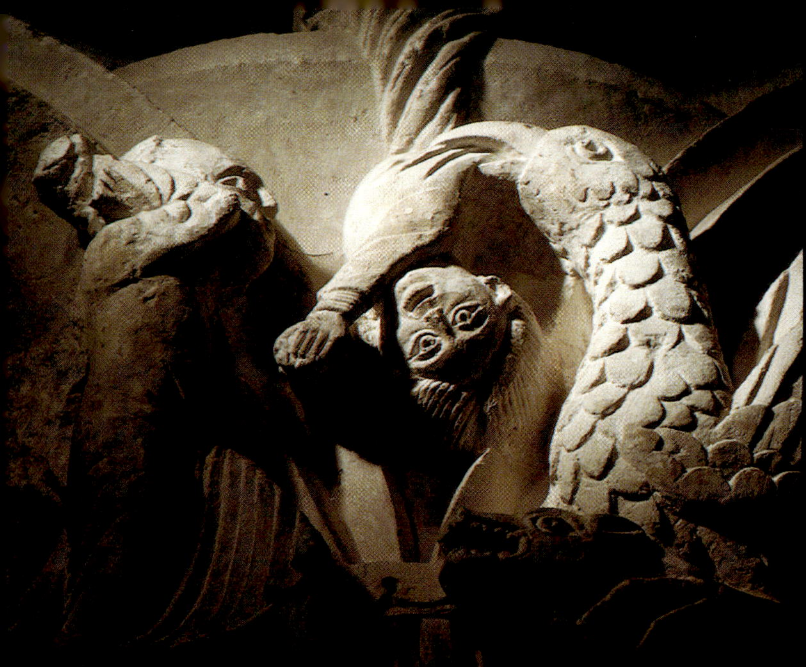

SIN AND REDEMPTION

Although throughout the nave a system of formal and thematic allusions prevails, some capitals seem designed to work together as matched pairs. Two scenes from a single story may interact with one another, like the two faces of a coin. There is a dialogue of this kind between the capital that shows the story of Adam and Eve and the one that shows the figures of the mortal sins of Lust and Despair, although these are found at opposite ends of the nave, on the ninth pier on the north and the second pier on the south. On the Adam and Eve capital, which shows the Garden of Eden, the sin of the first parents has already taken place. Eve covers her nudity with a large, lacy leaf, while with her other hand, she feels the weight of the forbidden fruit that the snake holds out to her with his mouth. Here

1

Heaven

THE ABDUCTION OF GANYMEDE 1

3 LUST AND DESPAIR

the fruit is not the traditional apple, but a bunch of grapes, and the upright around which the snake coils his body is a vine-brace. Adam, his hand on his cheek, seems to recoil from the scene, yet his other hand is already reaching for the fruit. The original sin has been committed. On the other capital, in a completely different style, three figures, including a snake and a naked woman move about in a luxuriant setting of palm trees. The woman, her hair styled in high rolls, pulls at her breast from which she nurses a snake who is climbing up her leg. This is, in fact, a traditional depiction of an allegory of Lust. On the other corner of the capital, a demon with his tongue hanging out, in what appears to be the ultimate defiance of reason, plunges a double-edged sword into his own back. He represents the madness and suicidal guilt of Despair.

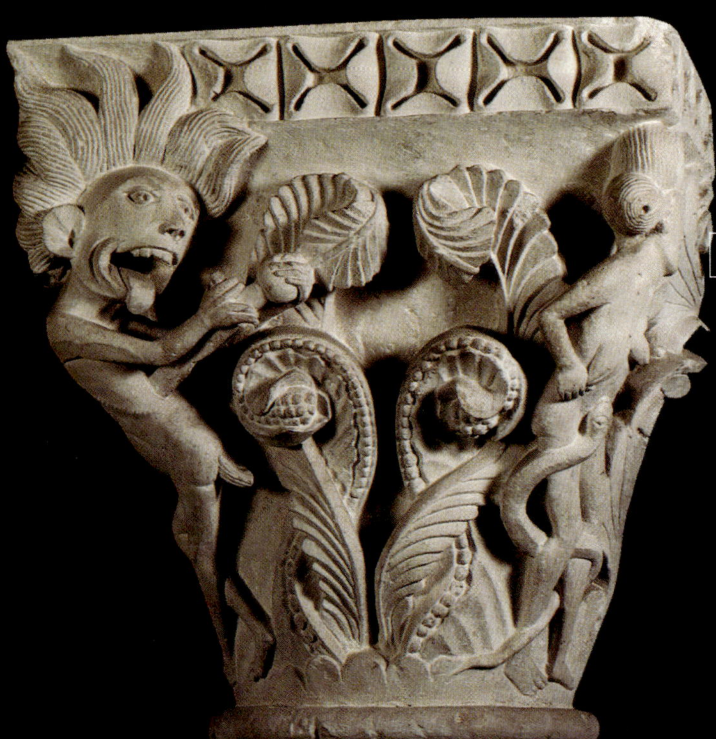

3

Although iconographically these two scenes are alike, their messages are deeply opposed. Lust and Despair symbolize arrogance, pain, and death; they disallow all redemption. However, even at the very moment of the fall of Adam and Eve, there are already signs of forgiveness. Adam is already beginning to repent even as he grasps the grape cluster, and the fruit of the vine that represents the Tree of Sin here, also suggests the ultimate Salvation of Christ. Elsewhere in the church, on the eighth pier on the south wall of the nave, the earthly paradise is represented by four rivers, each one personified by a crouching king from whose open mouth the river flows.

A similar duality can be seen in the depictions of the abduction of Ganymede, and the parable of Lazarus and the Rich Man, found on

2

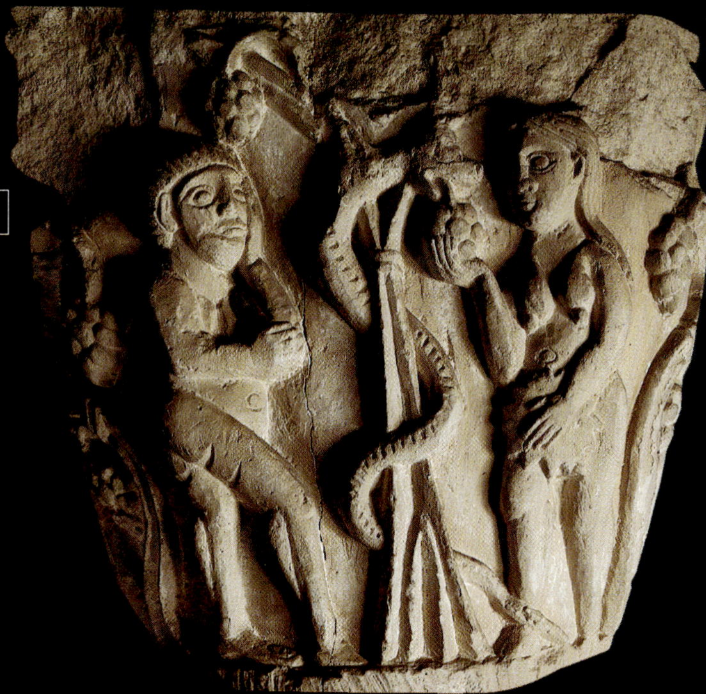

2 ADAM AND EVE

or Hell

4 THE DEATH OF LAZARUS

RIVER OF PARADISE

the south side of the fourth pier of the nave. While the heartless rich man dies, impotent despite his wealth, the poor man, Lazarus, also dies, crouched in the corner of the capital. Through his open mouth his soul, in the form of a small figure within a mandorla (below, right), takes flight. On the adjoining side of the capital, two angels appear, to carry his soul to Abraham's bosom (p. 150), which symbolizes the celestial paradise. In contrast, the boy Ganymede, swept up in a whirlwind, is carried off by an eagle. Behind the bird of prey, the demon applauds the scene, while to the left, a distraught figure, accompanied by his dog, tries to save the child. Both the mythological fable and the Christian parable are allegories of the destiny of the soul. One soul, in terror, is carried to hell, while the other, in glory, rises up to heaven.

4

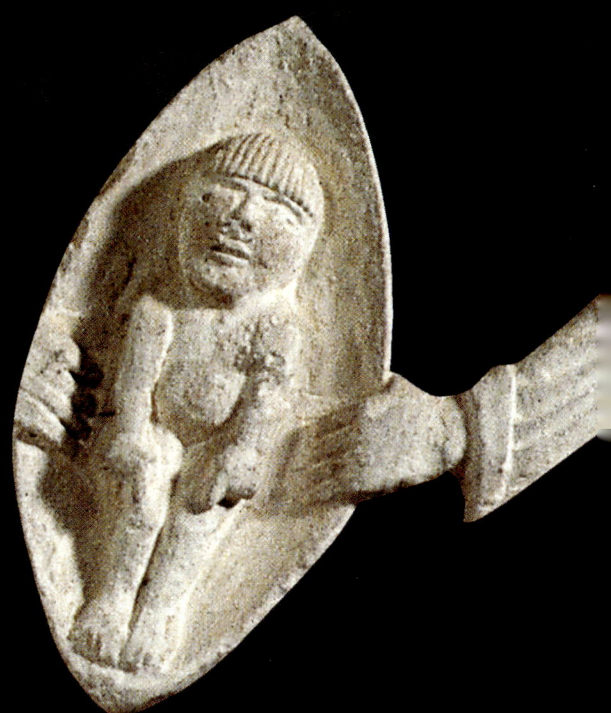

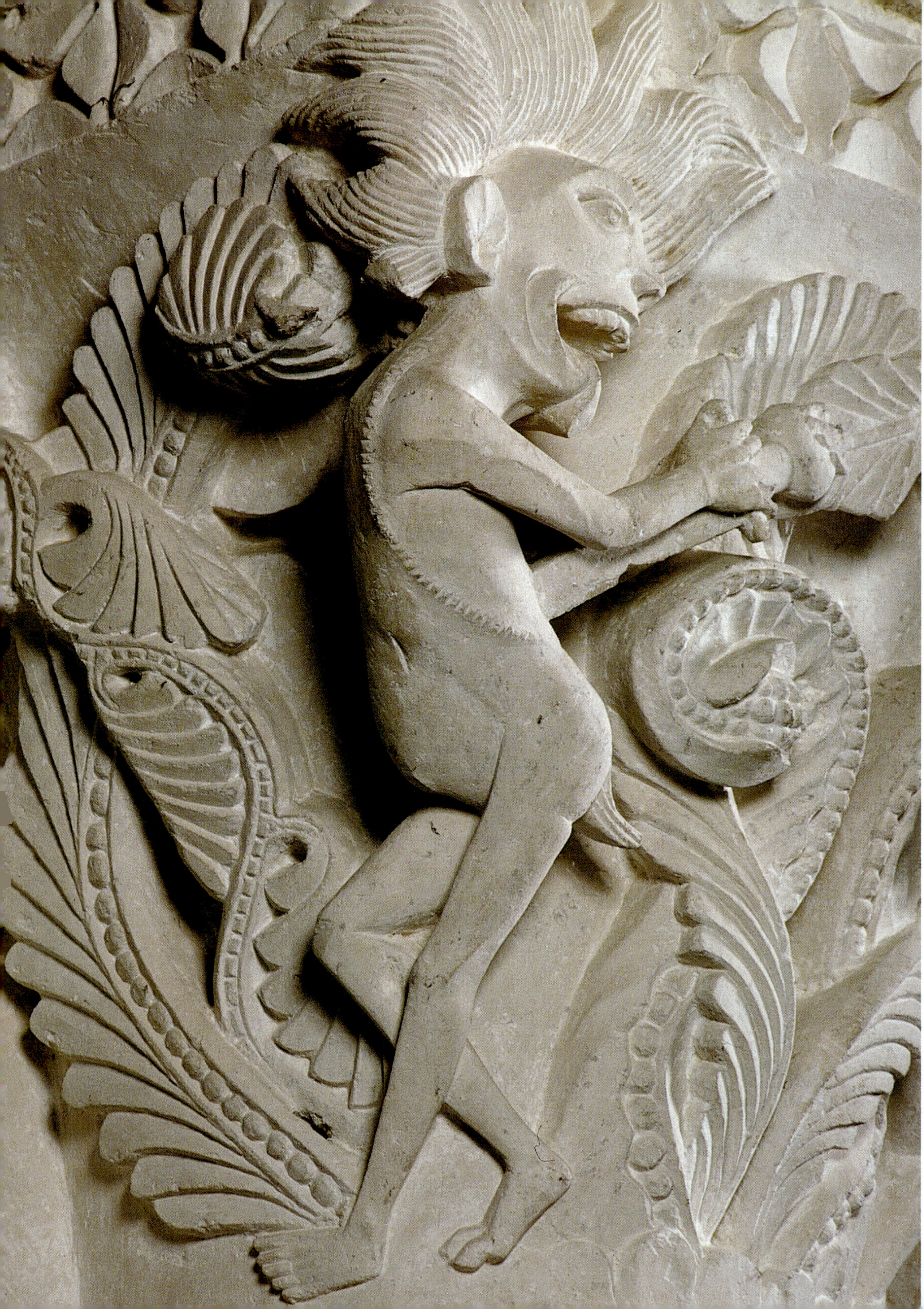

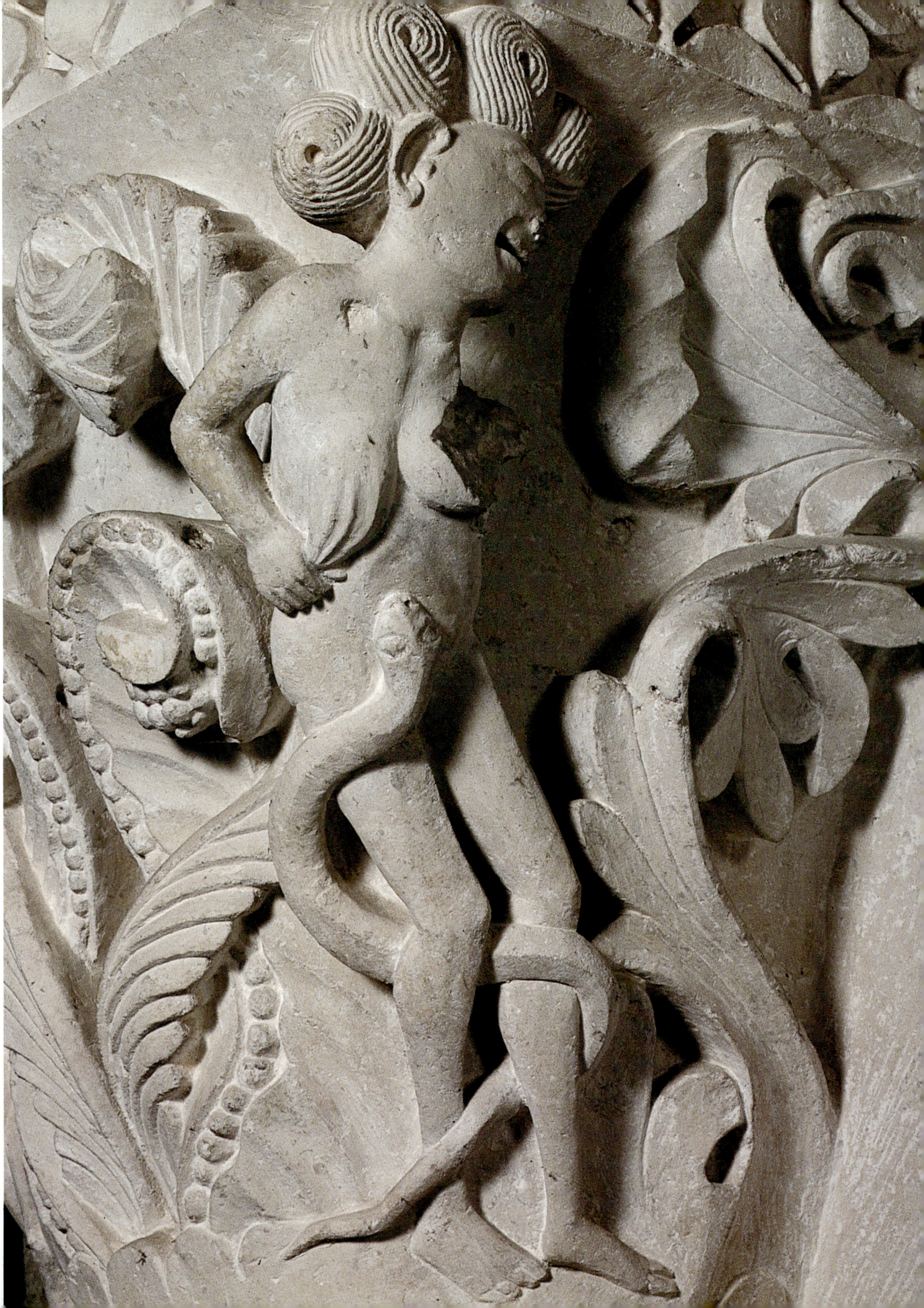

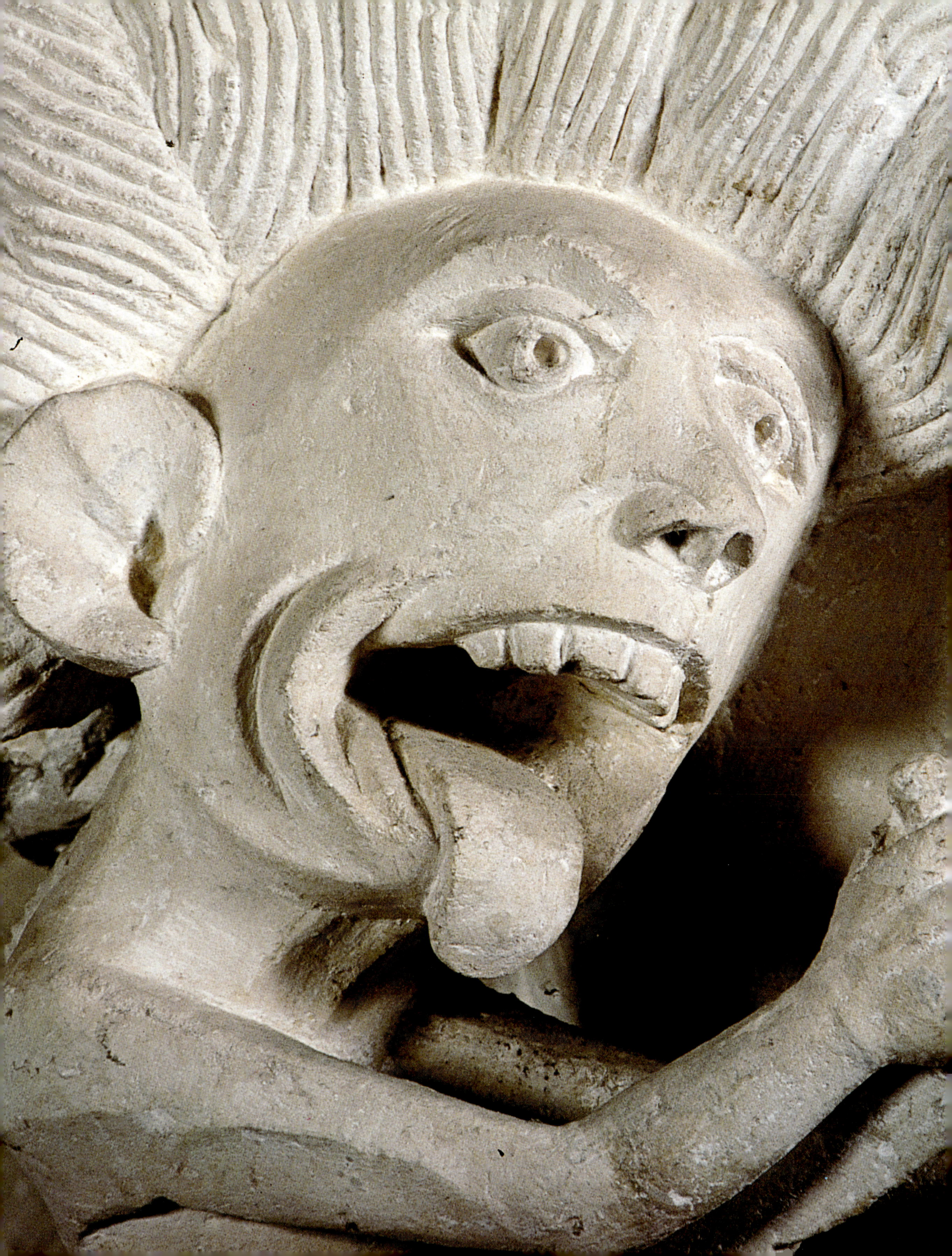

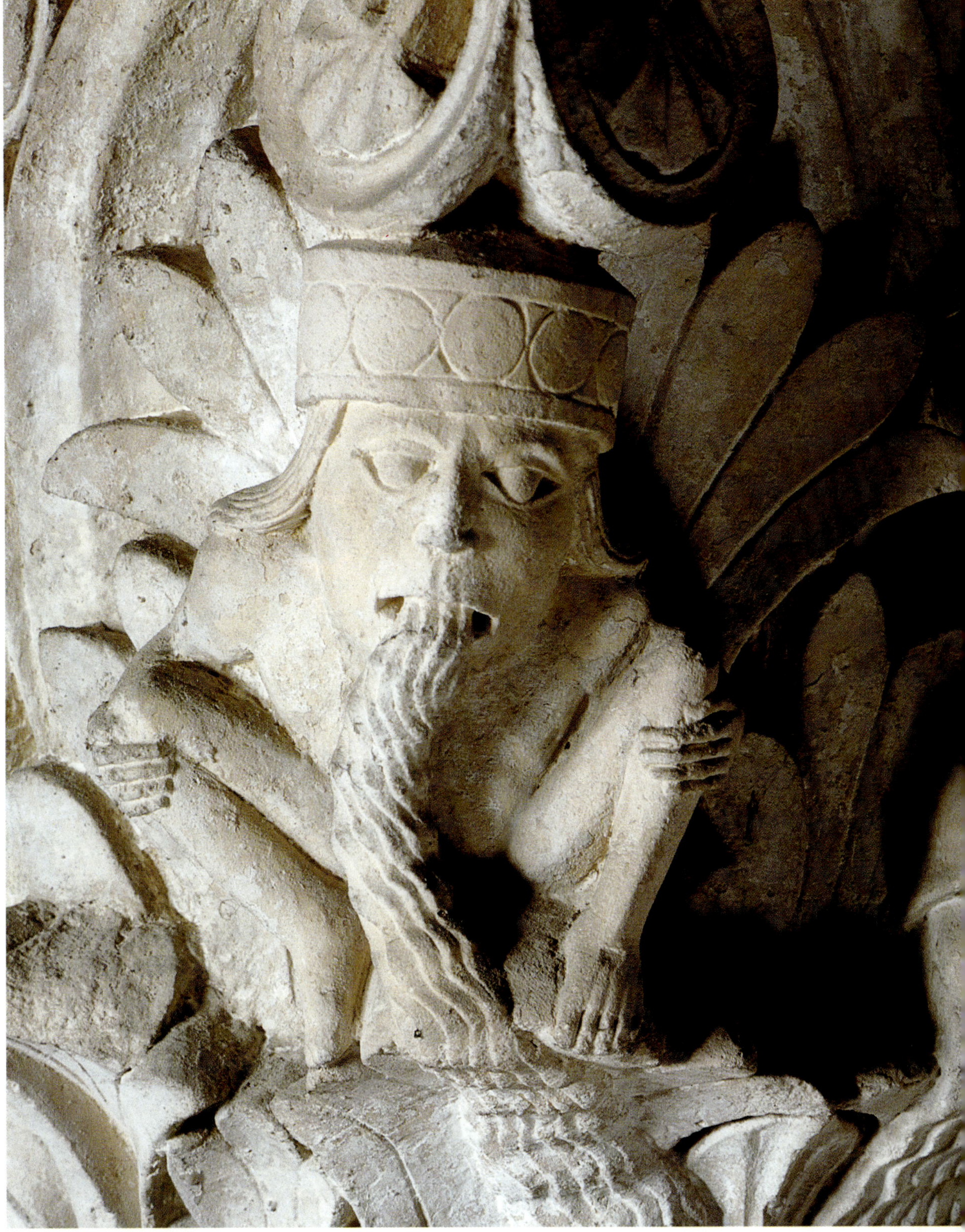

LEFT: THE SIN OF DESPAIR

RIGHT: ONE OF THE FOUR RIVERS OF PARADISE

PRECEDING PAGES: DESPAIR AND LUST

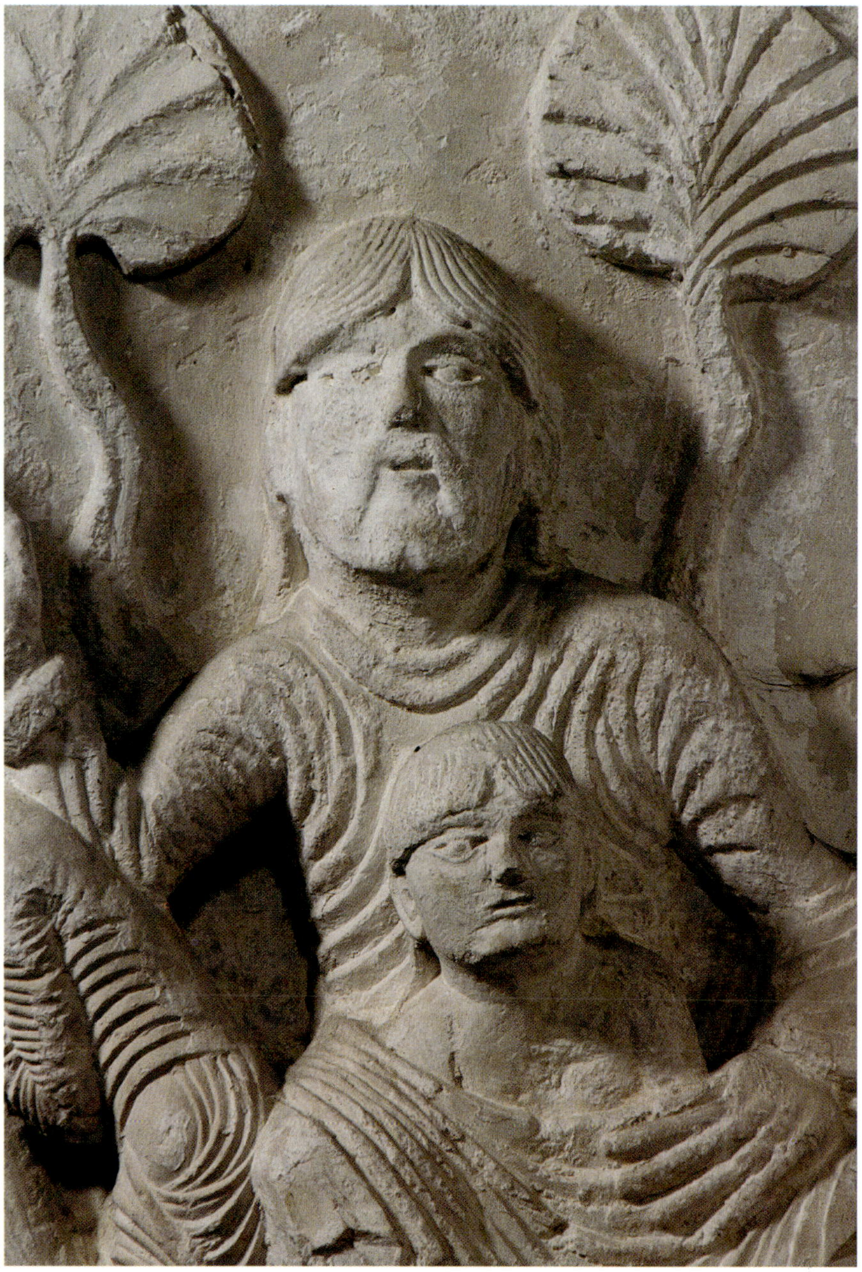

LEFT: LAZARUS IN THE
BOSOM OF ABRAHAM

RIGHT: GANYMEDE
CARRIED OFF BY THE EAGLE

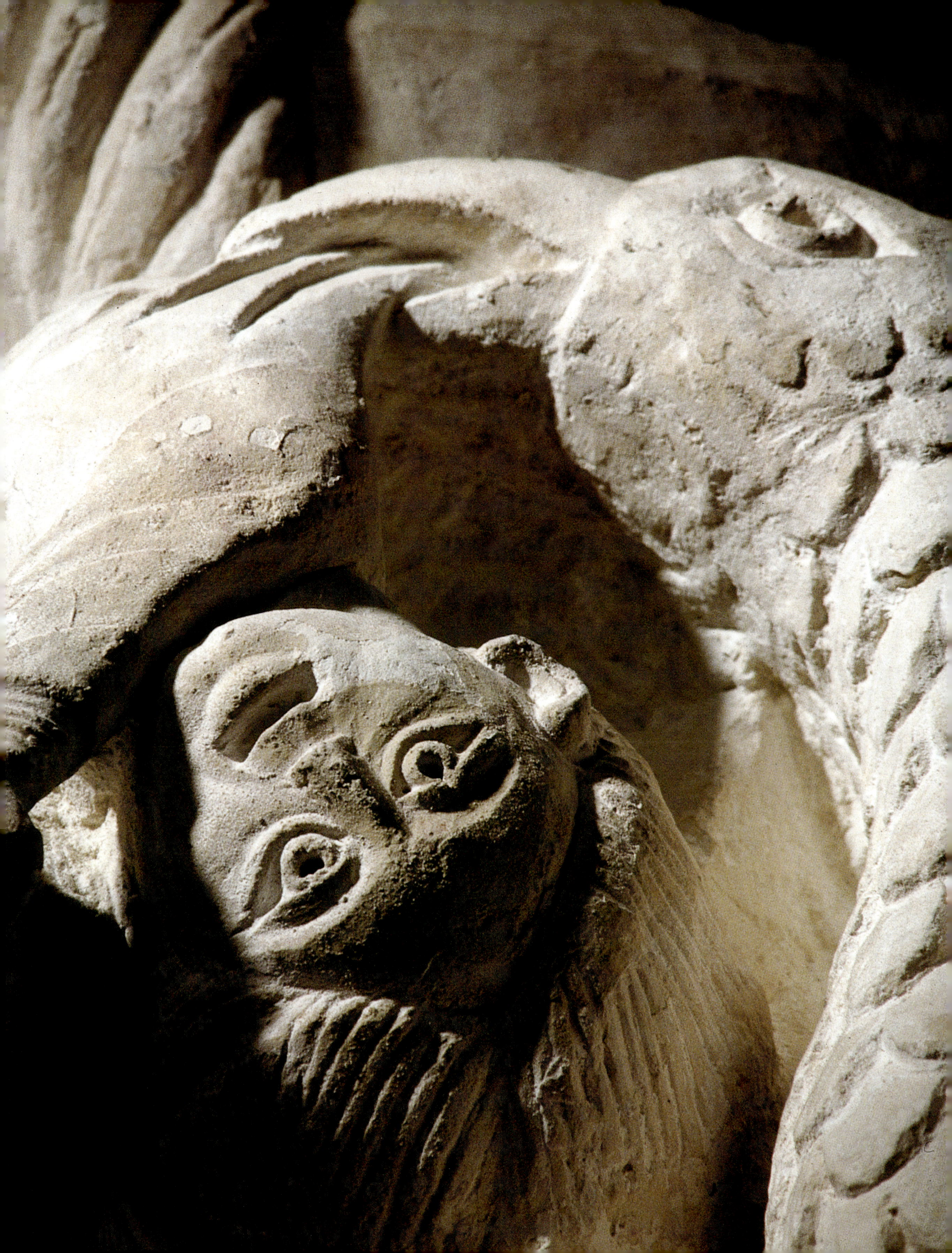

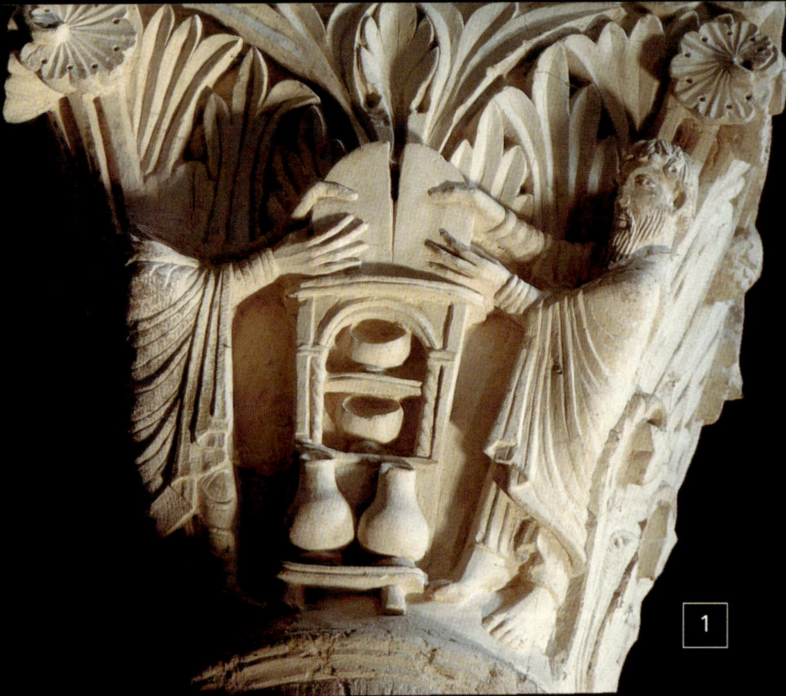

1

THE VICTORY OF CHARITY

Although many of the capitals at Vézelay represent demons, sin, temptation, and the dialogue of good and evil, there are also scenes of peace and splendid serenity. These precious moments are associated with the victory over death. On the seventh pier on the north aisle of the nave, death is personified by a basilisk, a legendary beast represented here as a cock with the tail of a dragon. Facing the basilisk is another fabulous creature, strange, but peaceable: a gigantic grasshopperlike animal with the beard and horns of a goat, fish scales on the side of its body, and the wings of a bird. According to Gregory of Tours, this heterogenous being symbolizes the Gentiles.

ST. BENEDICT RAISING A DEAD CHILD

2

The Reign

1

ST. PAUL THE HERMIT AND ST. ANTHONY BREAKING BREAD

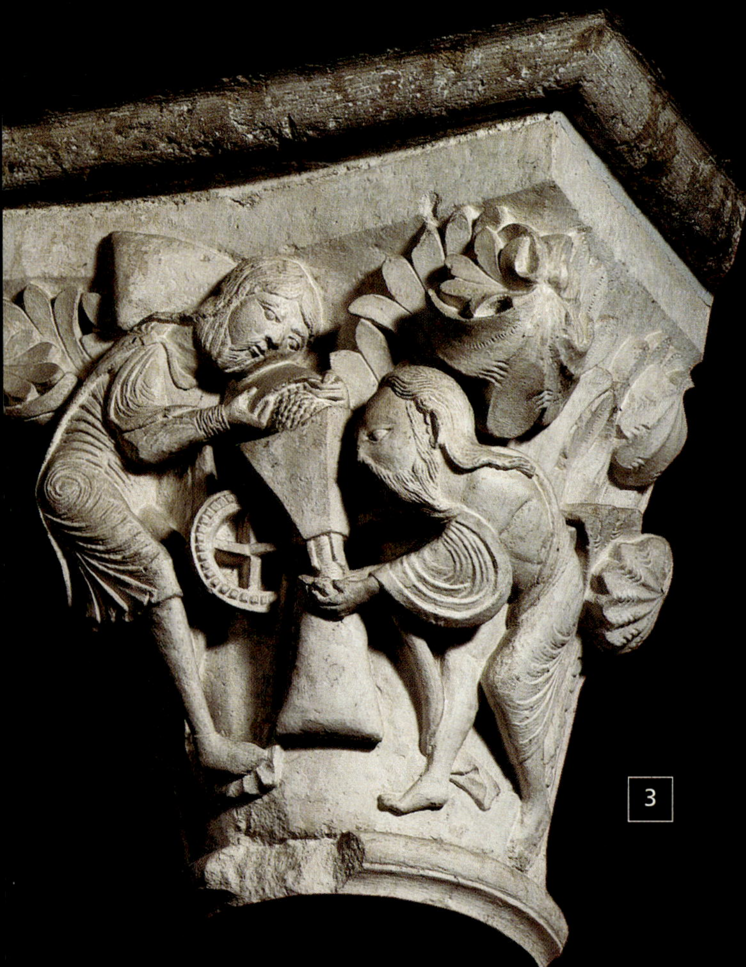

3

Standing next to the creature is a man raising a vessel to eye level. This is the leader of the converted pagans, who, just as mythological heroes avoided the fatal gaze of the Gorgon by holding up a mirror, tries to protect himself from the deadly gaze of the basilisk. The protective vessel that the man carries with such care is a chalice, which represents the Eucharist and thus Christ himself, humanity's only defense against death. On the second pier from the door on the north aisle of the narthex, death has already struck. Shown here is a father grieving for a child, whose body is tightly wrapped in swaddling. To the right of the dead child stands St. Benedict, carrying a book of Scripture. He, too, is about to triumph over death, by bringing the child back to life.

When death is vanquished, the reign of

God will be established. Leaning forward over the Mystic Mill, Moses and Paul work in harmony to spread the divine word. In the grain that the prophet pours, the people of the Old Testament, with their hopes, their temptations, and their sins, are brought together; they are taken in, and transformed and purified, by the Apostle of the New Law. For a believer of the twelfth century, the idea of the perfect harmony of the two Testaments suggested the conversion of the Jews, which would signal the Second Coming of the Messiah. This exemplary age, in which men will embrace God and love their neighbors, is symbolized by two scenes of breaking bread. On

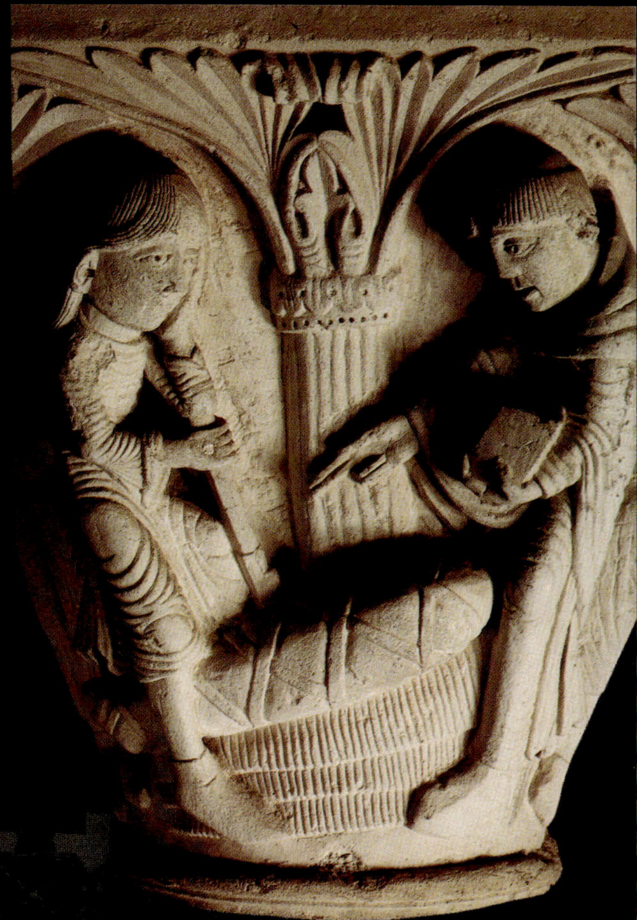

2

4 THE GRASSHOPPER AND THE BASILISK

ST. PAUL THE HERMIT AND ST. ANTHONY BREAKING BREAD

of God

3 THE MYSTIC MILL

the eighth pier of the north aisle of the nave, and also in the narthex, on the column that stands before the south tympanum, two hermits are shown breaking a loaf of bread into two equal portions with their bare hands. This is the meal of the two founders of monasticism, St. Paul the Hermit and St. Anthony of Egypt. According to legend, the crow who had brought half a loaf of bread every day for years to feed St. Paul had brought a whole loaf on the day of St. Anthony's arrival. On another capital, everything has been doubled: the bowls, the jars, even the shelves of the credenza that serves as a table for the two anchorites. After the many capitals that depict dramas, murders, and battles, the visitor's gaze comes to rest at last on the brotherhood of these two saints.

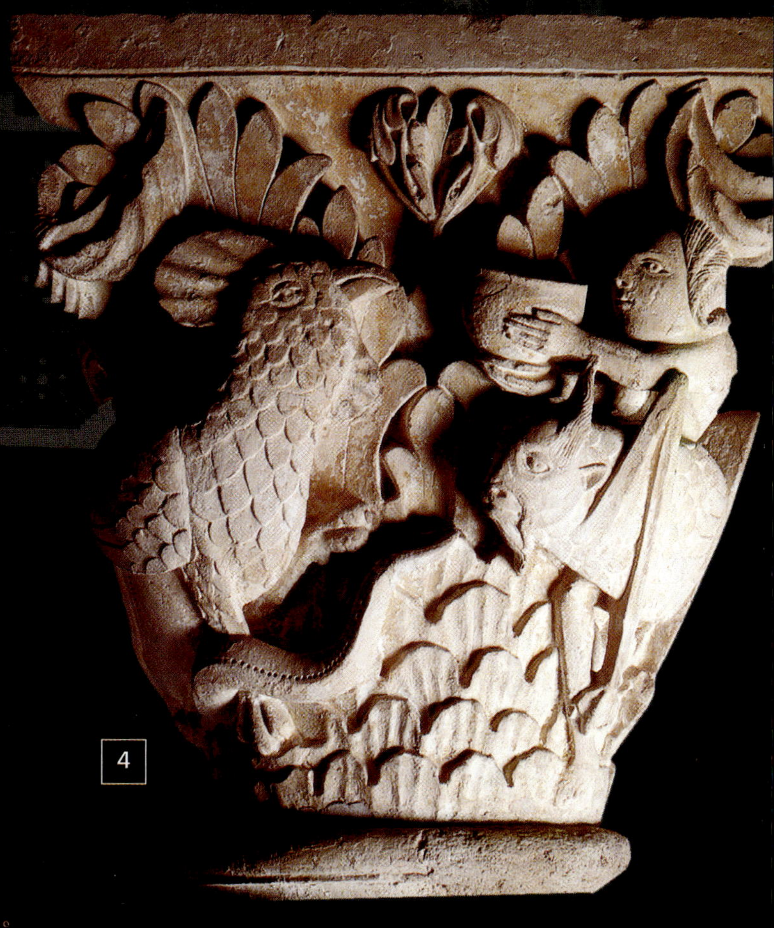

4

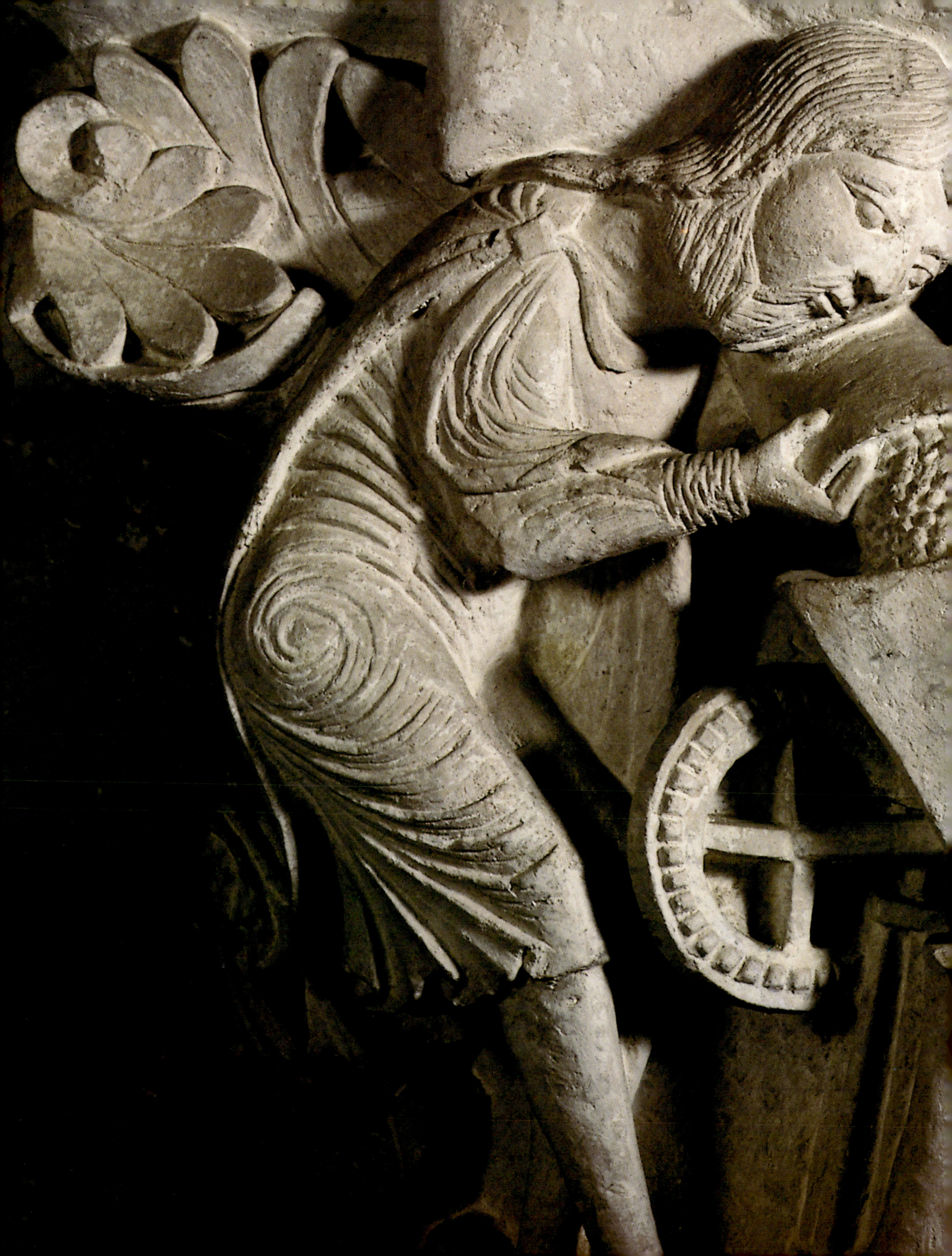

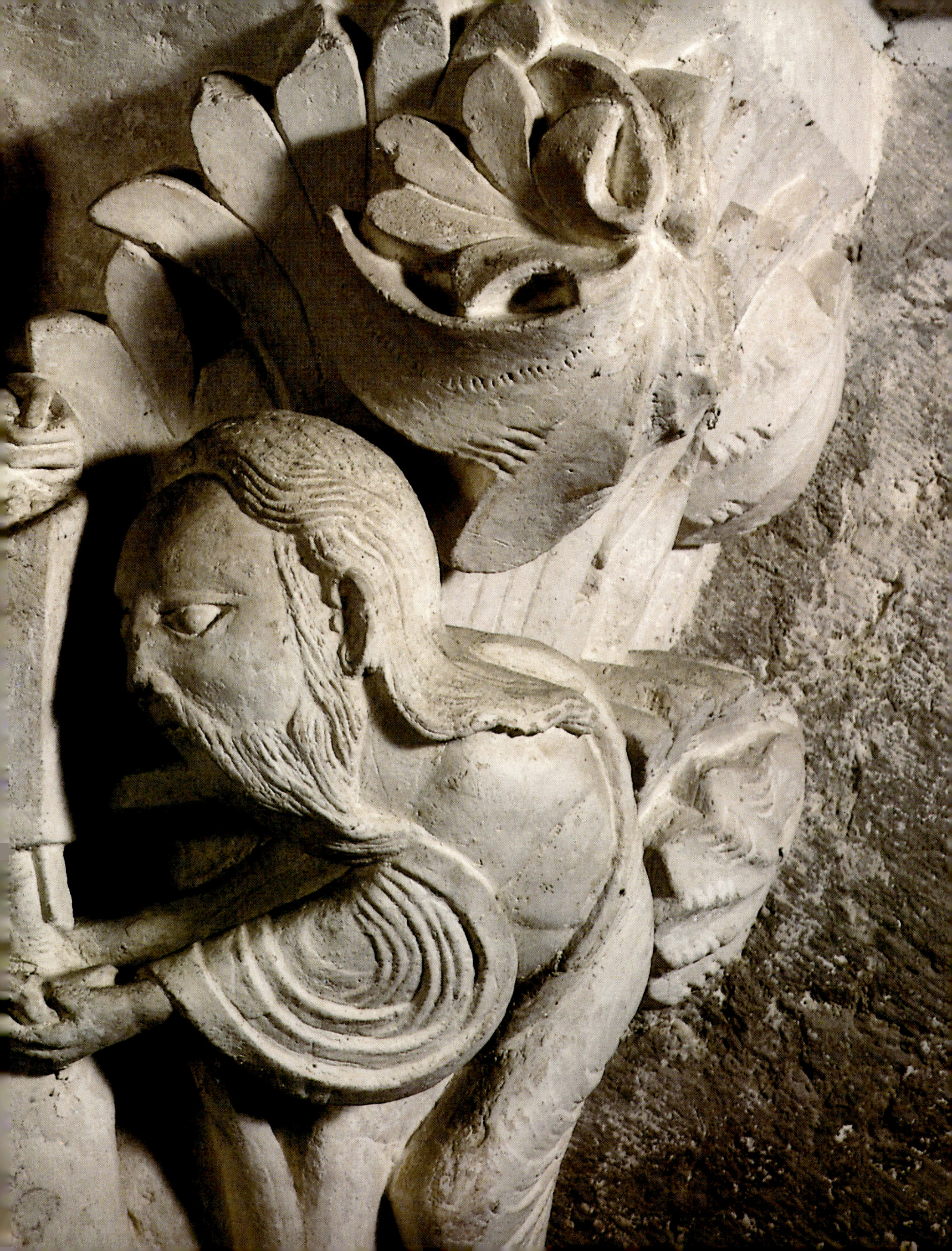

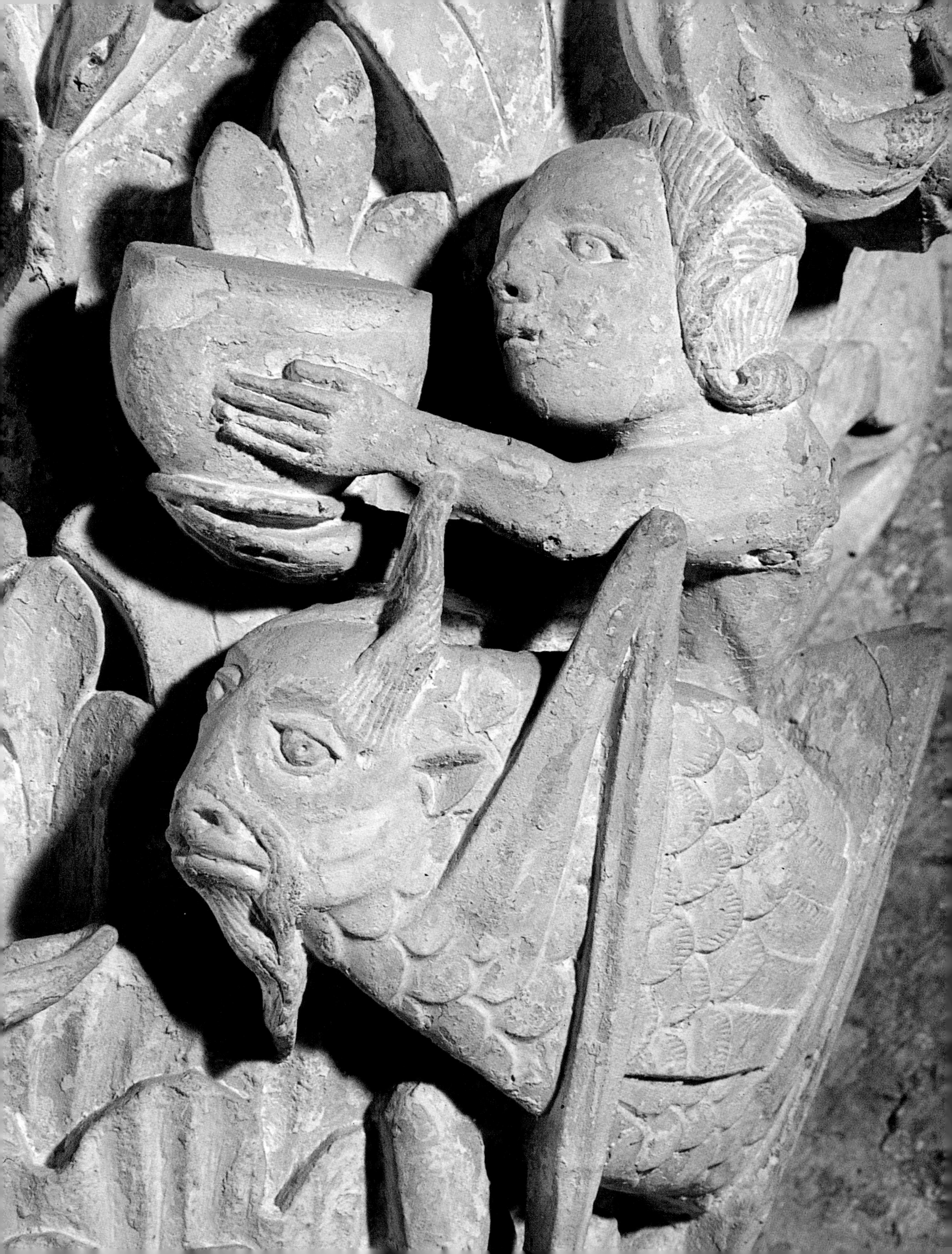

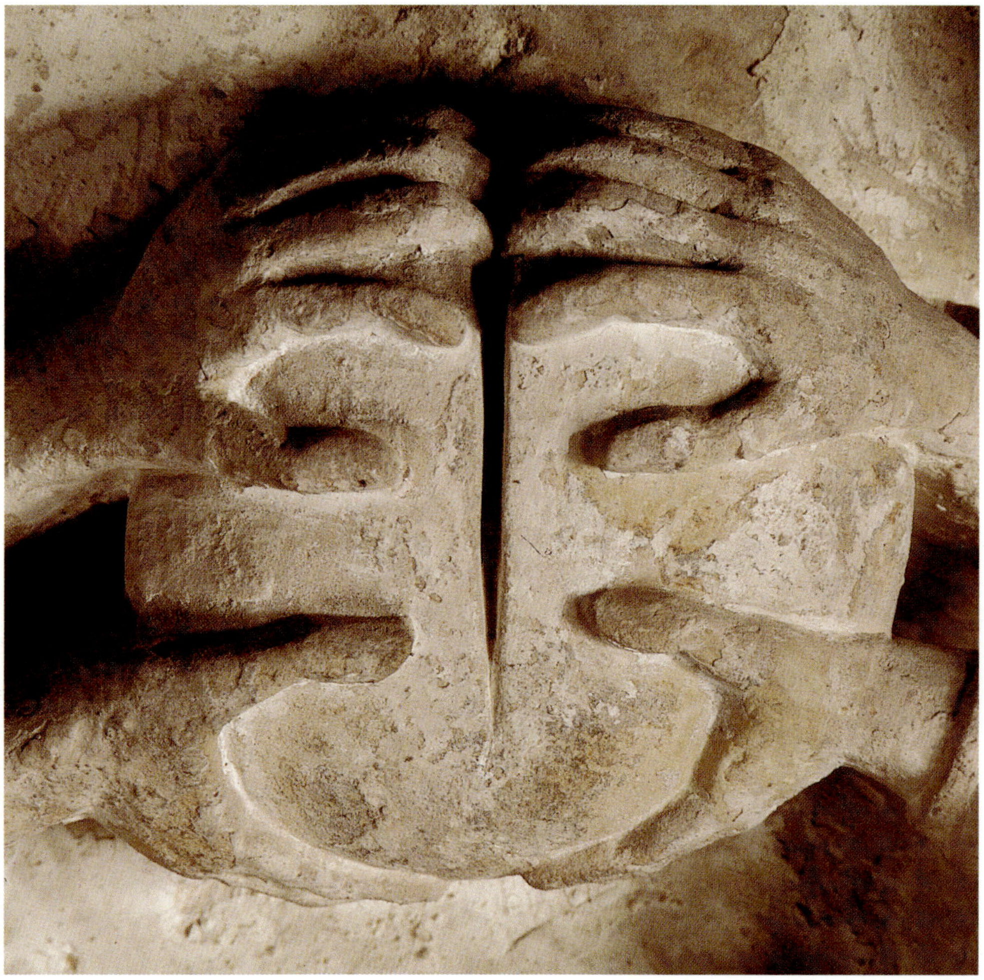

LEFT: THE GRASSHOPPER, SYMBOL OF THE CONVERTED PAGANS

ABOVE: THE BREAD OF BROTHERHOOD

BIBLIOGRAPHY

Barral i Altet, Xavier, François Avril, and Danielle Gaborit-Chopin, *Le Monde roman*, vol. 2, *Les Royaumes d'Occident*, Paris: Gallimard, "L'univers des formes" series, 1983.

Bernard de Clairvaux, *Textes politiques,* Paris, 18 October, 1986, selected and translated by Paul Zumthor.

Diemer, Paul, *Stil und Ikonographie der Kapitelle von Sainte-Madeleine Vézelay,* doctoral dissertation, Heidelberg, 1975.

Jean-Nesmy, Claude (Dom), *Vézelay, La-Pierre-qui-Vire*, Zodiaque, "Les travaux des mois" series, 1982.

Katzenellenbogen, Adolf, "The Central Tympanum at Vézelay," *The Art Bulletin*, vol. XXVI, 1944, pp.141–151.

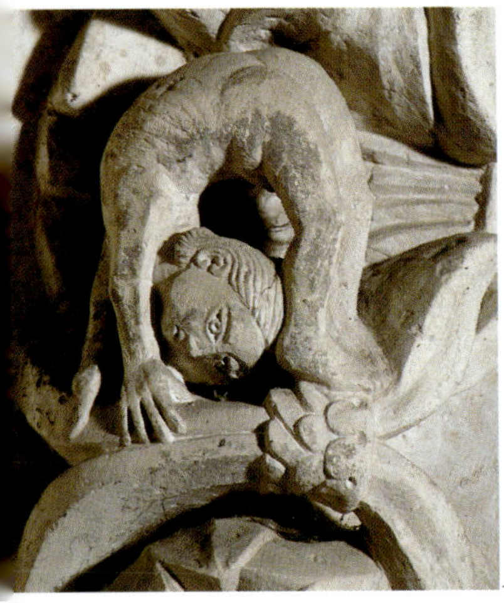

Panofsky, Erwin, *Gothic Architecture and Scholasticism.* Latrobe, Pa.: Archabbey Press, 1951.

Salet, Francis, *Cluny et Vézelay, l'œuvre des sculpteurs,* Paris: Société française d'archéologie, 1995. *La Madeleine de Vézelay,* Paris, 1948.

Vergnolle, Élaine, *L'Art roman en France,* Paris: Flammarion, 1994.

Vézelay, introduction by Victor-Henry Debidour, texts selected by E. M. Janet le Caisne, Paris: Plon, 1962.

Viollet-le-Duc, Eugène, *Monographe de l'ancienne église abbatiale de Vézelay,* Paris, 1873.

ACKNOWLEDGMENTS

The photographer wishes to thank the following people and institutions, who lent their assistance in the preparation of this work: the rectorate of the basilica of Vézelay; Father Daniel Rousseau; the Ministery of the Department of Yonne for Architecture and Heritage; M. Pierre Thiébaut, architect of the Bâtiments de France; the Office of the Mayor of Vézelay, and M. Bernard Chardon, Mayor; M. Jean d'Ogny; Father Dominique and the Franciscan community; M. Claude Stassart; and M. Jacques Fresnes.

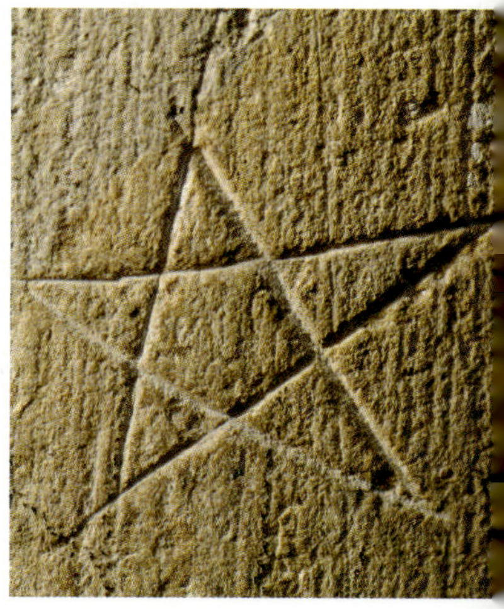

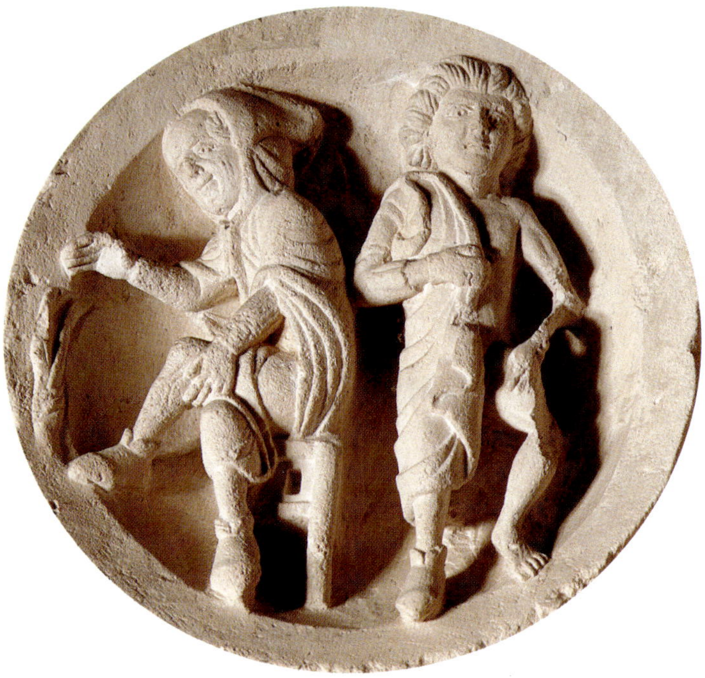

OPPOSITE:
THE LABORS OF THE MONTHS: FEBRUARY

Project Manager, English-language edition: Ellen Nidy
Editor, English-language edition: Elaine M. Stainton
Designers, English-language edition: Tina Thompson, Dirk Luykx

Library of Congress Cataloging-in-Publication Data

Rouchon-Mouilleron, Véronique.
[Vézelay. English]
Vézelay : the great Romanesque church / by Véronique Rouchon-Mouilleron ; photographs by Daniel Faure ; translated from the French by Laurel Hirsch.
p. cm.
Includes bibliographical references and index.
ISBN 0-8109-3937-1
1. Sculpture, Romanesque—France—Vézelay. 2. Sculpture, French—France—Vézelay. 3. Basilique de la Madeleine (Vézelay, France) 4. Sculpture, Romanesque—France—Vézelay—Pictorial works. 5. Sculpture, French—France—Vézelay—Pictorial works. 6. Basilique de la Madeleine (Vézelay, France)—Pictorial works.
I. Faure, Daniel. II. Title.
NB551.V45R6813 1999 99-43104

Published in 1999 by Harry N. Abrams, Incorporated, New York

Printed and bound in Italy

Harry N. Abrams, Inc.
100 Fifth Avenue
New York, N.Y. 10011
www.abramsbooks.com